THE MAKING OF THE MODERN REFUGEE

The Making of the Modern Refugee is a comprehensive history of global population displacement in the twentieth century. It takes a new approach to the subject, exploring its causes, consequences, and meanings. History, the author shows, provides important clues to understanding how the idea of refugees as a 'problem' embedded itself in the minds of policy-makers and the public, and poses a series of fundamental questions about the nature of enforced migration and how it has shaped society throughout the twentieth century across a broad geographical area—from Europe and the Middle East to South Asia, South-East Asia, and sub-Saharan Africa. Wars, revolutions, and state formation are invoked as the main causal explanations of displacement, and are considered alongside the emergence of a twentieth-century refugee regime linking governmental practices, professional expertise, and humanitarian relief efforts.

This new study rests upon scholarship from several disciplines and draws extensively upon oral testimony, eye-witness accounts, and film, as well as unpublished source material in the archives of governments, international organisations, and non-governmental organisations. *The Making of the Modern Refugee* explores the significance that refugees attached to the places they left behind, to their journeys, and to their destinations—in short, how refugees helped to interpret and fashion their own history.

Peter Gatrell was educated at the University of Cambridge. In 1976 he joined the University of Manchester where he is currently Professor of Economic History and affiliated to the Humanitarian and Conflict Response Institute. He teaches courses on refugees in modern world history, Russian economic and social history, the cultural history of war, and the history of humanitarianism. He is the author of several books including *The Tsarist Economy, 1850–1917* (1986), *A Whole Empire Walking: Refugees in Russia during World War 1* (1999), and *Free World? The campaign to save the world's refugees, 1956–1963* (2011).

The Making of the Modern Refugee

PETER GATRELL

OXFORD
UNIVERSITY PRESS

OXFORD
UNIVERSITY PRESS

Great Clarendon Street, Oxford, OX2 6DP,
United Kingdom

Oxford University Press is a department of the University of Oxford.
It furthers the University's objective of excellence in research, scholarship,
and education by publishing worldwide. Oxford is a registered trade mark of
Oxford University Press in the UK and in certain other countries

First published 2013
First published in paperback 2015

Published in the United States of America by Oxford University Press
198 Madison Avenue, New York, NY 10016, United States of America

British Library Cataloguing in Publication Data
Data available

Library of Congress Cataloging in Publication Data
Data available

ISBN 978–0–19–967416–9 (Hbk.)
ISBN 978–0–19–874447–4 (Pbk.)

For Martha Katz,
Erika Drucker,
And in loving memory of David Drucker

Preface

At the entrance to my local health club is a notice reminding guests not to leave their belongings in their car, 'to be on the safe side'. I have thought quite a lot about this phrase, which is something of a cliché in the English language. My book concerns people who were compelled to negotiate difficult journeys to a place of relative safety. It is primarily a work of history. What distinctive contribution can a historian make to refugee studies? My answer is that history as well as satisfying our curiosity about the past provides a fresh and unsettling perspective on issues of contemporary concern. Refugee crises are not a recent phenomenon. An historical approach enables us to track multiple crises from beginning to end, so to speak, analysing how they originated and what outcomes emerged and on whose terms. Looking back in time shows that current practices often uncannily echo earlier formulations, whether in relation to ideas around security or to problem-solving. History gives us insights into these complex genealogies. I draw on later nineteenth- and twentieth-century evidence to argue that states make refugees, but that refugees also make states; that the refugee regime broadly understood to include programmes of humanitarian assistance and the framework of international refugee law makes refugees into a category of concern; and that these processes are informed by cultural representation. This is not all. Refugees have called upon history to explain their displacement and to help negotiate a way out of their predicament. Refugees were created by violence and governed by regimes of intervention, but they gave meaning to their experiences through engaging with the past. History is a refugee resource.

There is nothing in my book of what the Canadian economic historian Harold Innes once described as an author's 'dirt experience'. Rather than conduct ethnographic fieldwork, I have consulted a large body of secondary literature and primary sources including oral testimony and other accounts by eye-witnesses, refugees included, and documents emanating from governments, international organizations, and non-governmental organizations (NGOs). I could not have written this book without the research undertaken by other scholars, most of whom I have never met, and who are knowledgeable about places I have never visited and fluent in languages I do not command. The footnotes give some indication of my debt to them. Any omissions or errors in understanding and interpreting their work are solely my responsibility.

I should like to thank all those students at the University of Manchester who enrolled on my final-year course, 'Refugees in Modern World History', and who helped me clarify my ideas. I have learned a lot from my doctoral students past and present, in particular Pete Borklund, Jenny Carson, Mateja Celestina, Rosaria Franco, Luke Kelly, Chris Lash, Joanne Laycock, Rosy Rickett, Laura Rubio, Junya Takiguchi, and Alice Tligui. Friends and colleagues in the UK and further afield have given plenty of support, including allowing me to read their unpublished work. I hope they will accept this general expression of thanks. The maps were drawn by Nick Scarle. Christopher Wheeler at Oxford University Press agreed to take this book on and offered the kind of encouragement that any author craves; I am also grateful to Cathryn Steele and Emma Barber, and to my copy-editor Elissa Connor. Three anonymous readers of the manuscript offered useful advice. I want to make special mention of Pam Ballinger, Anna Holian, and Laura Madokoro, generous and thoughtful interlocutors, Jérôme Elie and Francesca Piana who alerted me to relevant archival material in Geneva, Steven Lee and Janice Kim for advice on Korea, Laurence Brown who made valuable comments at an early stage, Jean-Marc Dreyfus, Urvashi Butalia, and Rubina Jasani, who commented on a draft chapter apiece, and above all Bertrand Taithe, who read a first draft in its entirety, and who has been a constant source of ideas as well as being a staunch friend. None of these kind people should be held responsible for the book's shortcomings.

My work on these topics has been supported over the past decade by the British Academy, the Leverhulme Trust, the Arts and Humanities Research Council, and the University of Manchester. I am indebted to them all. I would also like to thank the many librarians and archivists who have helped me, including Patricia Flückiger-Livingstone, Montserrat Canela Garayoa, and Hilde Haaland at UNHCR, Don Davis at the American Friends Service Committee in Philadelphia, and Joel Thoreson at the Evangelical Lutheran Church of America in Chicago.

In the light of its often sombre subject matter it is fitting that I should acknowledge the secure and privileged circumstances that made it possible for me to write this book. This is partly a matter of institutional support, but even more about the friendships that enrich my life. I take none of this for granted. I appreciate the kindness and hospitality of Peter and Zhenia Shoenberg in London and Cambridge, Lizzy Gatrell and Andrew Winstone in London, Dave Gatrell and Chloé Goudvis in Hong Kong, and Erika and David Drucker in Geneva, and the interest they have shown in my work. Jane, Dave, and Lizzy Gatrell fill me with pride and make everything worthwhile.

Preface to the Paperback Edition (March 2015)

A year and a half has elapsed since the first publication of *The Making of the Modern Refugee*. In June 2014 a UNHCR report timed to coincide with World Refugee Day put the total number of registered refugees at 50 million, the highest figure since the Second World War.[1] More than half of the total originated from Syria, Afghanistan, Somalia, Iraq, and Sudan. Syria barely warranted a mention in the first edition of my book. As a consequence of the civil war in Syria, some ten million people have fled their homes, three million of whom sought refuge in neighbouring states, notably Lebanon, Turkey, Jordan, Iraq, and Egypt. The influx of Syrian refugees increased the population of Lebanon by 25 per cent, and relations between the local population and refugees are reportedly acrimonious. There is immense pressure on housing, schools, and the health service. Kurds and Palestinians who have fled Syria face particular hurdles in finding temporary sanctuary in Lebanon. Much the same can be said about the situation of Syrian refugees in Jordan and Turkey, whose feelings towards the Assad regime may however become more ambivalent as a result of the threat posed by the forces of so-called Islamic State.[2] Other conflicts too have grabbed the headlines in recent months, as in Nigeria, where the concerted attacks by Boko Haram on villages in the north-east displaced nearly 650,000 people within the country and prompted others to cross into Chad, Niger, and Cameroon. According to UNHCR, 'refugees said that villages were mostly empty on the Nigeria side, with only old and disabled people remaining'.[3] In the first edition of *The Making of the Modern Refugee* I suggested that the collapse of the Soviet Union had not, in the main, resulted in massive crises of population displacement. From the standpoint of early 2015, however, the situation looks much less sanguine. Around one and a half million people have been displaced in eastern Ukraine, as a civil war rages between forces loyal to Ukraine and Russian separatists. The outcome of this conflict—fuelled by support from Western interests on the one hand, and Russian backing on the other—remains uncertain at the time of writing.[4]

The eruption of these crises and the intolerance shown by Western politicians to asylum seekers represent a depressing feature of contemporary society. The crises confront historians with the need to contribute to public debate by contextualizing mass population displacement. So far as Syria is concerned, in years to come it may be that the crisis will be understood not just as a terrible civil war in which refugees figure as miserable flotsam and jetsam, but as one element in a more complicated story that includes Syria's record not only as a refugee-hosting state but also as a polity whose original contours were shaped by refugees in the wake of the dismemberment

---

[1] <http://www.unhcr.org/53a155bc6.html> accessed Mar. 2015.
[2] See the briefing paper prepared by Rochelle Davis at <https://www.academia.edu/10978127/Backgrounder_for_Service_Providers_Refugees_from_Syria?auto=download&campaign=upload_email>
[3] <http://www.unhcr.org/541831e19.html> accessed Mar. 2015.
[4] Richard Sakwa, *Frontline Ukraine: Crisis in the Borderlands* (I. B. Tauris, 2015).

of the Ottoman Empire.[5] This reinforces one of the arguments in *The Making of the Modern Refugee*, namely that while refugees are the product of state-led practices, they also help to constitute the modern nation-state.[6]

The multiplication of refugee crises in a globalizing world may help to explain the burgeoning interest in refugee histories. Thanks to Matthew Frank, Jessica Reinisch, and others, we now have a clearer idea of the contours of the '40 years' crisis' from the end of the First World War to c.1960.[7] The situation in Europe at the end of the Second World War in particular continues to be a well-trodden field for research. Atina Grossmann traces the routes taken by Jewish refugees from Poland to Persia and India by way of the Soviet Union, and thence back to Poland in 1945–6, before they moved yet again to DP camps in Germany, and then finally resettled in North America, Israel, Australia, or South Africa. Her emphasis on how refugees maintained a sense of purpose in highly adverse circumstances is particularly compelling. Adam Seipp draws attention to the interaction of DPs, the local population, the military, and humanitarian aid workers in post-war Germany. His work—'an international history of a very small place', as he puts it—is a model of how historians can deploy a variety of sources to provide a sophisticated reading of refugee history.[8]

The creation of regional refugee regimes is also emerging as a vibrant topic to set alongside the more familiar story of how an international refugee regime came into being in 1951.[9] A stimulating body of work on the situation in East Asia in the wake of the Second World War opens up fresh research questions. Laura Madokoro and others emphasize the 'uneven development' of the refugee regime, pointing to its regional and local manifestations.[10] This is an important finding, although there is a risk that focusing on the proliferation of refugee regimes overlooks connections between different sites of displacement, such as the association that refugees have sometimes made between their circumstances and those of

[5] This is not just a post-1948 history of Palestinian refugees, but an inter-war history of admitting Armenians, Kurds, and others, as work in progress by Benjamin Thomas White establishes.

[6] On the problem with the nation-state as the primary point of analysis, see Philip Marfleet, 'Explorations in a Foreign Land: States, Refugees and the Problem of History' *RSQ*, 32, no.2 (2013), 14–34.

[7] Jessica Reinisch and Matthew Frank (eds), *The Forty Years' Crisis: Refugees in Europe, 1919–1959* (Bloomsbury Academic, 2015).

[8] Atina Grossmann, 'Remapping Relief and Rescue: Flight, Displacement, and International Aid for Jewish Refugees during World War II' *New German Critique*, 39, no.3 (2012), 61–79. Adam R. Seipp, *Strangers in the Wild Place: Refugees, Americans, and a German Town, 1945–1952* (Bloomington: Indiana University Press, 2013).

[9] Anna Holian and Gerald Daniel Cohen, 'Introduction: The Refugee in the Post-War World' *JRS*, 25, no.3 (2012), 313–25. On the background to the 1951 UN Convention, see Andrew Janco, '"Unwilling": The One Word Revolution in Refugee Status, 1940–1951' *CEH* 23, no.3 (2014), 429–46; Lucy Mayblin, 'Colonialism, Decolonisation, and the Right to Be Human: Britain and the 1951 Geneva Convention on the Status of Refugees' *Journal of Historical Sociology*, 27, no.3 (2014), 423–41. For a broader perspective, see Katy Long, 'When Refugees Stopped Being Migrants: Movement, Labour and Humanitarian Protection' *Migration Studies*, 1, no.1 (2013), 4–26.

[10] Laura Madokoro, Elaine Lynn-Ee-Ho, and Glen Peterson, 'Questioning the Dynamics and Language of Forced Migration in Asia: The Experiences of Ethnic Chinese Refugees' *MAS*, 49, no.2 (2015), 430–8, and the other articles in this special issue. See also Jessica Elkind, '"The Virgin Mary is Going South": Refugee Resettlement in South Vietnam, 1954–1956' *Diplomatic History*, 38, no.5 (2014), 987–1016.

other displaced persons, not to mention the outlook of aid workers who moved from one site to another on behalf of humanitarian organizations.[11] These agencies did not necessarily recognize the distinction between the international refugee regime and regional regimes. The history of non-governmental organizations can help to supply the 'common framework' that is needed to overcome analytical fragmentation.[12]

Some of the most interesting recent scholarship accepts the challenges of writing a refugee-centred history. One pitfall is to assume the homogeneity of 'experience'. Scott Soo avoids this risk by emphasizing the plural meanings of 'exile' that were articulated by and sometimes imposed upon Spanish Civil War refugees who settled in France. Their memories of 'composite interactions' cannot be pressed into a Procrustean bed.[13] Another challenge—which I confronted in *The Making of the Modern Refugee*—is to acknowledge that a refugee history cannot focus exclusively on refugees, but must instead also take into account various practices of external intervention. The consequences cannot be overstated, as demonstrated in Mimi Thi Nguyen's book on Vietnamese refugees who were obliged to express gratitude for their 'deliverance'.[14]

In a multi-faced study of refugees, Lynda Mannik draws upon the surviving photographic record of 350 Estonians who fled to Canada in 1948. In contrast to today's refugees who attempt the much shorter journey across the Mediterranean and place themselves in the hands of people whom they barely know, these refugees formed an incorporated company to pay for the refitting of an old minesweeper, the SS *Walnut*, to transport them from Sweden to Halifax, Nova Scotia, where they were held for a month in a detention centre before being granted asylum. The Canadian media construed this group as 'docile, northern, and white', and as victims of communism who arrived in 'little Viking boats', quite unlike others who faced a more hostile reception, notably Jewish refugees on the *St Louis*, which was turned back in 1939, and Tamil refugees in the mid-1980s. This has not prevented Canadian politicians and others from incorporating the experience of Estonian refugees into a narrative of Canadian humanitarianism and multiculturalism. Mannik locates the experiences of Estonian refugees in a larger framework of cultural representation and immigration policy. She demonstrates how Estonians were quite capable of holding a negative opinion of subsequent refugees whom they deemed to be 'economic migrants', whereas they were 'political' refugees, even though this was not in fact an accurate depiction of their own status, since they had the option of remaining in Sweden. Surviving Estonians and their children now dislike being described as 'the first boat people': 'I think [said one] of the Vietnamese who came, and we were not like that'.

---

[11] Peter Redfield, 'The Unbearable Lightness of Expats: Double Binds of Humanitarian Mobility' *Cultural Anthropology*, 27, no.2 (2012), 358–82.

[12] Matthew Frank and Jessica Reinisch, 'Refugees and the Nation-State in Europe, 1919–59' *JCH* 49, no.3 (2014), 477–90.

[13] Scott Soo, *The Routes to Exile: France and the Spanish Civil War Refugees, 1939–2009* (Manchester: Manchester University Press, 2013), 253.

[14] Mimi Thi Nguyen, *The Gift of Freedom: War, Debt, and Other Refugee Passages* (Durham, NC: Duke University Press, 2012).

The Atlantic crossing thus conveyed ideas of a heroic expedition, but it also carried an unfortunate association with those who in their opinion had a less genuine claim to asylum.[15]

The complex history of what the philosopher Ian Hacking calls 'making up people' emerges throughout *The Making of the Modern Refugee*.[16] It continues to preoccupy historians who have examined different sites of displacement. One way of proceeding is, as Laura Madokoro suggests, to 'think of refugees as people in motion rather than as subjects constructed in relation to the states that alternately refuse or receive them'.[17] Other scholars engage more directly with issues of categorization. Thus in her book on China under Japanese occupation and its aftermath, Janet Chen shows how officials in Shanghai wrestled with the issue of definition—who was a 'genuine refugee' and who belonged to the category of 'beggar'? Who had a valid call on government support and who was a sponger? The stakes were considerable, not only for millions of Chinese displaced by the Japanese military invasion and the prolonged occupation, but also for the occupation regime that was caught up in a crisis of its own making.[18]

One final issue is the choice of an appropriate register in which to write. The leading French migration scholar Gérard Noiriel urged fellow scholars to deploy 'new forms' of writing about migration, something that is evident in cultural studies.[19] Although my book largely adheres to established conventions of historical writing, I sought to demonstrate that multiple voices and portrayals of displacement circulate amongst refugees who write their own history. Reflecting on the experience of Palestinians in exile, Edward Said wrote that 'essentially unconventional, hybrid and fragmentary forms of expression should be used to represent us'. Such fragments are scattered throughout *The Making of the Modern Refugee*. So, too, are attempts by refugees to offer what they regard as a coherent version of the past. One of my favourite examples (see p. 295) is the 17-year-old Palestinian boy who said that 'my mother told us about Palestine, but she didn't know the plots'. Claims to speak with authority about the history of displacement come from many different sources, and it is idle to pretend that anyone has a monopoly.

[15] Lynda Mannik, *Photography, Memory, and Refugee Identity: The Voyage of the SS Walnut* (Vancouver: University of British Columbia Press, 2013), 55, 153–7.

[16] Ian Hacking, 'Making up People' *London Review of Books*, 17 Aug. 2006. See also Roger Zetter, 'More Labels, Fewer Refugees: Remaking the Refugee Label in an Era of Globalization' *JRS* 20, no.2 (2007), 172–92.

[17] Laura Madokoro, 'Borders Transformed: Sovereign Concerns, Population Movements and the Making of Territorial Frontiers in Hong Kong, 1949–1967' *JRS* 25, no.3 (2012), 407–27.

[18] Janet Y. Chen, *Guilty of Indigence: The Urban Poor in China, 1900–1953* (Princeton: Princeton University Press, 2012), 128. I owe this reference to Pierre Fuller.

[19] Gérard Noiriel, *The French Melting Pot: Immigration, Citizenship, and National Identity* (Minneapolis: University of Minnesota Press, 1996), 98. In addition to Nguyen, *The Gift of Freedom*, see Agnes Woolley, *Contemporary Asylum Narratives: Representing Refugees in the Twenty-First Century* (Palgrave Macmillan, 2014); and Amitava Kumar, *Passport Photos* (Berkeley, Calif.: University of California Press, 2000).

Contents

List of Maps and Tables

MAPS

TABLES

Abbreviations

ABBREVIATED TITLES OF JOURNALS

AAAPSS	*Annals of the American Academy of Political and Social Science*
AHR	*American Historical Review*
CEH	*Contemporary European History*
CSH	*Cultural and Social History*
CSSH	*Comparative Studies in Society and History*
HRQ	*Human Rights Quarterly*
IJRL	*International Journal of Refugee Law*
IMR	*International Migration Review*
JCH	*Journal of Contemporary History*
JEMS	*Journal of Ethnic and Migration Studies*
JMAS	*Journal of Modern African Studies*
JMGS	*Journal of Modern Greek Studies*
JMH	*Journal of Modern History*
JPS	*Journal of Palestine Studies*
JRS	*Journal of Refugee Studies*
MAS	*Modern Asian Studies*
MES	*Middle Eastern Studies*
RSQ	*Refugee Survey Quarterly*

OTHER ABBREVIATIONS

AFSC	American Friends Service Committee
ARA	American Relief Administration
CARE	Cooperative for Assistance and Relief Everywhere (originally Cooperative for American Remittances to Europe)
CO	Colonial Office, UK
DP	Displaced Person
EVW	European Volunteer Workers
FEWVRC	Friends' Emergency and War Victims' Relief Committee
FO	Foreign Office, UK
ICEM	Intergovernmental Committee for European Migration
ICRC	International Committee of the Red Cross, Geneva
IDP	Internally Displaced Person
IOL	India Office Library, British Library, London
IOM	International Organisation for Migration, Geneva
IRO	International Refugee Organisation
IWM	Imperial War Museum, London
JAI	Jami'at al Islam
JDC	American Jewish Joint Distribution Committee
LAC	Library and Archives Canada

LRCS	League of Red Cross Societies
LWF	Lutheran World Federation
MSF	Médecins sans Frontières
NARA	National Archives and Records Administration, Maryland
NCWC	National Catholic Welfare Conference
NGO	Non-Governmental Organization
OAU	Organisation of African Unity
ODP	Orderly Departure Programme
PRC	People's Republic of China
RSC	Refugee Studies Centre, University of Oxford
TNA	UK National Archives, Kew
UNCACK	United Nations Civil Assistance Command in Korea
UNHCR	Office of the United Nations High Commissioner for Refugees
UNICEF	United Nations International Children's Emergency Fund
UNKRA	United Nations Korean Reconstruction Agency
UNOG	United Nations Library, Geneva
UNRRA	United Nations Relief and Rehabilitation Administration
UNRWA	United Nations Relief and Works Agency
USEP	United States Escapee Program
WCC	World Council of Churches
WRY	World Refugee Year

Introduction: The Making of the Modern Refugee

Ours [the twentieth century] has been the century of departure, of migration, of exodus—of disappearance, the century of people helplessly seeing others, who were close to them, disappear over the horizon

(John Berger)

Today's information media are filled with reports of disasters that result in people being forced to flee. Sometimes they die before reaching a place of safety. The recent past provides abundant evidence of huge involuntary population movements in Iraq, Afghanistan and Syria, the Horn of Africa and the Great Lakes Region, and elsewhere. The dissolution of Yugoslavia and its violent aftermath in the early 1990s provided a salutary reminder that Europe was not immune from refugee crises; even today, by far the largest concentration of refugees per head of population anywhere in the world is in Armenia. Many of these conflicts persist. At the end of 2012, close on nine million refugees had been living in refugee camps and other settlements for more than a decade. The ordeal of 2.5 million Palestinians in the Middle East stretches back to 1948. Many of these instances are reasonably well known, at least in outline, but the circumstances of other refugees, such as Bhutanese in Nepal, Rohingya in Bangladesh, and Sahrawi refugees in West Africa rarely figure in the news. Western broadcasters occasionally touch on catastrophe, as when boats overloaded with refugees capsize at sea, but these accounts rarely illuminate the circumstances that compel them to flee. Instead public opinion is fed uninformative scraps about asylum seekers that disregard the fact that most of the world's refugees eke out an existence far from the borders of First World countries.

Something of the same applies to our grasp of more distant events. It is widely recognized that the great wars of the twentieth century, like those in previous eras, caused vast numbers of people to leave their homes. This reinforces the view that the link between war and population displacement is self-evident. But is it? Why has involuntary displacement been such a prominent feature of the modern era? Has it been episodic or systematic? Is there something peculiar about recent upheavals or do they form part of a twentieth-century continuum? What attempts were made to tackle crises in different parts of the world and at different junctures, and did these efforts have common aims and features? Under what circumstances did refugees return to their homes, and with what results? These questions suggest the need for a global history of displacement and relief programmes over time. They invite us to consider how refugees understood the myriad ramifications of flight and how they engaged with those who were left behind and with whom they might hope at some stage to reconnect. This process extends to exploring the meanings that they attached to the places of their departure, to their journeys, and to their destinations. This invites a history of, and in, displacement.

One aim of *The Making of the Modern Refugee* is to come to a better appreciation of what is distinctive about refugee crises in the new millennium, and what is not. My focus is predominantly on the twentieth century. To be sure, the historical record discloses numerous attempts to expel individuals and entire populations on grounds of political opinion or religious belief. Long before 1900, political disorder and war compelled vanquished or politically obdurate groups and religious minorities to seek refuge elsewhere. In 1492, Spain brought centuries of Moorish rule to an end and enforced Catholic conformity, causing 200,000 Muslims and Jews to flee. German Protestants who were expelled from the Palatinate in the seventeenth century made their way to Kent where they languished in vast tented settlements before proceeding to Pennsylvania. One million Huguenots left France rather than convert to Catholicism following the Revocation of the Edict of Nantes in 1685. Revolution in Haiti in 1791 caused white plantation owners to flee; some of them ended up in an isolated part of Cuba called Guantánamo Bay. These instances can be multiplied. They point to persecution and discrimination, but they belong to a more remote geopolitical universe and generated nothing like the institutional response that became familiar in the modern era. Twentieth-century displacement was unprecedented by virtue of being linked to the collapse of multinational empires, the emergence of the modern state with a bounded citizenship, the spread of totalizing ideologies that hounded internal enemies, and the internationalization of responses to refugee crises.[1]

Was the magnitude of population displacement in the late twentieth century of a different order compared to crises earlier in the century? The answer, which may come as something of a surprise, is that the size of the refugee population as recorded in official statistics and including data on internally displaced persons was highest in the middle years of the twentieth century. Given the rapid growth in world population the proportion of refugees was therefore smaller in relative terms in the late twentieth century (see the snapshot in Table 1). It is hard to avoid the conclusion that the most dramatic period of mass population displacement occurred in the 1940s as a result of war and political upheaval around the world.

What explains these dynamics and this magnitude? In the first phase, wartime mobilization raised the stakes by drawing attention to people whose mere presence was deemed to threaten the security of the state and the war effort. Entire communities in the Ottoman, Habsburg and Russian empires were deported

---

[1] Howard Adelman, 'Modernity, Globalisation, Refugees and Displacement', in Alistair Ager (ed.), *Refugees: Perspectives on the Experience of Forced Migration* (Continuum, 1999), 83–110.
  The publisher location for all references in this book is London, unless otherwise stated.

Table 1: Twentieth-Century Displaced/Refugee Population (millions, estimated)

	First World War aftermath	Second World War aftermath	Cold War aftermath
Continental Europe	10 [Eastern Europe] 2 [Balkans]	60	<7
Non-European continents	n/a	90 [China] 20 [South Asia] 1 [Middle East] 4 [other, incl. Hong Kong]	6 [South-East Asia and Middle East] 6 [Sub-Saharan Africa] 4 [other] 24 [IDPs]
Global total	>12	175	47
Total world population	1,800	2,300	5,300
Percentage displaced	<1.0%	7.6%	0.9%

Notes and sources: see chapters 1–6. For the Cold War aftermath (1992–96 average), see UNHCR data <http://www.unhcr.org/3bfa33154.html> supplemented by <http://www.internal-displacement.org/>.

before and during the First World War on grounds of their perceived disloyalty. These deliberate actions by imperial rulers multiplied the chaos brought about by the mass flight of civilians who sought to escape the wrath of enemy troops (chapter 1). In the Ottoman Empire, the Young Turks turned on Armenian and Kurdish minorities; those who escaped deportation and mass murder became refugees. Subsequently, revolution and civil war in Russia set class against class and offered another foretaste of what was to come, by linking social and political transformation to a further round of population politics.[2]

Targeting imperial subjects had unforeseen and ironic consequences, because patriotic leaders in each group appealed to refugees' sense of belonging to a belea-guered nation that could only be properly secured by detaching itself from the imperial core and being constituted as a sovereign entity. The end of the war led to the replacement of old imperial polities by new nation-states. But this created even more favourable conditions for the persecution of minorities who did not meet the criteria for political membership. Discriminatory practices reached their apogee in Germany where the Nazi state excluded Jews from political citizenship and then proceeded to exterminate them on occupied territory during the Second World War. Fascist terror was not, however, confined to Nazi Germany. Defeat in the Spanish Civil War forced Franco's opponents to flee to France. The cultural record created by Spanish refugees in designated camps or in transit to new destinations, spoke of loss and humiliation, tempered by a determination to transcend their displacement (chapter 2).

Nor was demographic engineering the sole preserve of totalitarian states. The rearrangement of population and territory in Greece and Turkey under the terms

---

[2] On population politics, see Zygmunt Bauman, *Modernity and the Holocaust* (Oxford: Polity Press, 1989); Amir Weiner (ed.), *Landscaping the Human Garden: Twentieth-Century Population Management in a Comparative Framework* (Stanford: Stanford University Press, 2003).

of the Treaty of Lausanne signed in 1923 was conceived as a means to prevent ethnic and social conflict by compelling the Muslim inhabitants of Greece to move to Turkey and insisting that residents of Turkey who professed the Orthodox religion depart for Greece. It created a substantial refugee population in both states. The growing acceptance of the argument that the modern state should be ethnically homogeneous had profound consequences: liberal politicians and diplomats embraced the 'unmixing of peoples' (in Lord Curzon's phrase) as a means of separating ethnic groups to reduce the possibility of conflict.[3]

This approach also characterized peace-making after the Second World War. The war uprooted civilians as well as soldiers. Invasion and deportation killed millions and left survivors stranded. In China the Japanese invasion led to a massive crisis of internal population displacement that destabilised the country politically and socially and contributed to the epoch-making communist revolution in 1949 (chapter 6). In Europe the victorious Allies embarked on a series of punitive expulsions as well as organized population transfers in Central Europe, forcing ethnic Germans out of Poland and Czechoslovakia. Given the widespread antipathy towards former enemies, the Allied powers focused not on their plight but on that of the so-called 'Displaced Persons' (DPs) who had been taken to Germany during the war as forced labourers. This was a polyglot group—the irony of Hitler bequeathing Germany a multinational population was not lost on contemporaries—held in camps so that arrangements could be made for their repatriation. The camp provided another opportunity for patriotic elites in historic émigré communities as well as Ukrainian, Polish, Lithuanian and other DPs inside Germany and Austria to engage with their co-nationals. Nationality was again reaffirmed. At the same time, a new crisis came about as people fled communist states in Eastern Europe. In a foretaste of things to come, Western governments pondered whether they might be more accurately described as 'economic migrants' rather than as persecuted individuals (chapter 3).

Turning 'insiders' into 'outsiders' became a familiar practice elsewhere in the twentieth century as colonial empires gave way to independent countries whose claims to legitimacy rested on the affirmation of popular sovereignty. The peace settlement after the First World War replaced Ottoman domination of the Middle East with a series of British and French mandates. British, French and Belgian rule in sub-Saharan Africa supported certain ethnic groups at the expense of others, stoking rivalries that had the potential to erupt into civil war when colonial rule came to an end. The map of the Middle East and the Indian sub-continent was redrawn yet again following the Second World War, culminating in the creation of new states whose history was bound up with large-scale refugee crises (chapters 4 and 5). Emerging nation-states established and defended their borders; governments defined the boundaries of citizenship

---

[3] Hannah Arendt, *The Origins of Totalitarianism*, 2nd edn (New York: Meridian Books, 1958), 267, 294; Aristide R. Zolberg, Astri Suhrke and Sergio Aguayo, *Escape from Violence: Conflict and the Refugee Crisis in the Developing World* (New York: Oxford University Press, 1989), chapter 1; Norman Naimark, *Fires of Hatred: Ethnic Cleansing in Twentieth-Century Europe* (Cambridge, Mass: Harvard University Press, 2001).

and engaged with ethnic minority and migrant populations: 'distinguishing migrants from locals, identifying and resettling refugees and displaced peoples—these endeavours became central to the new states' assertion of authority, and their definitions of citizenship'.[4] The conflict in Sri Lanka, which achieved independence from Britain in 1948, is a case in point. Here the new government discriminated against the predominantly Hindu Tamil minority in favour of the Buddhist Sinhalese majority. The result was a protracted civil war which by the 1980s displaced ten per cent of the total population.

In sub-Saharan Africa and South-East Asia the dissolution of colonial administration caused many white settlers to flee, although these 'returnees' struggled to find a place that they could call home.[5] But the mainsprings of population displacement lay elsewhere. Rival ethnic and social groups advanced claims to power in newly independent states. Revolutionary turmoil frequently accompanied the retreat from empire. As in Russia, radical leaders in China, Vietnam, Cambodia and Ethiopia defined membership of the political community in terms of class. Each of them added population resettlement to their repertoire. Revolution in Cambodia was followed by a prolonged refugee crisis when Vietnamese troops dislodged the genocidal regime of Pol Pot in 1979. Fledgling states targeted real or imagined opponents and enlisted supporters in the process of political transformation. Civil wars fuelled by external intervention created perfect conditions for manufacturing refugees. In Rwanda the refugee crisis had complex origins that can be traced back at least a generation prior to the genocide in 1994 (chapters 7 and 8).[6]

Seeking to understand the origins of population displacement is only one element in *The Making of the Modern Refugee*. We also need to consider how the modern refugee came to be construed as a 'problem' amenable to a 'solution'. Part of the answer is to be found in ideas of international action. The history of population displacement was closely linked to the creation and operation of an international refugee regime, meaning in the first instance a set of legal rules, norms and agreements between sovereign states about refugees and states' responsibilities towards them. But this regime was never a singular and unchanging entity. Its first incarnation followed the First World War when European states responded to the arrival of Russian and Armenian refugees with measures that were widely seen as ad hoc arrangements.[7]

After the Second World War, the new United Nations (UN) refashioned the refugee regime. This framework remains largely intact. For more than six decades the

---

[4] Sunil Amrith, *Migration and Diaspora in Modern Asia* (Cambridge: Cambridge University Press, 2001), 116.

[5] Andrea Smith (ed.), *Europe's Invisible Migrants* (Amsterdam: Amsterdam University Press, 2003).

[6] Aristide Zolberg, 'The Formation of New States as a Refugee-generating Process' *AAAPSS*, 467 (1983), 282–96.

[7] Claudena Skran, *Refugees in Inter-War Europe: the Emergence of a Regime* (Oxford: Clarendon Press, 1995); Nevzat Soguk, *States and Strangers: Refugees and Displacements of Statecraft* (Minneapolis: University of Minnesota Press, 1999); Emma Haddad, *The Refugee in International Society: between Sovereigns* (Cambridge: Cambridge University Press, 2008), 99–127.

main inter-governmental agency that supports refugees has been the Office of the United Nations High Commissioner for Refugees (UNHCR), formed in December 1950. UNHCR is responsible for supervising the application of the 1951 Convention Relating to the Status of Refugees, which safeguards the rights and welfare of persons 'outside the country of their nationality', provided they could establish a 'well-founded fear of being persecuted on grounds of race, religion, nationality, membership of a particular social group or political opinion'. This definition represented a departure from the pre-war doctrine whereby protection was offered to specified groups rather than an individual who could demonstrate persecution. It made implicit reference to Nazism but had Soviet totalitarianism even more in its sights (chapter 3). Signatories to the 1951 Convention agreed to the principle of non-refoulement, whereby no refugee could be returned to any country where he or she faced the threat of persecution or torture.[8] Like the pre-war League of Nations, UNHCR had no powers to intervene in the internal affairs of sovereign states who paid its bills and who ultimately decided asylum claims. Many states refused to endorse the Convention—even today only three-quarters of UN states have signed—and it took at least a decade for the UNHCR to gain international acceptance and to assist refugees in situations that its originators never envisaged (chapters 7 and 8).

The Convention left other forced migrants in the cold, including the person who left 'solely because political events were not to his liking', as well as internally displaced persons (IDPs) who did not cross an external frontier. Greater attention is now paid to people displaced by environmental change and natural disasters as well as development projects.[9] An important hallmark of change was the decision by the Organisation of African Unity in 1969 to adopt a Convention on Refugee Problems in Africa, according to which a refugee was any 'person who, owing to external aggression, occupation, foreign domination or events seriously disturbing public order in either part of the whole of his country of origin or nationality, is compelled to leave his place of habitual residence in order to seek refuge' (chapter 8). These decisions raised the visibility of internally-displaced persons who accounted for a significant proportion of the global total.[10]

UNHCR is not a fossilized entity: it too has a history.[11] Governments and intergovernmental agencies articulated a series of 'durable solutions' to displacement,

---

[8] A convention ratified by nine states including France and Britain in October 1933 introduced the principle of *non-refoulement* into international law. The 1951 Convention made an exception in the case of those deemed to be a threat to national security.

[9] Richard Black, *Refugees, Environment and Development* (Longman, 1998); Jennifer Hyndman and James Mclean, 'Settling like a State: Acehnese Refugees in Vancouver' *JRS*, 19, no.3 (2006), 345–60.

[10] Jacques Vernant, *The Refugee in the Post-War World* (Allen and Unwin, 1953), 6; Andrew Shacknove, 'Who is a Refugee?' *Ethics*, 95 (1985), 274–84; Oliver Bakewell, 'Conceptualising Displacement and Migration', in Khalid Koser and Susan Martin (eds), *The Migration-Displacement Nexus: Patterns, Processes, and Policies* (New York: Berghahn, 2011), 14–28; Susan Coutin, 'The Oppressed, the Suspect, and the Citizen: Subjectivity in Competing Accounts of Political Violence' *Law & Social Inquiry*, 26, no.1 (2001), 63–94.

[11] The key text is Gil Loescher, *The UNHCR and World Politics: a Perilous Path* (Oxford: Oxford University Press, 2001).

namely repatriation, resettlement or 'local integration'. To simplify a complex story, resettlement became the chief means (along with the deterrent effects of restrictive immigration policies) of resolving the situation of refugees who sought asylum between the wars. In the aftermath of the Second World War, the Allies anticipated that DPs would wish to return to their country of origin. As the Cold War intensified, however, policy-makers and officials devoted much of their efforts to resettling refugees from communism. Repatriation became a dirty word. The international response to other crises varied according to geopolitical considera-tions: the UN entrusted the care of Palestinian refugees to a specialized 'relief and works' agency as a kind of holding operation (chapter 4), but member states showed scant interest in the refugee crisis following the partition of India which they re-garded as a largely internal affair (chapter 5). The end of the Cold War took repatria-tion back to the top of the agenda—although repatriation had already been adopted in Cambodia and to a lesser extent in Vietnam during the 1980s (chapter 7).[12] This stance was accompanied by an emphasis among many wealthy countries on the need to deter mass displacement by focusing on conditions in 'refugee-generating' states.

Thus the twentieth-century refugee, as a person and as a category, was shaped by changing legal doctrine. We should not assume, however, that refugees were always defined according to a single formula. Those displaced as a result of the partition of India were excluded from the discussions leading to the 1951 Refugee Convention, because they were 'national refugees'. During the 1950s the British and the French resolved to keep the UNHCR out of refugee crises in Hong Kong and Algeria, on the grounds that they were a purely metropolitan responsibility. There has never been a 'one size fits all' definition of refugees in the Western and non-Western worlds.[13] It is more appropriate to think of multiple and overlapping regimes. Better still, we require a term that allows for different and contested doctrines and policies at a governmental, inter-governmental and non-governmental level. These practices are one of the constituent components of what I shall call refugeedom.[14]

The concept of a refugee regime can be probed more closely to take account of organized programmes of humanitarian assistance devised by non-governmental organizations (NGOs). These programmes did not begin in the twentieth century, but they became more ubiquitous and intrusive over time. The implications were

---

[12] Gervase Coles, 'Approaching the Refugee Problem Today', in Gil Loescher and Laila Monahan (eds), *Refugees and International Relations* (Oxford: Oxford University Press, 1989), 373–410; Howard Adelman and Elazar Barkan, *No Return, No Refuge: Rites and Rights in Minority Repatriation* (New York: Columbia University Press, 2011).

[13] Liisa Malkki, 'National Geographic: the Rooting of Peoples and the Territorialisation of National Identity among Scholars and Refugees' *Cultural Anthropology*, 7, no.1 (1992), 24–44; B.S. Chimni, 'The Geopolitics of Refugee Studies: a View from the South' *JRS*, 11, no.4 (1998), 350–74; Pamela Ballinger, ' "Entangled" or "Extruded" Histories? Displacement, National Refugees, and Repatriation after the Second World War' *JRS*, 25, no.3 (2012), 366–86.

[14] This is my translation of the Russian term *bezhenstvo* that gained currency during the First World War. 'Refugeedom' appears in Joseph Schechtman, *The Refugee in the World: Displacement and Integration* (New York: Barnes and Co., 1963). Schechtman lived in Russia until 1920, so he would have been familiar with the Russian usage.

enormous. Charitable organizations established, trained and supported teams of relief workers in the 'field' alongside a central administration charged with the task of disseminating publicity and fundraising. These institutions act in ways that are frequently taken for granted by public opinion in donor countries, but their operations need to be explained and contextualized historically. Most NGOs developed close links with governments and international organizations that commissioned programmes of assistance, thereby contributing to their budgets as well as raising their profile.[15]

NGOs trade upon their longevity and 'tradition' of humanitarian relief, but they rarely show anything other than superficial interest in their history. Nor, on the whole, do they seek to grasp the underlying causes of population displacement.[16] Part of my argument is that the humanitarianism they embody was an essential component in fashioning the modern refugee as a passive and 'traumatized' object of intervention as compared to the active, purposeful and much-travelled relief worker, a distinction that was not altered by the so-called shift from relief-based to rights-based humanitarianism. But the distinction is not just between the institutions of relief and the object of their concern. NGOs themselves might differ in approach, for example between faith-based and secular organizations. What was their relationship to intergovernmental bodies, to governments, to one another, and to refugees? What were their chosen instruments of action? What assumptions did staff workers take with them as they moved from one site of displacement to another?[17]

Critics point to a lack of accountability and transparency in the 'humanitarian international', reflecting the asymmetrical relations between donors and recipients.[18] Historical evidence suggests that good intentions derived from outrage at the treatment meted out to refugees. Cultural constructions of humanitarian purposefulness were an understandable response to human desperation and a tactic to stimulate public sympathy and generosity. Relief efforts were at times infused with

---

[15] Jonathan Benthall, *Disasters, Relief and the Media* (Tauris, 1993); Elizabeth G. Ferris, *Beyond Borders: Refugees, Migrants and Human Rights in the Post-Cold War Era* (Geneva: World Council of Churches, 1993), 35–65; Didier Fassin and Mariella Pandolfi (eds), *Contemporary States of Emergency: the Politics of Military and Humanitarian Interventions* (Brooklyn: Zone Books, 2010); Michael Barnett, *Empire of Humanity: a History of Humanitarianism* (Ithaca: Cornell University Press, 2011).

[16] William F. Fisher, 'Doing Good? The Politics and Antipolitics of NGO Practices' *Annual Review of Anthropology*, 26 (1997), 439–64; Fiona Terry, *Condemned to Repeat? The Paradox of Humanitarian Action* (Ithaca: Cornell University Press, 2002), 220–3, 236–7; Michael Barnett and Thomas Weiss (eds), *Humanitarianism in Question: Politics, Power, Ethics* (Ithaca: Cornell University Press, 2008).

[17] David Chandler, 'The Road to Military Humanitarianism: How Human Rights NGOs Shaped a New Humanitarian Agenda' *HRQ*, 23, no.3 (2001), 678–700; Nida Kirmani and Ajaz Ahmed Khan, 'Does Faith Matter? An Examination of Islamic Relief's Work with Refugees and Internally Displaced Persons' *RSQ*, 27, no.2 (2008), 41–50; Michael Barnett and Janice Gross Stein (eds), *Sacred Aid: Faith and Humanitarianism* (New York: Oxford University Press, 2012).

[18] Alex de Waal, *Famine Crimes: Politics and the Disaster Relief Industry in Africa* (Oxford: James Currey, 1997); Barbara Harrell-Bond, *Imposing Aid: Emergency Assistance to Refugees* (Oxford: Oxford University Press, 1986); Barbara Harrell-Bond and Eftihia Voutira, 'In Search of "Invisible" Actors: Barriers to Access in Refugee Research' *JRS*, 20, no. 2 (2007), 281–98.

a sense of displacement as a gendered calamity, persuading humanitarians of the need to provide for female refugees and orphaned children who had been abducted. Long-term plans also appealed to governments and relief workers, as in the doctrine of 'rehabilitating' refugees in order to prepare them for life as prospective citizens when they resettled. Aid agencies and politicians embraced the idea of 'development' as a means to support refugees and forestall future refugee crises. The antecedents of this idea stretch further back in time than is realized.

For many of the world's refugees the characteristic experience has been incarceration. This is not to discount those who managed to survive as 'self-settled' refugees: at the beginning of the twenty-first century, UNHCR estimated that around four in 10 registered refugees lived in a camp (the figure is higher in sub-Saharan Africa). The refugee camp too has a history, as a modern site of enumeration, categorization and assessment by officials and relief workers. When and for what reasons did this become an acceptable practice, and why did refugee camps emerge in some situations and not in others? What were the implications for the security and well-being of refugees? These questions have been addressed by human geographers, political scientists and social anthropologists, but historians have scarcely touched upon them. The refugee camp is something of a double-edged sword: a device for managing refugees, and a means of mobilizing refugees ideologically and militarily. History puts administrative practice and refugee experience alike into proper perspective.[19]

A focus on legal formulations, bureaucratic practices and material deprivation nevertheless supplies only a partial picture.[20] Refugees were (and are) regularly forced to live in extreme conditions, without necessarily being deprived of the capacity to exercise a degree of control over their own lives. As Aihwa Ong indicates, 'in official and public domains refugees become subjects of norms, rules, and systems, but they also modify practices and agendas while nimbly deflecting control and interjecting critique'.[21] Yet they are habitually portrayed as if they are without agency, like corks bobbing along on the surface of an unstoppable wave of displacement. In a banal manifestation of the extent to which speechlessness and passivity have become the norm, it is now possible to purchase a plastic 'model refugee family', whose miniatures can be assembled as part of a war-gaming scenario in order to lend it greater 'authenticity'. It consists of a small group of women and children, their headscarves giving them the appearance of 'Balkan refugees', disconsolately surveying an imaginary landscape. They are meant to

[19] Jennifer Hyndman, *Managing Displacement: Refugees and the Politics of Humanitarianism* (Minnesota: University of Minnesota Press, 2000); Terry, *Condemned to Repeat?*, 5–10; Sarah Kenyon Lischer, *Dangerous Sanctuaries: Refugee Camps, Civil War, and the Dilemmas of Humanitarian Aid* (Ithaca: Cornell University Press, 2005); Michel Agier, *Managing the Undesirables: Refugee Camps and Humanitarian Government* (Cambridge: Polity, 2011).

[20] David Turton, 'Conceptualising Forced Migration' RSC Working Paper, no.12 (Oxford: RSC, 2003); Oliver Bakewell, 'Research beyond the Categories: the Importance of Policy Irrelevant Research into Forced Migration' *JRS*, 21, no.4 (2008), 432–53.

[21] Aihwa Ong, *Buddha is Hiding: Refugees, Citizenship, the New America* (Berkeley: University of California Press, 2003), xvii; Peter Loizos, 'Misconceiving Refugees?', in Renos Papadopoulos (ed.), *Therapeutic Care for Refugees: No Place Like Home* (Karnac Books, 2002), 41–56.

convey a helpless inability to contain or comprehend what is happening to them. As we shall see, portraying refugees as bewildered and bereft victims has a long genealogy.

Anonymity too is a central conceit of modern representation. Mass displacement is taken to render refugees indistinguishable. The unnamed individual embodies the condition of refugees everywhere who cannot avoid their amalgamation into a collective category of concern. One major NGO issued a glossy booklet in 1970 to appeal for funds, making the point that 'this booklet bears no title, only a picture of an unnamed refugee. That is not an oversight. It is untitled as a token of respect for the vast number of nameless refugees whose tenuous claim to identity is constantly threatened; lost in the meaningless anonymity of the dismal statistics on human tragedy'.[22] No-one captured this better than the French critic Roland Barthes in his blistering attack on 'exotic' travel films of the 1950s that displayed 'a romantic essence of the fisherman, presented not as a workman dependent by his technique and his gains on a definite society, but rather as the theme of an eternal condition, in which man is far away and exposed to the perils of the sea, and woman weeping and praying at home'. He added that the same applied to refugees, 'a long procession of which is shown at the beginning, coming down a mountain: to identify them is of course unnecessary; they are *eternal essences of refugees*, which it is the nature of the East to produce'. This made it unnecessary to supply historical context. The image, so to say, speaks for itself.[23]

This 'eternal essence' informs much of the photographic record of displacement, which is largely how the twentieth century came to know refugees. A cluster of renowned mid-twentieth century photographers ensured that a visual record survived of civil wars in Spain and China (in the work of Robert Capa), the Partition of India (Margaret Bourke-White) and the Korean War (Bert Hardy). In recent times photographers such as Simon Norfolk and Alixandra Fazzina have added to the archive.[24] Sometimes the image serves as an aesthetic statement, as in the famous photograph taken in Nasir Bagh refugee camp by Steve McCurry of an 'Afghan girl', beautiful and exotic, but unidentified and de-contextualized.[25] Major international organizations and NGOs have employed staff photographers to record conflict as well as life in refugee camps. Only on rare occasions are people identified, and often (as in UNHCR photographs of successive High Commissioners) this is to highlight the stature of important officials, whose serious gaze implies authority and determination, or the compassion shown by humanitarian celebrities. The British fashion photographer Rankin took a series of photographs of Congolese refugees who settled in Mugunga camp, Goma, and created a small

[22] UNHCR Records of the Central Registry 1951–1970, Fonds 11, Series 1, 4/14, LWF, 1967–71.

[23] Roland Barthes, *Mythologies* (Vintage, 1993), 95–6, emphasis added; Anna Szörény, 'The Images Speak for Themselves? Reading Refugee Coffee-table Books' *Visual Studies*, 21, no.1 (2006), 24–41.

[24] See <http://www.simonnorfolk.com/>. Fazzina was awarded the UNHCR's Nansen Medal in 2010 for 'her striking coverage of the devastating human consequences of war'.

[25] McCurry announced in April 2001 that he had 'found' her again, and that her name is Sharbat Gula.

exhibition for Oxfam, 'to put faces to the statistics'. He added, without a trace of irony, 'I'd love to go back'.[26] These images are not straightforward snapshots of reality but rather constitute an 'iconography of predicament', which are framed in such a way as to stimulate compassion and loosen wallets.[27] Their timelessness neither explains displacement nor illuminates refugees' strategies for survival.

I have dwelt at some length on the question of anonymity because it is part of a larger issue, namely the general absence of refugees in historical scholarship. It may be that this invisibility reflects a belief—difficult to sustain in the new millennium—that refugees emerged only fleetingly on the stage of history before being restored to a more settled existence. There is still a tendency to regard refugee crises as temporary and unique, rather than as 'recurring phenomena'.[28] Their supposedly episodic appearance and tangential life renders refugees less prominent than other social groups that have left a clear footprint in the documentary record. It might be thought that refugees themselves contributed to this state of affairs by preferring to forget their ordeal, but as we shall see the evidence does not sustain such a blanket explanation. In respect of refugees we therefore need to explain the 'production of neglect'.[29]

Finally, to bring refugees closer to the centre of this story is to explore and go beyond their responses to displacement. The testimony of refugees speaks to a fundamental alteration in their lives. Tesfay, an Eritrean refugee told Caroline Moorehead that 'at home I always felt safe. I was respected, popular, I had friends. Here I knew no one. I dreaded having to tell my story again and again, to lawyers, to the doctor, to the Home Office. The only place I could find to live was the past'.[30] This disconsolate statement underscores the importance of human relationships and connections. They may, as in Tesfay's case, connect to officials who required him to list his credentials. But this hardly exhausts the significance of the networks in which refugees are enmeshed. Refugees have been linked to one another across time and space as well as being connected to host populations and to former friends and neighbours who stayed put. These relationships and networks are multi-faceted. To quote Joan Scott, 'How are those who cross the thresholds received? If they belong to a group different from one already "inside", what are the terms of their incorporation? How do the new arrivals understand their relationship to the place they have entered?'[31] These issues are threaded throughout *The Making of the Modern Refugee*.

---

[26] <http://news.bbc.co.uk/1/hi/entertainment/7680597.stm>, and his website at <http://www.rankin.co.uk/bio.aspx>.

[27] Terence Wright, 'Moving Images: the Media Representation of Refugees' *Visual Studies*, 17, no.1 (2002), 53–66.

[28] Barry Stein, 'The Refugee Experience: Defining the Parameters of a Field of Study' *IMR*, 15, nos.1–2 (1981), 320–30, at 321. For a pioneering attempt to survey the European dimension, see Michael Marrus, *The Unwanted: European Refugees in the Twentieth Century*, 2nd edn (Oxford: Oxford University Press, 2002).

[29] Joan Scott, *Gender and the Politics of History* (New York: Columbia University Press, 1988), 84.

[30] Caroline Moorehead, *Human Cargo: a Journey among Refugees* (Chatto and Windus, 2005), 233.

[31] Scott, *Gender and the Politics of History*, 178; Emanuel Marx, 'The Social World of Refugees: a Conceptual Framework' *JRS*, 3, no.3 (1990), 189–203; E. Valentine Daniel and John Knudsen (eds), *Mistrusting Refugees* (Berkeley: University of California Press, 1995).

I argue that refugees have helped to fashion themselves by recourse to history. In other words, the past has been a means to express their predicament and a channel for articulating and validating the possibilities of collective action. Whether engaged in politics, cultural activities or military campaigns, and whether retaliating, seeking restitution, or simply looking for a quiet life, a sense of history was often close to the surface of refugees' self-expression. To take this seriously is to think about the resources that refugees could call upon or create, such as memorial books commemorating the towns and villages that Jewish Holocaust survivors left behind in Central Europe after the Second World War and that Palestinians were forced to abandon in 1948. Financial and other tangible support from groups overseas also points to the presence of the past, because diaspora presupposes a history of migration, including forced displacement.[32]

Politics matters in affording refugees and their descendants the opportunity to engage with past episodes and sites of displacement and 're-placement'. The end of communism in Europe altered the terrain by creating conditions for the public commemoration of Soviet-era deportations, for example among Crimean Tatars, and of other displacements, such as those in the Italian-Yugoslav borderlands (chapter 9). But it is not always easy to establish a clear-cut link between political change and refugees' ability or willingness to confront the past. Those who were forced to flee as young adults following the Turkish invasion of Cyprus in 1974 have now reached middle age. A new generation has grown up knowing this history through the tales told by their parents and grandparents. What of other sites of displacement? How far have the children and grandchildren of Chinese refugees who fled to Hong Kong after 1949 begun to engage with the history of displacement? What role did 'refugee historians' play in tracing and commemorating refugeedom in Rwanda and Burundi during the 1960s–70s and in 1994, and for what audience did they write?

I draw things together by reflecting on the uses to which refugees have put history and how history has given them a voice, even where the consequences may be disquieting. Refugees appropriated and interpreted history as a key resource that helped them to make sense of their displacement. This is invariably a contested process, exposing multiple and divisive viewpoints.[33] Stories can become histories capable of perpetuating conflict and sustaining further episodes of displacement. Here we come full circle: displacement exposed refugees to the apparatus of the state and the power exercised by non-state actors. Refugees might consequently aspire to exercise power on their own behalf, perhaps to turn the tables on those who had persecuted them in the first place. The resolution of refugeedom might culminate in reconciliation with one's erstwhile enemies, but it could also summon retribution and a call to arms. Although one would still be left with the insistent

---

[32] Robin Cohen, *Global Diasporas* (London: UCL Press, 1997); Nicholas Van Hear, *New Diasporas: the Mass Exodus, Dispersal and Regrouping of Migrant Communities* (London: UCL Press, 1998).

[33] John C. Knudsen, *Capricious Worlds: Vietnamese Life Journeys* (New Brunswick: Transaction Publishers, 2005); Loring Danforth and Riki van Boeschoten, *Children of the Greek Civil War: Refugees and the Politics of Memory* (Chicago: Chicago University Press, 2011).

claims asserted by sovereign states, the most hopeful outcome (dare one say?) is to build cosmopolitan coalitions between refugees and non-refugees, promoting political debate, transparent justice, economic growth and social equality.

These considerations explain my decision to organize the material geographically and chronologically. Some episodes and sites necessarily get short shrift. I have said virtually nothing about refugees in countries such as Colombia, El Salvador, Nicaragua and Guatemala, partly because I did not want my discussion to be dominated by the history of US intervention, but I hope my approach will prove useful to students of protracted refugee situations in Central and Latin America. Notwithstanding this omission, my global history shows how the practices and legacies of population displacement were not limited to one particular time or place but extended far and wide.[34] The consequences are also better understood by stretching the canvas as wide as possible. Refugees frequently demonstrated an awareness of displacement elsewhere, and it would be strange indeed if historians overlooked these connections.

The Making of the Modern Refugee thus proposes a distinctive approach to the subject by bringing the causes and consequences of global population displacement within a single frame. It seeks to explain the circumstances, practices and possibilities of population displacement. It examines structures and networks of power, social experience and human agency in various situations. It asks how the lives that were dismantled by involuntary displacement might at the same time be re-assembled. Whose lives took on a more positive meaning, why and in what circumstances? Beyond this, it explores how a particular means of thinking about refugees was deployed—how refugees came to be recognized by and beyond the realm of law, including by those who never came face to face with refugees. Under what conditions did refugees break free of the designation? In what ways did they seek to transcend or, conversely, to embrace their displacement: might this be not only a condition of being in the world but also a means of self-realization?[35] What does history have to say about refugees, and to refugees? History can help answer questions as to how refugees became an omnipresent part of the twentieth-century world, and how they negotiated the turbulent currents of displacement and the conditions imposed by the refugee regime; how, in short, there were many ways to be a refugee.

---

[34] Dirk Hoerder, *Cultures in Contact: World Migrations in the Second Millennium* (Durham, NC: Duke University Press, 2002).

[35] E. Valentine Daniel, 'The Refugee: a Discourse on Displacement', in Jeremy MacClancy (ed.), *Exotic No More: Anthropology on the Front Lines* (Chicago: University of Chicago Press, 2002), 270–86.

PART I

EMPIRES OF REFUGEES

There were refugees everywhere. It was as if the entire world had to move or was waiting to move

(Homer Folks, 1920)

Most nineteenth-century Europeans did not encounter refugees, but the conflagration that consumed Europe during the First World War (1914–18) ensured that the word soon tripped incessantly and miserably off the tongue. Public opinion in belligerent and neutral states alike became accustomed to stories of the torment endured by civilian victims at the hands of invading troops, although in fact this offered a partial reading of events, which overlooked the domestic origins of population displacement. Relief efforts concentrated on alleviating civilian suffering until such time as the war ended and refugees could return to their homes. But 'home' itself changed as a result of war, revolution and the formation of new states. In post-war Europe, too, refugees emerged as a 'problem' requiring international action. How did all this come about?

In 1914 the territorial contours of Europe largely reflected the diplomatic settlement that ended the Napoleonic Wars a century earlier. The great continental empires—German, Austro-Hungarian, Russian and Ottoman—incorporated a diverse multinational population. Nineteenth-century revolts against dynastic rule had been suppressed and their leaders forced into exile where they carried the torch for liberalism and national self-expression. By 1918 these imperial polities vanished from the scene. The altered political cartography profoundly affected ordinary people who belonged to nation-states that claimed sovereignty in their name. Now the emphasis was on cultural and ethnic homogeneity, rather than the heterogeneity and pluralism that characterized imperial administration. There would be losers as well as winners in the fundamental transformation wrought by war and peace-making.[1]

Nothing prepared Europe for the terrible conflagration that consumed millions of lives during the Great War, or for the vast movements of refugees and prisoners of war that were a prominent feature of the continental conflict. Yet to imply that

---

[1] Jane Burbank and Frederick Cooper, *Empires in World History: Power and the Politics of Difference* (Princeton: Princeton University Press, 2010), 331–68; Aviel Roshwald, *Ethnic Nationalism and the Fall of Empires: Central Europe, Russia and the Middle East, 1914–1923* (Routledge, 2001). In *The Dark Side of Democracy: Explaining Ethnic Cleansing* (Cambridge: Cambridge University Press, 2005), Michael Mann argues that democratization opened the way for majority ethnic groups to persecute minorities. Compare Mark Mazower, 'Violence and the State in the Twentieth Century' *American Historical Review*, 107, no.4 (2002), 1158–78.

the period before the outbreak of war in 1914 was an era of uninterrupted peace would be to give a very one-dimensional reading of European history. Wars such as those between Russia and Turkey in 1877 and in the Balkan States in 1912–13 had momentous implications for domestic politics. Each big imperial polity extended its administrative and military capability. This process was contested, its outcome uncertain. State-building meant developing closer controls over ethnic minorities, some of whom had only relatively recently been absorbed into the state, as in Russia's annexation of the Crimea and the Caucasus. The same applied to Ottoman-ruled Eastern Anatolia, whose ethnically heterogeneous landscape was irrevocably altered by the settlement of Muslim refugees during the late nineteenth century. Population resettlement including forced migration and expulsion was a key instrument of state-building in this 'shatter zone' of empires.[2]

The First World War unleashed an unprecedented continental refugee crisis. Civilians no less than military personnel experienced war as a time of protracted displacement. In part this was because the eruption of fighting across large swathes of territory on the European mainland caused non-combatants to avoid the risk of enemy occupation by moving to the interior. But invasion-induced panic was not the only motor of displacement. Mobilization for 'total war' expressed itself with particular vehemence in imperial polities whose rulers knew that a challenge to their authority could come from any quarter, including minority populations. Although the strength and depth of nationalist sentiment should not be exaggerated, many minorities nevertheless had a counterpart amongst the inhabitants of adjacent empires. This made for an unsettling situation. Armenians lived under Ottoman jurisdiction but others were to be found among the subjects of the Tsar; Poles and Jews were scattered between the empires of Russia, Austria-Hungary and Germany; Ukrainians were not confined to the Russian Empire but lived under Austro-Hungarian rule as well. Might they not seize the chance to link up with co-ethnics, wrecking central authority and increasing the prospect of autonomy or even independence? We should be cautious about assuming that the outcome was preordained: as one historian writes, 'the road from the Ottoman imperial kaleidoscope to the rigidly defined world of the successor nation-states was full of false starts, reversals and uncharted alternatives'. The same was true elsewhere. But nervous imperial administrators took pre-emptive action by targeting and relocating 'suspect' national minorities.[3]

---

[2] Donald Bloxham, 'The Great Unweaving: Forced Population Movement in Europe, 1875–1949', in Richard Bessel and Claudia Haake (eds), *Removing Peoples: Forced Removal in the Modern World* (Oxford: Oxford University Press, 2008), 167–218; Eric Weitz, 'From the Vienna to the Paris System: International Politics and the Entangled Histories of Human Rights, Forced Deportations, and Civilizing Missions' *AHR*, 113, no.5 (2008), 1313–43; Mark Levene, 'The Tragedy of the Rimlands: Nation-state Formation and the Destruction of Imperial Peoples, 1912–1948', in Panikos Panayi and Pippa Virdee (eds), *Refugees and the End of Empire: Imperial Collapse and Forced Migration in the Twentieth Century* (Palgrave Macmillan, 2011), 51–78; Omer Bartov and Eric Weitz (eds), *Shatterzone of Empires: Coexistence and Violence in the German, Habsburg, Russian, and Ottoman Borderlands* (Bloomington: Indiana University Press, 2012).

[3] Reşat Kasaba, *A Moveable Empire: Ottoman Nomads, Migrants and Refugees* (Seattle: University of Washington Press, 2009), 136.

To advance these arguments is to bring population displacement, humanitarianism and politics into closer alignment. The creation of refugees opened up political possibilities. We enter a realm of political discourse in which refugees identified the source of their misery in actions taken by government officials. Displacement was framed as persecution. One ironic outcome was that minorities who were displaced on account of their nationality mobilized around the figure of the refugee. In the disintegrating Russian and Ottoman empires refugees helped to dig the foundations for new nation-states, thereby bringing about the very outcome that imperial administrators hoped to avoid.

International and transnational groups also entered the field of refugee relief. Diasporic organizations that emerged as a result of emigration to Western Europe and North America helped keep the suffering of minorities in the public eye. Disinterested humanitarians—those without direct ties to persecuted minorities in Eastern Europe and the Balkans—drew upon a prior history of compassionate action and a rhetoric that dwelled upon the behaviour of 'uncivilized' states. Cultural representations of enemy barbarity were not new: in Britain and France, for example, they reproduced stereotypes about Turkish brutality towards Armenian Christians. Sometimes these attitudes required adjustment, as when the publicity given to Belgian colonial rapaciousness in the Congo gave way to stories of German atrocity in occupied Belgium and the suffering endured by Belgian refugees in 1914. Late nineteenth-century conflicts, the Balkan Wars and above all the First World War enlarged the scope of humanitarian efforts and sometimes substituted for government intervention.[4]

When the war ended and the map of Europe was redrawn, refugees became a crucial element of efforts to rethink domestic and international politics. Empires were 'unmixed', and nation-states became a powerful instrument for the manufacture of new refugees.[5] The new League of Nations imposed minority treaties on the successor states of Central-Eastern Europe, in the hope that national minorities would live more securely in a state that bore the name of a titular majority. These expectations were often confounded. Elsewhere, Greece and Turkey fought over the carcass of the old Ottoman Empire, the outcome of which was an imposed exchange of population in order to realize the principle of national homogeneity. Revolution in Russia and the Bolshevik victory in the Civil War landed the League with a headache in the shape of a mass exodus of refugees from Russia who (it was said at the time) threatened to overwhelm neighbouring states.

In the longer term the battle lines were drawn in Spain, Italy and Germany, where Fascism demonstrated that political extremism retained its capacity to generate fresh displacement. Partly as a result of the immediate post-war crisis and the association between refugees and state security, European governments imposed tough border controls. Jews in particular suffered persecution and discrimination.

---

[4] Davide Rodogno, *Against Massacre: Humanitarian Interventions in the Ottoman Empire, 1815–1914* (Princeton: Princeton University Press, 2012).

[5] Rogers Brubaker, 'Aftermaths of Empire and the Unmixing of Peoples', in Karen Barkey and Mark von Hagen (eds), *After Empire: Multiethnic Societies and Nation-Building: the Soviet Union and the Russian, Ottoman and Habsburg Empires* (Boulder: Westview Press, 1997), 155–80.

A prominent American journalist spoke of 'a whole nation of people [that] although they come from many nations, wanders the world [and] batters at every conceivable door'.[6] In Southern Europe the bitter Spanish Civil War led to widespread internal population displacement before culminating in victory for the Nationalists and the flight of vanquished Republicans, men, women and children, to France and later to South America. Foreigners routinely regarded Spanish refugees not as heroic exiles from Fascism, but as a 'problem'.

Government budgetary constraints and the scale of the refugee crisis allowed NGOs to raise their profile. Officials from the German Red Cross assisted refugees from Poland. The Russian diaspora looked after refugees in Western Europe; Jewish and Armenian diasporic agencies did likewise. New transnational organizations appeared on the scene. Some were driven by religious beliefs that made Armenian Christians especially deserving clients. Save the Children Fund (established in 1919) on the other hand quickly established a reputation for impartial relief work, as did the Quakers. Humanitarianism thrived on notions of 'rescue', never more so than when it came to assisting women and children. It was infused too with ideas of 'rehabilitation' and 'development', doctrines that became widely disseminated in later decades but whose gestation can be traced back to the 1920s.

Where did this leave refugees? They were enlisted in fund-raising campaigns. They became the object of attention by patriotic leaders who mobilized them for political purposes and by professional experts for whom the presence of refugees validated their claim to intervene in society more broadly. Refugees were expected to be seen and not heard. They struggled to find a space in which to articulate their own aspirations. As we shall see, Spanish Civil War refugees constituted the clearest exception, refusing to see themselves as pure victims and instead being vocal custodians of a political alternative to Fascism. But to dismiss others is to overlook the ways in which ordinary refugees, whether from Armenia, Russia, Greece or Turkey made their presence felt as much through their deeds as their words. Their encounter with host societies could be compelling and transformative.

---

[6] Dorothy Thompson, *Refugees: Anarchy or Organisation?* (New York: Random House, 1938), 11; Annemarie Sammartino, *The Impossible Border: Germany and the East, 1914–1922* (Ithaca: Cornell University Press, 2010), 121–37.

1

Crucibles of Population Displacement
Before and During the Great War

Nous n'étions plus personne
(an unnamed Belgian refugee)

PRELUDE: CONFLICT AND DISPLACEMENT
ON THE EUROPEAN PERIPHERY

If asked to identify refugees at the turn of the century, contemporaries would have mentioned Jews who migrated to North America and Western Europe in order to escape poverty and discrimination in Eastern Europe. Tsarist Russia institutionalized discrimination and afforded no protection against the charge that they exploited peasants and workers. The large annual outflow of impoverished Jews created a diaspora that advertised the suffering of those who were left behind. But we need to cast the net more widely to grasp the more fundamental political and social processes that turned refugees into a 'problem' in the late nineteenth and early twentieth centuries. In South-Eastern Europe, at the edge of the three largest continental empires, economic competition compounded religious and ethnic differences. Christians, Muslims and Jews all felt the cold blast of persecution.

Territorial expansion, particularly on the part of the Russian Empire, raised the stakes much earlier. The Crimean War witnessed the mass flight of Orthodox Christian Bulgarian peasants in 1854 following reprisals by Ottoman troops. Bulgarian refugees also settled in Greece and Romania from where they campaigned against Turkish 'misrule' in Bulgaria. Another consequence of the conflict was the orchestrated departure of 300,000 Crimean Tatars to the Ottoman Empire. Notwithstanding evidence of these and other deportations, including Circassian and other Muslim groups expelled from the Caucasus during the 1860s, unsupported generalizations about 'ethnic cleansing' in the nineteenth century are unhelpful, because official policy was much less clear-cut. Nevertheless, these population movements contributed to land and religious disputes and further destabilized the region.[1]

---

[1] Justin McCarthy, *Death and Exile: The Ethnic Cleansing of Ottoman Muslims, 1821–1922* (Princeton, N.J.: Darwin Press, 1995), 17, 29, 47–8; Kasaba, *A Moveable Empire*, 108–22; Hakan Kirimli, 'Emigrations from the Crimea to the Ottoman Empire during the Crimean War' *MES*, 44, no.5 (2008), 751–73; Mara Kozelsky, 'Casualties of Conflict: Crimean Tatars during the Crimean War' *Slavic Review*, 67, no.4 (2008), 866–91.

Rivalry between empires made for an unsettling picture. The contest between the Habsburg and Ottoman Empires for supremacy stretched back for decades, but it acquired particular significance in the last quarter of the century when imperial rulers began to exert closer control over their borders and subjects of different faiths and ethnicity. In a sign of things to come, in 1873 a small group of Orthodox Christian merchants and peasants living in Bosnia and fearing for their safety and complaining of economic discrimination and hardship sought refuge in Habsburg-ruled Croatia where they demanded protection. The authorities in Vienna found themselves in a quandary, because they did not wish to pick a quarrel with the Sublime Porte. When Croatian activists agitated on behalf of refugees who arrived in 1875 following an uprising against Ottoman rule, Habsburg officials again disavowed their support for refugees whom they portrayed as insurgents to be repatriated, not as political innocents to be offered sanctuary. The numbers were substantial: at least 100,000 Ottoman subjects fled to Austria-Hungary from Bosnia-Herzegovina. The refugee crisis was quickly internationalized, because their claims to have been persecuted by Ottoman irregulars ('bashi-bazouks') were taken up by foreign sympathizers including in Serbia and Croatia. Vienna changed its stance in 1876, no longer opting to placate Constantinople but instead keen to exploit its weakness.[2]

War between Russia and Turkey, brought about by Ottoman suppression of the revolts in Bosnia-Herzegovina and Bulgaria, and by Russia's counter-attack, infused by ideas of Pan-Slavism, caused upwards of two million civilians to flee. Refugees spoke of the 'great unweaving of '93' (*93 sökümü*), the year 1293 in the Ottoman Rumi calendar equating to 1877. Bulgarian extremists were accused of massacring Muslim neighbours as well as Ottoman soldiers, and this behaviour in turn led to reprisals. Organized expulsions characterized the conflict: an Orthodox refugee described a 'complete clearing out of the Serbs of Bosnia'.[3] Muslims fled from Serbia and Bosnia-Herzegovina to Anatolia, where they were joined by Circassians and Kurds from the Russian Empire. The Treaty of Berlin made provision for Christian Orthodox refugees to return to their homes. Nevertheless Macedonia, having been absorbed by Bulgaria, was returned to Ottoman jurisdiction, with the result that Orthodox Christians now fled in large numbers to Bulgaria where they formed the backbone of revolutionary organizations dedicated to the overthrow of Turkish rule, and whose members attempted to recruit ethnic Bulgarians who remained in Macedonia. In Eastern Anatolia, the mass migration of Circassian and Chechen refugees triggered pogroms and the forced conversion of Armenians in 1895–96. Flows of refugees and returnees exacerbated land and religious disputes, making for an unstable situation throughout this economically underdeveloped region.[4]

---

[2] I draw, with the author's permission, on an unpublished doctoral dissertation by Jared Manasek, Columbia University.

[3] Quoted in Noel Malcolm, *Bosnia: a Short History* (Macmillan, 1994), 133. On Bulgaria, see McCarthy, *Death and Exile*, 71–6; Kasaba, *A Moveable Empire*, 117.

[4] Anastasia Karakasidou, *Fields of Wheat, Hills of Blood: Passages to Nationhood in Greek Macedonia* (Chicago: Chicago University Press, 1997), 99–107; McCarthy, *Death and Exile*, 77–81, 113; Uğur Ümit Üngör, *The Making of Modern Turkey: Nation and State in Eastern Anatolia, 1913–50* (Oxford: Oxford University Press, 2011), 19.

Regional instability resurfaced a generation later. The victory of the self-styled 'Young Turks' in 1908 alarmed Vienna by appearing to stimulate resurgent Ottoman claims to Bosnia, where a substantial Muslim population still remained. Austria's hasty annexation of Bosnia inflamed Serbia in turn. In 1912, Serbia, Montenegro, Bulgaria and Greece joined forces in an attempt to rid Europe of the vestiges of Ottoman administration. Ethnic Turks fled from Western Thrace when it became clear that Greece had in mind a programme of Hellenization. The violence inflicted on Muslim landlords and merchants in Macedonia by anti-Ottoman partisans caused a sudden influx of refugees of 180,000 Muslims to Constantinople and other towns in the first half of 1913. Greek merchants were attacked in turn. When the anti-Ottoman coalition broke apart later that year, Greece and Serbia sided with Turkey against Bulgaria. Thousands of ethnic Bulgarian refugees fled from Thrace, Macedonia, Dobrudja and Anatolia to the relative safety of Bulgaria. The short but bloody war between Turkey and Bulgaria ended with the Convention of Adrianople that sanctioned the 'voluntary' transfer of around 47,000 Christians from Eastern Thrace to Bulgaria and 49,000 Muslims from Western Thrace to Turkey if they lived within 15 kilometres from the frontier. Within a few months Greece and Turkey planned a similar population exchange. Displacement prior to and during the Balkan Wars thus carried echoes of previous conflicts and prefigured later upheavals.[5]

Relief measures also took place first and foremost within a local context. In the wake of the Crimean War, the Ottoman state built a new town in central Dobrudja (Megdidia, in present-day Romania) to accommodate refugees. In the 1870s bourgeois activists mobilized in Dubrovnik and Zagreb and further afield on behalf of refugees from Bosnia-Herzegovina, feeding the public a diet of graphic stories of Ottoman misrule. Later on, in what remained in Europe of the crumbling empire, traditional *millets* or communities organized on religious lines to support the newcomers, particularly those of non-Muslim faith. Muslim refugees including Circassians expelled from the Russian-administered Caucasus settled on the Ottoman periphery, in Syria, Jordan and Lebanon. A series of central government commissions dealt with those who moved to Eastern Anatolia. Refugees were housed in camps outside Constantinople, accommodated in over-burdened villages or assigned plots of land by the government. New settlements were named *Muhacirköy* ('Refugees' Village') or *Bosnaköy* ('The Bosnians' Village').[6]

Before long, humanitarian relief efforts acquired an international aspect. Two inveterate British travellers, Georgina Mackenzie and Pauline Irby, published a sympathetic account in 1865 of the Christian population in Serbia and Bosnia; it went through several editions in 1877, with the enthusiastic endorsement of

---

[5] McCarthy, *Death and Exile*, 150, 156–61; Karakasidou, *Fields of Wheat*, 122–4, 132.

[6] Kemal Karpat, 'Ottoman Urbanism: the Crimean Emigration to Dobruca and the Founding of Mediciye, 1856–1878', in Karpat, *Studies on Ottoman Social and Political History* (Leiden: Brill, 2002), 202–34; McCarthy, *Death and Exile*, 157; Alexandre Toumarkine, *Les migrations des populations musulmanes balkaniques en Anatolie, 1876–1913* (Istanbul: Isis, 1995), 79–103, at 89; Dawn Chatty, *Displacement and Dispossession in the Modern Middle East* (Cambridge: Cambridge University Press, 2010), 42–3, 89–91, 97–9, 110–20; Kasaba, *A Moveable Empire*, 110, 114.

Gladstone during his campaign for the 'emancipation of the Christians from the Turkish yoke'. Journalists such as W.T. Stead and scholars including E.A. Freeman and James Bryce also lent their support, helping to establish refugees as exemplars of a submerged Bulgarian 'nation'.[7] On the opposing side, the Tory millionaire Angela Burdett-Coutts established a 'Turkish Compassionate Fund', which denounced Russian interference and assisted Muslim peasants who were forced out of Bulgaria and Rumelia during the war of 1877–78. In what was to become a familiar scenario, first-hand testimony of refugees was conspicuous by its absence, the emphasis being instead on the atrocities perpetrated by one party or another, and the expertise deployed by sensitive foreign relief workers who flocked to the scene.[8]

Relief work continued with the formation by Noel and Charles Roden Buxton of the Macedonian Relief Committee (MRF) in 1903, which collected funds on behalf of those caught up in the revolt against Ottoman rule in Macedonia and Thrace. During the First Balkan War Charles Buxton invited his sister-in-law, Eglantyne Jebb to visit Macedonia to report on the hospitals that the MRF had established. She concluded that refugees might best create a 'self-supporting life' by being enabled to return to their villages: 'repatriation should appeal to all lovers of sound charity'.[9] Jebb combined her speaking engagements on behalf of Macedonian refugees with a new-found interest in agricultural cooperation, a connection that anticipated later developments. Later, in 1913, fresh fighting during the Second Balkan War exposed the suffering of more refugees who crowded into Bulgaria. The government struggled to cope. Politicians decided to settle Bulgarian peasants in the villages that Muslim farmers had abandoned. Alongside these measures, international networks of activists once again raised the standard of humanitarianism. The Anglo-Hellenic League was one such instrument of external relief, the International Committee for the Relief of Turkish Refugees another.[10]

The intensification of antagonism was nowhere more apparent than in the Ottoman Empire, where Armenians did not escape this disturbing combination of ethnic, religious and economic rivalry. Relations between Muslims and Christians had deteriorated in the late 1890s, culminating in forced conversions and massacres of Armenians in 1896, widely publicized in Western Europe by journalists such as E.J. Dillon. The situation was complicated by Tsarist Russia's ambitions in the region. The Sultan's concession to Armenians of some autonomy in Eastern Anatolia antagonized local Muslims, who found a ready ally among the Young Turks, one of whose leaders insisted that there should be 'no nationalities in Turkey.

---

[7] Their book was translated into Serbian at the time and regularly reprinted in the 1980s and 1990s. On Stead, Freeman and Irby and their links to Gladstone, see Rebecca Gill, 'Calculating Compassion in War: the "New Humanitarian" Ethos in Britain, 1870–1918' (unpublished PhD, University of Manchester, 2005), chapter 2.

[8] Gill, 'Calculating Compassion', 73–8, emphasizes that 'foreign relief work was used as a cover for covert diplomacy'.

[9] Linda Mahood, *Feminism and Voluntary Action: Eglantyne Jebb and Save the Children, 1876–1928* (Houndmills: Palgrave Macmillan, 2009), 149.

[10] McCarthy, *Death and Exile*, 119–20.

[We] do not want Turkey to become a new Austria-Hungary'. The outbreak of war in 1914 prevented the Sultan's measure from being implemented, but it unleashed an even more tragic series of events.[11]

Faced with an unending refugee crisis, Turkey established a new 'Directorate for the Settlement of Tribes and Immigrants' in 1913, charged with responsibility for finding refugees somewhere to live and, more ominously conducting ethnographic investigations of Ottoman society to map political affiliations and discover the extent of 'Turkishness'. Prominent victims of this pre-war downward social mobility, such as Mehmed Talaat Pasha, Dr Mehmed Nâzım, Dr Mehmed Reshid and Mustafa Kemal, expressed a desire for retribution:

> How [wrote Talaat Pasha] could a person forget the plains, the meadows, watered with the blood of our forefathers; abandon those places where Turkish raiders had stalled their steeds for a full four hundred years, with our mosques, our tombs...to leave them to our slaves. This was beyond a person's endurance. I am prepared to sacrifice gladly the remaining years of my life to take revenge on the Bulgarians, the Greeks and the Montenegrins.[12]

How far his uncompromising response was representative of Muslim refugees who settled in Anatolia is impossible to say. These turbulent and violent episodes reveal little of the perceptions that ordinary refugees held of their displacement. But the actions of Turkish officials and soldiers during the Great War indicate that they were prepared in the name of Muslim refugees to take revenge for their pre-war humiliation.

POPULATION DISPLACEMENT DURING THE GREAT WAR

The outbreak of war in July 1914 appeared to confirm the widely-held view that the conflict would be a largely military affair. European armies were expected to engage in military manoeuvres without significant costs for non-combatants. German troops invaded Belgium and France. Russia, which belonged to an Entente with Britain and France, mobilized its forces to attack Germany and Austria-Hungary. The German army pushed back Russian forces at the battle of Tannenberg, but Austria was unable to prevent Russia's invasion and occupation of Galicia. Although most informed observers anticipated a short and conclusive war, the Great War dragged on for more than four years. Each empire mobilized massive resources that fed the war machine, helping to prolong the conflict. This war effort required the recruitment of civilians to replenish the army but also entailed their contribution as producers and suppliers of munitions, equipment, food and fodder. The conflict

---

[11] Üngör, *The Making of Modern Turkey*, 33, 44–5; Nesim Şeker, 'Demographic Engineering in the Late Ottoman Empire and the Armenians' *MES*, 43, no.3 (2007), 461–74.
[12] Üngör, *The Making of Modern Turkey*, 45.

dissolved the boundaries between battlefield and home front, making this (in a phrase first popularized by the French authorities) a 'total war'.

The wartime refugee crisis reflected the huge numbers of civilians who were directly affected, but the war also posed challenging questions about the forms and extent of assistance. Questions arose such as how to classify and understand those who were displaced. Who counted as 'refugees' and how did they come to be displaced to begin with? Who determined their eligibility for assistance? How far should central government be responsible for managing emergency relief or should responsibility be devolved on to local and voluntary agencies and what would be the political implications of such a decision? What impact would the presence of large numbers of refugees have on the host community, and how might relations between refugees and non-refugees be managed in order to maintain wartime morale? To what extent would overseas communities become involved in assisting distant kin affected by displacement? How would the crisis be resolved—would refugees wish to return to their homes and if so how would repatriation be managed? These interrelated questions have continued to dominate discussions of refugee crises ever since.

'Belgium was invaded by an army; Holland was invaded by a people', wrote Ruth Fry in her account of Quaker relief work in wartime Europe.[13] Refugees fled from Antwerp and other towns and cities during September and October 1914. Stories of German military brutality gripped the public imagination. Entire villages were emptied of their inhabitants. Anyone caught helping Belgian men of military age to flee the country and fight the German army faced severe retribution. German occupation authorities invited refugees to return to their homes, and thousands did so before the first year of war was out. But the respite was only brief. The first destination was Holland, whose population of 6.3 million was swollen by one million Belgian refugees. Around 200,000 Belgians fled to France where they were put to work in agriculture or producing munitions. A similar number crossed the English Channel. By July 1918 the total number of refugees stood at 1.5 million. In France itself the German invasion in 1914 led to the flight or expulsion of French civilians to unoccupied parts of the country. By the beginning of 1915 the total number of internally displaced French stood at 450,000, rising to 735,000 in July. Refugees were quick to disseminate stories of robbery, pillage and burning, prompting government officials to accuse them of panic-mongering.[14]

Events elsewhere generated large movements of population. In Southern Europe, the entry of Italy into the war in May 1915 on behalf of the Entente powers caused 87,000 ethnic Italian residents of the Austro-Hungarian Empire, primarily workers from Trieste, Trento and Dalmatia, to flee to Italy and lend their support to the Italian war effort. The Habsburg officials sent 42,000 civilians, mostly women, children and the elderly, to internment camps where an emerging patriotic leadership

[13] Ruth Fry, *A Quaker Adventure: the Story of Nine Years' Relief and Reconstruction* (London: Nisbet & Co., 1926), 100.
[14] Philippe Nivet, *Les réfugiés français de la Grande Guerre (1914–1920): les 'boches du nord'* (Paris: Economica, 2004).

took every opportunity to foster Italian nationalist sentiment. By far the greatest impulse to population displacement came in October 1917, when the defeat of Italian forces at Caporetto brought about the flight of half a million civilians and one million bedraggled soldiers to cities such as Milan and Florence. Others were urged to stay behind in the northern rural borderlands, partly to alleviate the urban crisis and partly to make life difficult for the occupying Habsburg army; the government also hoped that their presence would strengthen Italy's territorial claims to Friuli and the Veneto.[15]

On the eastern front 870,000 civilians fled westwards when the Russian army invaded East Prussia (see Map 1), instilling in German public opinion a fear of 'Slav' and Cossack brutality and placing a huge burden on the economy. In Austria the number of refugees reached 500,000 by summer 1915, most of them from Russian-occupied Galicia and Bukovina where the newly-installed governor resolved to 'cleanse' his fiefdom prior to integrating it fully into the Tsarist Empire. Russian military commanders deported local notables and Galician Jews to the Russian interior. Ukrainian activists, who enjoyed the comparatively tolerant rule of the Habsburgs before the war, wisely decided to flee lest they feel the wrath of the new Russian administration. Vienna became home to around 140,000 refugees, half of them Jews. Others hid in towns in schools or barns in Bohemia and Moravia and in Hungarian towns. Some went back to their homes after the Austrian counter-attack in mid-1915, but the number of refugees grew again in 1916 in the wake of Russia's successful offensive and the second Russian occupation of Galicia and Bukovina.[16]

Following the assassination of Franz Ferdinand by a Bosnian Serb, Austria invaded Serbia in autumn 1914. Although the invasion was initially repelled, Serbian forces were defeated in November 1914 and thousands of civilians fled to the interior. The Habsburg army targeted Serbian guerrillas, in order to forestall what they most feared, a *levée en masse*, that is an uprising of the entire population. Worse was to come a year later, when a combined Austrian and Bulgarian invasion, backed by Germany, forced the remnants of Serbian forces to retreat across Kosovo towards the Adriatic. En route they were attacked by Albanian guerrillas. Half a million civilians followed suit to avoid the anticipated consequences of Bulgarian and Habsburg occupation. They found scant sympathy from Serbian officers who blamed them for obstructing the passage of military convoys and disrupting agricultural production. The population of the provincial town of Prizren swelled from 20,000 to 150,000 in a matter of days. All told, this catastrophic displacement of soldiers and civilians directly affected one-third of Serbia's population.[17]

---

[15] Matteo Ermacora, 'Assistance and Surveillance: War Refugees in Italy, 1914–1918' *CEH*, 16, no.4 (2007), 445–60; Julie Thorpe, 'Displacing Empire: Refugee Welfare, National Activism and State Legitimacy in Austria-Hungary in the First World War', in Panayi and Virdee (eds), *Refugees and the End of Empire*, 102–26.

[16] Peter Gatrell, *A Whole Empire Walking, Refugees in Russia during World War I* (Bloomington: Indiana University Press, 1999), 23; David Rechter, 'Galicia in Vienna: Jewish Refugees in the First World War' *Austrian History Yearbook*, 28 (1997), 113–30.

[17] Jonathan Gumz, *The Resurrection and Collapse of Empire in Habsburg Serbia, 1914–1918* (Cambridge: Cambridge University Press, 2007).

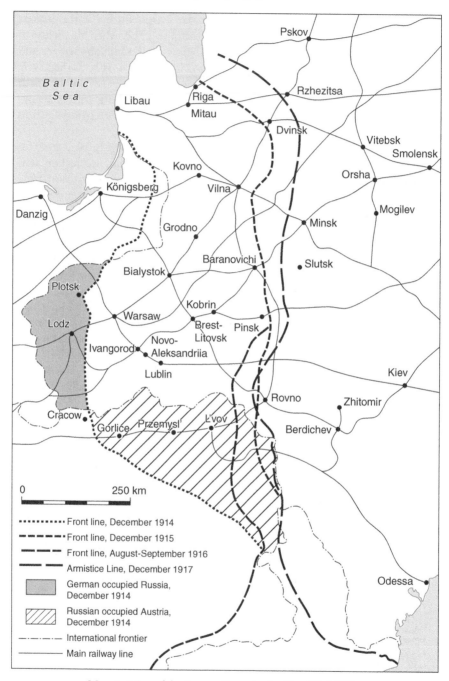

Map 1: Map of the Eastern Front in the First World War

A Scottish nurse described the retreat as 'the first stage of a Calvary which was to endure for several weeks. The stream of the refugees grew daily greater, mothers, children, bedding, pots and pans, food and fodder, all packed into the jolting wagons'. When the Bulgarian army continued its advance the party had no choice but to cross the mountains to seek sanctuary in Albania. Others headed for Montenegro where 'many died on those pitiless mountains, and the snow fell and covered up their misery for ever'. Displacement was characterized by class distinction. A British officer commented that 'the majority of the refugees were well to do people from comfortable homes; many of the poorer people, peasants, were clinging to their miserable homes towards the centre of the country'.[18] Those who could not escape faced incarceration in Austrian, Hungarian and Bulgarian camps. Small numbers of guerrillas (*chetniks*) took to the mountainous regions of Serbia and Montenegro and harassed the occupation regime. Refugees made their way to Salonika, Corfu and Brindisi. Serbian schools and orphanages were established in Nice, Tours, Grenoble, and in France's colonies in North Africa. A few even ended up as farm labourers in East Anglia. At least 140,000 Serbian refugees are thought to have died during the flight to Albania or in exile. These losses and struggles reinforced a sense of Serbian victimhood.

In the Russian Empire, the displacement of civilians reached three million in 1915 and may have climbed to seven million by the time Russia left the war in 1917. What gave rise to displacement on this scale? According to one explanation, 'as soon as our troops withdraw, the entire population becomes confused and runs away'. Sometimes they fled, lest they lose contact with fathers and sons who were currently serving in the Tsarist army. This did not necessarily imply a move to distant locations. During the initial phase of retreat refugees would often stay close to Russian troops, in the hope that the army would quickly recapture land from the enemy, allowing them to go home. Civilians also left their homes for fear of being terrorized by enemy troops. Nor were these fears misplaced: 'rumours are rife that the Germans have behaved abominably towards the local population'. These verdicts generally supported the view that population displacement was the product of mass panic. Politicians complained that the army should do more to encourage civilians to stay put, on the grounds that they could then disrupt the enemy's advance. Some patriotic provincial journalists argued that refugees 'quit their birthplace in order to give greater scope to our valiant army to spread its eagle wings'.[19]

Yet displacement was by no means solely dictated by a fearful civilian response to punitive action by the enemy. The Russian general staff disposed of sweeping powers to enforce the resettlement of civilians, and deemed this an appropriate strategy in the western borderlands where the loyalties of the local population were held to be doubtful. Within the extensive theatre of operations the Russian

[18] Charles Fryer, *The Destruction of Serbia in 1915* (New York: Columbia University Press, 1997), 70; M. I. Tatham, 'The great retreat in Serbia in 1915', in C. Purdom (ed.), *Everyman at War: Sixty Personal Narratives of the War* (Dent, 1930), 374–9.

[19] Gatrell, *Whole Empire Walking*, 15.

high command was accused of pursuing a scorched earth policy and driving civilians from their homes. Jews bore the brunt of this policy, but it affected Poles, Baltic farmers and others, including German colonists who had farmed in Russia for generations. Jews and German colonists found themselves put on the same train heading east. Tsarist officials deported Muslims on the Russian-Ottoman border and assigned their land to Russian settlers, an ominous foretaste of the Stalin-era deportations and expropriations. The Tsarist minister of the interior maintained that military behaviour had no bearing on refugeedom (*bezhenstvo*), which was 'caused by a desire for self-preservation'. Other commentators took a less coy line, openly acknowledging the routine use of compulsion. So widespread were the army's tactics that a leading Tsarist dignitary observed that 'refugees' constituted a minority of the displaced population, compared to the hundreds of thousands of those who had been forcibly displaced. For a while contemporaries distinguished between forced migrants and refugees: 'refugeedom is something spontaneous, whereas administrative resettlement [*vyselenie*] amounts to arbitrariness [*proizvol*]', wrote a Russian doctor. But the distinction soon ceased to mean anything.[20]

A similar distinction was drawn in Austria-Hungary, where the term 'evacuees' was reserved for those who were ordered to leave their homes, and 'refugees' who had left 'voluntarily', including for unpatriotic reasons. A citizens' committee in Prague contributed funds in the belief that charitable activities should reflect refugees' patriotic commitment to the Austrian cause—'these refugees are Austrian citizens, victims of Austria's war with Russia'. Jews from Galicia and Bukovina who fled to the interior in order to escape Russian rule confirmed their patriotism: 'better and truer Austrians [wrote one journalist] simply do not exist'; another commentator lauded the refugees as 'Austrians who have sacrificed everything for this state and can therefore claim their rights'.[21] A link was forged elsewhere between war, patriotic necessity and population displacement. Nevertheless, the presence of Jewish refugees from the shtetl inflamed existing anti-Semitic sentiment among the non-Jewish residents of Vienna, who all too easily fell into the habit of berating the refugees for their bad manners and profiteering.

By far the harshest impact of the war was to be found in the Ottoman Empire (see Map 2). Young Turk officers blamed Armenians for the successful incursion of the Russian army in Eastern Anatolia in the winter of 1914 and charged them with having instigated rebellion. Those who remained behind after the retreat of the Tsarist army in July 1915 suffered a terrible fate. Hundreds of thousands of Armenians were either murdered in their homes or driven out and forced to endure long

---

[20] Gatrell, *Whole Empire Walking*, 22, 33–48; Eric Lohr, 'The Russian Army and the Jews: Mass Deportations, Hostages, and Violence during World War I' *Russian Review*, 60, no. 3 (2001), 404–19; Joshua Sanborn, 'Unsettling the Empire: Violent Migrations and Social Disaster in Russia during World War I' *JMH*, 77, no.2 (2005), 290–324.

[21] Marsha Rozenblit, *Reconstructing a National Identity: the Jews of Habsburg Austria during World War I* (New York: Oxford University Press, 2001), 74; Thorpe, 'Displacing Empire', 109.

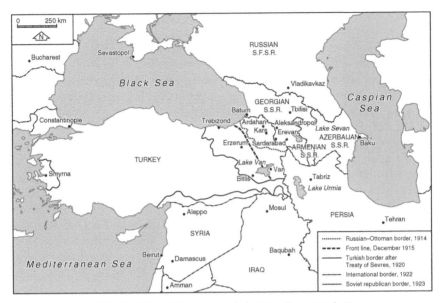

Map 2: Map of Armenia and the Near East, 1914–23

and degrading marches towards Syria in what *Manchester Guardian* correspondent Morgan Philips Price described as 'a condensation of agony that almost defies the human imagination'. Up to 250,000 Armenians evaded the deportations by crossing the Russian border in August 1915, although one in five died en route. More than 105,000 ex-Ottoman Armenians sought refuge in Erevan, quadrupling its size. Of those left behind in the Ottoman Empire, few survived the forced trek in the searing heat. Christian Assyrians along with many Kurdish inhabitants of the empire suffered terribly as well. The intended beneficiaries of these measures were Muslim refugees who had arrived in Turkey before and during the Balkan Wars, and who now wanted to ensure that surviving Armenians would be unable to reclaim their property. Turkish nationalists including many Muslim refugees had captured the state and wanted to make Armenians pay.[22]

Wherever the spotlight shone, it was clear that these civilians were deprived of the chance to decide whether to stay or to leave. No-one consulted them. They sometimes had only a few hours to pack. Most refugees had no itinerary, no maps, and normally no precise destination. There were few opportunities to confer with those who had gone on ahead. Whereas the motives for pre-war migration were clear and explicable, displacement seemed to be a meaningless momentum. Relief workers and refugees soon invested it with significance.

---

[22] Fatma Müge Göçek, Norman Naimark and Ronald Suny (eds), *A Question of Genocide: Armenians and Turks at the End of the Ottoman Empire* (New York: Oxford University Press, 2011); Üngör, *The Making of Modern Turkey*, 55–106, 108–14; Gatrell, *Whole Empire Walking*, 26.

REPERTOIRES OF ASSISTANCE

Against this complex background, involving large numbers of displaced persons, their abrupt departure, and the multiple interpretations given to their displacement, we can begin to trace the efforts made to deal with the consequences of wartime movements. Children urgently sought to establish whether their parents were alive or dead. Adults wished to be reunited with offspring with whom they had lost contact. Refugees needed legal advice about their status and entitlements to relief. Many wanted the opportunity to work or continue their education. Refugees took part in the relief programmes, but the war also provided an unprecedented opportunity for the demonstration of professional expertise by trained doctors, lawyers, teachers, psychologists, social workers and statisticians, who worked in government offices or in non-governmental organizations. In Vienna, for example, the Zionist activist Anita Müller created the *Verein soziale Hilfsgemeinschaft* that assisted pregnant refugees and young mothers and created day-care centres, employing hundreds of middle-class women and Jewish refugees and becoming 'instrumental in the professionalisation of Jewish social work in Austria'.[23]

The arrival of Belgian refugees in England unleashed a flurry of private charitable activity, supported by the notion that Britain owed the refugees a debt of gratitude for the suffering they had endured on behalf of the Allied cause. A War Refugees Committee (WRC), launched by Dame Flora Lugard made use of the 'hospitality lists' drawn up before the outbreak of war on behalf of the Ulster Unionist Council, whose leaders expected civil war in Ireland: what originated as a plan to rescue likely Protestant refugees thus became instead a programme to assist Belgian Catholics. Around 2,500 local refugee committees were established, along with a 'National Vigilance Association' whose local branches kept a watchful eye on young women. The Rothschilds contributed a large sum of money to support Belgian Jews who reached British shores and the Poor Jews' Temporary Shelter, in existence since 1885 to support immigrants from Eastern Europe, was given over to accommodate refugees in London's East End.[24] The WRC became a site of frantic activity. Lugard and her team of volunteers took pains to separate lower-class Belgian refugees from the better-off. The latter received a pink card entitling them to better transport and accommodation, whilst refugees with a blue card were housed in temporary camps such as those in Earl's Court and Alexandra Palace, where 'one does not want to take good class people', observed a British relief worker. The London Metropolitan Asylums board took charge of those who were unassigned and who ended up in the workhouse, an indication that officials increasingly played an important part in

---

[23] Rozenblit, *Reconstructing a National Identity*, 65–81.

[24] Peter Cahalan, *Belgian Refugee Relief in England during the Great War* (New York: Garland, 1982), 357–68; Jean Stengers, 'Pre-war Belgian Attitudes to Britain: Anglophilia and Anglophobia', in Martin Conway and José Gotovitch (eds), *Europe in Exile: European Exile Communities in Britain 1940–1945* (Leamington Spa: Berghahn Books, 2001), 35–52.

supporting indigent refugees. By the end of 1915 the WRC was the main channel for distributing state benefits to refugees.[25]

Although humanitarianism was buttressed by a belief that the devout Catholic inhabitants of Belgium deserved protection from 'pagan' Germany, this did not translate into unqualified admiration. One diarist wrote that: 'Everyone was Belgian mad for a time', but that 'the Belgians are not grateful. They won't do a stroke of work and grumble at everything and their morals! It may be true enough that Belgium saved Europe, but save us from the Belgians! As far as I am concerned, Belgianitis has quite abated'.[26] Other voices spoke out in support of refugees, noting their direct contribution to the British war effort by working in munitions factories. There was even a special settlement, 'Elisabethville', now part of Birtley in North-East England, named after the Belgian Queen and providing accommodation for 6,000 Belgian workers including disabled soldiers and refugees; the village had its own school, church and cemetery, and issued its own newspaper.

In the Russian Empire, refugees who had survived the journey from the vicinity of the front faced all manner of difficulties. The backward economy faced unprecedented demographic and social upheaval. Provincial and local *zemstvos* (rural local authorities), diocesan committees and private charitable societies provided underwear, shoes, linen, soap and other items for refugees. Railway stations, schools, empty factories, breweries, hotels, bathhouses, army barracks, monasteries, synagogues, theatres, cinemas, cafes and even prisons were converted into temporary accommodation. Towns and cities were transformed. One small town in the western province of Smolensk with a population of 28,000 before the war found itself home to 80,000 refugees by the late summer of 1915. Provincial governors filed reports complaining that they were 'crowded to the limit'. A year later refugees made up more than 10 per cent of the inhabitants of Russia's largest towns. Appeals for help made much of the expectation that refugees 'will not be staying long in our midst. The enemy will leave and the refugees will once more return to their own homes'. But probably few people believed this optimistic assessment: as the Union of Zemstvos argued in the autumn of 1915, 'we must not lose sight of the fact that refugees are our guests and not for a brief period either'. Municipal authorities lost no time in trying to 'evacuate' refugees to other parts of the empire. Initial hospitality rapidly evaporated as it became apparent that refugees had no money to pay for accommodation or food.[27]

The needs of refugees posed a particular challenge in economically less developed societies, not just in Russia and Serbia but also in Italy. Here the Ministry of the Interior took charge of the administration of relief and the settlement of refugees. Local authorities complained that they had insufficient means to support

[25] Anon., *The Condition of the Belgian Workmen now Refugees in Britain* (T. Fisher Unwin, 1917); Cahalan, *Belgian Refugee Relief,* 323–4; Kevin Meyer, 'The Hidden History of Refugee Schooling in Britain: the Case of the Belgians, 1914–1918' *History of Education,* 30, no.2 (2001), 153–62.

[26] Cahalan, *Belgian Refugee Relief,* 4; Pierre Purseigle, 'A Wave on to our Shores: the Exile and Resettlement of Refugees from the Western Front, 1914–1918' *CEH,* 16, no.4 (2007), 427–44.

[27] Gatrell, *A Whole Empire Walking,* 63; John Pollock, 'The Refugees at Kiev', *Fortnightly Review,* 585 (September 1915), 476–9.

displaced persons. As the size of the refugee population increased, the government created a central committee for refugee relief that worked in tandem with Catholic and socialist organizations such as the *Opera Bonomelli* and *Umanitaria*, as well as with the Red Cross, an indication that the scale of the task exceeded the capacity of central government.[28] The American Red Cross also supplied food, medicine and clothing from its warehouses in France. In Austria, where the authorities managed to impose some kind of control over the movement of refugees, the preferred option was to place them in refugee camps in order to facilitate their eventual repatriation. This happened to Poles, Ukrainians, Italians and Jews. Inmates described the conditions as primitive and 'unacceptable'. Groups deemed by the government to be more 'reliable' had to fend for themselves.

Wherever possible, refugees played an active part in making a tolerable life for themselves. In Holland they improvised accommodation by sheltering in makeshift structures such as greenhouses or finding emergency billets on barges and in apartments, hotels and warehouses. Later on, local authorities erected cheap bungalows, capable of being quickly dismantled and reassembled elsewhere. In order to appease the resident burghers in overstretched localities, the Dutch government housed the refugees in camps on the outskirts of towns such as Gouda, Ede and Nunspeet. This limited their room for manoeuvre. The authorities designated these camps as 'Belgian villages', in order to avoid the negative association with erstwhile 'concentration camps' during the South African War. Distinctions were drawn between 'dangerous elements' (*gevaarlijke elementen*), 'less desirable elements' and 'respectable refugees'. People in the first two categories, including suspected spies, prostitutes and juvenile delinquents, were sent to Nunspeet, which gained a terrible reputation. By contrast, the camp at Ede boasted canteens, schools, a church and a hospital, as well as an orchestra and sports clubs. The emphasis was on health, hygiene and hard work making toys and household goods. Refugees here could come and go.[29]

In France, government programmes of assistance were linked to the supervision of refugees' 'character', partly to spot security 'suspects' and also to identify potential workers for the war economy. This kind of surveillance was repeated time and again in relief programmes. In their anxiety about 'undesirable aliens', British government officials followed their French and Dutch counterparts by keeping a close track of the refugee population and establishing a register of the refugee population. Belgians complained that the restrictions on movement under the Aliens Restriction Act (4 August 1914), which required them to notify the police of any journey they made of more than five miles and confined them to specific areas of the country, amounted to being placed in a 'concentration camp'.[30] Their protest was to no avail.

[28] Ermacora, 'Assistance and Surveillance'.

[29] Fry, *A Quaker Adventure*, 103–15; Evelyn de Roodt, *Oorlogsgasten: Vluchtelingen en krijgsgevangenen in Nederland tidjens de Eerste Wereldoorlog* (Zaltbommel: Europese Bibliotheek, 2000), 159, 173–81, 192–4; Michaël Amara, *Des Belges à l'épreuve de l'Exil. Les réfugiés de la Première Guerre mondiale* (Bruxelles: Editions de l'Université De Bruxelles, 2008), 250–60.

[30] Cahalan, *Belgian Refugee Relief*, 357–68.

Elsewhere, the sheer numbers made it far more difficult to maintain a close watch on refugees. As we shall see, having displaced so many non-Russians from the western borderlands for reasons of national security, the Tsarist Empire found that the refugee population became the instrument of its eventual dismemberment.

REPRESENTATIONS OF REFUGEEDOM

Contemporaries struggled to comprehend the circumstances that led millions of their fellow men and women to leave their homes—or to remain behind. The result of this heart searching could be painful. Belgian public opinion during the war was sharply divided. Those who fled at the beginning of the war believed that people who stayed or returned to occupied Belgium grew fat on the proceeds of the black market, whereas refugees had no choice but to throw themselves on the mercy of foreign charities and to suffer in the national cause. On the other hand, those who stayed behind maintained that the refugees had abandoned their country at its time of need. There was thus a dialogue of the deaf. Elsewhere too, misunderstandings were common. Casual commentators blithely assumed that refugees numbered in their midst opportunists who lacked the stomach to resist. They portrayed refugees as 'deserters' who had failed to demonstrate sufficient fortitude or prowess in the teeth of the enemy onslaught. A British correspondent insinuated that young Serbian refugees in Oxford deliberately evaded military service, but in fact they were too young to enlist. Similar negative comments were made about Belgian refugees. Hostility towards refugees found expression in Northern France where local residents described French women as 'les Boches du Nord', because they were thought to have slept with German soldiers. Negative views were reinforced by the belief that refugees pushed up the price of food and housing, whilst competing for jobs and driving down wages. Stories surfaced of desperate refugees, for instance from Russia's western borderlands who stole or damaged farmers' property when they fled to the central provinces of European Russia. Other anxieties too, particularly about epidemic disease, crime and prostitution, were projected on to refugees.[31]

The contrary impulse to portray refugees as pure victims and to relieve their suffering rested upon the elaboration of compelling narratives of misery and despair. British charity workers and sympathetic newspaper columnists were wont (at least initially) to describe Belgian refugees as frightened, needy and depressed. One correspondent likened them to 'slow caravans of old women and children trailing along the high roads like modern Jews in search of new countries and new homes. Each of them has some sad history to relate, properties burnt, loved ones killed or lost'.[32] The Russian 'family journal' *Rodina* published a drawing of 'Two Flights', in which the plight of the refugee family was juxtaposed with the flight of Mary,

---

[31] Nivet, *Les réfugiés français*, 377–85; Gatrell, *A Whole Empire Walking*, 29.
[32] Amara, *Des Belges à l'épreuve de l'Exil*, 57, 73–5.

Joseph and baby Jesus to Bethlehem. Accompanying verses urged the refugees not to lose heart. Editors frequently focused upon a single refugee family; some of the poses were clearly contrived to create a genre photograph of the kind that had become fashionable at the turn of the century. Flora Scott, a nurse working with the Serbian Relief Fund, wrote that 'all the time you are reminded of Bible pictures'.[33] Other images emphasized instead the magnitude of the refugee movement; typical of these was a picture of the throng gathered outside a refugee sanctuary in Petrograd—'people of the most diverse condition and status, *now united by the single general term, refugee*'. Sometimes the photographic record drew attention not to refugees' degradation but rather to the impact of private benevolence. A picture timed for Christmas 1915 portrayed 'a child who has lost its refugee parents and who has found lodgings with a stranger'. Other photographs displayed refugees eating the remains of a soldier's meal, implying that the Russian soldier was the refugees' friend, not the source of their mass suffering and sorrow.[34]

Belgian refugees, disproportionately from an urban background, made a significant economic contribution in France and Britain to sectors whose workforce had been depleted by mobilization. The secretary of the Belgian War Refugees Committee applauded the efforts by local committees and refugees who sought to fill job vacancies. This helped offset the negative remarks that began to appear in the British press later in the war, when concerns were raised about the burden on the British taxpayer, the sacrifices made by British conscripts, and anxieties about the 'disreputable' sexual conduct of Belgian women. In France, too, the small number of Serb refugees initially found a relatively warm welcome; the municipality of Lyon, sold ribbons and medallions inscribed to the 'glorious defenders of Serb liberty'. Public opinion could quickly turn against refugees who were believed to have unreasonable expectations as to their living conditions. Refugees could not get it right: if they turned down work, then they faced accusations of shirking, but if they did take up the offer of a job they stood accused of causing qualified workers to be sent to the front.[35]

In Serbia dozens of foreigners volunteered to assist the country in its time of need, galvanized by the image of a suffering nation. Contemporaries spoke of Serbia's 'agony' and 'martyrdom'. The prominent philanthropist brothers Noel and Charles Roden Buxton commented about a 'fine race of peasants mangled and crippled'.[36] 'Slav committees' in Russia collected funds to pay for medical units. The British Red Cross and Scottish Women's Hospital, founded by Dr Elsie Inglis, recruited nurses to deal with the emerging health crisis in the first winter of the war. Medical assistance was extended to civilian refugees as well as soldiers. Lady Muriel Paget—the American wife of a former British minister to Belgrade, and

[33] Flora Scott collection, IWM, 77/15/1.

[34] Gatrell, *A Whole Empire Walking*, 74–5.

[35] Greg Burgess, *Refuge in the Land of Liberty: France and its Refugees from the Revolution to the End of Asylum 1789–1939* (New York: Palgrave Macmillan, 2008), 137–9.

[36] 'Serbia's Agony: Terrible Scenes among the Refugees and Wounded' *The Observer*, 7 February 1915.

a nurse during the First Balkan War—went to Serbia as part of the first unit of the Serbian Relief Fund (SRF), which promoted the Serbian cause and collected funds for hospitals and ambulances. Equivalent bodies supported displaced Poles, Armenians and Belgians. The SRF enlisted lawyers, businessmen, archaeologists, ethnographers and eminent historians such as R.W. Seton-Watson and G.M. Trevelyan, although the main driving force was Gertrude Carrington-Wilde. It sponsored 'Serbian Flag Day' and arranged exhibitions of Serbian sculpture and handicrafts. An analogous fund was created in the USA, where visits from eyewitnesses proved an effective means of persuading American bankers and others to dig deep. Seton-Watson was sufficiently well-connected to play an important part in British government discussions about the shape of post-war South-Eastern Europe.[37]

Volunteer nurses and relief workers described their work in Serbia in terms of adventure, courage and sheer hard work. Lucia Creighton, daughter of a prominent Church of England bishop, spoke of 'visiting many queer houses behind the front line'. In her diary she described a refugee camp, run by the British Red Cross, with eight marquees and 25 people to a tent, 'mainly women and children and old men. Some go out to work but many are too lazy and stay doing nothing as they are given just enough to live on'. Others lived temporarily in a disused factory. Later she wrote of being 'quite sick of the whole thing and [being] much more interested in the refugees outside' rather than having to work in 'practically a refugee workhouse'. She was impressed by the ground that relief workers and refugees covered together. Flora Scott wrote from Skopje on how 'everything is very strange, no looking glasses or anything civilised'. Serbia was both 'beautiful and sad'.[38]

One important element in this international humanitarianism concerned the risks to which female and child refugees were exposed. Certainly displacement afforded plenty of opportunities to exploit their vulnerability. Young females from the western borderlands of the Tsarist Empire were believed to be at the mercy of sexual traffickers or—no less troubling—to seek out possibilities to sell sex in order to survive. As with Belgian refugees, this formed part of a broader concern about the collapse of family discipline: as one Russian doctor proclaimed, refugees 'starve, run around naked, and live in appalling conditions and in such destitution that they drive their wives and daughters on to the street to join the ranks of prostitutes'. Some authors spoke in more positive terms of the scope for male siblings to substitute for parental authority and care, as in a short story that told of the reassurance offered a young girl by her brother, who guided her to safety across a river. A young Armenian farmer described how the Turks had tormented him and separated him from his family. He wanted to cry, 'but I pulled myself together and refused to cry; I realised that this was the women's way and that I had to cope differently'. He went out and killed a Turkish soldier who was holding women and children hostage. Melodramatic accounts such as these may have helped to restore confidence in the integrity of gender boundaries. Only rarely did the image of the

---

[37] Andrej Mitrović, *Serbia's Great War 1914–1918* (Hurst, 2007), 111–13.
[38] Diary of Miss L. Creighton, IWM, 92/22/1; Flora Scott papers, IWM, 77/15/1.

heroic female refugee find its way into the contemporary media, as in the tale of an anonymous refugee who had tricked a party of German soldiers into thinking that she could direct them back to their base camp. But instead of helping them she took out a bomb concealed in her bag, threw it in their midst and wounded all eight of them.[39]

The wartime crisis also drew attention to the versatility of refugees and their potential contribution to the national economy. Refugees contributed their labour to privately-owned farms and estates in the Russian interior; by the third year of the war refugees made up close on 10 per cent of the total labour force in the private farm sector. It helped that refugees included able-bodied workers whose skills were in short supply. A group from Riga that arrived in the Urals after a long journey soon found work as fitters, joiners and blacksmiths. In Kazan, refugees from Minsk worked as bakers, tailors, shoemakers and carpenters, as well as in the local abbatoir. Relief organizations applauded the initiative of craftsmen who settled in Smolensk and constructed anatomical models for use by medical students. The Russian rural intelligentsia imbued refugees with the capacity to impart a civilizing influence on the backward village. A priest in Simbirsk remarked that 'even in this lonely backwater the refugee movement has brought something new. Refugees who have arrived in the village, no matter how poor they may be, have shown the locals that there are shortcomings in their way of life and daily practices, that it is possible to work a good deal more productively'. Latvian patriots who settled in Russia's impoverished interior boasted that 'we have long forgotten what it means to suffer from a harvest failure or to go without bread'. Their displacement served to reinforce a sense of cultural distance between the virtuous Latvian yeoman and the backward Russian peasant, but it simultaneously undermined blanket negative representations of refugees.[40]

Condescension and genuine concern for human suffering—of men as well as women—went hand in hand. Claude Debussy composed the words and music to a song, 'Noel des enfants qui n'ont plus de maison'. A few lines convey the mawkish flavour:

> Nous n'avons plus de maisons!/Les ennemis ont tout pris, tout pris/
> Jusqu'à notre petit lit/Ils ont brûlé l'école et notre maître aussi/Ils ont brûlé l'église et monsieur Jésus-Christ/Et le vieux pauvre qui n'a pu s'en aller…

In an attempt at international solidarity, Debussy urged his listeners to avenge the children of France, Belgium and Poland who had suffered at the hands of German barbarians: 'If we forget any, forgive us'. 'Brave little Belgium' was a term much in evidence (and not just in the UK but in many parts of the world), a means of encapsulating the resistance that Belgian civilians offered the German army and their resolve to seek refuge in Holland, France or England. *King Albert's Book* allowed British dignitaries to pay 'tribute to the Belgian king and people'. Britain's

---

[39] Gatrell, *A Whole Empire Walking*, 115–27.
[40] Gatrell, *A Whole Empire Walking*, 132.

obligation towards Belgian refugees reflected the Allies' inability to stem the German onslaught, and public sympathy for Belgian refugees who reached the UK stemmed from a belief that they had suffered unspeakable torment at the hands of German troops.[41]

Attempts to disseminate appeals for assistance meant thinking imaginatively about the most suitable way of generating and sustaining public interest in the plight of refugees. One remarkable attempt to establish the contours of displacement was made at the end of 1916 by the Tatiana committee, a private charity which brought together members of the Russian aristocratic elite and members of the professions. It proposed a special exhibition designed to inform the Russian public about the living conditions and activities of refugees, who were not all 'beggars, idlers and spongers'. (A similar initiative took place in Vienna under the auspices of the Austrian Ministry of the Interior.) The aim was to address four main themes: conditions in Russia's borderlands before and during the war, including 'the destruction of settlements, property and artistic monuments'; the 'sorrowful journey' of refugees, including the background to their displacement, the course of the refugee movement and the assistance given by government and public organizations; living conditions in their new homes, including 'the work undertaken by refugees and their impact on the local population'; and finally the restoration of normal life in the regions cleared of enemy occupation. The Tatiana committee solicited material from refugees, who were encouraged to describe their experiences in their own words or to provide photographs, drawings, reports, memoirs, stories and *belles lettres*; 'the material that is collected will be collated and organized systematically and form part of a volume of "Collected materials on the history of the refugee movement during the world war".' Unfortunately the project was overtaken by the February Revolution, although not before Baltic artists contributed paintings and drawings in the expectation that they would eventually be brought together to form part of the collection for new national museums in Latvia and Lithuania. The committee's initiative retains its relevance nearly a century after: 'facts and observations, even if they seem at first to be insignificant and trivial, may prove to be of great interest. The most important thing is for the description to be sincere and truthful'.[42]

Muriel Paget made a point of reminding her audience back home of the sentiments that Serbian troops and refugees expressed towards the Serbian Relief Fund: 'the trust and the gratitude they give back is one of the most touching and beautiful things I have ever known, not too dearly purchased by any sacrifice'.[43] Similar statements emanated from relief workers elsewhere who moved from one country to the next and emphasized their privileged standpoint: 'only one who has witnessed the thousands of refugees can have any conception of the strain that has been put

---

[41] Tony Kushner and Katharine Knox, *Refugees in an Age of Genocide: Global, National and Local Perspectives during the Twentieth Century* (Frank Cass, 1999), 48; Glenn Watkins, *Proof through the Night: Music and the Great War* (Berkeley: University of California Press, 2003), 106–7.

[42] Gatrell, *A Whole Empire Walking*, 94–5; Thorpe, 'Displacing Empire', 112–13.

[43] Muriel Paget, *With Our Serbian Allies* (Serbian Relief Fund, 1915), 39–43.

upon the resources of the country'. Relief workers claimed a special kind of privileged insight; women, in particular, regarded themselves as defenders of 'civilization' against the 'tyranny' inflicted on helpless civilians. In Ruth Fry's words, 'to be idly happy and a refugee is a contradiction in terms. On the other hand, to enable them to help themselves has been to bring much happiness to many exiles'.[44] Kathleen Royds, who spent several months accompanying Serbian refugees from Albania to Corsica, described them as having 'quite a distinct psychology of their own'. She explained: 'to begin with their nerves are overstrained; they are flung among a strange people, frequently of different habits looking upon them with a certain amount of suspicion at any rate at first'.[45] Refrains such as these contributed to suppressing the voice of refugees, whose views and experiences were mediated by those claiming to have their interests at heart.

Humanitarian relief work could become a career choice. A small number of examples must suffice. Flora Sandes, a British woman who travelled to Serbia as a Red Cross volunteer before enlisting in the Serbian army later on devoted herself to post-war relief. (Later on she married a Russian émigré and achieved a kind of fame as the driver of Belgrade's first taxi.) Katharine MacPhail who was sent to Serbia on behalf of the Scottish Women's Hospital, stayed on to run a hospital in Belgrade, funded partly by the Yugoslav government and partly by Save the Children, and Evelina Haverfield's work in the Serbian Relief Fund's orphanage in Niš was only cut short by her premature death from typhus in 1920. Muriel Paget looked after Belgian refugees and then became a relief worker in Russia and the Baltic States. Like many Quakers, Florence Barrow began her career in Russia before moving to Poland and later the Middle East and Balkans to work with refugees. Hilda Clark, a qualified physician, worked on behalf of refugees in France during the First World War, and later with Spanish Civil War refugees and Jewish refugees from Nazi Germany.[46] Percy Alden, who worked for the Belgian Relief Committee in London and then became a government commissioner on behalf of Belgian refugees in the Netherlands, later served as chairman of the SCF, under whose auspices he worked in the Balkans on behalf of refugees. The American Spurgeon Keeny, having worked with Herbert Hoover's American Relief Administration, subsequently joined the YMCA to assist displaced persons after the Second World War. The ARA also launched the career of Arthur Ringland, who was instrumental in the creation of CARE, and Maurice Pate, who helped found UNICEF. Sometimes those with direct experience of displacement took up the challenge of assisting refugees. A notable example was the Dominican priest, Father Georges Pire, who having been forced to flee from Belgium as an infant, became a renowned champion of refugee children in Western Europe before and after the Second World War. This reminds us that refugees' lives could have astounding consequences.

---

[44] Fry, *A Quaker Adventure*, 140.

[45] Undated note, Papers of Kathleen Royds, KER6, IWM.

[46] Sybil Oldfield, *Doers of the World: British Women Humanitarians 1900–1950* (Continuum, 2006).

Refugees were the subject of critical comment: negative views of unhealthy and undisciplined refugees circulated alongside positive images. Bold metaphors expressed the sense of overwhelming threat to social order. The press and the public used language that was directly reminiscent of disaster, of river banks being broken—thus 'flood', 'deluge', 'wave', 'avalanche', 'deposit', 'lava'—and fertile land being laid waste by hordes of locusts in Russia. Having first described Belgian refugees as mere 'sojourners', British newspapers soon began to describe a refugee 'stream' that might yet become a 'cataract'. As Liisa Malkki puts it, these 'liquid names for the uprooted reflect the sedentarist bias in dominant modes of imagining homes and homelands, identities and nationalities'. This discourse was readily embraced by an emerging patriotic intelligentsia and by humanitarians. In Russia displacement was likened to the biblical exodus or to previous catastrophes such as the invasions of Europe in the early Middle Ages. Some witnesses believed that the 'boundless ocean' of refugees could never properly be navigated. The deployment of this language represented a departure from earlier characterizations of atrocity. It drew attention to a fundamental uncertainty about borders and belonging, about 'home' and the stability of the 'nation'.[47]

NATIONALIZING REFUGEES

Much of the responsibility for refugee relief fell upon national bodies that identified with the displaced population. This was true of Belgium. In Serbia, too, the canny government of Nikola Pašić claimed the mantle on behalf of all South Slavs and convinced the Allies that the emerging state of Yugoslavia should be led by Serbia. Polish and Ukrainian refugees from Galicia organized national committees in Vienna.[48] But the most dramatic manifestation of national mobilization occurred in Russia where the organization of relief along 'national' lines and the appropriation of the refugee for the national cause helped to create the possibility for a national politics in circumstances that were hitherto unpropitious. In the first place, as we have seen, the scale of displacement imposed an enormous strain on existing agencies. Where neither the state nor existing organizations could cope, national bodies stepped in to fill the gap. Secondly, refugeedom contributed to the sense of collective national danger and suffering. This allowed them to depict relief in national terms and to proselytize among a captive audience. Thirdly, diasporic groups in Western Europe and North America, the result of previous migrations, could also be harnessed to this cause. Lastly, national consciousness might be enhanced not only by a vision of national humiliation and danger but also by new social contacts that exposed ethnic particularism.

---

[47] Liisa Malkki, *Purity and Exile: Violence, Memory, and National Cosmology among Hutu Refugees in Tanzania* (Chicago: Chicago University Press, 1995), 15–16; Gatrell, *A Whole Empire Walking*, 200.

[48] Mark Cornwall, *The Undermining of Austria-Hungary: the Battle for Hearts and Minds* (Basingstoke: Macmillan, 2000); Thorpe, 'Displacing Empire', 114–17.

Non-Russian elites constantly reminded their audience that invading troops had lately violated their homeland. Members of the Latvian intelligentsia argued that refugees from the Baltic lands presented a living testimony of German barbarism; their presence brought home to the inhabitants of Petrograd and Moscow the consequences of territorial loss. Occupation—the infamous Land Ober Ost—and despoliation were bad enough, but these calamities did not exhaust the fears expressed by national leaders. Latvian, Lithuanian and Polish patriots lamented the prospect of 'national dispersion'. A spokesman for the Polish national committee outlined the implications as follows:

> Only continuous and close contact with the national group, whether in the distribution of allowances, the allocation of accommodation, the supply of clothing, the search for work, the offer of medical treatment, the satisfaction of all material and spiritual needs—only this can guarantee and secure refugees on behalf of the motherland.[49]

Armenian and Jewish spokesmen invoked the memory of torment and displacement, thereby linking past and present in a manner designed to mobilize the refugee population. Similar arguments held sway among the Polish patriotic intelligentsia who referred to the revolts against Tsarist rule in 1830 and 1863 to remind their audience of past suffering and heroic endeavour, using this as a justification for restoring an undivided Poland of the kind that existed prior to partition in the eighteenth century. This did not always convince prejudiced relief workers, particularly when they encountered Jewish refugees. Violetta Thurstan, a young British nurse on the eastern front, maintained that 'Jewish refugees do not suffer so acutely from the terrible homesickness that attacks the refugees of other countries; they are wanderers by nature or sub-conscious instinct, and are not so rooted to one particular soil as those with a heavier sense of nationality'.[50] Her view completely failed to take account of the dynamic results of displacement (see later in this chapter).

Lacking an equivalent history of dramatic resistance, Latvian patriots found it more difficult to make a similar case. Instead they tried a different approach, arguing (as did Jewish leaders) that the close bonds between Latvians would be severed permanently unless they resisted dispersion. The alarming prospect of an enlarged Latvian diaspora was articulated by the leading parliamentarian Jānis Goldmanis, who urged the need to find 'means of saving and preserving the Latvian people, who face the lot of the Jews—to be scattered across the entire globe'. Latvian refugees should in his view take the opportunity to convince Latvians who had settled in (or been exiled to) distant parts of the empire of the need to think of Latvia as their ultimate destination. For the Belarusian activist Eugene Kancher, writing

---

[49] Gatrell, *A Whole Empire Walking*, 156; Vėjas Liulevičius, *War Land on the Eastern Front: Culture, National Identity, and German Occupation in World War I* (Cambridge: Cambridge University Press, 2001).

[50] Violetta Thurstan, *The People Who Run: Being the Tragedy of the Refugees in Russia* (New York: G.P. Putnam's Sons, 1916), 150–3.

from a vantage point in Central Asia, the war was one more coffin in the nail of the nation: 'I pondered the fact that over hundreds of years Belarusians had likewise been forced to scatter and had perished, like autumn flies, and with their flesh had fertilized the soil for other peoples'.[51]

The enforced displacement of population created an entirely new framework for belief and behaviour. When they took to the road, refugees were by definition deprived of membership in a close-knit local community, but displacement offered them an opportunity to gain access to an enlarged national community, built on the foundations of a common sense of loss and the need for collective effort to regain what had been forfeited in wartime. It might even be possible to re-establish contact with those who had left the homeland long before the war: as one Latvian patriot put it, 'the unity of Latvia demands that we register all such settlers and ensure that they do not lose their identity'. The chronicler of Latvian displacement, Kristaps Bachmanis (1867–1942), described how these settlers 'had been left alone with their destiny and so became estranged from the life of our people, our common fate, our grief and our longing for better future'. Fortunately, he went on, 'at last our refugees have enabled us to establish contact with Latvian settlers in Russia. Our purpose should be to do everything to destroy the wall between us and them'. Displacement provided an opportunity to make amends for previous failures to assert national solidarity.[52]

According to Martynas Yčas, the Lithuanian activist who later served as president of the new republic, the Lithuanian refugee committee 'prepared the people for future action and created the foundations for a future cultural and political edifice ... It forced even non-Lithuanians to recognise that we ourselves were the masters of our country'. Allowing for a degree of retrospective exaggeration, Yčas neatly encapsulated the sense of political mobilization and the vision of national emancipation that refugeedom now made possible.[53] Patriotic rhetoric was combined with practical efforts in the Russian interior. National spokesmen hastily improvised schools, orphanages, clubs, workshops, canteens and barracks, with funds provided by a plethora of national committees. The state tolerated these efforts, partly as a means of lightening the burden on hard-pressed government officials and on the public purse. In Tsarist Russia, these national committees served another purpose so far as the government was concerned: they offered an alternative to the 'public organizations', whose leaders asserted a claim to organize refugee relief and resettlement. But by the autumn of 1915, contrasts were being drawn between the speed and efficiency of the national committees and

---

[51] Gatrell, *A Whole Empire Walking*, 159; Valentina Utgof, 'In Search of National Support: Belarusian Refugees in World War I and the People's Republic of Belarus', in Nick Baron and Peter Gatrell (eds), *Homelands: War, Population and Statehood in the Former Russian Empire, 1918–1924* (Anthem Books, 2004), 53–73, at 59.

[52] Kristaps Bachmanis, 'Musu agrakas kludas' (Our previous mistakes), *Dzimtenes Atbalss*, 18–19 (1916); Gatrell, *A Whole Empire Walking*, 158.

[53] Gatrell, *A Whole Empire Walking*, 157–62; Tomas Balkelis, *The Making of Modern Lithuania* (Routledge, 2009), 105–14.

the hesitant manner in which local authorities handled refugee relief, so the Tsarist government gained little by this stratagem.

Abrupt physical displacement entailed profound social and political consequences for the Jewish population of imperial Russia. In one sense the war liberated Russian Jewry, by forcing the Tsarist government to recognize that it could no longer continue to sustain the Pale of Settlement—in other words, that it was more important to defeat the real enemy than to maintain administrative controls over the Jewish population of the Russian Empire. As the liberal-minded minister of agriculture put it, 'one cannot fight a war against Germany and against the Jews'.[54] Certainly, Jews continued to suffer all manner of harassment and physical abuse at the hands of the Russian army. Yet once it became clear that their movement could no longer be controlled by government agencies, the Pale of Settlement dissolved itself. In August 1915 the government reluctantly conceded that 'Jewish war sufferers'—those who fled and those who had been deported—should be allowed to settle in provincial towns but not in Petrograd or Moscow. Consistent with pre-war Tsarist policy, Jewish refugees were also forbidden to settle in villages. Nevertheless, the consequences were dramatic enough: two-fifths of all Jewish refugees moved to areas of the Russian Empire that had previously been closed to them. Townspeople in the Russian interior who had scarcely set eyes on Jews now rubbed shoulders with them. The consequences could of course be troubling. The use of Yiddish in public places led some Russians to think that German was being spoken, and this compounded the fear of Jewish cultural difference; some municipal authorities made it clear that Jews should not venture out of doors.

The experiences of Jewish refugees in Russia and in the Habsburg Empire were very varied. Some Russian Jewish writers envisaged that hundreds of thousands of refugees could establish a 'Jewish centre' in Siberia, helping 'to transform this region into a powerful developing country'. Others, however, expressed serious reservations lest the solidarity engendered by confinement to the Pale of Settlement be undermined: 'we need to consider this from a national, not a narrow refugee point of view'. It was unwise to promote the dispersion of Jews throughout the Russian Empire, still less to tolerate their potential assimilation in the Russian interior.[55] More immediately, the war modified the dynamics among Russian Jewry by encouraging elite members to join with young, talented health professionals who imparted a more democratic complexion to Jewish relief work. 'Now [it was said] one flag has been raised, the Jewish banner. The wave of refugees has united all shades of Judaism and all languages. Jews who hitherto did not know or understand one another have been brought together. Mutual antagonisms have disappeared, to be replaced by excellent fraternal relations'.[56] Certainly the cultural and economic distance between the poor Jew from the shtetl and the relatively small

[54] Gatrell, *A Whole Empire Walking*, 146–7.
[55] Gatrell, *A Whole Empire Walking*, 146.
[56] Gatrell, *A Whole Empire Walking*, 148; Steven Zipperstein, 'The Politics of Relief: the Transformation of Russian Jewish Communal Life during the First World War' *Studies in Contemporary Jewry*, 4 (1988), 22–40.

and privileged Jewish communities in Moscow and Petrograd remained difficult to bridge. Where the gap narrowed, government officials interpreted this as a sign that their own obligations lessened: the governor of Tambov for example obstructed the distribution of allowances to Jewish refugees, giving as his reason the support they received from Petrograd's Jewish committee. Some things did not change.

In Vienna, too, middle-class Jews overcame their aversion to the *Ostjuden* and did what they could to alleviate the suffering of their destitute co-religionists by establishing soup kitchens and workshops, paying school fees and supporting rabbis. The philanthropist Sophie Grünfeld spoke optimistically of the contact between bourgeois Jews and the poor refugees who 'had other customs. But our contact with you has brought us closer and the bearing and dignity with which you bear your tragedy fills us with sincere admiration'.[57] Such optimism was overdrawn; as in Russia, social divisions remained acute. Wealthier Jews made use of their contacts in Vienna, whereas poorer refugees had to make do with substandard accommodation in barns or schools or else ended up in miserable refugee camps. Jewish charities in Austria and in the diaspora looked further ahead. Workshops were established to encourage young refugee women to learn a suitable trade or to assist men to become better farmers in anticipation of their return to Galicia or Bukovina. Schools prided themselves on providing instruction and vocational training. In this way displacement became linked to economic improvement in backward parts of the Habsburg Empire. Nevertheless, not everyone was satisfied: Zionists complained that too much attention was being devoted to refugees rather than encouraging emigration to Palestine.

Diaspora communities contributed assistance as well. American-Armenian immigrants established homeland societies at the turn of the century and kept them going long after the war came to an end. Poles did likewise, and drew on Polonophile opinion in the UK.[58] Wealthy British Jews collected money to assist Jewish refugees who arrived from Belgium. The position of Jews, particularly in the Tsarist Empire, posed a challenge for Anglo-Jewry. To highlight their suffering was to draw attention to pre-war persecution and pogrom in a state that was now a wartime ally. Some activists believed that it was insufficient to trumpet philanthropic activity and ignore the dreadful consistency of Tsarist conduct in peace and war. It was also difficult for British Jews to overcome internal social divisions in support of refugee co-religionists in the Tsarist Empire. Much more successful in terms of publicity and fundraising were Jewish groups in the USA, above all the Joint Distribution Committee of American Funds for the Relief of Jewish War Sufferers, later renamed the American Joint Distribution Committee (JDC). Until America entered the war there were no scruples about publicizing Tsarist brutality and Jewish suffering. One-third of the total funds at the disposal of the Jewish

---

[57] Rozenblit, *Reconstructing a National Identity*, 75.

[58] For example, a 'Chomaklou Society' was already in existence in the early twentieth century: <http://www.chomaklou.com/index.php>; Norman Davies, 'The Poles in Great Britain 1914–1919' *Slavonic and East European Review*, 50, no.118 (1972), 63–89.

committee in Russia came from a group headed by the leading New York banker Felix Warburg.[59]

Refugees came to embody the suffering of an entire 'people' or nation. Mention of 'brave little Belgium' indirectly drew attention to 'great' Britain but also encouraged a powerful and even apocalyptic rhetoric of 'civilization' versus the 'barbarism' embodied in the German perpetration of atrocity. (The entire rhetoric stood in sharp contrast to the condemnation of the Belgian government just a few years earlier for its actions in the Congo.) British officials acknowledged an obligation towards refugees, whose plight was a result of the Allies' inability to stem the enemy onslaught that exposed the Catholic population of Belgium to 'pagan' and 'atrocious' Germany. Refugees symbolized suffering that could be made good in part from reparations that the Allies planned to extract from the defeated foe. Christian rhetoric was also evoked on behalf of Serbian refugees, who 'once across [the pass] made the sign of the Cross. God be praised [they said], we have entered the threshold of Paradise'. Serbian refugees were construed as distraught but also devout, a trope that spoke to national interests as well as to foreign philanthropy.[60]

In short, collective action helped to bridge the gap between the educated national elite, refugee members of the national intelligentsia, and the ordinary refugee. Connections were also forged with diaspora organizations. It was no longer possible to retain a distinction between members of the educated intelligentsia and the 'unenlightened' masses, because they had all been exposed to the dehumanizing and debilitating consequences of refugeedom. Non-refugee members of national minorities bound themselves by levying 'taxes' on the entire community. The reiteration of a sense of loss and destruction of 'national' assets acted as a unifying device. By virtue of the disruption caused to other relationships by war, refugeedom created a situation in which nationality assumed enormous importance. 'Most of those who hitherto called themselves "Russian" are now beginning to think of themselves as Poles, Jews, Ukrainians, Armenians, Latvians, rather than as Russians', wrote the editor of *Sputnik bezhentsa* ('Refugee-Traveller') in September 1915.[61] Displacement conferred respectability upon the rhetoric of national consciousness and imparted vitality to a crusade couched in a national idiom.

REPATRIATION AND REMEMBRANCE

When the Great War finally came to an end the question of repatriation became urgent. The first priority was to repatriate soldiers including prisoners of war, but

[59] Henry Rosenfelt, *This Thing of Giving: the Record of a Rare Enterprise of Mercy and Brotherhood* (New York: Plymouth Press, 1923); J. Bruce Nichols, *The Uneasy Alliance: Religion, Refugee Work, and US Foreign Policy* (New York: Oxford University Press, 1988), 33–4; Samantha Johnson, 'Breaking or Making the Silence? British Jews and East European Jewish Relief, 1914–1917' *Modern Judaism*, 30, no.1 (2010), 95–119.

[60] David Mitrany, *The Effect of the War in Southeastern Europe* (New Haven: Yale University Press, 1936), 243–7.

[61] Gatrell, *A Whole Empire Walking*, 141.

attention soon turned to refugees. This took on a different aspect in different contexts. Grandiose plans drawn up in the UK to resettle Belgian refugees in Chile and South Africa came to naught, because Belgium insisted that refugees should contribute to its national reconstruction after the war. Most of the 140,000 Belgian refugees in the UK at the Armistice returned home by 1919. Ruth Fry described a visit to Brussels and Antwerp where 'there was a strange sense of places waking up after a long bad dream', but 'Belgium was thoroughly tired of foreign charity and was anxious to stand on her own feet'. However, the war had exposed a cleavage between Francophone and Flemish viewpoints.[62]

The situation elsewhere was more complicated. Serbian refugees went back home, partly with the assistance of the Serbian Relief Fund and Quaker relief workers. Social and economic reconstruction took many years to complete. Jewish refugees endured frequent harassment when they returned to Western Galicia. Others were prevented from returning by the vicious conflict in the new Polish-Ukrainian borderland; they struggled to survive in Vienna. A handful succeeded in enrolling in university and even obtained citizenship in the new Austrian state. Refugees from the western borderlands who wished to return from the Russian interior when the Bolsheviks sued for peace faced enormous hurdles: not just the German occupation of the Baltic, but also how to explain a lack of identity papers. Questions about their health status were inevitably intrusive. Meanwhile the Bolsheviks tried to discourage able-bodied and skilled men and women from leaving the struggling Soviet state. How all this worked out for one individual can be seen in the diary of Alfreds Goba, a young Latvian who returned from temporary domicile in Baku. He negotiated practical steps and the psychological difficulties associated with going home. In an entry from August 1918 he writes: 'Now I am working. I am working towards building a new Latvia'. Goba hoped that peace would bring freedom from German and Russian tutelage alike: 'Latvia, Latvia you have lived a hard and slavish orphan life, and still you are like a child. Will you survive? Will you be able to stand on your own two feet?' He saw a close fit between the need to establish his family on more secure material foundations and Latvia's search for national liberation. In Latvia, Lithuania and Poland, the new authorities paid close attention to the political opinion and ethnic identity of prospective returnees, particularly those who (unlike Goba) did not belong to the titular nationality. Jews regularly encountered discrimination and hostility.[63]

This is not to say that states necessarily embraced the figure of the refugee once the war came to an end. Refugees were frequently hidden from the officially sanctioned narrative. Post-war governments mostly drew a veil over the circumstances of mass displacement, particularly if they showed the state in an unfavourable light. Belgium and France had little to say about refugees, although popular memories of the crisis in 1914 were revived during the crisis of 1940 which afflicted the same regions and often

[62] Fry, *A Quaker Adventure*, 118.

[63] Aija Priedite, 'Latvian Refugees and the Latvian Nation State during and after World War I', in Baron and Gatrell (eds), *Homelands*, 35–52; Tomas Balkelis, 'In Search of a Native Realm: the Return of World War I Refugees to Lithuania, 1918–1924', in Baron and Gatrell (eds), *Homelands*, 74–97. I am grateful to Aldis Purs for his translations from Goba's diary.

affected the same people. Mussolini had no interest in talking about the mass exodus of Italians following the debacle at Caporetto, preferring instead to associate his regime with the glories of ancient Rome. In Russia the Bolsheviks derived their legitimacy from the Russian Revolution and relegated the 'imperialist war' and its refugees to the margins of political significance. The successor states that emerged from the wreckage of the old continental empires devoted little attention to the history of refugee politics during the war, being more preoccupied with building the new state than with en-couraging wartime commemoration. Although the experience of refugees might be slotted into a narrative of national salvation and deliverance, politicians trod quite carefully lest they draw attention to the wartime chaos or encourage refugees to claim compensation.

In Hungary, Armenia and Serbia on the other hand, mass displacement—and in Armenia's case, mass murder—contributed to the cultivation in the new state and among the diaspora of memories of national catastrophe. A Serbian teacher who taught refugee children in France during the war in France asked his pupils to write an assignment entitled 'My departure from the fatherland and arrival in France'. He published the results in 1923, in a book entitled *The Hopes of the Serbian Golgotha*. It comes as no surprise that it was re-issued in Serbia eight decades later or to learn that other stories of suffering were revived in Belgrade in the late 1980s and 1990s, with titles such as 'Golgotha and Serbian resurrection', helping to legitimize independence as communist rule collapsed.[64]

The post-war disengagement from the experience of the Great War reflected the fact that a fresh crisis erupted during the 1920s, causing international organizations (notably the League of Nations) and relief workers to focus on the immediate needs of new refugees. But political uncertainty in this enormous and contested space only served to multiply the dilemmas and difficulties associated with repatriation. The refugee population was swelled by newly displaced persons, the result of German military occupation of the western borderlands of the former empire. Subsequently, the prolonged dislocation of the Russian civil war, battles between Polish, Lithuanian, and Ukrainian troops, the Soviet-Polish War, and continued turmoil in the Caucasus prompted additional displacement, as well as sizeable emigration. Some people stayed where they were, but found that borders had moved instead, bringing about their political expatriation. Thus the years of war, revolution, and peacemaking between 1917 and 1921 were marked by renewed demographic disturbance on a pan-European scale. Its implications are explored in the next chapter.

CONCLUSIONS

The First World War brought about momentous movements of population, adding to the legacy of war and displacement in South-Eastern Europe and the Balkans

---

[64] Silvija Ćurić and Vidoslav Stevanović (eds), *Golgota i vaskrs Srbije 1915–1918* (Belgrade: Parti-zanska knjiga, 1986), with thanks to John Paul Newman for the reference.

during the 1870s and in 1912–13. Millions of civilians fled in order to escape the threat of invasion. To construe this as panic and 'spontaneity' was to direct attention either to a lack of patriotism—true patriots stood their ground—or to a loss of self-control by people who would need to be taught how to regain their reason before they could rebuild their lives. Others fled because their own governments gave them no choice: they were deported as punishment for perceived disloyalty. The decision by the Ottoman leadership to target Armenians, and the Russian high command's relentless pursuit of Polish, Jewish, Latvian, German and other minorities, reflected a strategic choice to excise entire groups not on grounds of their conduct (although some were blamed for military defeat), but by virtue of their unalterable ethnicity. Others stood to benefit materially, such as Muslim inhabitants of the Ottoman Empire, many of them refugees from Bulgaria and Greece, who were assigned the property of expropriated Armenians and Assyrians.

How far did the displacement of population during the Great War anticipate subsequent refugee crises? One striking anomaly in relation to what happened later on is that most countries decided not to establish refugee camps and instead dispersed refugees to towns and villages. Holland was a notable exception. Camps were also used to incarcerate refugees from Galicia and Bukovina as well as Habsburg subjects from the Italian borderlands who were deported to the interior of Austria where they could be kept under close surveillance. Other poor states, notably Italy and Russia, overwhelmed by the scale of the refugee crisis, shifted much of the responsibility for supporting refugees on to public organizations and private charitable bodies, leaving the central government to concentrate resources on the direct war effort. Russia despatched its 'suspect' minorities to remote locations, far from the centre of power where there was no need for a labyrinth of camps.

Other aspects of the wartime crisis pointed more clearly to the way ahead. The speed and size of displacement encouraged emergency improvisation at first. Subsequently bureaucratic administration did not lessen but rather enhanced the importance of efforts by private or semi-official organizations. All this went hand in hand with an energetic attempt to distinguish and to classify refugees as a precondition of providing assistance. Almost always the refugee was imagined to be the victim of unstoppable forces, whether a brutal enemy or a state engaged in national mobilization. The category of the refugee became part of the common currency of politics and public opinion: 'the word "refugees" signifies [in Russia] a numerous body of people, of any age, sex and social status'.[65]

To be labelled as a refugee had demeaning consequences, stripping away attributes of social distinction and class to leave oneself exposed to a sense of pure deprivation. The consequences of this silencing are eerily familiar to the modern reader. A Belgian refugee spoke from the heart when he summed up his feelings: 'One was always a refugee—that's the name one was given, a sort of nickname (*sobriquet*). One was left with nothing, ruined, and that's how people

---

[65] Gatrell, *A Whole Empire Walking*, 96–7.

carried on talking about "the refugee". We weren't real people any more'.[66] It was rare to find alternative readings of displacement, such as by the deputy mayor of the border town of Hazebrouck who expressed that hope that 'the war will have permeated the different regions of our country; we in the north have our qualities, they in the Midi have theirs'.[67] How refugees reacted to their circumstances and to the arrangements made on their behalf is difficult to tell. A voice from Russia rejected the refugee category: 'we are living people [with] the misfortune to have been displaced, but we are human beings all the same. We long to become people once again'.[68]

Yet if prevailing images tended to homogenize the refugee, creating a single category of difference, nationality offered a means of distinguishing between refugees. Refugeedom contributed to the intensification of a sense of national identity, not because one ethnic group alone had been singled out but because it created the prospect that the 'nation' might be permanently uprooted and scattered. Tormented yet valiant Belgian refugees came to stand for the country as a whole. Italian deportees were placed in internment camps by the Austro-Hungarian army, and became a ready-made audience for patriots to disseminate nationalist propaganda. Serbian refugees symbolized the travails of an entire nation waiting for deliverance. In Russia newly-minted national organizations claimed the refugee for themselves, arguing that they had a responsibility to the nation, which in turn would not shirk its responsibilities. Refugees whether Poles, Latvians, Armenians or Jews belonged somewhere after all.

The war provided new opportunities for manifestations of humanitarian sentiment and relief efforts. Relief workers described their wartime work in terms of romance and adventure and the exercise of calm judgement in sharp contrast to their perception of refugees as inert, traumatized and lacking in self-control. Although relief efforts had an ephemeral purpose, their legacy mattered in ways that were not always evident at the time. One outcome was that individuals drew upon their experience of wartime displacement to commit themselves to further action. Engagement with refugees paved the way for careers in humanitarianism. External aid too played an important role. Foreign well-wishers manifested a sentimental attachment to Serbians, Belgians and above all Armenians. They collected money and kept the plight of refugees in the public eye. Even more significant was the growth of diaspora associations where ideas about victims and perpetrators circulated alongside the message of national endurance. To be sure, diasporic groups did not necessarily embrace refugees from a different social background with equal fervour. Generally speaking, however, foreign sympathizers and diasporas traded on perceived national characteristics, turning refugees into emblems both of historic suffering and national self-realization.

---

[66] Sophie de Schaepdrijver, *La Belgique et la Première Guerre Mondiale* (Frankfurt: Peter Lang, 2004), 104–5.

[67] Nivet, *Les réfugiés français*, 555.

[68] Editorial, *Bezhenets*, 18 October 1915.

The war confirmed that cosmopolitanism was not an option. Cosmopolitan identities had already been weakened in the Ottoman Empire during the latter part of the nineteenth and early twentieth centuries: 'new notions of identity and sentiments of commonality and difference were created'. Nationalists treated this as a preordained outcome. As the leading Latvian poet and playwright Jānis Rainis put it in 1917, commenting on the refugees who moved from Tsarist Russia's borderlands to the interior: 'one cannot circumvent the national phase of social development and pass directly to a non-national cosmopolitanism'. Such types, he added, 'if they reject their own people, will not embrace a non-national state of the future, but will instead be submerged in a different oppressor nation'. This—the nationalization of the refugee—was the First World War's disquieting legacy.[69]

[69] Karakasidou, *Fields of Wheat*, 142; Gatrell, *A Whole Empire Walking*, 141. Rainis himself supported the rights of national minorities in Latvia.

2

Nation-states and the Birth of a 'Refugee Problem' in Inter-war Europe

The new refugees were persecuted not because of what they had done or thought, but because of what they unchangeably were—born into the wrong kind of race or the wrong kind of class

(Hannah Arendt)

INTRODUCTION

On 3 November 1918, exhausted by the war effort and unable to count any longer on the support of Austria-Hungary, the Ottoman Empire and Bulgaria, Germany agreed to an armistice; the guns fell silent on the Western front eight days later. The peacemakers who assembled in Paris in January 1919 redrew the map of Europe. Already in October 1917 the Russian Revolution brought the Bolsheviks to power with a commitment to bread, land and peace, and in this volatile political situation the non-Russian parts of the empire asserted the right of self-determination. Germany exploited this weakness in the Allied war effort and its troops occupied swathes of Russian territory, but the eventual defeat of the Central Powers allowed the Allies to impose their will on Berlin, Vienna and Istanbul. A series of peace treaties dismembered Austria-Hungary and trimmed German and Ottoman territory. Each state faced enormous problems of reconstruction. Serbia, for example, now part of the new Yugoslavia, had to reknit the entire fabric of society and economy. Post-war conflicts paved the way for further upheaval. Civil wars gripped Russia, Finland and Ireland, and a brief but bloody revolution convulsed Hungary. The Soviet-Polish War (1919–20) and war between Greece and Turkey (1919–22) led to further bloodshed. The consequences reverberated across the continent.

The aftershock of the First World War had momentous implications for displaced people—demobilized soldiers, returning prisoners of war and civilian refugees. Revolution, imperial collapse and territorial changes meant that repatriation returned them to places that were unrecognizable. For others repatriation was not an option. In Russia, the Bolshevik victory led to the mass exodus of their 'White' opponents. International attention was lavished on these displaced Russians, as well as Armenian refugees who survived the massacres in the Ottoman Empire. Other new states, diametrically opposed to Bolshevism, appeared on the scene. Estonia, Latvia and Lithuania became sovereign states. Poland emerged as an independent polity, with territory ceded from Austria-Hungary, Germany and Russia. The outcome of the post-war settlement was far from stable. Europe's 'successor states' aspired to a high degree of national homogeneity, yet minorities accounted for one-quarter of the total population. The legacy of wartime movements of population and widespread poverty and privation compounded the problem: 'the keen struggle for existence in these countries has kept alive the chauvinism of the war period'.[1]

One option was to escape social or political subordination by putting oneself beyond the reach of unsympathetic states. Ethnic Hungarians who feared for their future in Romania, Czechoslovakia or Yugoslavia fled to the truncated state of Hungary, a defeated country in which most of them had never set foot. Having forfeited the privileged position they enjoyed as landed gentry or as government officials in the old Habsburg Empire, they demanded admittance and formed the backbone of a reactionary and revanchist politics. By contrast, many Hungarians from a more modest background decided to remain, such as peasants who hoped to benefit from the redistribution of land that new states embarked upon. In the medium term they gained relative to their social superiors who fled to Hungary.[2]

The term refugee acquired a new resonance as large numbers of people were displaced and as states in turn erected barriers to asylum. In the words of Sir John Hope Simpson, author of a classic study on refugees, 'the whole system is based on a scheme of national states, with populations which fit into the scheme of nationalities. [The] person without a nationality does not fit into that system'.[3] The League of Nations that began work in January 1920 made the protection of national minorities a cornerstone of its programme, but the successor states regarded the minority treaties as an unwarranted interference. The Soviet Union appeared to resolve the issue by providing political and cultural opportunities for non-Russian minorities, but the presence of ethnic groups in neighbouring, non-communist states—Poles in 'bourgeois' Poland, for example—raised the spectre of cross-border subversion. Here too, the way ahead pointed to the persistence of wartime practices of targeting 'unreliable elements', which reached a crescendo in 1937 with the deportations of Germans, Poles, Koreans, Chinese, Greeks, Bulgarians and others.[4]

The collapse of the Ottoman Empire had equally pronounced consequences, not unexpected given its turbulent pre-war history. In 1919 the Greek government decided to exploit what appeared to be Turkey's weakness by invading Western Anatolia on the pretext of assisting its ethnic Greek inhabitants. Greek and Armenian guerrillas attacked Turkish villagers, turning the region into a 'wilderness'.[5] Three

---

[1] 'Report of David Bressler and Joseph Hyman to the JDC on Present Conditions of the Jews of Eastern Europe' (1930), JDC Archives.

[2] István Mócsy, *The Uprooted: Hungarian Refugees and their Impact on Hungary's Domestic Politics, 1918–1921* (New York: Columbia University Press, 1983).

[3] John Hope Simpson, *The Refugee Problem: Report of a Survey* (Oxford: Oxford University Press, 1939), 230.

[4] Terry Martin, *The Affirmative Action Empire: Nations and Nationalism in the Soviet Union, 1923–1939* (Ithaca: Cornell University Press, 2001); Oleg Khlevniuk, 'The Objectives of the Great Terror, 1937–1938', in David Hoffmann (ed.), *Stalinism: the Essential Readings* (Oxford: Blackwell, 2003), 87–104.

[5] McCarthy, *Death and Exile*, 278.

years later, troops under the command of Mustafa Kemal (Atatürk) mounted a counter-offensive. In September 1922 the port city of Smyrna (Izmir) fell to his troops. Thousands of Greek survivors of the ensuing bloodshed were deported to Anatolia or else made their escape to Greece. These repercussions were immense. Allied diplomats meeting in Lausanne agreed to support a permanent exchange of population between Greece and Turkey in an attempt, as one British official put it, to 'de-Balkanise the Balkans'.[6] Lausanne legitimized mass displacement as a prophylactic device to promote ethnic homogeneity. Individuals were given no choice but to submit. Here refugeedom was the product of deliberate international action.

What was to be done to assist these victims of persecution and diplomatic wrangling? Russian and Armenian refugees were scattered across Europe, the Middle East, the Far East and North America. While impressive humanitarian efforts addressed their material needs, little attempt was made to understand the root causes of their displacement. Member states insisted that the League of Nations should keep 'political' questions out of refugee relief. This encouraged a sense that refugees were miserable flotsam and jetsam. Politics nevertheless formed an inescapable part of the equation. Anxieties surfaced over political and economic security, given the explosive impact of the Bolshevik Revolution. Not everyone saw things in negative terms: Italy's representative in Geneva appeared to welcome 'a vast nomadic movement, leading to the dawn of a new era in the old world of Europe. New slips are being grafted on the old tree of Western Europe'. Surveying the continental upheavals, one precocious English child imagined a land called 'Refugia' that might become a homeland for the dispossessed, but this generous fantasy likewise underscored the magnitude of social upheaval.[7]

As this vision implied, expressions of humanitarian concern emanated from a variety of sources. The League relied upon private philanthropic bodies and NGOs to carry out programmes of relief and reconstruction. The American-based Near East Relief (originally the Armenian Relief Committee) endorsed 'the forwarding of economic rehabilitation [as] probably the most important service that could be rendered' in the Balkans and the Middle East. The broad agenda encompassed improved health care, the education of women, and the dissemination of 'organized recreation', so that in due course 'the natives [could] help themselves'. External intervention was vital in the short term, lest the countries that accommodated them, 'lying at the very doorstep of modern western civilisation, constitute an even greater menace to that civilisation today than they have in centuries past'.[8]

Diasporic groups too mobilized substantial funds, with the specific purpose of supporting refugees for whom they had a particular affinity. This was most marked in respect of Armenians and Jews, but the much smaller Russian diaspora also mobilized on behalf of White émigrés with the support of Tsarist charities that

---

[6] Matthew Frank, *Expelling the Germans: British Opinion and Post-1945 Population Transfer in Context* (Oxford: Oxford University Press, 2007), 19.

[7] Soguk, *States and Strangers*, 113, 123. The boy in question was nine-year old Chad Varah (1911–2007), who went on to create the Samaritans.

[8] Frank Ross, Luther Fry and Elbridge Sibley, *The Near East and American Philanthropy: a Survey* (New York: Columbia University Press, 1929), 280; Simpson, *Refugee Problem*, 176–9.

moved abroad after the Bolshevik Revolution. Humanitarian organizations sought to galvanize public opinion by proclaiming the need to address historic injustices, but this tactic did not suit each and every case. Russian and Spanish refugees needed to find an alternative rhetorical strategy. Those affected by the Lausanne population transfer had a yet harder job to make themselves heard on the international stage.

POPULATION DISPLACEMENT IN THE FORMER RUSSIAN EMPIRE

The Russian Revolution set in train a brutal confrontation between those who supported the Bolsheviks and those who opposed them for a variety of motives. Civil war produced widespread internal displacement: '[W]e have [wrote one academic] lived through so much these past seven years that it is a rare citizen of the Republic who has not felt like a refugee at least for a short while'.[9] Having failed to overthrow the new regime, the Bolsheviks' opponents fled Russia. Most never returned, settling instead in 'temporary' refugee camps in Turkey, Bulgaria, Yugoslavia and Greece. By 1922, more than a quarter of all Russian refugees had settled in Germany, 360,000 in Berlin alone. One-fifth lived in Poland; the Balkan states, France and China accounted for most of the remainder. Thousands of refugees were admitted to Czechoslovakia which expected them to return in due course to a Russia free from Bolshevism. Mutual disillusionment soon set in; Cossack refugees especially felt that they were being exploited by local farmers. Other Russians ended up in the Belgian Congo and Tunisia, where they fantasized about reviving an aristocratic life. The flow of refugees was not entirely one-way. Korean patriots who opposed the Japanese occupation of their country fled to the Russian Far East after the brutal suppression of the independence movement in 1919; they joined other refugees who had sought sanctuary in 1910 following Japan's annexation of Korea.[10]

Governments looked to minimize their responsibilities towards Russian refugees. The International Committee of the Red Cross (ICRC) approached the League of Nations, which appointed the renowned Arctic explorer Fridtjof Nansen as High Commissioner for Refugees in September 1921, a post for which he refused a salary. Nansen was given a temporary mandate to assist 'any person of Russian origin who does not enjoy or who no longer enjoys the protection of the Government of the USSR, and who has not acquired another nationality'. The ICRC in particular emphasized that this assistance should be understood as politically neutral humanitarianism.[11]

---

[9] Donald Raleigh, *Experiencing Russia's Civil War: Politics, Society, and Revolutionary Culture in Saratov, 1917–1922* (Princeton: Princeton University Press, 2002), 187.

[10] Samantha Johnson, 'Communism in Russia Only Exists on Paper: Czechoslovakia and the Russian Refugee Crisis, 1919–1924' *CEH*, 16, no.3 (2007), 371–94.

[11] Simpson, *Refugee Problem*, 227; Dzovinar Kévonian, *Réfugiés et diplomatie humanitaire: les acteurs européens et la scène proche-orientale pendant l'entre-deux-guerres* (Paris: Publications de la Sorbonne, 2003), 388–91.

The League invited Nansen to organize the repatriation of refugees or arrange for 'their allocation to the various countries which might be able to receive them and to find means of work for them'. Initially, he entertained hopes of promoting the repatriation of Russian refugees from overcrowded places such as Varna and Constantinople, so that they might contribute to the reconstruction of Russia. Soviet leaders sought thereby to nip anti-Bolshevik agitation in the bud. Pro-communist organizations in the West encouraged repatriation, but few refugees took the bait. Nansen eventually abandoned the idea.[12]

With no funds at his disposal Nansen could not assist refugees directly, although he made a point of employing refugees as clerical staff in local branches. (They were also represented in the Geneva office.) His main achievement was to conduct a census of refugees and provide those who could afford five francs with a 'Nansen passport' to enable them to travel to a third country to find work, the underlying purpose being to help distribute Russian and Armenian (and subsequently Assyrian) refugees more 'equitably' among member countries of the League of Nations. The passport offered no assurances about the right of abode or the right to work. European governments were loath to make substantial contributions to the League's relief efforts for reasons of financial retrenchment. Their stance also reflected an element of contempt for refugees which, in the British case, translated into a highly restrictive immigration policy. The Under-Secretary for Foreign Affairs, Cecil Harmsworth, derided 'Cossacks, Kalmucks, priests, generals, judges and ladies' whom he regarded as 'an intolerable burden'. But this did nothing to address the question of their offspring who, in the words of a more insightful observer, were 'in danger of becoming useless and harmful elements in the Europe of tomorrow'.[13]

By no means all refugees came from a privileged background, although this stereotype tended to predominate, as Harmsworth's description suggests. Those with existing contacts found work relatively quickly. French employers recruited Russian workers in the refugee camps in Constantinople and Bulgaria—Renault took on refugees at its factory in Billancourt. Others became taxi drivers, accountants, clerks, bank guards and prostitutes. Their prospects diminished considerably as a consequence of the Great Depression at the turn of the decade. Harbin in the Far East turned into a miniature Russian metropolis, home to some 200,000 refugees. In Shanghai around 8,000 Russian refugees formed an active cultural community, although they remained an underclass among the privileged foreign mercantile elite.[14]

While prominent Russian artists, composers, lawyers, politicians and academics left behind diaries and correspondence describing their lives in exile, and

---

[12] Katy Long, 'Early Repatriation Policy: Russian Refugee Return, 1922–1924' *JRS*, 22, no.2 (2009), 133–54; Martyn Housden, 'White Russians Crossing the Black Sea: Fridtjof Nansen, Constantinople, and the First Modern Repatriation of Refugees Displaced by Civil Conflict, 1922–1923' *Slavonic and East European Review*, 88, no.3 (2010), 495–524.

[13] Skran, *Refugees in Inter-War Europe*, 83–4, 149, 285; Soguk, *States and Strangers*, 104. On the complex Assyrian situation see Simpson, *Refugee Problem*, 47–61.

[14] Catherine Gousseff, *L'exil russe: la fabrique du réfugié apatride, 1920–1939* (Paris: CNRS, 2008).

while Russian émigrés maintained a vibrant culture—Harbin was home to a notable orchestra and opera house—the voices of those who were unable to trade on artistic talent or social connections were usually concealed. One disquieting example survives in the form of a letter by one Madame Mouravieff who petitioned the British Commissioner of Police in Bombay, explaining that she landed in jail, having been charged with prostitution. In her letter, written in hesitant English, she describes herself as 'simply nervous and hysterical' (sic), and that 'nobody understands me here. I am so tired, I have been suffering too much and I am overwhelmed with grief, I am living like a "dead body"'. The Commissioner decided to keep her in prison rather than send her to the refugee camp in Belgaum, some 400 miles south, on the grounds that she was a 'nymphomaniac' who would be a 'nuisance' in the camp. She ended her letter with the plaintive words: 'I am so lonely here, be interested in me'.[15] How she came to be in this position, and what happened to her, we can only speculate. All we know for certain is that any romance that attached to the narrative of 'Russia abroad' simply passed her by.

With only a small administration under the aegis of the League of Nations, assisting Russian refugees became instead a story of self-help and private philanthropy, in which the Russian Red Cross and exiles from Zemgor (the most important public organization in Tsarist Russia for the relief of civilian victims of war) took a lead role in providing schooling, vocational training, basic medical treatment and assistance for children and the elderly in Constantinople and on the Greek island of Lemnos. A Russian Aid Society supported indigent White Russians; so too did the Russian Orthodox Church and the American Red Cross. Notwithstanding their efforts and those of Nansen, Simpson concluded that after 20 years of action, specifically in the Far East, 'things could scarcely be worse from the refugee standpoint, and unless steps of some kind are taken the mass of the emigration will sink into a condition of moral degradation and economic misery which will disgrace Western civilisation'.[16]

The attitudes struck by those in influential positions such as Simpson were informed by notions of refugees' physical and mental affliction. Doubts about their political opinions added a complicating factor—there was talk of Bolshevik 'infiltration'. This febrile atmosphere also governed policy towards internally displaced persons who wished to return to their homes that now came under the jurisdiction of a new state. Following the collapse of the Provisional Government in Russia, the desperate economic situation in Bolshevik-held territory encouraged these refugees to make their way west. Not that material considerations were always paramount—patriotic Poles and Balts wanted to participate in the reconstruction of their 'homeland'. Between 1918 and 1924 around 130,000 people returned to Latvia and 215,000 to Lithuania; by 1925 the total number of Polish citizens who had been

---

[15] Letter dated November 1920, IOL, Political and Secret Annual Files, 1912–30, L/PS/11/177.

[16] Simpson, *Refugee Problem*, 513; Dzovinar Kévonian, 'L'organisation non-gouvernementale comme acteur émergent du champ humanitaire: le Zemgor et la Société des Nations dans les années vingt' *Cahiers du monde russe*, 46, no.4 (2005), 739–56.

repatriated from the Soviet Union stood at 1.26 million. In addition to formal repatriation agreements between the relevant governments, refugees returned under their own steam, adding to fears that they would spread infectious disease. But these successor states operated a discriminatory policy favouring those who belonged to the titular nationality. Thus ethnic Poles were welcome in Poland, whereas Lithuanians and Jews found it far more difficult to secure Polish citizenship. There were stories of patrols forcing refugees back across the frontier to Soviet Russia to an uncertain fate.[17]

Humanitarian relief efforts faced an uphill struggle. The American Jewish Joint Distribution Committee (JDC) sent investigators to Poland and Lithuania, from where Boris Bogen sent back depressing reports about 'refugee concentration camps'.[18] Florence Barrow, a Quaker social worker, helped refugees who returned to Poland, after being forced to leave their homes in 1915. Her single-minded pursuit of refugee families is touching and remarkable; she tracked Polish refugees whom she had first encountered during 1916, in the Quaker settlements in the mid-Volga region. The extant stories mix despair and hope in equal measure, as in the account of the Harek family, three sisters who had been orphaned in 1915 after the family had been expelled from a village south of Brest-Litovsk. The elder sister was adopted by a school teacher in Pinsk, leaving the younger ones to move eastwards, where they eventually settled in the Quaker home in Buzuluk district, Samara province. In 1920 the sisters made the long journey home, only to find their house occupied by another refugee family.[19]

A labyrinthine bureaucracy vetted the returnees to ensure that only those with the 'correct' political opinions were admitted, that they were physically fit, and preferably that they had practical skills to offer. Polish returnees from Siberia—many of whom were the children of Tsarist exiles and had never set foot on Polish soil—were asked if they 'felt Polish'. Latvians and Lithuanians too, having been caught up in the maelstrom of the revolution, faced tough questions about their political beliefs. While returnees from the titular majority linked their own prospects to the foundation of the state, and were rewarded with land, minorities who wished to repatriate fared badly. The new states of Eastern Europe did not hesitate to deter and expel those whose presence was deemed harmful. Discrimination against Jews was widespread: a conservative newspaper published in Lithuania complained that Jews 'are streaming into our country bringing with them many different dangers and unhappiness to the true citizens of our country [sic] and to the state itself'.[20] This encouraged a sense that the nation was the exclusive property of the dominant ethnic group.

---

[17] Elizaveta Isaakova, 'A Testimony' (manuscript *c.*1962), 236, Bakhmeteff Archive, Columbia University; Tomas Balkelis, 'In Search of a Native Realm: the Return of World War I Refugees to Lithuania, 1918–1924', in Baron and Gatrell (eds), *Homelands*, 74–97.

[18] 'Through the Ukraine with Bogen' (April 1922), JDC Archives. Boris Bogen was the JDC's director of East European relief.

[19] 'Poland: refugee problems, conditions, and relief work', FEWVRC, Box 9, Parcel 1, Folder 3; Florence Barrow, 'Refugees in Poland', *The Friend*, 29 September 1922.

[20] Balkelis, 'In Search of a Native Realm', 91.

ARMENIA: RECONSTRUCTION AND RESETTLEMENT

In the aftermath of the genocide on the territory of the Ottoman Empire in 1915, Western Armenian politicians and refugee activists in diaspora organizations such as the Armenian General Benevolent Union held out hopes that the refugee question could be settled by an organized programme of repatriation to a 'recovered' Anatolia under Armenian jurisdiction. According to one estimate, around 800,000 Armenians were thought likely to resettle in a 'national home', to include Eastern Anatolia. Armenian dignitaries spoke of 'taking possession of our homeland, which has been irrigated by the blood of countless martyrs and heroes'.[21] Inevitably, Turkey opposed any kind of independent Armenian state, let alone one carved out of its territory.

Although Armenian refugees were scattered far and wide, many of them found homes in the fledgling Soviet republic of Armenia. An American visitor came face to face with the effects of famine and typhus on youngsters whom he described as 'wizened and ancient dwarfs. Those attenuated bodies clad in a shagginess of filthy rags, seemed centuries removed from civilisation. You felt that you had stumbled into prehistoric man's den'.[22] American philanthropy would relieve suffering, re-store sanity to 'crazed' refugees and re-establish civilization. Yet this analysis dis-counted the efforts of Soviet authorities, whose public works were supplemented by enterprises owned and managed by refugee entrepreneurs. Officials allocated land and inputs to refugee farmers, and levied a special 'refugee tax' on the settled population. Nansen praised the development of the country 'under an apparently stable government' and pointed to the need for sustained investment to allow 50,000 refugees to settle permanently. Erevan lay at the heart of 'a wonderful land which needs only one thing and that is water to become a Garden of Eden'. But his attempts to raise the necessary funds came to naught.[23]

The only alternative to irrigation was emigration. A leading Quaker wanted to 'give the young a chance of developing as far away as possible from the Turks and from the race hatred of the past. There are, as you know, vast tracts of land in Australia quite unoccupied—they want a white Australia'. Nansen looked to Latin America, but in vain. Most refugees preferred to settle in Syria, Cyprus, Palestine and Lebanon, rather than so far afield.[24] Syria became home to around 200,000 refugees. This did not imply an easy passage to a place of safety. The child of one family, Sarkis (b.1934), recounted what he had been told of his grandfather's odys-sey that took in Marash, Aleppo, Rayyak and Damascus:

> In the beginning it was very hard...My grandfather was privileged. He was given some space at the cemetery of the Armenians. Eventually some relatives came from

---

[21] Richard Hovannisian, *The Republic of Armenia, 1918–1921*, volume 1 (Berkeley: University of California Press, 1971), 460, 476.

[22] Melville Chater, 'Land of Stalking Death' *National Geographic Magazine*, 36 (November 1919), 403–18.

[23] Report by Dr Nansen to League of Nations, 28 July 1925, IOL, L/E/7/1315/3774; Skran, *Refugees in Inter-War Europe*, 170–7, 180.

[24] UNOG, Fonds Nansen, Box C1586, doc.17729, Marshall Fox to Nansen, 7 January 1930.

Aleppo with more resources and they worked together and established a 'camp'. This became the Armenian 'camp' near Bab Musalla. After a time, my grandfather moved us to a very small house with two rooms. We had a small space where we made small goods for selling in the souq near the Umayyad Mosque. My grandmother used to cook in a big pot for the whole family.[25]

Refugee camps were a legacy of the failure to find a durable solution to the plight of Armenians. Soon these camps were being described as 'regular settlements' of people who 'have always lived surrounded by hostile elements; their dwellings, however primitive, constitute a small capital'. Outside observers endorsed the view that Armenians manifested a 'free spirit' that should be given a chance to flourish outside the camps, which threatened a 'paralysis of character'.[26]

The situation in Greece was especially desperate. Armenians jostled with Greek refugees from Asia Minor, and the Greek government arranged with the USSR for their repatriation to Soviet Armenia; some 30,000 Armenian refugees and others took up this offer. In Palestine the long-established Armenian community objected to the newcomers who attached themselves too willingly to the religious authority of the Patriarchate, a subordination they resented. Cyprus seemed to offer a more promising sanctuary, because of its longstanding Armenian community of farmers and shopkeepers, and others who escaped Ottoman persecution in 1894–96 and 1909. However, as in Palestine, the 'natives' (*deghatsi*) kept their distance from the refugees (*kaghtagan*). It took years before the two groups intermarried or spent time together. The school curriculum stressed the distinctiveness of Armenian language and faith, whilst conversations at home reinforced the message about the history of persecution, escape and survival, and the duty of survivors to preserve Armenian culture.[27]

This became a common theme among Armenian patriots. Whether in Syria or Lebanon, which was home to an established Armenian community (many of whom were originally from Western Anatolia and spoke Turkish), or elsewhere, the problem was that life beyond the Armenian homeland or in the confines of the camp exposed refugees to a dual challenge. One was the troubling possibility of 'assimilation' in a different culture. A more immediate issue was the social and religious division among the Armenian population. Ironically, the attacks launched by Muslim leaders in Lebanon and Druze rebels in Syria helped bring about unity between the recently arrived Armenian refugees and the older Armenian communities. The French mandatory authorities cemented this process. By the late 1920s refugees had a chance to join other elements of the Armenian diaspora under the aegis of the Armenian Revolutionary Federation (Dashnaks), the leading nationalist and anti-Soviet political party which dedicated itself to the creation of 'true

---

[25] Chatty, *Displacement and Dispossession*, 176.

[26] Georges Carle, report dated 1925, IOL, L/E/7/1315/3774. 'Paralysis of character' was the term used by James Barton, Director of Near East Relief.

[27] Susan Pattie, *Faith in History: Armenians Rebuilding Community* (Washington: Smithsonian Institution Press, 1997), 50–70; Bedross Der Matossian, 'The Armenians of Palestine 1918–48' *JPS*, 41, no.1 (2011), 24–44.

Armenians'. Refugee camps played a part—but only a part—in this political project, which sustained Armenian enclaves for decades.[28]

In France, where the numbers were much greater, 60,000 Armenian refugees were housed in former POW camps. The best known of these institutions, Camp Oddo in Marseille, boasted Armenian churches, shops, hospitals and schools administered by staff who carefully compiled lists of arrivals and registered the occupation, status and place of origin of refugees as part of an ongoing project to ensure that Armenians retained a sense of 'nation'. The qualities that French authorities professed to admire in Armenians—'dedication to labour, family spirit, love of the home, frugality, sobriety, and saving'—coincided with their own sense of virtue. Nevertheless a collective sense of persecution was reinforced by the decision of the French authorities to close down Camp Oddo in 1927. With the French state reluctant to assume the financial costs of maintaining Armenian refugees, they were expected to find work in the automobile industry, in metalworking and in textiles. Fortunately the buoyant labour market afforded reasonable opportunities. The Armenian diaspora also invested in the reconstruction of villages in Soviet Armenia. Some refugees turned victimization on its head by resorting to acts of terror against the symbols of Turkish authority—a reminder that the phenomenon of 'refugee warriors' goes back a long way.[29]

Their depiction as courageous survivors and adherents to a common Christian 'civilization' appealed to the values and wallets of foreign philanthropists. Armenophiles such as Arnold Toynbee and James Bryce addressed a British audience. Dudley Northcote, a British army officer serving in Mesopotamia and familiar with conditions in the Baqubah refugee camp, described Armenians' strong work ethic and willingness to learn. He bemoaned the decision by the British government to reward their loyalty to the Allies by incarcerating Armenian and Assyrian refugees in 'concentration camps', yet also feared the consequences of closing these down. The Arab population of Iraq was unreceptive, so local settlement was not a feasible option; there was neither demand for unskilled labour nor 'respectable' work for women. In Northcote's words, the proposal 'certainly means the end of them as a community and the complete abandonment of them to the Arabs'.[30]

The League of Nations and NGOs embarked upon the task of 'reclaiming' Christian women and children from the spiritual and moral 'corruption' of Islam. As they had done during the 1896 massacres, British parliamentarians expressed concern about women who were 'being retained in Turkish harems'.[31] Emma Cushman, an American missionary, got the League to underwrite a 'neutral house' in Constantinople, which cared for children who developed a 'distorted mentality' as captives, but who could now learn the Armenian language, sing hymns and

---

[28] Ronald Suny, *Looking toward Ararat: Armenia in Modern History* (Bloomington: Indiana University Press, 1993), 219–22.
[29] Maud Mandel, *In the Aftermath of Genocide: Armenians and Jews in Twentieth-Century France* (Durham: Duke University Press, 2003), 132; Burgess, *Refuge in the Land of Liberty*, 153.
[30] Joanne Laycock, *Imagining Armenia: Orientalism, Ambiguity and Intervention* (Manchester: Manchester University Press, 2009), 171.
[31] Edmund Harvey MP, 14 July 1924, IOL, L/E/7/1315/3774.

learn Armenian craftsmanship. The Danish missionary and social worker Karen Jeppe established a sanctuary in Aleppo, causing friction between the newcomers and local Bedouin tribes. Jeppe added a fresh twist: 'the rescue always required a special effort on the part of the persons rescued; they had to decide for themselves whether they would leave the houses where they were detained or not. We only helped them to carry out their own intentions'. She used her extensive case notes to record traces of ineradicable 'Armenianness'.[32]

The appropriation of refugee experience reached its apogee in the ordeal of Aurora Mardiganian (1901–94), a young girl who managed to survive and to make her way to the USA in 1917. She soon came to the attention of a screenwriter who encouraged her to write a memoir that became the basis of a feature film that survives only in fragmentary form. In an extraordinary twist, Aurora found herself starring in a film of her own life. The publicity brochure boasted that 'the chaste figure of Aurora is seen not acting, but living again through the horrors of those two years of captivity', and the film included graphic scenes of rape and crucifixion. In other words, what appears on one level to be an instance of a female refugee who claimed the right to tell her own story emerges on closer inspection as her exploitation by film producers who sought to make a profit through offering an 'authentic' representation of slaughter and deportation. Aurora's nakedness and powerlessness were clearly of great significance to the film makers, and her ordeal, her youth and gender turned her into the archetypal Armenian refugee.[33]

'UNMIXING' THE BALKANS

In the Balkans, population displacement came about from a combination of flight and population transfer. Between 1912 and 1926, a quarter of a million ethnic Bulgarian refugees fled to Bulgaria from the Ottoman Empire, Romania, Greece (which accounted for nearly half of the total), and the newly created state of Yugoslavia. One component resulted from the agreement signed with Greece in 1919 to implement a population exchange. Refugees accounted for 5 per cent of the total population of Bulgaria in the 1920s, but a much higher proportion in the country's remote Macedonian enclave that Bulgaria retained after the Balkan Wars. The government in Sofia, dominated by the Agrarian Party led by Aleksandr Stamboliiski, devised a series of ad hoc measures to provide refugees with land. Artisans who settled in urban centres were expected to take over the properties of Greeks, but the large numbers created a housing shortage. Bulgaria appealed successfully to the League of Nations for a large loan to help cover the costs of resettlement, astutely

---

[32] Miss E. D. Cushman, report to Secretary-General of League of Nations, 16 July 1921, and Karen Jeppe, note 28 July 1927, IOL, L/E/7/1230/1585; Simpson, *Refugee Problem*, 35; Keith Watenpaugh, 'The League of Nations' Rescue of Armenian Genocide Survivors and the Making of Modern Humanitarianism, 1920–1927' *AHR*, 115, no.5 (2010), 1315–39, at 1337.

[33] IOL, L/PS/11/159/P7105, my emphasis; Leshu Torchin, '*Ravished Armenia*: Visual Media, Humanitarian Advocacy and the Formation of Witnessing Publics' *American Anthropologist*, 108, no.1 (2006), 214–20.

claiming that without international support the refugees' presence risked fomenting communist revolution. Refugees who received financial support from the League were obliged to renounce their previous citizenship. Additional help came from Save the Children which built a model village for refugees on reclaimed swamp land.[34]

These efforts served to remind Bulgarians of the country's defeat in the Balkan Wars and the First World War, and of their generosity in looking after their own. In other words the crisis said as much about Bulgaria's 'national hospitality' as it did about the experience of displacement. Refugees took a different view, arguing that 'we were expelled from our places of birth because we are Bulgarians, yet here we are not afforded [recognition] because we are refugees'. The inadequate measures for accommodating them created a profound sense of disappointment.[35] Their status as refugees marked them out as marginal people. This story has a postscript: Bulgarian refugees displaced by the Balkan Wars and the First World War returned to their homes when the Axis powers occupied Greece and Yugoslavia, although the turn of the military tide in 1944 meant that their triumph was short-lived.

Even more dramatic changes took place to the south. The protracted war between Greece and Turkey culminated in the destruction of Smyrna in September 1922 and an alarming refugee crisis. People on both sides spoke of widespread harassment, brutality and the suicide of women who wanted to evade capture. Around 350,000 Muslim refugees had already moved to Turkish territory in 1921–22. Ottoman Christians were stranded on the coast when Turkey recaptured the city. British and American Red Cross officials spoke of 'a disorganised flood of refugees' who urgently required food, shelter and medical assistance. Foreign governments made hasty arrangements to evacuate hundreds of thousands to Athens, Salonika and Corfu.[36]

Although many refugees planned to recover their homes when things calmed down, these hopes were quickly dashed. The League of Nations agreed to extend Nansen's mandate to help resettle refugees in Greece without needing to call on member states for significant funds. Against the backdrop of continued violence and depleted resources, diplomats and officials embarked on a radical project that would transform the social and ethnic composition of both countries. The liberal Greek political leader Eleftherios Venizelos regarded the transfer of population from Eastern Thrace as an opportunity to 'Hellenise' the land that Greece had recently acquired from Bulgaria, in other words to settle Greeks in Western Thrace and in Macedonia: if (as he said) he could not establish 'Greater Greece', then he

---

[34] King Boris III named it Atolovo, in honour of the Duke of Atholl, president of SCF. *The League of Nations Reconstruction Schemes in the Inter-War Period* (Geneva: League of Nations, 1945), 101–8; Kathleen Freeman, *If Any Man Build: the History of the Save the Children Fund* (Hodder and Stoughton, 1965), 35.

[35] Theodora Dragostinova, 'Competing Priorities, Ambiguous Loyalties: Challenges of Socio-economic Adaptation and National Inclusion of the Interwar Bulgarian refugees' *Nationalities Papers*, 34, no.5 (2006), 549–74, at 565.

[36] Henry Alden Shaw, 'Greek Refugees from the Caucasus and the Work of the American Red Cross at Salonique' *Journal of International Relations*, 12, no.1 (1921), 44–9, at 45; McCarthy, *Death and Exile*, 303; Kévonian, *Réfugiés et diplomatie humanitaire*, 107–8.

would settle for a 'Great Greece'. At the Lausanne conference British Foreign Secretary Lord Curzon welcomed the proposed 'homogenisation' of population that
would bring an end to 'old deep-rooted causes of quarrel'. No-one consulted those
directly affected.[37]

Both Greece and Turkey were poor and badly damaged by warfare, and unprepared for this mass transfer and the ensuing health crisis. The American Red Cross
and Save the Children deloused refugees and distributed food and clothing in
Greece, although not in Turkey where they were denied access, leaving the field to
the under-funded Turkish Red Crescent. The American diplomat Henry Morgenthau, who combined sentimental attachment to Greece with an undisguised
antipathy to Turkey, described how fortunate refugees from Asia Minor found
temporary accommodation in the Athens Opera House and in former mosques.
A refugee camp in Salonika reminded him 'very much of the concentration camps
for Russians we visited in Lemberg [L'viv] in 1919'. Not content with showing his
disgust, Morgenthau told his readership of his own part in the scene: 'I at the
moment, above all others, pledged to redeem this throng! What an awful responsibility!' But refugees had a capacity to respond positively to external assistance, by
virtue of being the descendants of Homer and Philip of Macedon. They needed
'guidance' rather than what he termed the 'government' that the British exercised
over its colonial subjects in India.[38]

Strictly speaking, the 'Convention Concerning the Exchange of Greek and
Turkish Populations' did not create 'refugees'. Instead it stipulated that 'as from
1 May 1923 there shall take place a compulsory exchange of Turkish nationals of
the Greek Orthodox religion established in Turkish territory and of Greek nationals of the Muslim religion established in Greek territory'. Greeks who moved from
Turkey acquired Greek citizenship and vice versa. But substantial numbers had
been displaced by the war, and the term 'refugee' was already in widespread use.
Official terminology recognized this state of affairs by creating a Refugee Relief
Fund, followed soon after by the Refugee Settlement Commission (RSC). Established by the League of Nations and ratified by the Greek Parliament in October
1924, the RSC survived until 1930. Nor was this terminology confined to bureaucratic documentation: refugee associations published newspapers with titles such
as *Prosfygikos Kosmos* ('Refugee World').[39]

Bare statistics convey something of the immediate social, economic, political
and cultural consequences of Lausanne for Greek and Turkish refugees (see Map 3).
In all, around 1.22 million Greeks were obliged to leave Asia Minor, while 400,000
Turkish refugees moved from Greece, carried in Turkish vessels at the behest of the
government which refused to entrust the human cargo to any other party.[40] Greece
absorbed the equivalent of around 25 per cent of its pre-war population, the numbers swollen by refugees arriving from Eastern Thrace and Pontic Greeks from the
Black Sea littoral; there were around half a million of these. In numerical terms

[37] Frank, *Expelling the Germans*, 22–3; Skran, *Refugees in Inter-War Europe*, 158–9.
[38] Henry Morgenthau, *I Was Sent to Athens* (Garden City: Doubleday, 1929), 9, 98–102, 124.
[39] Charles Eddy, *Greece and the Greek Refugees* (George Allen and Unwin, 1931), 7, 71–82.
[40] Kasaba, *A Moveable Empire*, 138.

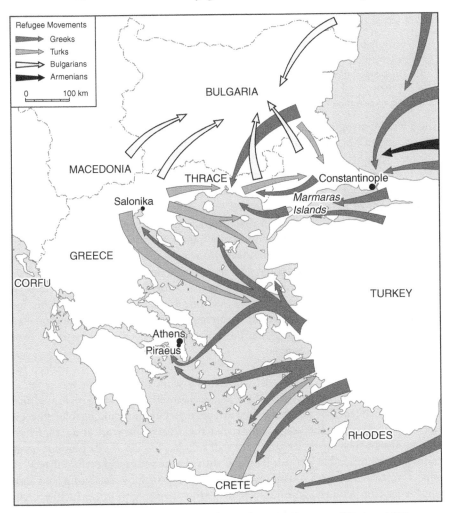

Map 3: Map of the Population Exchange between Greece and Turkey, 1923

Turkey, with a much larger population (13.5 million in 1922) shouldered a relatively smaller burden. Both states became more homogeneous. The Muslim population of Greece dropped from 20 per cent to 6 per cent of the total. Before 1923 around one-fifth of the population of Turkey was non-Muslim, but thereafter the figure fell to just 3 per cent (although it was 10 per cent in Istanbul). Greeks who remained in Turkey faced an uncertain future, being accused of having 'collaborated' with the Greek army during its operations in western Anatolia.[41]

[41] Raoul Blanchard, 'The Exchange of Populations between Greece and Turkey' *Geographical Review*, 15, no.3 (1925), 449–56; Alexander Pallis, 'Racial Migrations in the Balkans during the Years 1913–1924' *Geographical Journal*, 66, no.4 (1925), 315–31.

Red Cross officials urged Greece to relocate refugees from camps quickly:

You can't make John Jones self-supporting while he is living in a great camp and being fed by relief machinery, put to bed at seven o'clock and got out at five. That is not the way the people make their living. Every day that they stayed in those camps they were losing their moral grip; they were becoming weaker and pauperising themselves; becoming accustomed to being taken care of, and becoming poor citizens of Greece.[42]

The government agreed. Around half of the refugees from Anatolia were duly settled on land in Macedonia and Western Thrace that had previously been farmed by Muslims who fled before the war or who sold up before the Convention was enforced. Here refugees made up 45 and 35 per cent of the respective population in 1928. The Refugee Settlement Commission, with a mandate 'to promote the establishment of refugees in productive work either upon the land or otherwise' provided loans for the purchase of draft animals and timber. Greece expropriated properties belonging to Muslim farmers and Italian, French and English landowners. Some 2,000 new villages were created on reclaimed marsh land. Only after they discharged their debts did refugees receive title deeds, but many of them refused to pay as a matter of principle, arguing that 'indemnities payable for properties abandoned in their former homes should be offset against debts payable to the Commission'. The RSC betrayed little awareness of the experiences of newcomers, notably in Macedonia, where powerful local elites managed to secure their own economic and political advantage.[43]

The Commission believed that it could 'inspire the refugees as a class with courage and determination, [although] whether the work of settlement was to be a success or failure depended upon the refugees themselves'.[44] Morgenthau told international bankers that the credit they extended to Greece would enable refugees to be self-supporting. The League applauded 'the capacity for work and receptivity to new ideas which characterise the mass of refugees', while another author contrasted 'those miserable Turkish hamlets' with the new 'large cheerful villages—what a miracle!' Refugees contributed to economic growth by reclaiming land and improving crop rotation, and the RSC helped by investing in infrastructure such as roads and schools. Commission members visited experimental agricultural undertakings, irrigation projects and stud farms. Americans welcomed the increased cultivation of tobacco which was turned into 'Lucky Strike' and 'Camel' brands of cigarette. Greeks were employed by the RSC as engineers, agronomists, health workers, accountants and other technical specialists. Teachers too had a vital role to play, not least by ensuring that the children of newcomers rapidly learned to speak and read Greek, making this a 'truly national enterprise'.[45] This looks very like the development agenda after the Second World War.

[42] George Kritikos, 'The Agricultural Settlement of Refugees: a Source of Productive Work and Stability in Greece, 1923–1930' *Agricultural History*, 79, no.3 (2005), 321–46, at 324–5.

[43] League of Nations, *Greek Refugee Settlement* (Geneva: Greek Resettlement Commission, 1926), 81; Karakasidou, *Fields of Wheat, Hills of Blood*, 143–66.

[44] Eddy, *Greece and the Greek Refugees*, 94, 174.

[45] Morgenthau, *I Was Sent to Athens*, 112–13, 190, 274–5; Eliot Mears, *Greece Today: the Aftermath of the Refugee Impact* (Stanford: Stanford University Press, 1929), 17, 235, 291–2.

The face of Greece changed in other respects too. Refugees settled in Athens and its environs. The new suburb of Kokkinia soon boasted a population of 33,000 inhabitants. Morgenthau reported that the 'somnolent streets of Athens' had become 'bustling [and] thronged with new faces'. He was particularly impressed by the simple but clean houses whose low construction costs appealed to his banker's temperament. The port city of Piraeus, where contemporaries complained that refugees built 'unauthorised structures in the streets and vacant lots adjoining their houses', bore the imprint of refugee settlement at least until the 1970s. The RSC prided itself on having built dispensaries, kindergartens and schools here too, as well as installing water supply, although the rate of construction failed to keep pace with the needs of the new population. Occupational change was also under way. Female refugees boosted rug and carpet-making and silkworm breeding. Other trades included spinning, dress-making, carpet weaving, pottery and the manufacture of copper goods. Industrialists hoped to take advantage of the additional labour supply to keep wages at a minimum. Although Greek union leaders invited refugees to join, the outcome was disappointing, and refugee labour remained in a weak bargaining position.[46]

Economic opportunities could not disguise the negative image of the newcomers whose cultural differences were regularly emphasized. One local made it clear that 'there is no way I will accept the Caucasians. Venizelos brought shit to Macedonia'. This was an extreme but by no means an isolated view.[47] The Greek foreign minister set the tone by suggesting that 'Greece is already saturated with refugees'. Hostile observers spoke of an 'oglokratia', a reference to the Turkish surnames that carried the suffix –oglu. The Populist Party maintained that the newcomers represented a 'refugee dictatorship' and demanded that refugees be excluded from political participation or confined to non-Greek associations. Likewise anti-Venizelist factions spoke of a 'refugee menace'. Whether the popularity of Punch and Judy shows in the villages of Macedonia owed something to the deteriorating relations between newcomers and their neighbours or betokened its lessening is difficult to tell. In an ominous foretaste of events in Nazi Europe some refugees were instructed to wear yellow armbands in order to distinguish them from locals.[48]

Native Greeks portrayed them as 'Orientals', 'baptised in yoghurt' (*giaourtovaftesemeni*) and 'Turkish seeds' (*Turkosporoi*), as well as 'stupid'. Refugees were accused of having imported low-class and 'immoral' music—(*rebetika*) along with drugs. But *rebetika* provided remarkable evidence of the cultural creativity of displaced singers and composers who drew upon a rich musical tradition in the urban centres of Anatolia. They mischievously appropriated the idea that they disturbed conventional mores, creating songs that described seductive or promiscuous women and the pleasures of cannabis; titles such as 'Hashish Harem' and 'Bordello

---

[46] Morgenthau, *I Was Sent to Athens*, 50, 242; Eddy, *Greece and the Greek Refugees*, 191–4.

[47] Elisabeth Kontogiorgi, *Population Exchange in Greek Macedonia: the Rural Settlement of Refugees 1922–1930* (Oxford: Clarendon Press, 2006), 187.

[48] George Mavrogordatos, *Stillborn Republic: Social Coalitions and Party Strategies in Greece, 1922–1936* (Berkeley: University of California Press, 1983), 194; Mears, *Greece Today*, 258; Karakasidou, *Fields of Wheat*, 157.

Blues' give some idea of the content. These were sung in villages, but they achieved a greater impact in the townships of Greece. Gramophone companies vied with each other to bring out new records. One song, *Neva hedzaz* ('Like a dry and drifting leaf'), recorded by Marika Kanaropúlu, asked: 'How much longer will my fate condemn me to drag myself through foreign lands like a withered leaf?' Kanaropúlu (1914–90), a native of Bursa (Turkey) was nicknamed Turkalítsa or 'The Turkish girl'. Her recording career in Greece lasted from 1930 until 1936, when she left for the USA. In another song, 'The exile's grief', the prolific composer/singer Andónis Dalgás spoke of the 'pain of *ksenityá*', the condition of having to live in a foreign land called Greece and being separated from his home:

> It is for you I weep, oh mother dear/and suffer in this land as one exiled/
> I beg you, mother, never shed a tear/but light a candle for your child.

The melody came from a Turkish song, 'Every place, darkness' that was often recorded in Turkey and Greece. Other lyrics spoke of the impoverished circumstances into which refugees from Asia Minor had fallen, an ironic comment on the fact that it was precisely this low life that attracted a respectable audience seeking a vicarious thrill.[49]

Music could do only so much to counter the negative qualities to refugees. Maria Birbili described the reception she was given when she reached Crete in October 1923:

> Somebody gathered us to pick olives in Paliochora. It took us two days and one night to reach there. Once we arrived at the village, he wanted to get us to sleep in a hen-coop. I told him, 'I do not go inside. Had I wanted to be captured I would have remained in Asia Minor'. A crowd gathered round us and eyed us with curiosity like being another race [asking] 'Do you speak any Greek? Do you have churches in your country?'[50]

Refugees from Smyrna were described as 'frivolous, quarrelsome and prone to gossip'. Of course not all refugees were tarred with the same brush: refugees from Bulgaria were deemed to be 'a progressive factor and a rural element of the first class'. In other words, whereas government propaganda spoke of a universal 'Greek idea', available in principle to all refugees, public opinion deployed a differentiated lexicon that made life intolerable for many newcomers. It may be that the murder of two refugees in 1933 inspired Nikos Kazantzakis to begin his famous novel, *Christ Recrucified* (1948), which described a village deeply affected by the arrival of a party of refugees from Asia Minor.[51]

Refugees from Asia Minor fought back politically and culturally. Pontic Greeks became firm supporters of Venizelos, saying that 'if it wasn't for Venizelos, none of us would be left, they [the Turks] would have exterminated us, as they did the

[49] *Greek-Oriental Rebetica: Songs and Dances in the Asia Minor Style, 1911–1937* (Folklyric CD 7005, 1991).

[50] Kritikos, 'The Agricultural Settlement of Refugees', 349.

[51] Mavrogordatos, *Stillborn Republic*, 182; Renée Hirschon, *Heirs of the Greek Catastrophe: the Social Life of Asia Minor Refugees in Piraeus* (New York: Berghahn, 1998), 24; Dimitri Pentzopoulos, *The Balkan Exchange of Minorities and its Impact on Greece* (Hurst, 2002), 101–2.

Armenians'. But by the mid-1930s politically active refugees had abandoned liberal politics in favour of the Communist Party, a consequence in part of their disillusionment with the policies of the Greek state, which sought a rapprochement with Turkey and renounced any attempt to compensate them for the properties they had been forced to abandon. Culturally, the refugees from Constantinople regarded themselves as superior to their hosts, and were in turn held to be 'stuck up'. They poked fun at the conservative tastes of the local Greek population. Cultural rivalry was illustrated by the former residents of the Marmaras islands who settled on remote Ammouliani, off the coast of Salonika and poured scorn on the outmoded dress sense of local Greeks and affirmed a kind of cosmopolitanism: '[W]e wore the latest fashions. In our home we had a mania for Russian styles'. Other refugees too subscribed to an open-mindedness which they contrasted with parochial host society.[52] Pontic Greek newcomers—Turkish-speaking, but Greek Orthodox by faith, and including men who had engaged in guerrilla warfare against the Ottoman state—claimed to be 'authentic Greeks' whose ancestors had set out from Greece to colonize the littoral coast and who now claimed to be returning 'home'. These characterizations persisted: an elderly Greek refugee woman from Asia Minor whose family had settled in Piraeus told a visiting scholar in the 1970s that: 'Before we came here, what were they? We opened their eyes. They didn't know how to eat or dress. They used to eat salt fish and wild vegetables. It was we who taught them everything'. Like other refugees who expressed their cosmopolitanism in terms of food, dress and locality, she thought of local Greeks as 'country bumpkins'.[53]

The consequences for socio-economic and political life in Turkey were equally troubling. Interviewed several decades later, Turkish informants described the hardships of travel, and the humiliating circumstances of their departure, when some of them had been forced to dance naked as they left the villages of Macedonia.[54] The loss to the Ottoman economy of Greek artisans and merchants was keenly felt. Existing communities were ruptured no less than in Greece, and the refugees had to work hard to re-establish them. The newcomers, described as *muhacir* or as *mübadil* (literally, 'exchanged people'), drew a sharp distinction between the standard of life they enjoyed in Greece and the difficult conditions they found in Turkey. 'I do miss it', said one informant: 'I want to go back, but I cannot. Those are the lands of the infidels'. Ironically, local Turks described the settlers in similar terms, demanding that they speak Turkish and imposing fines on those who refused to do so.[55]

---

[52] Stephen Salamone, *In the Shadow of the Holy Mountain: the Genesis of a Rural Greek Community and its Refugee Heritage* (New York: Columbia University Press, 1987), 39, 102, 201.

[53] Hirschon, *Heirs of the Greek Catastrophe*, 25–33; Triadafilos Triadafilopoulos, 'The Political Consequences of Forced Population Transfers: Refugee Incorporation in Greece and West Germany', in Rainer Ohliger (ed.), *European Encounters: Migrants, Migration and European Societies since 1945* (Aldershot: Ashgate, 2003) 99–122.

[54] Karakasidou, *Fields of Wheat*, 151–2.

[55] Bruce Clark, *Twice a Stranger: How Mass Expulsion Forged Modern Greece and Turkey* (Granta, 2006), 32; Tolga Köker, 'Lessons in Refugeehood: the Experience of Forced Migrants in Turkey', in Renée Hirschon (ed.), *Crossing the Aegean: an Appraisal of the 1923 Compulsory Population Exchange between Greece and Turkey* (New York: Berghahn, 2003), 193–208, at 203–4; Aslı Iğsız, 'Documenting the Past and Publicizing Personal Stories: Sensescapes and the 1923 Greco-Turkish Population Exchange in Contemporary Turkey' *JMGS*, 26, no.2 (2008), 451–87, at 456.

A new Ministry of Exchange, Reconstruction and Resettlement arranged for the allocation of land to refugees, but its procedures were chaotic and arbitrary. Tobacco farmers from Thrace and Macedonia converted vineyards, only to find that the land was unsuitable for its cultivation. Properties that had belonged to Greeks and Armenians were badly damaged and required years to restore. Turkish police and army officers frequently appropriated them, forcing refugees to go to the back of the queue, as they had done before 1914. The government planned to invest in 'new villages' to dilute the proportion of refugees in established communities: 'the proportion of refugees, settled in a town or village, whose language and traditions are of a race other than Turkish will not exceed 20 per cent', but little came of this either.[56]

Turkey's political leaders hoped that the refugees would contribute by their presence to building the new nation-state. Prime Minister İsmet Paşa wrote in 1924 in terms that connected Turkish refugees to the broader diaspora and to the new state:

> There is no doubt that the country is in dire need and suffering. Nevertheless, it is our responsibility to make the newcomers not feel strangers and give them utmost assistance. We encourage the desires of our friends abroad who want to come to their motherland. The empty building is doomed to perish [unless] it be filled.[57]

In similar vein, Atatürk's readiness to 'gather in' Turkish populations found expression in their organized 'repatriation' from Romania, Bulgaria and Yugoslavia after 1931. One enthusiast commented that the newcomers possessed 'vigour and ambition so that they are making a genuine contribution to the country'.[58] But Turkey curbed any attempt by refugees to organize on their own behalf; a pro-refugee 'Free Republican Party' triumphed in the municipal elections in 1930 but was quickly suppressed, turning refugees into 'a silent crowd to be integrated into the system according to the terms of the political leadership'.[59] Meanwhile harsh measures were taken against the remaining Greeks and the Kurdish population of Turkey in 1925 and 1934, some of whom evaded internal deportation by fleeing to Iran, Iraq and Syria. Eighty years later their descendants continue to live a marginal existence. Deportee families in Eastern Anatolia went on to form the nucleus of the modern PKK (Kurdistan Workers' Party).[60]

How did displacement become part of commemorative activities? Although Greek politics were suffused with the refugee question, official efforts to commemorate the displacement were conspicuous by their absence, largely because the Greek government did not want to disturb a diplomatic rapprochement with Turkey. Only in 1994 did local and national politicians approve the construction

[56] Onur Yıldırım, *Diplomacy and Displacement: Reconsidering the Turco-Greek Exchange of Populations, 1922–1934* (Routledge, 2006), 149; Stephen Ladas, *The Exchange of Minorities: Bulgaria, Greece and Turkey* (New York: Macmillan, 1932), 706–7, 714.

[57] Yıldırım, *Diplomacy and Displacement*, 155.

[58] Joseph Schechtman, *Population Transfers in Asia* (New York: Hallsby, 1949), 102.

[59] Yıldırım, *Diplomacy and Displacement*, 186–8.

[60] Üngör, *The Making of Modern Turkey*, 169.

of memorial sites on behalf of the Pontic Greeks who were targeted by the Ottoman Empire, declaring 19 May a day of remembrance. Impressive cultural and educational initiatives owed more to refugee initiative than to government. For example, the intellectual life of Macedonia was boosted by the foundation of the University of Salonika, to which refugees made a major contribution. The unpropitious political climate did not prevent the formation of an impressive Centre for Asia Minor Studies, which had its origins in a project during the 1930s by the musicologist Melpo Logotheti-Merlier to collect popular songs from across Greece. She collected testimony from 5,000 refugees and fashioned a story of survival amidst suffering.[61]

Beyond the realm of formal politics, the legacy of the Greek-Turkish population exchange became entrenched in historiography, in family history, in music and in the geography of settlement. Memories of displacement remained vivid for survivors and for locals. To establish oneself in Greece was fraught with difficulty. In Macedonia the divisions between refugees from various backgrounds and the local population remain acute; their descendants refuse for example to participate in one another's saints' days. Additionally, many refugees who arrived in Greece thought of Asia Minor as a 'place of Greek loss, rather than as a place of Turkish presence'.[62]

All the same, these divisions overlooked the complex, 'multicultural' history of localities where Slavic-speaking and Greek-speaking inhabitants lived side by side for generations prior to the commotion of war.[63] The 92-year-old George Siamanides, who lived most of his life in Salonika, having been forced out of the Turkish village of Imera, southeast of Trebizond, described a long and difficult journey via Constantinople, Giresun and Piraeus, before he and his family arrived in the small town of Naoussa. Decades later he spoke of how, 'When I close my eyes, I can still recall the aroma from the blue flowers that wafted down from the meadows above our house. I can taste the milk from our three cows, and I remember the tang of the butter'. His vivid memories included the realization that the men of the village worked on the other side of the Black Sea: 'Greece itself was remote from our consciousness. The country that loomed in our imaginations was Russia'. These historic ties with Russia led the people who took them in to believe that they were 'communists'. There were other 'trials' as well: 'We found ourselves in a former army camp used by French colonial troops during the First World War, where there were millions of lice. It was a moonscape, with not a tree in sight. We remembered our mountain valleys and cried'.[64]

Meanwhile in Turkey in 1999 a group of second generation 'exchanged people' from Greece set up the *Lozan Mübadilleri Vakfı*, literally 'foundation for those exchanged at Lausanne', which arranged for the descendants of the population

[61] <http://www.helleniccomserve.com/centreasiaminorone.html>; Penelope Papailias, *Genres of Recollection: Archival Poetics and Modern Greece* (Palgrave Macmillan, 2005).

[62] Elif Babül, 'Claiming a Place through Memories of Belonging: Politics of Recognition on the Island of Imbros' *New Perspectives on Turkey*, 34 (2006), 47–65, at 54.

[63] Karakasidou, *Fields of Wheat*, 125, 159.

[64] Clark, *Twice a Stranger*, 123–9.

exchange to make return visits to Greece. The inspiration came from a double blow, namely the earthquake that devastated Izmit in North-Western Turkey in August 1999 and a smaller earthquake that affected Athens a month later, leading to a diplomatic rapprochement between the two countries. Widespread interest in the consequences of Lausanne was aroused by the publication in 1998 of a novel by Kemal Yalçın, *The Entrusted Trousseau: Peoples of the Exchange* [*Emanet Çeyiz*] telling of the efforts made by a Turkish 'resettler' to visit Greece in order to seek out the Greek Orthodox family that entrusted its Muslim neighbours with a wedding trousseau in 1923, in the belief that they would soon be able to go back to their homes in Asia Minor. Yalçın's book caused a stir, on the grounds that it 'offended' Turkish national pride. Films, TV programmes and cookery books contributed to a recent explosion of interest in this history, reflecting in part a search for Turkey's 'cosmopolitan' past—not a bad marketing tactic for the tourist industry—but it also personalized the population exchange, as a means of re-appropriation of history by 'ordinary' people.[65]

The longer term impact of Lausanne emerged in a classic piece of ethnography based upon fieldwork conducted during the 1970s by Renée Hirschon, who found that the families of Greek refugees who settled in Piraeus retained a strong sense of a distinctive 'refugee' identity. A series of 'pan-refugee' congresses contributed to that process. Six decades later their descendants continued to refer to one another as 'refugees' (*prosfiges*) and as *mikrasiátes* (referring to their place of origin in Asia Minor), affirming a sense of separate identity from 'locals' and underpinning claims for adequate housing and other kinds of compensation from the Greek government. The older generation of refugees recalled difficult encounters with the local population and officialdom, and this no doubt contributed to their sense of disappointment. Their children and grandchildren were not expected to retain any sense of affiliation with the 'homeland'; they had, so to speak, become part of 'modern' Greece.[66]

REFUGEES AND THE SPANISH COCKPIT

The refugee crisis brought about by the Spanish Civil War had equally serious consequences. Fighting between supporters of the Republic and Franco's Nationalists displaced around three million so-called 'evacuees' within Spain. A pro-republican Evacuation Committee sent around 400,000 people from Madrid to places of safety in Valencia, Murcia and Catalonia. The crisis quickly became internationalized. Refugees were looked after by various organizations including Save the Children, the Quakers and Mennonites. Francesca Wilson painted a vivid picture of the arrangements made to process refugees in Barcelona's 80,000-seater

---

[65] See also the website of the Population Exchange Museum, in Çatalca <http://mubadelemuzesi.net/museum.aspx>.

[66] Hirschon, *Heirs of the Greek Catastrophe*; Pentzopoulos, *The Balkan Exchange of Minorities*, 228–9.

sports stadium, adding that 'I realised how much easier it is to deal with crowds now than it was in the last war—because of the wireless and loudspeakers—and how much better it is to call on refugees to cooperate than to herd them like cattle'. Basil Wright made a documentary film, 'Modern Orphans of the Storm' (1937) to raise funds for Basque child refugees. Aldous Huxley did the same by endorsing the publication of children's drawings.[67]

As early as June 1936, 60,000 refugees fled Spain, following the routes made familiar by generations of labour migrants in more peaceful times. By October 1937 five times that number entered France thanks to the relatively benign environment created briefly by Léon Blum's Popular Front government. Their expectations of a temporary exile were soon confounded. In the wake of Franco's march on Barcelona, which fell to Nationalist forces in February 1939, some 300,000 refugees gathered at the French border. French border officials were urged to turn them back and restrict the issue of entry permits, and upwards of 200,000 refugees were consequently obliged to return to Spain by the end of that year. The rest were disarmed and admitted to France. A film by John Wigham showed streams of refugees leaving Barcelona and slowly making their way to the French border, where they encountered French Senegalese guards who caused them to recall the unforgiving treatment they received at the hands of Franco's African conscripts.[68]

Whether those who fled to France were more fortunate than opponents of Franco who stayed in or returned to Spain is a moot point. Women and children were held in triage centres where officials separated them from adult males who were sent to refugee camps on the grounds that they were combatants. One refugee, Lluís Ferran de Pol recalled arriving in France:

> Our only welcome was the distant sight of an immense beach, darkened by the crowd of the first arrivals. Suddenly we are in front of a barbed-wire fence. We pass through a vast entryway where, with bayonets fixed, black soldiers stand sentry nearby. We can't believe our eyes, we feel something akin to panic. We are just prisoners and will have to get used to the idea.[69]

Conditions in the camps in Roussillon were rudimentary. Black humour was one response—camps were called 'Hotel des Mil Una Noches' and 'Gran Hotel de Catalunya', but understandable bitterness led to others being named after Judas and French Prime Minister Daladier. At one time 80,000 refugees lived in cramped and unhygienic conditions on the beach at Argelès; three times as many passed through the camp between 1939 and 1941. Others were placed in camps at Saint-Cyprien and Le Barcarès, before being shipped to Algeria. Survivors described malnutrition and exposure to the elements. Refugees improvised by making nails out of barbed wire and scavenged for driftwood to build shelters that were laid out in

---

[67] Francesca Wilson, *In the Margins of Chaos: Recollections of Relief Work in and between Three Wars* (John Murray, 1944), 190–7.

[68] Helen Norris Nicholson, 'Shooting in Paradise: Conflict, Compassion and Amateur Filmmaking during the Spanish Civil War' *Journal of Intercultural Studies*, 27, no.3 (2006), 313–30.

[69] Francie Cate-Arries, *Spanish Culture behind Barbed Wire: Memory and Representation of the French Concentration Camps, 1939–1945* (Lewisburg: Bucknell University Press, 2004), 147.

'streets' corresponding to the towns they fled. Accounts of guards' brutality added
to the dismal picture. Josep Bartolí sketched a grotesquely fat and hairy 'monstrous
gatekeeper of hell' who guarded the gate; in the background skeletal figures stared
out from the barbed wire. Inmates caustically placed a notice at the entrance, advertising France as the country of 'liberté, fraternité, égalité', and made a point of
celebrating the 150th anniversary of the French Revolution.[70]

In the ensuing months and years Spanish refugees described how they encountered local animosity. Businesses complained that 'the Red invasion has killed tourism'. There was a general concern about immigration and its perceived impact on
the 'national character'; France had already become 'the world's dumping ground'
according to one French official. The prevailing mixture of contempt and fear
proved conducive to a regime of 'permanent surveillance' in which Spanish refugees were exposed to intermittent brutality, particularly if they were identified as
communists or anarchists and sent to concentration camps at Collioure and Le
Vernet.[71]

In a show of solidarity the Soviet Union embarked on so-called rescue expedi-
tions and admitted 5,000 refugee orphans from Spain. Unsurprisingly the Franco
regime denounced this 'barbaric export' of children. They were housed in state-run
institutions bearing the names of Bolshevik heroes. Educationalists and psychologists assessed their background and moral bearing. Their letters home (which never
reached their parents) described how they navigated life in the dangerous shoals of
Stalin's Russia. Children wrote of everyday experiences but also how a proletarian
brotherhood helped them to feel 'at home' and to prepare them, as they hoped, to
return as trained soldiers or skilled workers. Recent research paints a disturbing
picture of tensions between refugee children and adult minders as well as reports
of physical and sexual abuse. This abrupt relocation to the Soviet Union did not
bring an end to their odyssey: many were evacuated to the Urals and Central Asia
during the Second World War. Some *niños* returned to Spain when repatriation
became possible in 1956; many of those who married Russians opted to remain in
the USSR.[72]

Other destinations likewise proved unsettling and exciting in equal measure.
One young refugee brought to the UK recalled later in life that 'when we arrived,
I'd never seen a tent before in my life, only in films with Indians and cowboys'. The
'Red Duchess', Katharine, Countess of Atholl, Eleanor Rathbone and Ellen
Wilkinson were prominent sympathizers; so too was the young communist Chris-
topher Hill who subsequently became the pre-eminent historian of seventeenth-

---

[70] Louis Stein, *Beyond Death and Exile: the Spanish Republicans in Exile, 1939–1955* (Cambridge,
Mass: Harvard University Press, 1979), 58; Geneviève Dreyfus-Armand, *L'exil des républicains espag-
nols en France: de la Guerre civile à la mort de Franco* (Paris: Albin Michel, 1999), 67; Pierre Marqués,
La Croix-Rouge pendant la guerre d'Espagne 1936–1939: les missionnaires de l'humanitaire (Paris:
L'Harmattan, 2000), 359.

[71] Burgess, *Refuge in the Land of Liberty*, 160–2, citing Marcel Paon; Wilson, *In the Margins of
Chaos*, 225; Stein, *Beyond Death and Exile*, 72–3.

[72] This is explored in the powerful film by Jaime Camino, *Los Niños de Rusia* (2002). Glennys
Young, 'Implications of a Micro-history: Home, Gender and Power in the *Casas de los Niños* in the
Leningrad Region' (unpublished, 2008).

century England. Labour politician Edith Summerskill organized a National Women's Appeal for Food for Spain, and the National Joint Committee for Spanish Relief underwrote the travel expenses and care of children in the UK. But the politics of humanitarianism did not run in just one direction. A strong pro-Franco sentiment took hold in some circles; the maverick anti-communist and anti-Semite Charles Sarolea devoted as much time to denouncing Republicans as he did working on behalf of refugees as the Belgian consul in Edinburgh during the First World War.[73]

A Fascist apologist wrote of the 'Reds' that they 'will wither away without glory in the most remote reaches of the globe. It is, when all is said and done, the history of all emigrants—the history of all migrants is one of a slow disappearance without glory'.[74] Refugees were determined to prove him wrong. In France, self-appointed camp leaders organized choirs, football tournaments, classes and workshops. Their survival became a form of resistance to the Franco regime and a means of self-affirmation: 'those who were not leaving were for the enemy', wrote Dolores Torres, in uncompromising fashion.[75]

Stories and songs encapsulated feelings about the passage to France, Mexico, Argentina or other destinations in which exhaustion and tangible loss were combined with images of a disciplined journey to a place of safety, as well as survival in unpropitious conditions. The Basque Children's Committee published a journal that enabled refugees to keep in touch and to publish their memoirs; it was entitled *Amistad*, a reference to the ship seized by slaves who were being taken to Havana in 1839 and who were eventually allowed to return to Africa. Exile narratives revealed a complex pattern. Certainly refugees encountered hostility and endured taunts at the hands of French officials and the public, and something of the same happened in Argentina, where the government was less accommodating than in Mexico. Testimonies speak of endurance and a belief that exile taught lessons about managing adversity. 'Each earned there his or her halo of blessed saintliness, the martyr's palm', wrote one refugee from Mexico in 1945, adding that a clear distinction should be drawn between political refugees and mere 'economic migrants' (*gachupines*) whose national consciousness was open to question.[76]

During the German occupation of France, which gave the French something else to think about, refugees were made to work on the construction of the Atlantic coastal defences. Their situation remained precarious after the war, when they were assigned to back-breaking work in agriculture, mining and construction. By the

---

[73] Peter France, 'Sarolea, Charles Louis-Camille (1870–1953)', *Oxford Dictionary of National Biography*, Oxford: Oxford University Press, 2004 <http://www.oxforddnb.com/view/article/66974>, accessed 31 May 2012; Kevin Myers, 'The Ambiguities of Aid and Agency: Representing Refugee Children in England, 1937' *CSH*, 6, no.1 (2009), 29–46; Susan Cohen, *Rescue the Perishing: Eleanor Rathbone and the Refugees* (Vallentine Mitchell, 2010).

[74] Cate-Arries, *Spanish Culture behind Barbed Wire*, 14.

[75] Sharif Gemie, Fiona Reid and Laure Humbert, *Outcast Europe: Refugees and Relief Workers in an Era of Total War, 1936–48* (Continuum, 2012), 35.

[76] Cate-Arries, *Spanish Culture behind Barbed Wire*, 51; Patricia Weiss Fagen, *Exiles and Citizens: Spanish Republicans in Mexico* (Austin: University of Texas Press, 1973). Ironically, the Mexican government hoped to recruit skilled workers from among the refugees.

early 1950s around 120,000 refugees in France still held out hopes—soon dashed—of an Anglo-American campaign to remove Franco and enable them to return to Spain, rather like the fantasies of an anti-Soviet crusade expressed by refugees from Eastern Europe after 1945. But this understates the intense politicization of Basque and other refugees who located their exile in relation to a socialist and republican tradition.[77]

Narratives were suffused by ideas connecting personal bereavement to displacement, as in the memoir of Juan Rejano, the editor of an exiles' journal, *Romance*, who wrote in 1959 of 'dragging my bones from one place to another in the anxiety-ridden sands of the Argelès-sur-Mer concentration camp'. When he learned of the death of the poet Machado: 'it was as if his death gave new life to the beloved ghosts still so near by, because before my mind's eye paraded the images of the frozen fields of Castilla, Andalusian olive groves, provincial little squares with the bubbling sound of fountains and children's laughter, the silent orchards of lemon trees, of blackbirds, the Guadalquivir and the legendary language of the Duero'. Although Rejano, like others, refused to regard the time spent in refugee camps as (in his words) a 'void', the pain of separation was nevertheless acute. Bartolí drew a devastating picture of an arm clutching a strand of barbed wire; the rest of the body is submerged beneath the sand and rock of the beach at Argelès. The caption read, 'The others left; you stayed behind'. The poet Celso Amieva published a poem in 1960 about the torment he experienced together with his sense of pride in being an exile:

> Spaniard/Loaded down with your knapsack/May the gods preserve/Your Spanish pride and identity'/Amen. I wouldn't trade/The hunger, the misery and the sorrow/ That this knapsack carries/From the camps to the work crews/For all the bags of gold/ Of the slave masters and assassins.[78]

Displacement ultimately helped forge a sense of common identity as a refugee nation-in-exile that symbolized the 'real Spain', in contrast to the land that had been appropriated by Fascists, under whose iron heel millions of ordinary Spaniards were condemned to suffer and whose propaganda insisted that Franco was the guardian of Spanish 'tradition'. The mass exodus (*retirada*) was construed as survival against difficult odds and a means of forging solidarity.[79]

THE COMING OF WAR

In his mammoth study of 'the refugee problem', Sir John Hope Simpson despaired at the missed opportunity and the need for renewed efforts by private humanitarian agencies: bemoaning 'the exaggerated nationalism that creates the refugee and

---

[77] Laurence Brown, 'Pour aider nos frères d'Espagne': Humanitarian Aid, French Women, and Popular Mobilisation during the Front Populaire' *French Politics, Culture and Society*, 25, no.1 (2007), 30–48.

[78] Quotations from Cate-Arries, *Spanish Culture behind Barbed Wire*, 47–8, 187.

[79] Sharif Gemie, '"The Ballad of Bourg-Madame": Memory, Exile and the Spanish Republican Refugees of the *Retirada* of 1939' *International Review of Social History*, 51, no.1 (2006), 1–40.

also creates most of the difficulties which beset him in the country of refuge', he nevertheless added that those difficulties have 'been partly offset by the halting development of international solidarity'. New methods of communication enabled private American philanthropic bodies such as the Rockefeller Foundation, Near East Relief and myriad diaspora associations to get involved. Their officials in Shanghai and Istanbul cabled Geneva and New York for help, to 'let the public know'.[80] Nevertheless this provided only a small crumb of comfort. Humanitarianism exposed the failings of political leaders to meet the challenge posed by fascism.

Jewish refugees fleeing Nazi persecution derived little benefit from 'international solidarity'. In the 1920s there were signs of hope. The JDC channelled remittances to relatives in Poland—the 'diaspora in the diaspora'—who had suffered during the war. Programmes of 'rehabilitation' gathered momentum as American Jews funded social work, orphanages and credit cooperatives. The JDC threw its weight behind plans to relocate Jews from Russian towns to farmland in Soviet Crimea, the idea being that they would be better protected from pogroms and accusations of 'rootlessness'. Joseph Rosen, the plan's architect, regarded resettlement in Ukraine as preferable to emigration, describing the Zionist project in Palestine as a 'mockery'. The Kremlin's endorsement of the scheme reflected a wish to counter the presence of Muslim Tatars. Few Jews took the plunge before collectivization turned their lives upside down once more.[81]

Was the record of liberal democracies any better? Hannah Arendt thought not. She pointed out that receiving states used the same language and adopted the same discriminating practices as persecuting states: 'the constitutional inability of European nation-states to guarantee human rights to those who had lost nationally guaranteed rights made it possible for the persecuting governments to impose their standard of value even upon their opponents'.[82] The Evian Conference called by US President Franklin Roosevelt in July 1938 was an attempt to get other countries to accept a greater share of refugees, but participants lined up to demonstrate their intransigence and the conference was widely regarded as a fiasco. Not only did it fail to improve the prospects of escaping persecution, it also (as the former High Commissioner for Refugees, James G. McDonald, pointed out) avoided addressing the ultimate cause of the crisis, which clearly lay in the policies pursued by the Nazi state.[83]

Jews were blamed by the Vichy regime for France's collapse in 1940, a sorry coda to the torment that afflicted them throughout the previous decade. Around 200,000 Belgians hastily fled to Paris and its environs—older people recollected

---

[80] Simpson, *Refugee Problem*, 10, 178.

[81] Joseph Van Gelder, 'Activities of the Refugee Department in Europe, 1921–23' (1924), JDC Archives; Yehuda Bauer, *My Brother's Keeper: a History of the American Jewish Joint Distribution Committee, 1929–1939* (Philadelphia: Jewish Publication Society of America, 1974), 64; Jonathan Dekel-Chen, *Farming the Red Land: Jewish Agricultural Colonization and Local Soviet Power, 1924–1941* (New Haven: Yale University Press, 2005).

[82] Arendt, *Origins of Totalitarianism*, 269, 294–6.

[83] Skran, *Refugees in Inter-War Europe*, 230–40.

the painful events of 1914. Plans were drawn up for an influx of 800,000 Belgian refugees, one-quarter of whom were to be sent to Britain. Initially, the French public were relatively unconcerned by their presence and the first flurry of departures even took on a holiday character. But this mood soon gave way to alarm. Germany's occupation of France led to a sharp increase in the number of Parisians fleeing the French capital. Some justified their departure not in terms of blind panic but as a stratagem to deny the enemy French manpower. Within a matter of weeks, following the armistice, many civilians resolved to go home. Those who stayed in the unoccupied zone were placed in reception centres.[84]

The crisis produced contested readings of displacement. Internally displaced civilians drew on memories of the First World War. Onlookers regarded the farm wagons rolling along the streets of the capital as a harbinger of desperate times. A fascist sympathizer spoke of a reversion to a past when France found itself 'at the gates of a medieval famine'.[85] Such images underplayed the purposefulness of refugees who portrayed themselves as heroes of a nascent resistance. When they reached provincial towns further south they met with a frosty response because they embodied defeat and national disgrace. In due course, most of them returned to their homes. For French Jews, however, war and occupation meant internment and deportation. The Francophile British historian Richard Cobb mischievously suggested that the exodus inspired French people to discover their country anew. Whether or not this was the case, it encouraged a general amnesia after the war.[86]

CONCLUSIONS

Political upheaval in post-1918 Europe created a huge refugee population that led the new League of Nations and NGOs to devise programmes of assistance. Russian refugees found it hard to make a claim on foreign charity by portraying themselves as a persecuted minority: had they not been the instruments of persecution towards Jews, Poles and Balts in the old Tsarist Empire? Their best recourse was to draw attention to Russia's cultural wealth that faced imminent destruction at the hands of an atheistic and proletarian dictatorship. By contrast, the Bolsheviks sought to change the course of history. Their exiled opponents denounced what they took to be hasty and ill-conceived programmes of economic modernization and social experimentation. Russian refugees believed in restoration, the Bolsheviks in transformation. Western governments, contemptuous of both, were happy to let Nansen pick up the pieces.

[84] Gemie, Reid and Humbert, *Outcast Europe*, 76–102; Vicky Caron, *Uneasy Asylum: France and the Jewish Refugee Crisis, 1933–1942* (Stanford: Stanford University Press, 1999).

[85] Valerie Holman, 'Representing Refugees: Migration in France, 1940–44' *Journal of Romance Studies*, 2, no.2 (2002), 53–69, at 56.

[86] Hanna Diamond, *Fleeing Hitler: France 1940* (Oxford: Oxford University Press, 2007), 147–9, 180, 197, 212.

Other aspects of international diplomacy were troubling in ways not always recognized at the time. This was most apparent in relation to the Greek-Turkish population exchange. The Lausanne experiment became an important precedent, demonstrating the potential appeal of programmes to 'unmix peoples'. Dissident voices struggled to make themselves heard, as when the international lawyer Georges Scelle lambasted the transfer, describing the process of 'transplantation and uprooting [as] contrary to human freedom'.[87] Here too was a straw in the wind, disclosing the possibility that human rights could be abrogated by governments that claimed the moral high ground whilst simultaneously deporting people against their will. The population exchange had equally disquieting consequences at a local level. Surgical metaphors about 'excision' and references to an organized exchange disguised a chaotic and even violent process in which the pursuit of ethnic harmony foundered on the rock of economic self-interest. Many of those who were 'exchanged' found themselves marginalized from the outset. The inflated claims made on behalf of population transfer must be evaluated accordingly.

The sense of loss felt by Greek refugees from Asia Minor translated into political radicalism: not an irredentist politics (as among Hungarian elites who fled Czechoslovakia, Yugoslavia and Romania) but a leftist politics, indicating that their quarrel was with successive Greek governments that failed to make adequate provision for them. The Metaxas dictatorship targeted the left after 1936. During the Axis occupation of Greece, rivalry between left and right intensified; German forces supplied arms to 'refugee villages' in Macedonia. In the ensuing civil war of 1945–49 the Communist Party was forced underground. At this juncture, Pontic Greek refugees threw in their lot with right-wing parties because their devout Orthodoxy was at odds with communism.

By contrast, Armenian refugees kept their heads down and stayed out of politics, perhaps fearing the consequences of too much exposure. In France, Lebanon and Cyprus the home, school and church became the chief sites for the articulation of national identity, and this appealed to philanthropists who valorized Armenians as hardworking Christians. Exiled Dashnak leaders in the Middle East maintained a close interest in Soviet Armenian politics, leading Moscow to suspect external meddling. But Armenian refugee politics was a largely passive affair that appealed to a tight circle of exiles.

Refugees from the Spanish Civil War were less emasculated and maintained an intense interest in politics, but their impressive intellectual and cultural achievements made little impact in Spain, which became a backwater until foreign tourists helped open the country to closer international scrutiny in the 1960s. Their valorization by foreign governments and relief workers varied according to political persuasion: for those on the left, Spanish refugees embodied the anti-fascist struggle, whereas conservative forces demonized them as a dangerous anticlerical species, to be neither trusted nor tolerated.

---

[87] Kévonian, *Réfugiés et diplomatie humanitaire*, 259.

Class was an important variable. Hungarian peasants resolved to stay on their farms now under Yugoslav, Czech or Romanian jurisdiction, whereas government officials, business leaders and landlords were disproportionately represented among the refugee population in Hungary. Refugees fleeing the Bolshevik regime experienced downward social mobility. All the same, social class and conditions in the job market do not explain everything. Demeaning attributes were ascribed to refugees in the aftermath of war no less than during the Great War. Ethnic Greeks who were transferred from Turkey had to endure resentment from the local populace irrespective of class—although it helped to be 'respectable'—as well as having to negotiate corrupt officials. In neither instance did refugees contribute overtly to cementing nationhood. Refugees in Greece and Turkey remained socially segregated and economically deprived; oftentimes their fate was to be the whipping-boys of conservative nationalists. Nevertheless, population displacement indirectly played a part in nation-state formation as it had in 1914–18, since it forced the state to confront the meaning of membership in the new political community.

Incarceration offered a provisional solution to the Armenian refugee crisis as well as to the Greek refugee crisis in 1921. These arrangements had a habit of turning into a lengthy stay, as with refugees from the Spanish Civil War who spent months in French camps that the famous Catalan cellist Pablo Casals likened to Dante's Inferno.[88] In Baqubah the British authorities confined Armenians and Assyrians to camps, which meant hard graft: Dudley Northcote argued that refugees needed to be put to work, to be self-supporting and maintain morale. But the issues were complex: if Armenians had 'a homing instinct', where precisely was their 'home'?[89] Most Armenians in the diaspora had no intention of making a home in the Soviet Union. The vision of an enlarged Armenian state was dashed on the rocks of geopolitics. Eventually Armenian and Spanish refugees left the camps behind, but their departure produced mixed emotions. Confinement made possible an intense politicization: would this be diluted by resettlement?

Refugees' experiences were frequently appropriated by non-refugees. That is to say, their experience was not 'innocent' or unmediated, but was instead framed by the views and tactics of politicians, for whom refugees embodied an ideological viewpoint, by humanitarians and diplomats such as Henry Morgenthau, for whom Greece's response to Lausanne amounted to a national epic, and by diasporic groups. Some accounts emphasized expert knowledge, as in Salonika where engineers organized sanitary improvements and recommended the use of 'sanitary squads for policing the refugee camp', and where Greek refugee women proved to be 'remarkably adaptable'.[90] These attitudes and practices were disseminated further afield, part of a transnational process embracing ideas about external intervention and self-help, along with humanitarian norms and concepts of international law.

---

[88] Stein, *Beyond Death and Exile*, 157.
[89] Laycock, *Imagining Armenia*, 166; Simpson, *The Refugee Problem*, 49.
[90] Shaw, 'Greek Refugees', 47–9.

In the larger scheme of things, the fate of Jews rather than ethnic Russians, Armenians, Greeks, Turks, Catalans and Basques cast the longest shadow, not by virtue of their displacement but because their failure to be enabled to flee contributed to their eventual extermination. The consequences of the insipid international response in the 1930s to the situation of Jews in Nazi Germany only became fully apparent in 1945. Jews who managed to get out were stripped of everything, including occupation, citizenship and the right to an opinion. In vain did French jurist Noël Vindry assert that 'the state has no right to say, "this individual no longer pleases me, keep him on your territory as a doubtful element and do with him as you please"'.[91] Vindry belonged to a tiny minority: 'doing as you please' culminated in the refusal of all but a handful of activists to confront the pernicious ramifications of Nazi German policies during the 1930s.

---

[91] Kévonian, *Réfugiés et diplomatie humanitaire*, 253–4. Vindry was writing in 1925.

PART II

MID-CENTURY MAELSTROM

There is a kind of grim and tragic monotony to this century's stereotype of large-scale relief and reconstruction and refugee aid: Spanish refugees, Jewish and political refugees, displaced persons, expellees, escapees, Pakistan, Palestine, Korea, South Vietnam. Where next do the vast governmental and the small voluntary agencies trek in the wake of these problems?

(Lou Schneider, 1954)

The hazards and challenges discussed in Part I paled into insignificance alongside the enormity of global population displacement during and immediately after the Second World War. Hitler's European empire relied upon invasion, occupation, terror and forced labour. Its collapse left the victorious Allies with the challenge of reconstructing war-torn societies and returning combatants and refugees to their homes. The demise of other empires had equally profound consequences. In the Far East, Japan's defeat signalled both the demise of its Korean empire and its occupation of mainland China, where the number of refugees beggared belief. Communist victories in North Korea and China generated a fresh refugee crisis in the region. In 1947 Britain brought the curtain down on its empire in South Asia by granting independence to India and Pakistan, where a combination of uncertainty and widespread 'communal' violence uprooted 18 million people. A year later the British government renounced its mandate in Palestine, where the attempt to curb Jewish immigration took on extra resonance in the light of the Holocaust. The formation of the state of Israel went hand in hand with the displacement of Palestinians, adding a new dimension to the global refugee crisis.

The post-war world was full of people who were 'out of place'. This was equally true of Europe, Asia and the Middle East. The Allies did not stop at redrawing international frontiers, but embarked on demographic engineering as well. An organized transfer of population between Poland and Soviet Ukraine involved 1.3 million people in 1944–46. Germans were unceremoniously expelled from Poland and Czechoslovakia, largely for punitive reasons, although prophylactic considerations also came into play. The Quaker internationalist Bertram Pickard noted wryly that 'post-war political and psychological conditions will necessitate, even though some suffering may be involved, certain exchanges and transfers of population and the migration of many individuals from countries of origin to countries willing to accept them'.[1] Others looked to such exchanges as a means

---

[1] Bertram Pickard, *Europe's Uprooted People: the Relocation of Displaced Population* (Washington D.C.: National Planning Association, 1944), 50.

to eliminate root causes of war. Diplomats conceived of a partition of Palestine on the grounds that it would do for Arabs and Jews what Lausanne supposedly did for the Balkans, where 'the ulcer has been clean cut out and Greco-Turkish relations, we understand, are friendlier than ever before'.[2] The appeal of a population exchange extended to the Indian sub-continent, although plans for Partition in 1947 envisaged that the frontiers for India and Pakistan would be drawn in such a way as to minimize cross-border flows of people.

Allied preparation for post-war reconstruction came to fruition in the final stages of the war in Europe. Planners were keen to avoid what they regarded as a serious gap in post-war preparedness after 1918. The purpose of the new United Nations Relief and Rehabilitation Administration (UNRRA) was to channel resources to countries shaking off the consequences of wartime occupation. The UN hoped to 'put back into running order those segments of a nation's economy which were necessary to carry out the relief programme, and give each country and its people some of the tools to begin to help themselves'. These bold aims were suffused with the lofty ideal of closer international cooperation. UNRRA's responsibilities included assisting those directly affected by the war in Europe to return to their homes in liberated territories. However, as the Cold War intensified, in 1947 UNRRA gave way to an International Refugee Organisation whose primary purpose was not to repatriate European refugees but to enable them to find new homes beyond Stalin's reach.[3]

The preoccupation of politicians and planners with the situation in Europe was blinkered but understandable. They could point to the sheer scale of population displacement brought about by the flight of refugees and the deportation of workers from occupied countries to sustain the Nazi war effort. Another consideration was the connection made between population displacement, on the one hand, and the legitimacy of the Allied war effort on the other—in other words, how to ensure that 'traumatized' victims of war could become healthy citizens capable of playing a full part in democratic societies. Development thus went hand in hand with resettlement. Here, too, international cooperation was needed. A new Intergovernmental Committee on European Migration acknowledged that 'the problems of European migration could not be left to the whim of individual initiative or private organisations' or bilateral action. The resettlement of refugees had to extend beyond European shores.[4]

In the medium term the Western powers crafted a regime that protected refugees under the auspices of the United Nations High Commissioner for Refugees (UNHCR), charged with ensuring that signatory states adhered to the 1951

[2] Simpson, *The Refugee Problem*, 433–5.
[3] George Woodbridge, *UNRRA: the History of the United Nations Relief and Rehabilitation Administration* (New York: Columbia University Press, 1950), 3 vols, vol. 1, 29; vol. 2, 425; *The Story of UNRRA* (New York, 1948), 5. Refugees of pre-war vintage were the responsibility of the Intergovernmental Committee on Refugees (IGCR), established by the Evian Conference in 1938.
[4] CUA Archives, NCWC Collection, Series 3, Box 170, General Secretary/Executive Department, Office of UN Affairs, Folder 11, Migration, Memos.

Refugee Convention that enshrined in international law the concept of protection from persecution. This in turn raised questions such as how refugee status would be determined and what the obligation of states should be towards recognized refugees. In addition to pushing ajar the doors of wealthy countries in North America, Australia and Western Europe, investment in technical assistance and development programmes held out the possibility that less developed countries would admit refugees. Underlying these programmes was a belief that the 'free world' had to convince refugees that they had made the right choice in fleeing communism. In South Korea, for example, the refugee crisis afforded an opportunity to link rehabilitation to a 'free economy and a democratic way of life'.[5] But resettlement held little attraction to refugees in the Indian sub-continent or in Hong Kong, let alone German expellees who looked instead to local integration as a panacea. UNHCR's mandate in any case did not extend to these groups. The refugee regime that emerged in 1951 did not encompass refugees in all parts of the globe. It assumed a partial, not a universal form.

One vital component in the project of post-war relief and rehabilitation was the part played by voluntary organizations, including those that could point to a history stretching back to the First World War. Some NGOs earmarked funds for specific groups of refugees, as the JDC did for Europe's surviving Jews. Others developed ambitious programmes of relief, reconstruction and resettlement that took in China, Korea, India and Palestine as well as Germany and Austria. For Catholic Relief Services, the focus was on society as a whole, not on a particular group. NGOs also developed innovative means of fundraising. A newcomer on the scene, CARE (Cooperative for American Remittances to Europe), made it possible for donors to express 'direct and personalised concern' with designated individuals in war-torn countries by purchasing relief packages, which it guaranteed to deliver within three months or else refund the purchase price, 'a totally new form of enterprise' in the relief field. The efflorescence of these NGOs and the rehabilitation agenda went hand in hand with recruitment of qualified personnel—social workers, psychologists, engineers, nutritionists and statisticians—alongside volunteer relief workers.[6]

Cold War considerations suffused the refugee camp. Europe's DP camps were sites for the articulation of anti-communist beliefs that went hand in hand with the hope that Soviet domination of Eastern Europe would eventually cease. Patriotic leaders backed impressive efforts among DPs to organize cultural and educational programmes that had a clear political purpose, including among Jews who looked to Palestine as a place of safety. Beyond Europe, too, the refugee camp was far more than an instrument of external management. It provided scope for intense social, cultural and political activity, particularly on the part of Palestinian refugees in the Middle East but also among the internally displaced Koreans. But questions re-

⁵ David Ekbladh, *The Great American Mission: Modernization and the Construction of an American World Order* (Princeton: Princeton University Press, 2009), 9, 139.

⁶ Report to Board of Directors by Harold Miner, 15 October 1951, CARE Archives, Box 1, Annual Reports, 1946–49; Reuben Baetz, *Service to Refugees, 1947–1952* (Geneva: LWF, 1952).

mained. What of self-settled refugees, such as those in 'colonies' in Calcutta or Lahore? Would refugees be granted a degree of autonomy, by governments, international organizations or NGOs? Who spoke for the refugees, and might they be granted the opportunity to speak on their own behalf? Whose experience counted?

These questions arose most acutely in sites where it was more difficult to specify the Cold War as the main motor for action. With no powerful Western state to speak up for them, Palestinian refugees found themselves outside the IRO and UNHCR regime, and it was left to host governments in the Middle East and NGOs to justify their relief efforts as a means to keep communism at bay. In other sites, such as Hong Kong, colonial officials wanted to keep the lid on the refugee crisis, although they succeeded only up to a point. In South Asia the refugee crisis brought about by the partition of India was largely an internal affair. Political considerations of a different kind came into play. Arguments around the 'rehabilitation' of refugees circulated among politicians and officials who sought to determine their responsibilities towards refugees and refugees' responsibility towards the new state.

Cultural production had a hand to play in these arguments. In South Asia it directed attention to the potential capacity of some (but not all) refugees to become fully-fledged citizens, and the assumptions that were made about the guidance they required in order to do so. Ideas around relief, rehabilitation and development were invested with cultural content, and refugees responded accordingly—and not necessarily in the way that government officials hoped. Among Palestinian refugees the politics of cultural representation manifested itself in a determination not only to advertise the magnitude of their loss but also to establish and maintain by various means a connection to ancestral territory. Like refugees in India and Pakistan, they began to construct 'a more self-conscious relationship to place [and] to re-concretise a connection to the land that had been violently sundered'.[7]

Would this dislocation resonate further afield? How might ordinary people in the new states of India and Pakistan be made to sit up and take notice of displaced persons in their midst? Might Palestinian refugees find a sympathetic audience among global humanitarians, and who would be the conduit? The general secretary of the World Council of Churches recognized the dilemma when he compared the refugee crisis in the Middle East to the situation in Europe: '[T]he needs of the millions of refugees in Europe are a constant concern, but we recognise that hopeless and appalling as is the situation of this group, they at least have behind them the lame economy of Western Europe as a final buffer between them and actual starvation. Between the refugees from Palestine and starvation there is nothing but the desert in all its arid unfriendliness'.[8]

---

[7] George Bisharat, 'Exile to Compatriot: Transformation in the Social Identity of Palestinian Refugees in the West Bank', in Akhil Gupta and James Ferguson (eds), *Culture, Power, Place: Explorations in Critical Anthropology* (Durham, NC: Duke University Press, 1997), 203–33, at 217.

[8] WCC Archives, File 425.1.032, Palestine folder, W.A. Visser 't Hooft, draft letter to *The Times*, 27 September 1948.

3

Europe Uprooted

Refugee Crises at Mid-century and 'Durable Solutions'

The massive homelessness of millions of people, which is to say, the war, is sickening. More than the danger and the risk, it is really the homelessness.

(Emmanuil Kazakevich)

INTRODUCTION

Europe bore much of the brunt of the dramatic political and social transformations that took place around the globe in the middle years of the twentieth century, and that helped shape the post-war refugee regime and the lives of refugees. The war wrenched civilians as well as soldiers from their homes. At least 40 million European non-combatants were displaced during the war, many within the pre-war borders of their own country. As in the First World War the rapid German advance into Belgium, France and Poland in 1939, and the Nazi invasion of Soviet Russia in 1941, brought about mass displacement. German occupation regimes ruptured social and economic ties. Organized deportations were repeated on systematic scale under the Nazis. Eastern Europe became a huge site of exploitation and colonization that was limited only by the extent of the Wehrmacht's advance. Hitler's territorial ambition entailed 'clearing' the land of Jews, ultimately by transporting them to the death camps in Eastern Poland, Belarus, Ukraine and the Baltic States. Soviet occupation of Eastern Poland and the Baltic in 1939–41, followed by Stalinist deportations (discussed in chapter 9) and finally the Red Army's re-conquest of Eastern Europe in the later stages of the war added to the social and demographic turbulence. These continental convulsions wreaked havoc.[1]

As the war came to an end the Allies were confronted by millions of survivors who were 'out of place'. Jews who survived the Holocaust wished to leave Central and Eastern Europe at the earliest opportunity, demanding that as refugees they be

[1] Malcolm J. Proudfoot, *European Refugees: a Study of Forced Population Movements* (Faber, 1957), 32–4; Alfred J. Rieber (ed.), *Forced Migration in Central and Eastern Europe, 1939–1950* (Frank Cass, 2000); Philipp Ther and Ana Siljak (eds), *Redrawing Nations: Ethnic Cleansing in East-Central Europe, 1944–1948* (Oxford: Rowman and Littlefield, 2001); Jessica Reinisch and Elizabeth White (eds), *The Disentanglement of Populations: Migration, Expulsion and Displacement in Postwar Europe, 1944–49* (Palgrave Macmillan, 2011).

allowed to settle in Palestine. As early as 1942 the Allies had begun to think about reconstruction, including enabling those whom the Nazis had drafted as forced labour as they conquered territory to return home. But significant numbers of these Displaced Persons (DPs) were determined to resist being repatriated to countries that now fell within the Soviet sphere of influence. Hannah Arendt pointedly remarked that 'a very large proportion will regard repatriation as deportation'.[2] They regarded themselves as fleeing from communism, as well as being victims of Nazism: Hitler had uprooted them, but Stalin was the chief source of their persecution. The situation in Germany and Austria was complicated by the steady influx of civilians who fled west when the victorious Red Army swept through Eastern Europe towards Berlin. Who would provide for them?

Territorial adjustments and political change complicated matters further. The Allied agreements at Yalta in 1944 and Potsdam in 1945 altered the shape and ethnic composition of Poland and Ukraine, legitimized the Soviet annexation of the Baltic States and entrenched Communist power throughout the region. Furthermore, far from bringing an end to organized deportation, the defeat of Nazism helped to popularize the idea. French officials entertained the idea of uprooting 13 million Germans and transferring them overseas, partly for punitive reasons but also because they could make way for the influx of refugees who were shortly expected to arrive from Eastern Europe. Elements of this fantasy were brutally realized when the Allies expelled virtually all ethnic German inhabitants of Poland and Czechoslovakia. The emerging post-war international refugee regime passed them by. Nor did it take account of Italians who abandoned the disputed territory of Venezia Giulia or who fled Italy's colonial possessions to 'return' to 'homes' they had never known. The same was true of the 20,000 Greek and Macedonian children who were evacuated by the Greek Communist Party during the civil war in 1947–49 and taken to Eastern Europe, much as their Spanish counterparts had been ten years earlier.[3]

International agencies and NGOs focused on Europe's DPs. The Allies expected that most would sort themselves out with a modicum of external assistance from the United Nations Relief and Rehabilitation Administration (UNRRA). The priority was to assist the surviving victims of war (excluding ex-enemy civilians), and to provide emergency relief prior to their repatriation. By late 1945, around seven million men and women had been repatriated, including more than five million to Soviet territory. But at least 1.5 million Poles, Latvians, Lithuanians, Ukrainians and others resisted. As the Cold War intensified and inter-Allied cooperation dried up, their fortunes were entrusted to a new body, the International Refugee Organisation (IRO), which the USSR refused to join. IRO officers determined the eligibility of 'genuine refugees and Displaced Persons' for protection and made

---

[2] Quoted in G. Daniel Cohen, *In War's Wake: Europe's Displaced Persons in the Postwar Order* (New York: Oxford University Press, 2012), 4.

[3] Pamela Ballinger, 'Borders of the Nation, Borders of Citizenship: Italian Repatriation and the Redefinition of National Identity after World War II' *CSSH*, 40, no.3 (2007), 713–41; Michael Fleming, 'Greek "Heroes" in the Polish People's Republic and the Geopolitics of the Cold War, 1948–1956' *Nationalities Papers*, 36, no.3 (2008), 375–97.

plans for their resettlement. By the end of the 1940s Western officials argued that the outstanding issues in Europe had largely been solved through a mixture of resettlement and local integration. Any remaining concerns would be dealt with by a small successor agency with a limited mandate. This paved the way for the creation of the Office of the United Nations High Commissioner for Refugees in December 1950, which thus emerged as a sickly creature with a limited life expectancy.

Whether repatriated or not, refugees and DPs had to negotiate their incarceration in 'assembly centres' and camps. The refugee camp provided patriotic leaders amongst the DPs as well as in the diaspora with an opportunity to advertise ideas of historic suffering and the potential for national deliverance, as they had done during the First World War. Non-refugees, including government officials and experts responsible for the care of refugees, construed DPs in more problematic terms, as impaired and in need of psychological intervention. Their constitution as a 'problem' brought together political, legal, cultural and economic considerations. Under what circumstances could they be admitted to third countries? What about new waves of refugees from communism, in Hungary, East Germany and Yugoslavia—could they become good citizens in the West or might they be fifth-columnists? How far did new cohorts of refugees seek economic betterment rather than sanctuary from persecution? A combination of factors—the Cold War in Europe, and the revival of the world economy—created favourable conditions for the resettlement of DPs and refugees in the 1950s, but Western governments expected this to be on their terms.

Difficult questions were asked about the policies pursued by Western governments. As the 1950s drew to a close, the contrast between Western affluence and the degradation of a 'hard core' of DPs still in camps amounted to a scandal. Significant efforts were made to 'clear the camps', either by relocating refugees in third countries or facilitating their integration locally. World Refugee Year (WRY) (1959–60) typified international efforts to assist refugees and to publicize the work of UNHCR. WRY owed much to the dissemination of images of damaged and distraught refugees. The campaign also made a statement about the responsibilities of citizens in the 'free world' towards refugees. This humanitarian initiative, like the post-war refugee regime as a whole, sought to define the boundaries of citizenship. But to repeat: the officials who operated this regime looked the other way when it came to deported and 'transferred' persons, whose experiences were obscured from view.

TRANSFERS AND EXPULSIONS

Transfers, expulsions and deportations were pursued with great vigour during and after the Second World War (see Map 4). German troops ordered the expulsion of Jews, Roma, communists and others when they occupied Alsace-Lorraine in 1940. The Molotov-Ribbentrop Pact (1939) paved the way for the colonization of Polish territory by German settlers and ultimately the extermination of East European

Jewry. Nazi officials forced Poles out of their homes in the Warthegau, replacing them with ethnic Germans from Eastern Poland, which now formed part of the Soviet sphere. In Poland, huge changes took place under the Soviet occupation. Jewish refugees arrived in large numbers in the towns of Galicia, seeking to escape German-occupied territory to the west. In Volhynia, military colonists were arrested and their land expropriated. Around 40,000 Poles, Jews and Ukrainian nationalists were deported to Central Asia and Siberia between February 1940 and May 1941. Polish women faced constant humiliation and sexual violence. Holding on to a sense of connectedness to the 'homeland' assumed critical significance in their lives.[4] In the wake of the Nazi invasion Stalin followed in the footsteps of the last Tsar by demonizing German farmers, Crimean Tatars, Chechens and others and deporting them to Central Asia on grounds of 'treason' (see chapter 9).

Politicians engaged in a merry-go-round of demographic engineering after the Second World War. Winston Churchill advocated a 'clean sweep' of ethnic Germans from east of the Curzon Line, describing it (with a nod towards the Greek-Turkish population exchange) as a means of 'disentangling' groups in order to create friendship between nations. Events on the ground ran ahead of bureaucratic decision-making. The Czech leader Edvard Beneš spoke of providing a 'humane and orderly' transfer that was consistent with 'civilised' norms of conduct; for him, national minorities were 'always a real thorn in the side of individual nations'.[5] At Potsdam Stalin claimed that 'all the Germans had run away' from Poland; Churchill agreed. Neither claim was accurate. Instead ordinary Czechs and Poles took matters into their own hands, forcing Germans from their homes in the summer of 1945. Concerted state intervention led to seven million Germans being driven out of Czechoslovakia, Poland, Hungary and Yugoslavia between 1945 and 1950. Put in charge of the new Polish Ministry of Recovered Territories, Władysław Gomułka categorically stated that 'we must expel all the Germans, because countries are built on national lines and not on multinational ones'. Poland also rid itself of ethnic Ukrainians who were given just a few hours' notice to quit and forced to identify themselves by means of the letter 'U' that appeared on the identity papers issued by the recently-dislodged Nazi occupation regime. These measures caused enormous bitterness and hardship.[6]

Another vindictive bit of post-war reckoning took place in Bulgaria, where the new Communist government expelled 250,000 ethnic Turks. Turkey quickly

---

[4] Aleksander Wat, *My Century: the Odyssey of a Polish Intellectual* (New York: New York Review Books, 2003); Katherine R. Jolluck, *Exile and Identity: Polish Women in the Soviet Union during World War II* (Pittsburgh: University of Pittsburgh Press, 2002), 199–278; Jan T. Gross, *Revolution from Abroad: The Soviet Conquest of Poland's Western Ukraine and Western Belorussia* (Princeton: Princeton University Press, 2002); Kate Brown, *A Biography of No Place: from Ethnic Borderland to Soviet Heartland* (Cambridge, Mass: Harvard University Press, 2004), 10, 149, 185–91.

[5] Arendt, *Origins of Totalitarianism*, 276.

[6] Eugene M. Kulischer, *Europe on the Move: War and Population Changes, 1917–1947* (New York: Columbia University Press, 1948), 285–6; Naimark, *Fires of Hatred*, 110; Frank, *Expelling the Germans*, 74–90; Timothy Snyder, *The Reconstruction of Nations: Poland, Ukraine, Lithuania, Belarus, 1569–1999* (New Haven: Yale University Press, 2003), 197–8. Czechoslovakia additionally expelled 200,000 Hungarians under the 'Košicky Programme'.

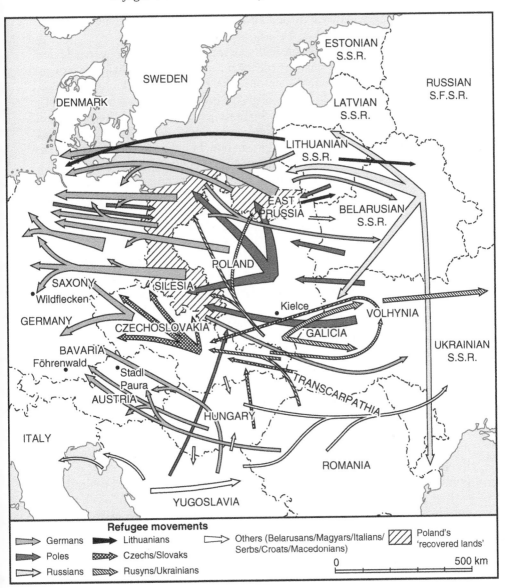

Map 4: Map of Population Movements in Central Europe, 1944–48

closed the border in turn, 'because the Bulgarian government was infiltrating through the frontier many persons without the required visas or with false visas as well as a number of gypsies'. Meanwhile, Armenian refugees who settled in Romania between the wars now lived under a Communist government. A UN official wrote, 'prior to the advent of Communism in Romania, all of these Armenians were highly productive citizens', but the Romanian authorities decided to expel them to Turkey, where they were doubly unwelcome as Armenians and as former residents of a Communist state.[7]

UNRRA disclaimed any responsibility for these expellees and transferred populations. The welfare of German expellees was a matter for the individual German states (*Länder*). Beyond Germany, no-one apart from some religious groups paid much attention to their immediate plight.[8] Although 'treated as self-respecting individuals and not to be dealt with by bureaucracy as beings belonging to an inferior category', they were 'nonetheless refugees in the wider sociological sense, because their social and economic integration into the national community which has accepted them is far from complete'.[9] Some expellees spent years in transit camps. Sir John Hope Simpson worried about their impact on the new Federal Republic: there is (he wrote) 'no peace safe while masses of people live in conditions intolerable in a civilised era. In Central Europe the ground lies ready prepared for the seed of revolutionary propaganda'.[10] Local people spoke unfavourably of the cultural differences between themselves and the newcomers ('Pollacks' and 'Pimoks', 'Poles' and 'strangers'). The camps enabled expellees to sustain a connection to the 'homeland' and 'Homeland societies' kept alive faint hopes of territorial restitution. (In East Germany the expellees found it difficult to vent their experiences in public, because the communist state regarded the issue as closed.) The situation worsened when around three million new refugees poured into West Germany from the east; their position was less clear-cut than that of the expellees.[11]

DISPLACED PERSONS AND THE ALLIES

Policy-makers had first to determine the conditions under which people had been displaced. One contemporary drew a distinction between 'war fugitives', who fled from (or were evacuated from) the immediate zone of conflict; 'refugees' ('the product of ideological policies'), including those forcibly expatriated or deported, such as Jews; and forced labourers. Others held that 'refugees [are] civilians not outside the national boundaries of their country, who desire to return to their

---

[7] AFSC Archives, Folder, DPs Services—Commissions, Organisations, Report of the UNHCR Refugee Advisory Committee, 4 December 1951; H. Wilbrandt, Refugee Service Committee, Istanbul, to G. van Goedhart, UNHCR, 25 August 1952, Fonds UNHCR 11, Series 1, Folder 15/39, Armenian Refugees 1952–63.

[8] Elfan Rees, spokesman for the World Council of Churches urged members to 'fight against "the spirit of Potsdam" which divided human beings into "eligible" and "uneligible" categories of merchandise'. Memo dated February 1947, WCC Archives, File 425.1.033 ERC, Different Countries and Refugee Groups 1947–48.

[9] Vernant, *The Refugee in the Post-War World*, 142.

[10] Foreword to Henry Carter, *The Refugee Problem in Europe and the Middle East*, (Epworth Press, 1949).

[11] Rainer Schulze, 'The Politics of Memory: Flight and Expulsion of German Populations after the Second World War and German Collective Memory' *National Identities*, 8, no.4 (2006), 367–82; Meryn McLaren, '"Out of the Huts Emerged a Settled People": Community-building in West German Refugee Camps' *German History*, 28, no.1 (2010), 21–43.

homes, but require assistance to do so, who are: (a) temporarily homeless because of military operations; (b) at some distance from their homes for reasons related to the war'.[12] The Bermuda Conference (April 1943) agreed that the repatriation of those displaced by the war would be a priority, describing this as the power of 'the homing instinct'.[13] The term 'Displaced Person' was a deliberate decision to categorize those who were the unwitting or innocent victims of Germany's war machine; they were 'civilians outside the national boundaries of their country by reason of the war, who are desirous but are unable to return to their home or find homes without assistance'.[14] Hannah Arendt offered a more dyspeptic analysis, arguing that the label 'was invented during the war for the express purpose of liquidating statelessness once and for all by ignoring its existence', since the term 'stateless person' (in widespread use before the war) at least implied the loss of the protection afforded by the state. DPs lived in limbo; they belonged not to any country, but to the internment camps where they were held prior to repatriation and the restoration of their nationality.[15]

The broader context had already been laid down in November 1943 when President Roosevelt addressed representatives of the 'United Nations' in the White House, inviting 'each nation to provide relief and help in rehabilitation for the victims of German and Japanese barbarism', lest they suffer mass starvation and disease. He proposed an organization that would 'restore to a normal, healthy and self-sustaining existence' the oppressed countries, thereby enabling 'our own boys overseas to come home'. The priority was to assist in the 'resumption of urgently needed agricultural and industrial production and the restoration of essential services', and at the same time to return 'prisoners and exiles to their homes'. Accordingly UNRRA began its work the following month. One of its first decisions was to agree that relief work was 'not political', even though Roosevelt spoke of 'fighting to cleanse the world of ancient evils, ancient ills'.[16]

As the war came to an end UNRRA created 'spearhead' teams, more than 300 of which were in the field by June 1945. By the end of the year 6,000 staff had responsibility for the administration and welfare of DPs in a series of rapidly arranged assembly centres. Few people had kind words to say about the organization, whose staff were frequently characterized as incompetent, wasteful and inconsiderate. Allied officers moved DPs from one camp to another. In the 12 months following VE Day, more than two million Russians had been repatriated, along with 450,000 Poles. Analysts praised the combined efforts of the Allied military and UNRRA in preventing a 'wild stampede', but since its main purpose was to prepare

---

[12] Proudfoot, *European Refugees*, 115.
[13] Herbert Emerson, 'Postwar Problems of Refugees' *Foreign Affairs*, 21, no.2 (1943), 211–20, at 213.
[14] Proudfoot, *European Refugees*, 115.
[15] Arendt, *Origins of Totalitarianism*, 279, 284. 'The concept of statelessness is a very difficult one for the army to grasp', wrote Joseph Schwartz of the American JDC. Quoted in William I. Hitchcock, *Liberation: the Bitter Road to Freedom, Europe 1944–1945* (Faber and Faber, 2009), 230.
[16] Woodbridge, *UNRRA*, vol. 1, 3–4, 29; Jessica Reinisch, 'Internationalism in Relief: the Birth (and Death) of UNRRA' *Past and Present*, Supplement 6 (2011), 258–89.

the ground for them to return home, UNRRA forfeited any vestige of respect from the DPs.[17]

UNRRA sought to persuade non-Jewish DPs that it was in their interests to return to homes where they would 'find familiar patterns and a way of life more in keeping with their national culture than if they were to seek resettlement in strange lands'. DPs were invited to contribute to the task of 'building a new home in which everyone will feel happy'.[18] Films with titles such as *The Road Home* and *Home for the Homeless* were designed to create a positive impression of life in Poland and the Baltic States. Soviet repatriation officials operated in France, Iran, Greece, Egypt and other countries and published newspapers in support of homecoming: *Vesti s rodiny* ('News from Home'), *Schastlivyi put'* ('Happy Journey'), and *Rodina zovet* ('The Motherland Calls'). Soviet security forces maintained 'verification-filtration points'. Where doubts arose, however, for example about Ukrainian nationalists, returnees were held in 'filtration camps' and then used as forced labour. The fact that any returnee might spread information about the West among the Soviet population, in ways calculated to undermine morale, rendered everyone suspect.[19]

In a separate but related development the Soviet press made much of the idea of 'homecoming', by appealing to Armenians who were living abroad to 'return' to Soviet Armenia. Pro-Soviet diasporic organizations such as the Armenian National Council of America joined the chorus of approval, and American well-wishers argued that Russia was the 'good Samaritan' who would rescue displaced Armenians, improve their prospects by lobbying for an increase in Armenian territory at Turkey's expense, and preserve Armenian civilization. Unsurprisingly, anti-Soviet groups bitterly opposed the idea of repatriation, just as they had done during the 1920s. Most of those who took up the Soviet offer had never set foot in Erevan, and they soon discovered that 'home' was less attractive than they had been led to believe. The more fortunate managed to get out before being caught up in Stalin's late purges.[20]

This left other DPs in Germany or Austria, praying for an Anglo-American victory over the Soviet Union (see Table 2). A series of polls conducted in spring 1946 established the strength of their anti-communist sentiment, although this did not stop UNRRA officials from arguing that 'the political explanation serves merely as

---

[17] UNRRA Archives, S-0520-0252-0010, Welfare Guide, 'Services to United Nations Nationals Displaced in Germany' (marked restricted, 15 March 1945); Vernant, *The Refugee in the Post-War World*, 30; Mark Wyman, *DPs: Europe's Displaced Persons, 1945–1951* (Ithaca: Cornell University Press, 1998), 40; Kathryn Hulme, *The Wild Place* (Frederick Muller, 1953), 35–7.

[18] Laura J. Hilton, 'Pawns on a Chessboard? Polish DPs and Repatriation from the US Zone of Occupation of Germany', in Johannes-Dieter Steinert and Inge Weber-Newth (eds), *Beyond Camps and Forced Labour* (Osnabrück: Secolo Verlag, 2005), 90–102, at 96.

[19] Nick Baron, 'Remaking Soviet Society: the Filtration of Returnees from Nazi Germany, 1944–49', in Peter Gatrell and Nick Baron (eds), *Warlands: Population Resettlement and State Reconstruction in the Soviet-East European Borderlands, 1945–1950* (Basingstoke: Palgrave, 2009), 89–116.

[20] Charles Vertanes, *Armenia Reborn* (New York: Armenian National Council of America, 1947), 35; John Carlson, 'The Armenian Displaced Persons' *Armenian Affairs*, 1, no. 1 (1949–50), 17–34; Joanne Laycock, 'The Repatriation of Armenians to Soviet Armenia, 1945–49', in Gatrell and Baron (eds), *Warlands*, 140–61.

a convenient justification and cover for underlying motives which are essentially personal and economic'.[21]

By 1949, at which point the door closed on repatriation, a further 73,000 DPs had returned home. However, an impressive number refused repatriation: 650,000, including 200,000 Poles, 110,000 Ukrainians and 150,000 Balts. Others—prisoners as well as DPs—evaded repatriation, either because (like Ukrainians from Galicia) they were not citizens of the USSR before the cut-off date, or because they obtained forged documents to pass themselves off as citizens of pre-war Poland. Poles who served in the Allied armies during the war were not classified as DPs, and many of these former combatants remained in Britain or France. From a Soviet standpoint, however, they could not qualify as 'refugees'.[22] This stance contributed to a breakdown of trust between Soviet repatriation officers and the IRO.

The Cold War came to the rescue of DPs who were reluctant to repatriate, enabling some to be resettled in the USA or other countries while others were permitted (or obliged) to remain in Central Europe. Subsequently their numbers were swelled by newcomers fleeing the Communist seizure of power in Eastern Europe. Anti-Communist opinion regarded them as heroic 'escapees' from totalitarianism. The first UN High Commissioner for Refugees, Dutch lawyer and journalist Gerrit Jan van Heuven Goedhart, did his best to speak the language of apolitical humanitarianism, but the broad consensus in the West held that unless DPs found somewhere to live and work they would otherwise be prey to Communist influence. Thus the post-war refugee crisis rapidly became politicized.[23]

Table 2: DPs from Central/Eastern Europe in West Germany, 1945–46

Nationality	September 1945	December 1945	June 1946	December 1946
Polish	816,012	553,000	419,000	272,712
Latvian	64,979	86,000	97,000	93,357
Lithuanian	47,269	54,000	59,000	57,154
Russian, Ukrainian	33,146	45,000	45,000	45,000
Yugoslav	27,699	40,000	23,000	19,455
Jews	22,580	47,000	107,495	139,613
Estonian	21,453	27,000	32,000	28,936
Czech/Slovak	3,000	3,000	2,000	927
Total	1,036,138	855,000	784,495	657,154

Source: UNRRA data, reported in Proudfoot, *European Refugees*, 291.

[21] 'Why the Displaced Persons Refuse to go Home' (May 1946), in Yury Boshyk (ed.), *Ukraine during World War II* (Edmonton: Canadian Institute of Ukrainian Studies, 1986), 209–22.

[22] Iu. N. Arzamaskin, *Zalozhniki vtoroi mirovoi voiny: repatriatsiia sovetskikh grazhdan v 1944–1953gg.* (Moscow: Focus, 2001).

[23] Kim Salomon, *Refugees in the Cold War: Toward a New International Refugee Regime in the Early Postwar Era* (Lund: Lund University Press, 1991).

THE DP CAMP: INCARCERATION AND NATIONAL SELF-EXPRESSION

Whether awaiting repatriation or trying to evade it, Displaced Persons survived as best they could in the designated assembly centres in the four occupation zones of Germany and in Austria and later on in numerous camps or as self-settled groups ('free-livers'). How were DPs assigned to particular camps? How was the camp managed, and how did DPs arrange their daily routine? How did they interact with the local population and with the occupying forces? What was the connection between incarceration and political self-expression? How did their experience compare with DPs—up to one-fifth of the total—who made their own arrangements? (For Jewish DPs, see chapter 4).

Few reception centres and DP camps conformed to the bureaucratic ideal of a well-ordered institution: one Polish DP described living 'like nomads [in] a huge gypsy camp'.[24] Over time, however, camps became better organized, and DPs were simultaneously subject to greater constraints. For example, outgoing and incoming correspondence was restricted and subject to inspection by Allied authorities, and letters had to be written in English, French, German or Russian, languages that the Allies could most easily understand without having recourse to translators. This regime explained why anger quickly surfaced. A young Polish man asked, 'Is there really much difference between "now" and "before"? I was a number. I am a number. I was called "Polish dog", now I am called "wretched Pole"'. Another DP wrote in scathing terms about his feelings of betrayal and degradation: 'When we were drunk, our greatest pleasure was to picture the day when we in turn would see our "Allies" as DPs in Siberia and how "they" would feel when they could get the same treatment of humiliation as the military and so many UNRRA officers do not spare to give us'.[25]

From an Allied point of view, the camps were a convenient device to prepare for repatriation, as well as to marshal available resources in a difficult economic climate, rather than being an instrument of discipline for its own sake. DPs were hired by UNRRA as teachers, nurses, secretaries and security staff. In due course they assumed responsibility for much of the day-to-day administration of the camps. UNRRA argued that 'in the long run, by practice and persuasion, but not by order and command, committees could be taught to act fairly and human beings rehabilitated'.[26] Sometimes an oppressive regime was imposed on fellow inmates, not by the occupation authorities or by UNRRA, but by the camp committees that controlled the supply of food, cigarettes and clothing. The Allies welcomed this practice as a sign that DPs could learn the habits of self-reliance and 'fairness' after their prolonged exposure to Nazi brutality.[27]

---

[24] Anna D. Jaroszyńska-Kirchmann, *The Exile Mission: the Polish Political Diaspora and Polish Americans, 1939–1956* (Athens: Ohio University Press, 2004), 65.

[25] Ben Shephard, *The Long Road Home: the Aftermath of the Second World War* (Bodley Head, 2010), 269.

[26] Woodbridge, *UNRRA*, vol. 2, 525–32; Wyman, *DPs*, 113–14, 117–18.

[27] Anna Holian, *Between National Socialism and Soviet Communism: Displaced Persons in Postwar Germany* (Ann Arbor: University of Michigan Press, 2011), 48–50.

The occupation regime nevertheless imposed limits on political agitation, particularly if it threatened to spread beyond the camp. Organizing camps on national lines made this a contentious issue. Whereas the US authorities made deliberate provision for Ukrainians to be housed in Ukrainian camps, the British initially objected that this caused unnecessary difficulties: '[T]here is no objection to DPs organising themselves for their moral and physical welfare, but "national committees" of nations who have been incorporated, at least de facto, into the Soviet Union have ensured a great deal of trouble by conducting anti-Soviet propaganda'.[28] By the middle of 1946, as the Cold War intensified, the Foreign Office came round to the idea. Most relief workers accepted this fait accompli, but Quakers expressed misgivings, urging 'vigilance against competitive nationalism' that hindered reconciliation between former enemies. Given the mutual suspicion between DPs and their German neighbours, this was easier said than done.[29]

Most DPs understood that a more pressing issue was how to pass long hours in the camp. They supplemented food rations by various methods including black market transactions with local Germans, who promptly accused DPs of being wedded to criminal behaviour. Allied officials deplored these and other unorthodox tactics:

> In general they appreciated the efforts made on their behalf, but some of the more ignorant or prejudiced were unwilling to participate in the health programme. It was forbidden to keep livestock in the camps, but on one occasion some refugees had managed to keep some pigs in one of the modern billeting quarters. A search was made without success, and it was learned afterwards that the pigs had been shut in a lift which had been kept in motion between floors in order to evade the search team.[30]

Other voices added to the chorus of complaint. DPs gained a reputation in some distant quarters for being 'bums, criminals, black marketeers, subversives, revolutionaries and crackpots of all colours and hues', in the words of one US Congressman whose colourful language evidently reflected his opposition to looser controls on immigration.[31]

The maintenance of order and hygiene became a recurrent feature of camp life in ways that anticipated the management of refugees elsewhere. Refugees regarded as degrading the intimate physical inspections and X-rays to which they were subjected, typically in order to establish their eligibility for resettlement: these health checks (for which they had to pay from their own pocket) might identify infectious diseases and bodily ailments that affected their status—even poor teeth might send

---

[28] Marta Dyczok, *The Grand Alliance and Ukrainian Refugees* (Basingstoke: Macmillan, 2000), 130.

[29] Wyman, *DPs*, 157; Roger Cowan Wilson, *Quaker Relief: an Account of the Relief Work of the Society of Friends, 1940–1948* (Allen and Unwin, 1952), 234; Jenny Carson, 'The Quaker Internationalist Tradition in DP camps, 1945–48', in Gatrell and Baron (eds), *Warlands*, 67–86.

[30] Louise W. Holborn, *The International Refugee Organization: a Specialized Agency of the United Nations, its History and Work, 1946–1952* (Oxford: Oxford University Press, 1956), 250.

[31] Matthew J. Gibney, *The Ethics and Politics of Asylum: Liberal Democracy and the Response to Refugees* (Cambridge: Cambridge University Press, 2004), 137.

one to the back of a very long queue. Inmates complained of a complete lack of privacy in the overcrowded and dilapidated buildings that housed them, and some outside observers complained of 'promiscuity'. Allied officials offered a different perspective, believing that 'compassion' helped to restore 'moral order', and that this required a rigorous regime. Bureaucrats wished to keep refugees on their toes. The British Foreign Office spoke of the need to promote 'welfare work [among DPs] in order that they should not go to pieces as a result of forced inactivity'. As a leading Canadian psychiatrist put it, 'the autocratic paternalism of the camps is not only almost a necessity; it is probably beneficial'.[32]

Tedious routine was leavened by creativity. Exhibitions of their craft work enabled DPs to demonstrate their capacity for useful work and thus to advertise their potential employability in a third country or, as one Polish exhibition catalogue put it to show how 'they worked on themselves, improved their knowledge of old professions and acquired new ones'. An emphasis on competitive sports had a similar purpose, cultivating an image of DPs—both for themselves and the resettlement officers—as sturdy and healthy rather than decrepit and diseased. Young, professional inmates created an active political and cultural life. Theatrical performances had a didactic purpose. Newspapers recounted stories of wartime displacement and enjoined DPs to remember important dates in the national calendar, such as the adoption of the Polish constitution on 3 May 1791 and Independence Day on 11 November commemorating the dramatic events in 1918 that established the First Republic. It was a sign of the commitment of DPs to the 'national order of things' that they insisted on renaming the camps to reflect national affiliation and identity by giving them historically resonant names. Camp Haren in Lower Saxony was renamed Maczków in honour of a prominent Polish general. Maczków was akin to a town, earning the title of 'capital of little Poland'. Elsewhere a link between exile and cultural life emerged in a Lithuanian exhibition of folk art that assembled 'precious relics for us, exiles. Handfuls of Lithuanian soil, the dried crumbs of country bread, a little hank of flax'.[33]

Diasporic connections reinforced the message. Non-Jewish exiles in far-flung locations disseminated 'romantic national sagas informed by the traditional vision of their nations as heroes and martyrs in the struggle for freedom and democracy against evil forces of oppression'. DPs with connections to anti-Communist Polish exiles in London were reminded that their schools should 'save [the youth] for Poland' and inculcate a 'spiritual bond with the entire nation and its new destiny [sic]' by being 'enlightened by a certain sum of knowledge [and becoming] a new person, internally restructured'. In 1945 the United Ukrainian American Relief Committee joined forces with its Canadian counterpart to establish a Central Ukrainian Relief Bureau. There were equivalent organizations in Italy, Belgium

---

[32] Henry B.M. Murphy, *Flight and Resettlement* (Paris: UNESCO, 1955), 58; Dyczok, *The Grand Alliance*, 129.

[33] Jaroszyńska-Kirchmann, *The Exile Mission*, 66; Dalia Kuizinienė, 'National Identity and Lithuanian Literature in the Displaced Persons Camps in Germany in 1945–1950', in Kuizinienė (ed.), *Beginnings and Ends of Emigration: Life without Borders in the Contemporary World* (Kaunas: Versus Aureus, 2005), 193–203, 263–7.

and France. In the first instance this meant protecting DPs from involuntary repatriation, but a more extensive cultural politics came into play, even though some DPs regarded the diaspora as a remote and elitist agglomeration of exiles, insufficiently attuned to the needs of ordinary people.[34]

Patriotic rhetoric raised the political stakes. The experience of the camps taught Ukrainian DPs to think in terms of a 'united' Ukraine free from Soviet domination. Ukrainian activists portrayed themselves as the heirs to a political struggle in the tradition of the eighteenth-century Cossack leader Ivan Mazepa. Heirs to a proud national past, DPs were the embodiment of the heroic exile who awaited the liberation of their country. They served the cause of the 'fatherland' by dint of committing themselves to a reluctant exile, 'until a free and joyful return home'. As with refugee communities during the First World War, Ukrainians were enjoined to stick together for spiritual sustenance as well as self-help. Ideas of national loss, remedial action and duty were encapsulated in an editorial by a prominent Ukrainian DP:

> We must face the fact that our people will be scattered in small groups around the globe. These small Ukrainian islands will be washed by foreign seas until the seas cover them and swallow them up. But will they really be swallowed up? Will we allow this to happen? One thing we can have that will preserve our people for our nation and its cause—the Ukrainian press and book. That is the only weapon which remains in our hands as we scatter around the globe. The book and press will unite us over countries, seas and continents.[35]

From the complex encounters between ordinary DPs, displaced intelligentsia and the émigré community, there emerged a dominant narrative of the homeland as a potential paradise on earth that was presently polluted by Communist rule. However, attempts at creating a single Ukrainian 'nation abroad' were undermined by the bitter political rivalry between OUN-B (anti-Soviet nationalist insurgents inspired by Stepan Bandera), and other factions. OUN-B members described the armed struggle on Soviet territory as 'invaluable capital without which we are nothing but a cluster of homeless refugees'.[36]

Thus the nationality factor continued to be an inescapable part of DPs' self-perception. Hannah Arendt observed that 'the more they were excluded from right

---

[34] Ewa Morawska, 'Intended and Unintended Consequences of Forced Migrations: a Neglected Aspect of East Europe's Twentieth-century History', *IMR*, 34, no.4 (2000), 1049–87, at 1064; Jaroszyńska-Kirchmann, *The Exile Mission*, 86–7; Holian, *Between National Socialism and Soviet Communism*, 87–8; Aldis Purs, '"How those Brothers in Foreign Lands are Dividing the Fatherland": Latvian National Politics in DP Camps after the Second World War', in Gatrell and Baron (eds), *Warlands*, 48–66.

[35] Roman Ilnytzkyj, 'A Survey of Ukrainian Camp Periodicals, 1945–1950', in Wsevolod Isajiw, Yury Boshyk and Roman Senkus (eds), *The Refugee Experience: Ukrainian Displaced Persons after World War 2* (Edmonton: Canadian Institute of Ukrainian Studies Press, 1992), 271–91, at 287–8.

[36] OUN is the acronym for the Organisation of Ukrainian Nationalists, *Orhanizatsiya Ukrayins'kykh Natsionalistiv*. Volodymyr Kulyk, 'Political Emigration and Labour Settlement: Construction of an Émigré Community in the Media Discourse of Ukrainian Displaced Persons in Germany and Austria, 1945–1950', in Ohliger, *European Encounters*, 213–37, at 227.

in any form, the more they tended to look for reintegration into a national, into their own national community'.[37] DPs conceived of themselves as erstwhile citizens of a vanished state that might yet be reconstituted. They drew on a 'conservative and static notion of an essentialised Latvian identity'.[38] This particular historical consciousness emerged in the DP camps, and it re-emerged when European Volunteer Workers (EVWs) transferred their sense of Latvianness to the textile mills of Lancashire. Others had more difficulty negotiating their identity. Long after he left a DP camp, the Lithuanian émigré Jonas Matulionis recalled that:

> Emigration ended our nomadic period of life, which was temporary, uncertain and exhausting. Thank God, the Western world did not leave us alone, but how difficult it is to live on the mercy of others! Will we be happy in our new countries? I doubt it. Without our country, without our homeland, whose juices slaked our thirst, we will always feel like uprooted trees dumped by a storm on strange earth.[39]

In this context it is worth recalling Louise Holborn's distinction between Jewish DPs and DPs from Poland and the Baltic States: '[T]he Jewish population directed their energies towards the future; it was a hope within the realm of possibility. The non-Jewish group looked back to what had been'.[40]

Something of these tensions emerged in the camp as well. There were complaints that the Lithuanian camps were run by 'venerable nationals' who behaved like landed gentry towards their 'serfs', justifying their action in terms of safeguarding the good name of Lithuania, although a rather different version emerged in the comment by a Ukrainian historian that the camp encouraged 'some of the ideas of western democracy [and] little remained of the stylised symmetry between *pan* [lord] and *khlop* [peasant]'.[41] Perhaps this was a sign of anxiety about social disappointment. The association between displacement and downward social mobility was widely held, including among DPs themselves who had been part of the professional intelligentsia: 'Not long ago we were the avant-garde of democracy, but now we live like the last of the homeless, stand before the gates of military barracks, hoping to get work in the kitchen—washing dishes or cleaning trash cans, in order to have food'.[42]

Amidst the evidence of nationalist sentiment in the DP camps, a contrary tendency can also be detected. As one Lithuanian newspaper put it, 'we, the DPs are the great concern of the world. But the world has become a great concern for us too'.[43] DPs created the 'UNRRA University' in Munich under whose auspices around 2,000 students from 28 different nationalities attended lectures and language

[37] Arendt, *Origins of Totalitarianism*, 293; compare Cohen, *In War's Wake*, 85.

[38] Linda McDowell, *Hard Labour: the Hidden Voices of Latvian Migrant 'Volunteer' Workers* (London: UCL Press, 2005), 19.

[39] Thomas Balkelis, 'Living in the DP Camp: Lithuanian War Refugees in the West, 1944–54', in Gatrell and Baron (eds), *Warlands*, 25–47, at 43.

[40] Holborn, *The International Refugee Organization*, 192.

[41] Balkelis, 'Living in the DP Camp', 36; Ihor V. Zielyk, 'The DP Camp as a Social System', in Isajiw, Boshyk and Senkus (eds), *The Refugee Experience*, 461–70, at 465.

[42] Holian, *Between National Socialism and Soviet Communism*, 18.

[43] Balkelis, 'Living in the DP Camp', 32.

courses between 1945 and 1948. Its rector fostered a cosmopolitan outlook.[44] A group of concerned American citizens who visited camps in Germany ten years later was impressed by the political purpose evident in a workshop that employed 'five people—five different nations. One might think that there would be a new Babel: quite the contrary. Today we can say that the workshop has become a little UNO, in the best sense of the word'. The same ethos emerged in the camp at Stadl Paura in Upper Austria where one visitor anticipated the shape of things to come: 'here the idea of a United Europe has begun to come true'.[45] Nationalist self-expression did not go unchallenged.

We have already alluded to the fact that Allied treatment of DPs created bitterness. One DP wrote to the Canadian relief worker Mabel Geldard-Brown that 'your mention that I must hate the name of DP is right. I do not like it [and] sometimes hate it, because of the many meanings which are attached to it. Usually a DP here is a trouble maker and whether I like it or not I come under the same denomination'.[46] Sometimes DPs adopted an ironic tone, as in a ditty that went the rounds of the camps: 'Would you please excuse me/that I nothing know/I am only a number/in the IRO long row'. Estonians coined a new word, 'Dipiistumine', to describe the process whereby they lost a sense of being connected to the past, while Lithuanians referred to DP as *Dievo paukšteliai*, literally, 'birds of God', a term that entertained the possibility of flight to a better life. Other witty expressions emerged also in a Russian 'DP alphabet' according to which the letter E stood for 'ekhat' ('to go...nowhere'), N for 'no documents' (*net dokumentov*), and S stood for *slukhi* or 'rumours', 'the most panic-inducing of which travel at 300,000 kilometres per second'. Others likened the DP camp to a Soviet collective farm that 'turned us into dull and banal people'. A Lithuanian cartoonist depicted the overcrowded conditions in one camp with a wealth of 'types'—the 'housewives' and the butcher, the professor and the chess players, the lovers and the peeping tom.[47] This rich material suggests a greater capacity for creativity and humorous reflection than many relief workers managed.

REPRESENTATIONS OF DISPLACEMENT: PSYCHOLOGY, CULTURE AND HUMANITARIANISM

Generally speaking, whether they lived in camps or not, DPs were characterized as 'disorderly', demoralized and uncooperative. One official could scarcely hide his distaste for East Europeans 'with their unkempt, unwashed appearance and their makeshift clothes'. The Allied military authorities condemned their 'banditry' and

[44] Anna Holian, 'Displacement and the Postwar Reconstruction of Education: Displaced Persons at the UNRRA University of Munich, 1945–1948' *CEH*, 17, no.2 (2008), 167–95.

[45] Peter Gatrell, *Free World? The Campaign to Save the World's Refugees, 1956–1963* (Cambridge: Cambridge University Press, 2011), 57, 133.

[46] LAC, Mabel Geldard-Brown Fonds, MG30-E497, vol. 3, folder 5, UNRRA, correspondence with DPs and others, 1944–48, dated 15 May 1948, signature indecipherable.

[47] Irina Saburova, *Dipilogicheskaia azbuka* (Munich: n.p., 1946); Murphy, *Flight and Resettlement*, 87.

described them as 'the scum of Europe'; another officer added that 'when suspected of wrong-doing they could of course seldom explain their actions in any language that a military government officer could understand'.[48] But these impoverished attitudes overlook the resourcefulness of refugees who adapted to abnormal economic conditions and devised strategies to avoid detection by Soviet commissars, such as the young Russian schoolteacher who passed herself off as Greek.[49]

Over time arguments about unorthodox and disruptive behaviour or about the options for employment gave way to a more durable concept of helplessness and apathy, a 'psychosis which expresses itself in reluctance to face the responsibilities of a normal community life'.[50] This diagnosis linked displacement to alienation. A leading psychologist suggested that: 'On arrival at some place of safety the individual refugee becomes submerged in a sea of his fellows. Personal problems and personal differences do not count. When conditions get easier he has become merely one segment of an ever-reforming queue'.[51] In this interpretation, the 'refugee problem' was about a state of mind, and the question was how to repair psychological damage. Sociologist Edward Shils suggested that DPs were apathetic, 'cantankerous' and incapable of 'rational political thought' and looked to the DP camps to become 'experiments in group therapy', designed to prepare the displaced for resettlement in a third country or failing that, to allow them to settle in Germany. Displaced children caused particular anxieties. 'I've just seen two Europes', wrote an official from CARE in 1949: 'I visited refugee camps and saw boys and girls of 10, with eyes that looked ten times ten'. According to Shils, 'they live in hordes and live by marauding, they promise to become the new gypsies, undisciplined, untrained, ready for any political disorder and without any sense of communal responsibility'. The children of refugees and DPs needed particular care in order to help them become good citizens.[52]

The concept of 'DP apathy' was rooted in psychological expertise. (Apathy had also been a feature of pre-war discussions about the impact of long-term unemployment.) Murphy attributed this condition to segregation, lack of privacy and 'a sense of dependence' on others. He noted but did not comment on the fact that refugees' energy was mostly taken up with petitioning the authorities for resettlement. Murphy dismissed the democratic credentials of DPs, on the grounds that they originated from countries that 'voluntarily [sic] relinquished democracy between the wars'. In a deliberate juxtaposition, Murphy offered his readers two pictures from the archives of the IRO. On one side was a photograph with the caption:

[48] Proudfoot, *European Refugees*, 177–8; Modris Eksteins, *Walking Since Daybreak: a Story of Eastern Europe, World War II, and the Heart of our Century* (Boston: Houghton Mifflin, 1999), 112, 119.

[49] Harvard University Refugee Interview Project, Schedule A, Vol.35, Case 386.

[50] UNHCR, *Final Report on the Ford Foundation Program for Refugees Primarily in Europe* (Geneva: UNHCR, 1958), 31.

[51] Murphy, *Flight and Resettlement*, photo section III.

[52] Edward A. Shils, 'Social and Psychological Aspects of Displacement and Repatriation' *Journal of Social Issues*, 2, no.3 (1946), 3–18, at 9–10; William J. Cole, Unpublished report, CARE Archives, Box 4, Subseries 1.1 General/historical, Bloomstein's research files; Tara Zahra, 'Lost Children: Displacement, Family, and Nation in Postwar Europe' *JMH*, 81, no.1 (2009), 45–85.

DP Apathy or depression is well illustrated in this picture of a group of Estonians singing a national song as they see their compatriots set out for settlement. The occasion is naturally a melancholy one, probably meaning the splitting of families, but the general impression of sadness is one which was to be found in any Baltic DP camp in 1946 and 1947.[53]

This was a strange gloss on a photo showing a group of women whose stance could just as well be described as one of defiance and affirmation rather than 'melancholy'. The caption overlooked the solidarity that is evident in the picture. It took a heroic stretch of the imagination to interpret this image as conveying 'depression'.

The second photograph displayed a group of men (there are no women this time). The caption read:

Ready for resettlement. The difference from the previous picture lies deeper than the difference in situation and in nationality although both these factors play a part. There is nothing in this picture of a very mixed group of DPs in an emigration camp to identify them as refugees [nor is there in the first picture! PG] unless it be their clothing. They could be a group of workers or repatriates anywhere in central Europe. They are psychologically ready for resettlement and though they may later lose some of their present confidence they do not show here any of the stigmata of the typical refugee.[54]

Murphy clearly made up his mind that these men—he does not give their nationality—were sturdy and strong. Most of them smiled for the camera. They lacked, in his extraordinary choice of words, the 'stigmata' of displacement.

NGOs shared this broad evaluation. In November 1946 the World Council of Churches noted 'a growing depression amongst refugees and DPs [at] having to spend a second winter in the camps or under other abnormal conditions'. This meant more resources for professional services. Military authorities, voluntary agencies and UNRRA employed social workers in a new 'Personal Counselling Service'. In 1948 the IRO took over this service, managing a case-load of DPs who required advice prior to resettlement. By July 1949 IRO officials planned to give each refugee an individual 'plan for his future', something that the understaffed League of Nations could never have contemplated.[55]

Roberto Rossellini's neglected classic, *Stromboli* (1949), presented a psychological study of displacement and resettlement in fictionalized form. The film addressed the soul-searching of a young DP (played by Ingrid Bergman) who marries a Sicilian fisherman—revealingly, Rossellini could not make up his mind if she is supposed to be Czech or Lithuanian, as if it is her 'DP-ness' in general that drives the narrative forward. The central highlight of the film is a breathtaking extended shot of tuna fishing, which embodies the 'traditional' way of life that she finds so oppressive. In the final shot Bergman is shown climbing towards the threatening volcano, as if to suggest that her wartime torment at the hands of Nazis and the

---

[53] Murphy, *Flight and Resettlement*, photo section XII.
[54] Murphy, *Flight and Resettlement*, photo section XIII.
[55] Holborn, *The International Refugee Organization*, 265.

stifling oppression of a closed society can only be resolved by succumbing to an unstoppable force of nature.

Other films too provided a means of personalizing and dramatizing the plight of DPs and camp life. A notable example was Fred Zinnemann's film, *The Search* (1948). Zinnemann visited DP camps in 1947 and was shocked by what he termed the 'remnants of various decimated nationalities'. He filmed among the ruins of German cities, with Montgomery Clift in an early screen role as an American GI who befriends a young Czech refugee boy whom he hopes to take back to the USA. These plans come unstuck when the boy is eventually reunited with his mother, thanks to the energetic efforts of UNRRA. Mother and son make arrangements for repatriation, not resettlement. An obscure film, *Umanità* (Humanity) was shot by Jack Salvatori in 1946 in the makeshift refugee camp in Cinecittà, with the assistance of UNRRA and the Italian Sub-Ministry for Post-war Assistance. Like *The Search*, it had American protagonists and a lost child, a *sciuscà* or shoeshine boy, as well as Italian survivors of the brutal German occupation. The film included shots of the labyrinth of partitioned wooden dormitories on the site of the film studio. Ironically, refugees appropriated this enclosed space just at the time when Italian neo-realist film makers were seeking to abandon the studio and take cameras on to the street. The film critic Antonio Baracco described how 'one solitary displaced person used as his bedside table one of those luminous metal signs on which is written "*Alt! Silenzio, si gira!*" [Stop! Silence, we're rolling]'.[56]

For their part relief workers described an ethos of service that was occasionally tinged with modesty but more commonly entailed putting themselves at the heart of the narrative. Tales of sacrifice, particularly of the comforts of home life, were accompanied by observations of the distressed circumstances of those in DP camps and their corresponding impact on DPs' 'personality'. The novelist Iris Murdoch was employed by UNRRA in Austria in 1946; DPs figured in her early work, *The Flight from the Enchanter* (1956). Kathryn Hulme (1900–81) had even greater success with her account of Wildflecken, originally a SS training camp. Polish DPs renamed it Durzyń, alluding to ancient Slavic tribe of Durzyńcy who lived in Bavaria in the fifth and sixth centuries AD. In *The Wild Place* she described a 'strange half world' and a 'queer inverted life', where 'a tiny band of UN workers brought new hope to more than 100,000 of [Hitler's] homeless and helpless victims, small wandering tribes from Babel'. Hulme did not hesitate to complain about 'professional DPs' whom she described as scroungers. (Absent from her book was any mention of the German expellees who moved in large numbers to the Wildflecken area.) The psychological no less than the physical consequences of war appeared incalculable: '[T]he DPs' prompt obedience to anger and threats seemed almost the worst discovery I had yet made about them'.[57]

---

[56] Noa Steimatsky, 'The Cinecittà Refugee Camp (1944–1950)' *October*, 128 (2009), 22–50; Sharif Gemie and Louise Rees, 'Representing and Reconstructing Identities in the Postwar World: Refugees, UNRRA, and Fred Zinnemann's film, *The Search* (1948)' *International Review of Social History*, 56, no.3 (2011), 441–73.

[57] Hulme, *The Wild Place*, 67–9; see also Adam Seipp, *Strangers in the Wild Place: Refugees, Americans, and a German Town, 1945–1952* (Bloomington: Indiana University Press, 2013).

Other accounts were more probing, both of the circumstances of refugees and of the motivations of relief workers. Roger Wilson, the General Secretary of the Friends Relief Service, remarked that some Quakers 'wanted to find out if our pacifism had any link with physical cowardice, and went looking for danger'.[58] Quakers worked for the spiritual enrichment both of themselves and of displaced persons. Here the imperative of a 'gift of service' reached its apogee, yet not without soul-searching at having to cooperate with the military authorities—the wearing of khaki uniforms caused particular unease. The Quakers sent workers into the field hoping that they would 'live adaptably and imaginatively in unforeseen circumstances, maintaining inward balance in a world full of tensions and frustrations. To develop and maintain a capacity for purposeful living in the midst of degradation, a sense of confident daring in human relationships is of supreme importance'.[59] Quakers castigated relief workers who overstepped the line by adopting a superior attitude towards DPs. Francesca Wilson observed that some women had 'begun well [only to] turn overnight into dictators. Obscure women in their own home towns, they exact obedience from their subjects once they are the Queens of the Distressed Ruritanias'. This was reminiscent of criticism that surfaced during the First World War when Belgian refugees arrived on British shores, a history with which Wilson herself was familiar. Sacrifice and 'simplicity of living' were the qualities she prized. Self-effacement included protestations by relief workers that should 'tell a story from the point of view of the refugees themselves'. This story was one of torment and escape, and of the possibility that freedom might yet be denied by Allied policy. One critic even suggested that the Allies were guilty of 'genocide' because DPs were denied the chance of 'psychic recovery'. Quakers did not go this far, but they protested that DPs were 'softened up' for repatriation by being turned into compliant and dependent objects. DPs were individual human beings, not an anonymous mass.[60]

COMPONENTS OF THE POST-WAR REFUGEE REGIME

The Cold War added a crucial dimension to the post-war refugee crisis by putting paid to bilateral US-Soviet cooperation. The American administration withdrew from UNRRA at the end of 1946, regarding it as too willing to accede to Soviet interests, and advocated a temporary agency to resettle rather than repatriate refugees. The constitution of the new International Refugee Organisation (IRO) was formally agreed on 15 December 1946. Its remit extended to victims of Nazism and Fascism, Spanish Republicans and 'other pre-war exiles' (there were some

---

[58] Roger Wilson, *Authority, Leadership and Concern: a Study in Motive and Administration in Quaker Relief Work* (Allen and Unwin, 1949), 7.

[59] Wilson, *Quaker Relief*, 109; Johannes-Dieter Steinert, *Nach Holocaust und Zwangsarbeit: Britische humanitäre Hilfe in Deutschland* (Osnabrück: Secolo Verlag, 2007).

[60] Francesca M. Wilson, *Advice to Relief Workers* (John Murray, 1945), 7; Leo Stole, 'Why the DPs Can't Wait' *Commentary* (January 1947); Edgar H.S. Chandler, *The High Tower of Refuge: the Inspiring Story of Refugee Relief throughout the World* (Odhams Press, 1959), 11.

550,000 pre-war refugees under IRO aegis), as well as more than one million people who were 'unable to return as a result of events subsequent to the outbreak of war'. The preamble spoke of 'genuine refugees and displaced persons' as an urgent problem. DPs—formally defined as civilians who were 'outside the national boundaries of their country by reason of the war'—would continue to be assisted to return to their country of origin, but if they had 'valid objections' were now to be enabled 'to find new homes elsewhere'. Communist governments denounced the West for protecting 'war criminals' or regarding DPs as a source of cheap labour (see later in this chapter). Of greater long-term significance was the IRO's emphasis on refugees as victims of 'persecution', a doctrine that gave Western governments a hefty stick with which to beat the Soviet bloc for years to come. Political and economic considerations were therefore closely intertwined.[61]

In 1949 the IRO had a pointed exchange with a group of leading intellectuals including Bernard Shaw, Albert Einstein and Bertrand Russell, who suggested that refugees and DPs could be regarded as harbingers of 'world citizenship': 'by sheer force of events they have acquired the feeling of belonging to a community larger than one nation [sic]. History made them citizens of the world, and they should be treated as such'. This did not go down at all well with the IRO: 'Here are people to whom you say, be proud of your statelessness'. Much better, its officials countered, for them to be rid of that status. Paul Weis, the IRO's chief legal adviser, argued that 'it is through his connection with a particular state by the ties of nationality that the individual finds his place in international law'.[62] Weis was on the side of the patriotic intelligentsia, whether in the diaspora or in DP camps. Cosmopolitanism was for him a dirty word.

What would follow the IRO, once post-war resettlement schemes solved the 'DP problem'? Debates in the UN, as in the pre-war League of Nations, revealed a range of views. American officials saw no need for a large international bureaucracy, particularly if it risked undermining the USA's freedom of manoeuvre. Some governments, including the British government, entertained a generous and open-ended commitment to refugee protection but found themselves in a minority. Most member states disliked the idea of a 'blank cheque' that would have to be honoured in the future. Eventually the UN's Economic and Social Council hammered out a compromise in 1950 that created the Office of the United Nations High Commissioner for Refugees (UNHCR) to provide international protection on their behalf and to seek 'permanent solutions' to refugee problems. The relevant legal instrument, the 1951 Refugee Convention, circumscribed the category of refugee and imposed a clear time restriction:

> For the purposes of the present Convention, the term 'refugee' shall apply to any person who...as a result of events occurring [in Europe] before 1 January 1951 and owing to well-founded fear of being persecuted for reasons of race, religion, nationality, membership of a particular social group or political opinion, is outside the country

---

[61] The standard institutional history is Holborn, *The International Refugee Organization*.
[62] Cohen, *In War's Wake*, 89–90.

of his nationality and is unable or, owing to such fear, is unwilling to avail himself of the protection of that country.

This definition discounted claimants who 'merely disliked'—as was said at the time—the political characteristics of the state in which they resided. Crucially, signatories to the Convention undertook to protect recognized refugees from being forcibly returned to their countries of origin ('non-refoulement').[63]

UNHCR had a limited geographical and temporal mandate. International acceptance of the new agency was at best lukewarm. Communist countries refused to participate, on the grounds that the Convention politicized population displacement. Other governments objected to the possibility that it might poke its nose into their business. Like the League of Nations, UNHCR faced serious financial shortcomings, and only a one-off grant from the Ford Foundation helped to keep it afloat in the early years. Many US politicians had reservations about the powers—albeit limited—vested in any international organization that was not subordinated to American interests. The likeable first High Commissioner wanted to give individual refugees 'the feeling that they are protected', but conceded that 'direct contact' with individual refugees might be frustrated by national governments.[64]

There was widespread agreement among signatories to the Convention that UNHCR should be a 'non-operational' body dependent upon voluntary organizations to assist refugees. To long-established agencies such as Save the Children, the AFSC and National Catholic Welfare Conference, and organizations that assisted specific ethnic groups such as the American JDC, were now added Inter-Church Aid (the forerunner of Christian Aid), CARE, the Lutheran World Federation, and many others. These NGOs secured lucrative contracts from the Intergovernmental Committee for European Migration (ICEM) and the US Escapee Program (USEP), both outside the UN framework, as well as from UNHCR, in order to resettle refugees. Without exception each agency proclaimed that it abjured politics in favour of a universal claim to 'humanitarianism'. Yet one only had to scratch the surface to find the politics of intervention. As the Cold War gathered momentum, DPs and refugees were construed as the standard bearers of democracy even if their previous actions were thought to be dubious or even collaborationist.

REFUGEES, RESETTLEMENT AND CITIZENSHIP

Eugene Kulischer, author of an informative study of population movements in Europe during the first half of the twentieth century, argued that 'Germany found itself submerged by a human flood' of refugees and expellees. What was to be

---

[63] Kazimierz Bem, 'The Coming of a "Blank Cheque": Europe, the 1951 Convention and the 1967 Protocol' *IJRL*, 16, no.4 (2004), 609–27; Skran, *Refugees in Inter-War Europe*, 143–4. The 'non-refoulement' provision did not apply to refugees who were deemed to threaten state security or who because of a serious criminal record 'constituted a danger to the community of the country' in which they sought sanctuary.

[64] Goedhart to Paul Weis, 4 February 1951, in Weis Papers, Social Sciences Library, University of Oxford, PW/WR/PUBL/9; Loescher, *UNHCR*, 42; Cohen, *In War's Wake*, 151–4.

done? Land reform was one option, but its effects were limited by the number of 'claimants'. Italy, economically backward, war-torn and home to a large refugee population, was in even more dire straits. The preferred solution was to encourage emigration to Canada, Australia and South America. Without planning—the opposite to the 'elementary forces' of 'migratory currents'—Kulischer believed that there was a risk of war: 'to admit immigration is better than to be obliged to repel invasion'. In a phrase evoking the American New Deal he called for a 'TVA of human migratory currents'.[65] Planned migration gained plenty of adherents by the late 1940s, and the ICEM, which was dominated by the Americans, promoted planned migration from 'over-populated' countries in Europe that were believed to be vulnerable to social unrest and political radicalism.

As repatriation lost its appeal for Western officialdom, DPs were despatched to new destinations. One 'durable solution' in 1947 envisaged the creation of a huge Ukrainian 'colony' in Canada or Argentina. Relief workers spoke up for DPs who wished to move to North America and Australia, formulating their appeals with a 'human interest' angle rather than concentrating on legal formulas. Recruiting officers subjected DPs to various tests that reminded them of Nazi practice. Around 400,000 DPs travelled to the USA under the Displaced Persons Act that came into force in June 1948. Canada took 160,000. Others went to Western Europe, Latin America and Australia, where they became a point of reference for those other immigrants known as 'Ten Pound Poms' who were admitted under the assisted places scheme, and who sometimes complained that they were treated as 'bleedin' DPs'.[66]

Other schemes enabled Poles and Balts to work in Belgian mines and Lancashire's cotton mills. The British devised two schemes entitled 'Westward Ho' (for DPs in general) and 'Balt Cygnets', for women to be employed on domestic duties in hospitals. Belgium mounted 'Operation Black Diamond' and Norway admitted 400 Jewish DPs under the title of 'Northern Lights'. The new recruits to the UK economy were labelled 'European Volunteer Workers' (EVWs). Some 20,000 young women arrived in Britain between 1946 and 1950 to take jobs in domestic service and in textiles. These schemes did not go unchallenged. One attack concentrated on the qualities of the DPs. An editorial in the *Daily Mirror* ('Let them be displaced') complained that 'other countries had taken the cream and left us most of the scum. They must now be rounded up and sent back'. The *New Statesman* called for a 'rigid selection' of Ukrainians, in order 'to exclude the illiterate, the mentally deficient, the sick, the aged, the politically suspect, and the behaviourally disruptive. [We should] clear out the rubbish amongst those who have already come'.[67] A very different critique came from Quakers who denounced this 'slave market horribly reminiscent of another similar offer made by the Germans not so

---

[65] Kulischer, *Europe on the Move*, 254, 266, 290, 319–25, referring to the Tennessee Valley Authority.

[66] A. James Hammerton and Alistair Thomson, *Ten Pound Poms: Australia's Invisible Migrants* (Manchester: Manchester University Press, 2005), 179–80.

[67] Diana Kay and Robert Miles, *Refugees or Migrant Workers? European Volunteer Workers in Britain, 1946–1951* (Routledge, 1992), 116–17; *Daily Mirror*, 20 July 1948.

very long ago', while Soviet officials condemned the IRO as an 'employment agency' enabling 'the West to enrich itself by resettling the so-called refugees to the countries making the highest bid for their labour'.[68]

Resettlement plans went ahead. Louise Holborn asserted that 'planned migration'—the resettlement of more than one million displaced persons between 1947 and 1951—counted as the IRO's 'greatest achievement'. Where earlier attempts at resettlement had been undertaken by refugees themselves, the IRO coordinated the efforts of 18 member governments. The expansion of the post-war global economy helped translate these plans into practice, but they required exploratory missions both to Germany and Austria and to areas of potential resettlement such as Latin America, and—for DPs—interviews, medical examinations, 'selection' and 'orientation'.[69]

DPs nevertheless had to show that they merited resettlement. Ostensibly non-political organizations such as the World Council of Churches (WCC) collected 'human interest stories' of refugees who fled Communist rule in Bulgaria, Romania and Albania. For example, Haki F., born in Albania in 1919 and arriving in Greece via Yugoslavia in 1953, stated that 'people in Albania are only waiting for the moment they will be assisted to start a revolution against the present regime; war has never been over for them. Misery, terrorism and uncertainty of life have constituted the daily routine of the average Albanian since 1945'. He planned to migrate to Australia and resume his life as a farmer. The WCC described him as 'brave and conscientious', a fitting candidate for resettlement. Other stories told of ethnic Greeks who fled from Asia Minor to Romania in 1922, thence to Greece to escape persecution by the Communist government in 1947. Angela H., who left for Australia under the auspices of the USEP to join her son, exemplified the possibility of 'starting again', beginning with a formulaic account of starvation, harassment, torture, expropriation and eventual 'rescue'. This served a Cold War purpose and established a link with past episodes of displacement.[70]

The next big challenge came from Hungary, where the outbreak of revolution in 1956 produced the most dramatic refugee-generating crisis in continental Europe between the end of the Second World War and the collapse of Yugoslavia in 1991. In the aftermath of the 1956 uprising, nearly 190,000 people crossed the border to neighbouring Austria by early 1957. Another 20,000 refugees made their way to Yugoslavia, but the difficult conditions in refugee camps caused them to leave for Austria as well. The West's response was governed not only by ideas of rescuing Hungarians from persecution but also by the fear that social instability in Austria could encourage political radicalism. Refugees were portrayed as victims of communist tyranny who had escaped 'carnage and deportations' in order to find 'liberty and justice'. UNHCR incorporated Hungarian refugees within its mandate, even though the Convention referred to events that took place in Europe prior to

[68] Margaret McNeill, *By the Rivers of Babylon: a Story of Relief Work among the Displaced Persons of Europe* (Bannisdale Press, 1950), 202–16; Proudfoot, *European Refugees*, 401.
[69] Holborn, *The International Refugee Organization*, 366, 369, 373–4.
[70] WCC Archives, File 425.1.043, Human Interest Stories.

1 January 1951. Acting on legal advice UNHCR decided that the Hungarians were eligible on the grounds that their 'persecution' could be traced back to the Communist revolution in 1947–48. UNHCR now became the primary organization for coordinating international assistance to Hungarian refugees and administering relief in adjacent countries.

Hungarian refugees were placed in more than 250 makeshift refugee camps in Austria. The government called upon Austrian citizens to donate money to support the refugees; much was made of the need for Catholic solidarity. In a short while, however, complaints were made about the burden that the refugees placed upon the public purse. They were described as economic migrants rather than political refugees and as a 'flood' that threatened to 'inundate' Austria. When Hungarians entered the coffee bar or tried to set up a small business, no longer content to play the prescribed role of poor and helpless refugees, public opinion turned against them. Other problems arose because 'some Hungarians also told lies to the authorities, to members of relief organizations; how could they know—trained as they were in dissimulation during the years of terror—that here evasions and lies were no longer necessary?'[71] Psychologists reported that refugees lacked the character to become full citizens of new Austria. Here too a tension emerged between the valorization of refugees as heroic escapees and their 'confused' psychology.[72]

Although some refugees were repatriated to Hungary following protracted negotiations, the Hungarian 'brain drain' brought significant economic benefits to host countries in the West.[73] This point surfaced ten years on in a dispute between UNHCR and the Hungarian authorities concerning refugees who had fallen sick and wished to return to Hungary. The Hungarian Ministry of Foreign Affairs responded icily to a request for sympathetic consideration: 'The Hungarians of 1956 who were admitted to Western European and overseas countries were checked and rechecked by those countries which meant to get important economic and even political gains. It seems to be only proper that the receiving country which benefited from the influx of Hungarians should bear also the burden of a few cases where their selection was not quite happy'. He added that, 'seen from the other angle, it does not seem warranted that Hungary, i.e. the Hungarian people which remained here and suffered a loss by the mass emigration of 1956, should take care of those who got into situations like Mrs X. [To admit her] would prove to be inhuman towards those ill and poor who need subsistence in Hungary.'[74]

---

[71] *Migration News*, 7, no. 1 (January–February 1958); Brigitta Zierer, 'Willkommene Ungarnflüchtlinge 1956?', in Gernot Heiss and Oliver Rathkolb (eds), *Asylland wider Willen: Flüchtlinge in Österreich im europäischen Kontext seit 1914* (Vienna: Jugend und Volk, 1995), 157–71, at 163, 169–70.

[72] Susan Carruthers, *Cold War Captives: Imprisonment, Escape and Brainwashing* (Berkeley: University of California Press, 2009).

[73] The Hungarian diaspora sent over photos of American film stars and cars so that refugees would learn something of the culture of the country that was admitting them. Carl Bon Tempo, *Americans at the Gate: the United States and Refugees during the Cold War* (Princeton: Princeton University Press, 2008), 66–75.

[74] Endfe Ustor, Ministry of Foreign Affairs, to Francisco Urrutia, UNHCR regional Representative, New York, 28 August 1965, Fonds UNHCR 11, sub-fonds 1, file 6/1/1 HUN.

From his point of view, those who left the country were 'economic migrants', not refugees, an argument which as we have seen came to be shared by officials in the West.

The Hungarian refugee crisis is significant for several reasons. It extended UNHCR's remit. Officials in Geneva argued that Hungarian refugees fell within its mandate, since although the Convention excluded events that happened after 1 January 1951, it was not meant to 'exclude persons who may become refugees at a later date as a result of events before then or as a result of after-effects which occurred at a later date'. UNHCR held that the term 'events' could relate to the establishment of the People's Democratic Republic in Hungary in 1946.[75] Second, UNHCR helped several thousand refugees to go back to Hungary, and its role as a mediator anticipated other kinds of action. Third, many Hungarian refugees were regarded as having the capacity to 'adapt', having exercised a conscious choice to flee from tyranny: 'rather than being treated as persons in need of "welfare", from the outset the responsibility for adapting to their new society was placed squarely on them'.[76] They were expected to demonstrate their potential as citizens.

This left the 'hard core'. This demeaning term was already in circulation by 1946 and referred to those whose claims for resettlement had been turned down on grounds of physical or mental disability, or for having a criminal record or for other reasons. Since many families chose to stay together, a 'black mark' against one member had serious consequences. Irrespective of their achievements in resettling refugees and DPs, the IRO and UNHCR failed to address their needs, which the US regarded as best met through economic growth and 'integration' in Germany and Austria. Personal acts of generosity provided for schemes such as the 'Homeless European Land Program (HELP)' which the American actor Don Murray and his wife Hope Lange established in 1956, buying up land in Sardinia on behalf of refugees in the hope that 'as this community grows and becomes self-supporting, it will stimulate the founding of new communities and that the refugees themselves will return a portion of their earnings to bring in other refugees'.[77] Their project was backed by the Food and Agriculture Organisation, CARE, and by Protestant charities who regarded it as an object lesson in resettling refugees and encouraging migrants from 'over-populated' parts of South-eastern Europe to contribute to long-term development.[78]

A different approach emerged in 1958 when three aspiring young Conservative British politicians and journalists announced their intention to launch a year-long campaign to draw public attention to the plight of the world's refugees. Although aware of recent events in Hungary, they were particularly concerned about the legacy of the Second World War which had left tens of thousands of displaced

---

[75] 'Eligibility under the [1951] Convention of Refugees who left Hungary because of the Events of 1956', 2 September 1959, Fonds UNHCR 11, sub-fonds 1, file 6/1/1 HUN.

[76] Barbara Harrell-Bond, 'The Experience of Refugees as Recipients of Aid', in Ager (ed.), *Refugees*, 136–68, at 151.

[77] *Refugees in Europe, 1957–1958* (New York, 1959), 51.

[78] MS Eng. c.4659, Papers of John Alexander Sinclair (1906–88), UN Career Records Project, Special Collections, Bodleian Library, Oxford.

people in camps in Europe. They convinced the UN to lend its support to a 'World Refugee Year' (WRY), to include refugees in Hong Kong and the Middle East. The new UN High Commissioner for Refugees, Auguste Lindt, summarized its aim as seeking to 'foster a world-wide movement of sympathy for refugees by acquainting the public at large with all the economic and social aspects of the problem and by opening up vistas of progress'. WRY was intended to 'attract public attention to refugees as a social and humanitarian problem on a strictly non-political basis'. In addition to promoting 'personal knowledge' of the multitude of 'unknown citizens', the aims were to swell the coffers of NGOs and to encourage third countries to overcome their reluctance to admit elderly or sick DPs. This emphasis on generating public goodwill, loosening purse-strings and, where possible, finding 'solutions' set the tone for the campaign. In truth, the campaign was driven by a strong sense of Western guilt and a willingness to atone for failing to prevent the creation of the 'hard core'.[79]

WRY was conceived as a bold and imaginative campaign, characterized by the use of specially commissioned documentaries, plays, exhibitions and advertising. Stamps played an important part in raising money and depicting the 'refugee world'. There had been precedents, although they were overprinted rather than original designs: Norway issued stamps to raise funds for the Nansen International Office for Refugees in 1935, and France did likewise in 1936 and 1937 in support of refugees from Nazi persecution. China issued stamps in aid of 'war refugees' in 1944 and the PRC followed suit in 1954 on behalf of 'the flight of Chinese from Vietnam'. The Dominican Republic issued stamps on behalf of Hungarian refugees. WRY stamps had an instructive purpose, allowing 'the refugee story [to be] told, a story always beginning with flight and despair, and ending, sometimes, in hope and resettlement'. One popular image was the Holy Family. The Vatican reproduced Fra Angelico's 'Flight into Egypt'. Jean Cocteau designed a first-day cover that echoed the religious theme. France chose a design of a young girl drawn against the background of a ruined city, reminiscent of scenes of devastation in Europe at the end of the Second World War. The US stamp showed a stark wall against which refugees were silhouetted, 'facing (as the publicity stated) down a long dark corridor towards a bright exit, symbolizing escape from the darkness of want and oppression into the brightness of a new life'. The imagery reinforced the point that WRY enabled refugees to replace despair with hope, to enjoy a trajectory that would take them from the deplorable camp to a place of comfort and modernity.

Fake 'refugee camps' in London, Geneva, Manchester and other cities highlighted the conditions in which refugees were forced to live; the camps were immensely popular with visitors. Photographs added to the drama of displacement and the 'iconography of predicament'. Yet refugees were not expected to speak. Rather they looked out from photographs or figured as part of the background scenery when visiting celebrities reported on their plight and needs, as when the

---

[79] See Gatrell, *Free World?*

president of the Canadian Committee for WRY was despatched to Geneva with instructions to be photographed 'in some sort of refugee setting'.[80] Occasionally a more reflective voice was heard above the hubbub. A journalist for the *Manchester Guardian* wrote that 'sharply drawn portraits of men, women and children living in the refugee camps of Europe bring one face to face with highly individual persons, not all admirable or even likeable, but all intensely alive and full of character, real people evoking a response of sympathetic interest and concern; whereas to speak in general terms of "the refugees" may prompt only the image of a faceless indistinguishable horde, moving pity without hope or help'.[81] Drawing attention to each human being implicitly reaffirmed the importance that the Refugee Convention attached to the individual.

CONCLUSIONS

Far from bringing them to an end, peace only multiplied the crises of displacement. These crises cast a long shadow over the lives of millions. The Nazi regime bequeathed the Allies the problem of repatriating forced labourers to France, Belgium, Poland, Ukraine and other countries. Older vintages of refugees also faced a dismal prospect. Exiled Spaniards who fled during the Spanish Civil War abandoned hopes of returning to Spain; in 1950 more than 110,000 remained on French territory. Other situations, however, were of the Allies' making, notably the expulsion of ethnic Germans. The paradox was that the Western powers simultaneously insisted on the right of individual refugees as defined by the 1951 Convention to be acknowledged as victims of persecution, whilst trampling on the rights of German expellees. The Convention itself marked an important advance: '[I]t is not [according to a leading Quaker] a very noble or liberal document, but it is a worthy step forward in human progress or it can be so, if it is made to live and work, in that it establishes certain vital human rights for a most helpless, forlorn and unprotected segment of humanity'.[82]

Western governments took steps to resettle refugees and DPs in third countries or to integrate them locally. The shift from UNRRA to IRO operations in 1947 marked this new dispensation, a far cry from the situation in 1945 when Allied governments and military officers envisaged offloading them by means of rapid and often brutal repatriation. DPs who protested this policy acquired a reputation for being 'displeased people'. Tens of thousands remained in camps in Germany, Austria and Italy until they died. Others were eventually enabled to move to better accommodation, but in some cases this took more than a decade. In 1951 the UN spoke of a 'final solution' to the refugee crisis in Europe, before adopting 'durable solution' as a less emotive term, less capable of being confused with the Holocaust.

[80] Canadian Committee for WRY, Box 4, Folder 1, Bob Torrance to Douglas Deane, World Alliance of YMCAs, 8 June 1959.
[81] 'Refugees are People', *The Guardian*, 3 May 1960.
[82] Colin Bell, 'Toward Human Rights for Refugees' *AFSC Bulletin* (December 1951).

Post-war support for refugees reflected Cold War considerations, although the meanings attached to displacement were contested and fluid. UNRRA regarded those who resisted repatriation as a nuisance, but by the late 1940s and early 1950s refugees were being re-valorized as emblems of resilience in the teeth of Communist domination in Eastern Europe, as victims of persecution, and as prospective citizens. At least, this was true up to a point. Insistence on individual persecution as the chief criterion for recognition represented a significant departure in legal practice, and an indication that human rights were beginning to make an appearance in international law. Beyond legal corridors, however, the individual continued to be amalgamated within the broad entity of 'refugee'. NGOs were really not interested in the ordinary person except as the embodiment of totalitarian oppression or as the author of a brief history demonstrating the worthiness of humanitarian intervention. Public fixation with the category lumped refugees together. Everyone—NGOs, privileged citizens, diasporic organizations—looked on refugees as a single category, 'regardless of their vast variations in personal background, motives for leaving, reasons for escape, and plans for the future'.[83]

Expert knowledge accompanied the crisis of post-war displacement. It created opportunities for the accumulation of knowledge about refugees. Social workers, psychologists and others flocked to the scene under the aegis of UNRRA, the IRO and NGOs. Their findings were sometimes very wide of the mark. Specifically the diagnosis of 'DP apathy' demonstrated an extraordinary myopia in view of the tactics that refugees devised in order to survive. Such pathologization formed part of a broader litany of complaint. Refugees and DPs who decided to 'dig in' and resist attempts at repatriation constituted a problem either by virtue of their assertiveness or because they were 'lazy'. Displaced persons could not get it right: too much determination, and they were deemed unruly or ungrateful; too little, and they were regarded as helpless or even 'norm-less' people with a 'low predisposition to change'. Such assumptions revealed more about professional expertise than they did about refugees.[84]

Expert knowledge was one thing. It may have accurately captured the underlying sentiments of those adults for whom incarceration manifested itself in feelings of loss, estrangement and boredom. But the evidence does not point in a single direction. Youngsters might have a very different perspective of camp life. One DP reminisced that 'we lived there for three years. I was a teenager and there was a lot going on'. For her the DP camp held exciting prospects. Another Latvian informant who was placed in a camp in Mannheim told her interviewer, 'I grew up there'. A 16-year-old Austrian Jewish boy, when asked how he felt when he had to leave his home country, replied: 'I felt curious as to what the rest of the world was like. I was rather glad that we had to leave, because I thought were it not for Hitler's

---

[83] Daniel and Knudsen, 'Introduction', in Daniel and Knudsen (eds), *Mistrusting Refugees*, 3.

[84] Professor Fricis Gulbis, May 1946, UNRRA Archives, S-0408-0007-02, Germany Mission, Welfare, DP Study Centre Hamburg, 20 February 1946–23 April 1947; Judith Shuval, 'Refugees: Adjustment and Assimilation', *Encyclopedia of the Social Sciences* (New York: Macmillan, 1968), 373–7; Shephard, *The Long Road Home*, 267–8; Salomon, *Refugees in the Cold War*, 153.

invasion, I would never have been able to see the world'. As the dust settled, however, the prevailing view amongst social workers and psychologists was that displacement and the DP camp had been entirely detrimental in weakening family ties and parental discipline.[85]

While the UN and many NGOs were committed to 'rehabilitation' as the basis for economic recovery in the short term, Quakers understood this to be a means of fostering better relations between human beings. From this standpoint, material welfare and emotional sustenance required an atmosphere of mutual respect. This admirable reflexivity corresponds to the injunctions of critics of the modern refugee regime. Quakers also pointed to other shortcomings, including the absence of analysis of the circumstances that created conflict in human society. This made them harbingers of a critical discourse. But they were only one element in a growing humanitarian Babel.

The most significant institutional development in the long term was the emergence of UNHCR as a major player on the international stage, with a mandate to protect refugees who came within the terms of the Convention. This was by no means evident in its early years during which it struggled to gain funding and recognition. To be sure, it received an early accolade when it was awarded the Nobel Peace Prize in 1954 (the funds were used to liquidate the refugee camp on the Greek island of Tinos). Yet only in the aftermath of the Hungarian revolution did UNHCR begin to gain legitimacy, and only with the crisis in Algeria did it begin to spread its global wings. By the early 1960s UNHCR spoke of fresh responsibilities, and there was already talk of the need for the Commissioner to free himself from the constraints of the 1951 Convention and use his 'good offices'. As one well-informed insider said, 'for years nations lulled themselves into the belief that the unending stream of refugees torn from the fabric of society was a transitory phenomenon'.[86] As it dawned that refugees were a permanent feature of the postwar scene, UNHCR could justify its rationale and claim greater authority.

Other histories and other trajectories were connected to the geo-politics in the aftermath of the war. One aspect of this dynamic was the role of East European exiles in supporting the USA during the Cold War, although their political leverage should not be exaggerated. More crucial still were the claims of Jewish DPs to a place of safety and thus to a 'homeland' in Palestine. Zionist leaders expressed pleasure that thousands of young Jewish men wanted to leave the camps and enlist in the armed forces. The IRO did not stand in their way. Their confrontation with the indigenous Arab population with whom their fate became closely interwoven forms the backdrop to the following chapter.

---

[85] McDowell, *Hard Labour*, 79; Jaroszyńska-Kirchmann, *The Exile Mission*, 68, 95–7; Tara Zahra, ' "The Psychological Marshall Plan": Displacement, Gender, and Human Rights after World War II' *Central European History*, 44, no.1 (2011), 37–62, at 54.

[86] James M. Read, 'The UN and Refugees: Changing Concepts' *International Conciliation*, 537 (1962), 1–60, at 5–6.

4

'Nothing Except Commas'

Jews, Palestinians, and the Torment of Displacement

I tried to put the displacement between parentheses, to put a last period [full stop] in a long sentence of the sadness of history, personal and public history. But I see nothing except commas

(Mourid Barghouti)

INTRODUCTION

The Palestinian poet Mourid Barghouti (b.1944) expresses the forlorn feelings of someone whose displacement has no end.[1] His poignant formulation captures the acute and overwhelming burden shouldered by refugees. Barghouti alludes to the events of 1948 that came to be known among Palestinians as the 'great disaster' (al-Nakba), as a result of which many of them lost their homes and either fled to neighbouring states or became internally displaced within the new state of Israel. The hope for a 'full stop' in the sense of being allowed to reclaim their property and forge a state dominated Palestinian politics through to the present day, inflecting the entire politics of the Middle East. These politics were embroiled with the equally strong attachment of Zionists to a state that guaranteed the security of Jews, a sentiment owing a great deal to the catastrophe that was the Holocaust. Choosing Palestine for their ultimate destination paved the way for a series of dramatic confrontations with the majority Arab population.[2]

In these ways, two seemingly distinct 'episodes' in population displacement—the persecution and elimination of European Jews, on the one hand, and the displacement of Palestinians after the Second World War on the other—were inextricably linked. As the poet Mahmoud Darwish put it, 'what brings us together is at the same time a point of conflict between us'.[3] To establish this association between Palestinian Arab and Jewish history it is necessary to recognize their respective ideas of a homeland, the shared sense of being victimized, and their dual aspiration to

---

[1] Mourid Barghouti, *I Saw Ramallah* (Bloomsbury, 2004), 163.

[2] James L. Gelvin, *The Israel-Palestine Conflict: One Hundred Years of War* (Cambridge: Cambridge University Press, 2005); Chatty, *Displacement and Dispossession*, 180–230; Seteney Shami (ed.) *Population Displacement and Resettlement: Development and Conflict in the Middle East* (New York: Center for Migration Studies, 1994).

[3] Barbara M. Parmenter, *Giving Voice to Stones: Place and Identity in Palestinian Literature* (Austin: Texas University Press, 1994), 3.

seek restitution through 'return'. The Zionist search for 'a land without people for a people without land' was refined under the British mandate in Palestine. The idea gained ground among the surviving remnants of European Jewry (*She'erit Hapleta*) who had little prospect of a tolerable life in Eastern Europe. Palestinian nationalism was by contrast a less developed ideology: most Palestinians regarded themselves as members of a specific village, rarely as part of a broader Arab 'nation'.

Both currents of nationalist thought gained strength from arguments over territory, population, archaeology and history—a 'struggle between two memories' in Darwish's words. Palestinian nationalist doctrine resisted the erosion by others of the rights of peasant farmers to their land: '[T]here is no possibility of the Arabs accepting as consolation for the loss of their homeland a few more cinemas and a few more dentists', as a pro-Palestinian MP remarked in the British House of Commons in July 1939.[4] One strand of Zionism envisaged the relocation of Palestinian Arabs to facilitate the settlement of more Jewish immigrants in an independent state. The ensuing refugee crisis affected 750,000 Palestinians who, it was said, 'have become refugees on the borders of our own country to make room for other refugees from many parts of the world'.[5]

These intertwined histories can also be brought together by focusing on Jewish and Palestinian diasporas. The worldwide mobilization of Jewish opinion that extended from continental Europe to North America unleashed a vision of a national home and profoundly altered the region's politics, even if this project never gained the support of all Jews. The displacement of Palestinians in turn created a diaspora that likewise demonstrated a remarkable political and cultural energy, albeit without surmounting political differences. But no diaspora is an unchanging entity. In the last 20 years the Palestinian diaspora has been badly affected by the lack of economic opportunities in Arab states and the need to look for work further afield. This plebeian experience is a world apart from that of the exiled Palestinian elite.

A striking feature of the commemoration of Palestinian displacement is an insistence upon collective loss. Palestinians initially described their flight as *al-hujayj*, meaning an escape from grave danger or as *sanat al-hijra*, the 'year of migration', referring to the flight of the Prophet Muhammad from Mecca to Medina. The term, *al-Naqba* (or *Nakba*), which construed the events of 1948 as a national disaster, was disseminated by Palestinian historian Arif al-Arif in the late 1950s in a six-volume history published in Beirut. Commemorating dispossession and displacement increased following the 1967 Six-Day War and continued, notwithstanding setbacks such as the Israeli army's dismantling of the archives of the Palestine Research Centre in Beirut. Palestinians in Israel as well as in the diaspora commemorate 'Nakba Day' on 15 May.[6] *Nakba* helped to legitimize

[4] Schechtman, *Population Transfers in Asia*, 94.
[5] Per-Olow Anderson, *They Are Human Too: a Photographic Essay on the Palestine Arab Refugees* (Chicago: Henry Regnery, 1957), 23.
[6] Salman Rushdie, *Imaginary Homelands: Essays and Criticism, 1981–1991* (Granta, 1992), 179; Nur Masalha, *The Palestine Nakba: Decolonising History, Narrating the Subaltern, Reclaiming Memory* (Zed Books, 2012), 241–5.

Palestinian militancy. An obvious point of comparison is the *Shoah* or Holocaust, which underpins Israel's claims to national legitimacy. Here again the two histories converge.

ANTECEDENTS OF THE REFUGEE CRISIS

To make sense of these upheavals we have to retrace our steps. Attempts to resettle Jewish refugees in Western Europe and North America were hindered by racial prejudice and bureaucratic indifference. In the Dominican Republic the dictator Rafael Trujillo hoped simultaneously to improve his international image, to introduce more advanced farming methods and to dilute the country's Afro-Caribbean profile by relocating 100,000 Jews. The scheme failed.[7] Shanghai held out more promising prospects. By 1939 2,600 Jewish refugees were living there; several thousand Jews from Poland and elsewhere added to their number in 1940–41. Refugee camps soon became overcrowded. One refugee welcomed 'their deep sense of human dignity and refusal to accept the standards of the German concentration camp as the model by which to measure human living conditions'. Enterprising men and women set up small businesses repairing bicycles or providing other services. Other developments were less positive; there were complaints of petty crime and family breakdown. Conditions deteriorated during the Japanese occupation, although some businesses carried on. The Allied victory in 1945 enabled refugees to recover a semblance of normality and to prepare for a new life in the USA, Australia, Palestine and even Germany.[8]

The most serious initiative to improve the fortunes of European Jewry took place elsewhere. During the First World War the British Foreign Secretary Arthur Balfour announced that the government 'viewed with favour the establishment in Palestine of a national home for the Jewish people', provided that it did not 'prejudice the civil and religious rights of existing non-Jewish communities in Palestine'. Zionists made a direct link between Jewish settlement and what they regarded as the cultural and economic retardation of the indigenous Arab population. Dorothy Thompson wrote that Jewish settlement in Palestine offered 'a really grandiose scheme for developing backward territories with displaced Europeans'. Visiting Palestine in 1934, the liberal British parliamentarian Eleanor Rathbone, later to become a resolute critic of government policy towards persecuted Jews in Nazi Europe, was so incensed by what she took to be the demeaning treatment of women in Palestine that she asked rhetorically: '[W]ould it matter to the progress of civilisation if all the Arabs were drowned in the Mediterranean?', in order to

---

[7] Simone Gigliotti, '"Acapulco in the Atlantic": Revisiting Sosúa, a Jewish Refugee Colony in the Caribbean' *Immigrants and Minorities*, 24, no.1 (2006), 22–50; Marion A. Kaplan, *Dominican Haven: the Jewish Refugee Settlement in Sosua, 1940–1945* (New York: Museum of Jewish Heritage, 2008).

[8] Felix Gruenberger, 'The Jewish Refugees in Shanghai' *Jewish Social Studies*, 12, no.4 (1950), 329–48, at 330; Marcia R. Ristaino, *Port of Last Resort: the Diaspora Communities of Shanghai* (Stanford: Stanford University Press, 2001).

leave the field clear for 'progressive Zionism'.[9] Economic backwardness—deeply disturbing when given the Rathbone treatment—figured in the depiction of Palestine's mosquito-infested swamps, which became a site for drainage schemes that promised to eradicate malaria and also sustained an idea of progressive Zionism and contributed to a discourse of the 'strong and healthy Jew'. Hannah Arendt offered a different perspective when she bemoaned the consequences of separate economic spheres: '[W]hat had been the pride of the Jewish homeland, that it had not been based upon exploitation, turned into a curse when the final test came. The flight of the Arabs would not have been possible and not have been welcomed by the Jews if they had lived in a common economy'.[10]

British civil servants, missionaries and others, including Zionists, discussed at length the implications of organized immigration and the 'absorptive capacity' of Palestine. These debates took place against the background of a revolt by Palestinian labourers in Haifa in 1936 that lasted until 1939 and embittered relations between Jews and Arabs. The British, alarmed at the ensuing political and social instability, began to contemplate renouncing the Mandate. In 1937 a commission of enquiry under William Peel recommended the territorial division of Palestine between Jews and Palestinians. Its members cited the consequences of the Lausanne Convention, which (they agreed) had removed the 'ulcer' of communal antagonism, promoting harmony between Greeks and Turks. Given that Peel believed Palestine to be 'diseased', he advocated surgery in the form of an organized transfer of population.[11] Under the proposed partition a Jewish state would be assigned approximately one-fifth of Palestine. Peel's recommendations were hotly contested by Arab public opinion, and overturned by a government White Paper in 1939 that proposed strict limits on Jewish immigration in order to prevent the creation of an Arab landless proletariat, and advocated the creation of a unitary Palestinian state within a decade. Unsurprisingly this encountered strong opposition in turn from Jewish leaders.[12]

Analogous debates about displacement had already taken place among Zionists whose ultimate goal was a separate Jewish state, with a clear majority Jewish population. Israel Zangwill stated in the early 1920s:

> We cannot allow the Arabs to block so valuable a piece of historic reconstruction. And therefore we must generally persuade them to 'trek'. After all, they have all Arabia with its million square miles. There is no particular reason for the Arabs to cling to these

[9] Susan Pederson, *Eleanor Rathbone and the Politics of Conscience* (New Haven: Yale University Press, 2004), 262; Dorothy Thompson, *Refugees: Anarchy or Organisation?* (New York: Random House, 1938), 102–3.

[10] Hannah Arendt, *The Jewish Writings* (New York: Schocken Books, 2007), 444; Sandra Sufian, *Healing the Land and the Nation: Malaria and the Zionist Project in Palestine, 1920–1947* (Chicago: Chicago University Press, 2007).

[11] *Palestine Royal Commission*, Cmd. 5479 (HMSO, 1937), 390–1; Ted Swedenburg, *Memories of Revolt: the 1936–1939 Rebellion and the Palestinian National Past* (Minneapolis: University of Minnesota Press, 1995).

[12] Anglican leaders agreed. Gardiner H. Shattuck, 'Weeping over Jerusalem: Anglicans and Refugee Relief in the Middle East, 1895–1950' *Anglican and Episcopal History*, 80, no.2 (2011), 117–41.

few kilometres. 'To fold their tents and silently steal away' is their proverbial habit: let them exemplify it now.[13]

This view commanded some support elsewhere. A British MP suggested transferring Palestinian Arabs to Iraq, and Sir John Hope Simpson envisaged that the Palestinian peasant would 'always migrate to any spot where he thinks he can find work'.[14] David Ben-Gurion, the future Prime Minister of Israel, maintained in 1944 that '[the] transfer of Arabs is easier than any other type of transfer. There are Arab states in the area and it is clear that if the [Palestinian] Arabs are sent [to Arab countries] this will better their situation and not the contrary'.[15] Such 'transfer thinking' gained ground among a younger generation of Jewish settlers. Maps and statistics formed part of this strategy to redesign Palestine, its Arab population already being written out of the picture.

Jews in Europe were of course literally being erased—persecuted by the Nazis after 1933 and exterminated in the course of the Second World War. Only a small proportion survived. The victorious Allies deliberated over their future. Jewish Displaced Persons were initially not recognized as a separate category but instead assigned to camps according to their official nationality as Poles, Ukrainians and so on, a tactic meant to encourage them to repatriate but also (as was said) to 'avoid creating the impression that the Jews are to be singled out for special treatment, as such action will tend to perpetuate the distinctions of Nazi racial theory'.[16] The American authorities relented and established separate camps for Jews, but the British stood their ground. Few Jewish survivors wished to leave the camps and return to their homes in Eastern Europe. This had nothing to do with the prospect of a communist takeover and everything to do with a persistent sense of vulnerability. Emigration to Palestine or to North or South America held attraction because these paths were well-trodden.[17]

Surviving Jewish DPs were incarcerated in a variety of accommodation: former military barracks, converted hotels, apartment blocks, schools, hospitals and monasteries. They regarded the camps as an indictment of Allied foot-dragging and a mark of the failure of American Jewish organizations to make strongly enough the case for their resettlement. A minority demanded that Germans be forced to give up their homes, but American officers insisted that 'two wrongs don't make a right [and] they must help rehabilitate themselves'.[18] Some DPs found themselves behind barbed wire—'liberated, but not free' was a common refrain. In a famous report for President Truman, Earl G. Harrison, former US Commissioner of Immigration, described the dreadful conditions in which they

---

[13] Karl Sabbagh, *Palestine: A Personal History* (London: Atlantic Books, 2006), 212.

[14] Schechtman, *Population Transfers*, 91, 100.

[15] Benny Morris, 'Revisiting the Palestinian Exodus of 1948', in Eugene Rogan and Avi Shlaim (eds), *The War for Palestine: Rewriting the History of 1948* (Cambridge: Cambridge University Press, 2001), 37–59, at 47.

[16] Angelika Königseder and Juliane Wetzel, *Waiting for Hope: Jewish Displaced Persons in Post-World War II Germany* (Chicago: Northwestern University Press, 2001), 18.

[17] Holian, *Between National Socialism and Soviet Communism*, 153–85.

[18] Hitchcock, *Liberation*, 332; Königseder and Wetzel, *Waiting for Hope*, 95–7.

were living in Germany, and concluded that 'we appear to be treating the Jews as the Nazis treated them, except that we do not exterminate them'.[19] Irving Heymont, the American commandant of the Bavarian camp at Landsberg, recognized that what they most wanted was a degree of autonomy ('the word they use over and over'), adding that 'after their sacrifices and sufferings, they undoubtedly find it galling to be objects of charity. They must surely find it rankling to have their private lives regulated and subjected to constant inspection while the Germans live a relatively free life'.[20] Yet it is worth remembering, in Atina Grossmann's words, that 'registrations which only days, certainly weeks, before would have meant deportation and death now had concrete benefits in terms of housing and increased rations'.[21]

Jewish DPs practised a sophisticated collective politics and cultural life in the camps. The camp became a site for the affirmation of solidarity. Föhrenwald in Bavaria, with a population of more than 4,000 at its peak in early 1947, boasted a synagogue, police force and courts, clinics, schools, kindergartens, newspaper press, library, orchestra and sports clubs. Physical exercise cultivated tough and virile men and women, willing and able to help build a new Jewish state. One drama society went by the name of Bar Kokhba, after the heroic but abortive revolt against Roman rule in Palestine in the second century CE. The motto of the camp newspaper, *Bamidbar* ('The Desert') was as follows: 'In the desert/In the wilderness/On the way/We will remain/In the desert/In the wilderness/On the way/We will not return/One goal: Erets Yisrael'. Other newspapers boasted titles such as 'Liberation', 'Our Hope', 'A Home', and 'The Free Word'. In a symbolic gesture both of defiance and anticipation, Jews constructed a kibbutz on land that had belonged to Julius Streicher, editor of the notorious newspaper *Der Stürmer*. In July 1945, delegates to a Conference of Liberated Jews in Germany demanded the immediate creation of a Jewish state in Palestine. Jewish underground organizations in the British zone provided military training to DPs and recruited them for the fledgling Israeli army.[22]

The number of DPs was swollen by Jews who left Eastern Europe to escape continued anti-Semitism and a resurgence of pogroms, the most terrifying of which took place in the Polish town of Kielce in July 1946. Between 1945 and 1947 around a quarter of a million Jews trekked westward; they included an unknown number who had repatriated soon after the war but who decided to leave of their own accord.[23] Frederick Morgan, the head of UNRRA in Germany, argued

[19] Michael Brenner, *After the Holocaust: Rebuilding Jewish Lives in Post War Germany* (Princeton: Princeton University Press, 1997), 11; Königseder and Wetzel, *Waiting for Hope*, 31–41; Jay Howard Geller, *Jews in Post-Holocaust Germany, 1945–1953* (Cambridge: Cambridge University Press, 2005), 23–8.

[20] Hitchcock, *Liberation*, 327.

[21] Atina Grossmann, 'Versions of Home: German Jewish Refugee Papers out of the Closet and into the Archives' *New German Critique*, 90 (Fall 2003), 95–122, at 109.

[22] Königseder and Wetzel, *Waiting for Hope*, 121–3, 142; Brenner, *After the Holocaust*, 19–22, 30; Margarete Feinstein, *Holocaust Survivors in Postwar Germany, 1945–1957* (Cambridge: Cambridge University Press, 2010), 107–22, 153–7.

[23] Königseder and Wetzel, *Waiting for Hope*, 43–53.

that the exodus of Jews from Poland (labelled as 'infiltrees') was part of a broader Zionist 'racket' to settle them in Palestine. British Prime Minister Clement Attlee dismissed an 'artificial movement engineered largely with a view to forcing our hands over Palestine', not an unreasonable assessment of the tactics adopted by *Brichah*, the clandestine network that helped Jews to leave Europe. The stakes were raised when Jews who left Europe on unseaworthy vessels were interned in Cyprus by the British-led 'Operation Igloo', generating a storm of bad publicity.[24]

Amidst all this uncertainty, many Jewish DPs simultaneously looked back to a history of oppression and terror, and forwards to a life in a sovereign Jewish state. The stage was set for a resolute emphasis on suffering during the war, which their leaders located in a lengthy history of destruction (*khurbn*) and catastrophe. The enormity of wartime suffering seemed to Jewish and non-Jewish observers to have ushered in a new era. Nazi policy was documented by a Historical Commission that collected testimony from Holocaust survivors and formed the basis for the renowned Yad Vashem in Jerusalem.[25] Not everyone applauded the attention devoted to history. The educational director of the American Jewish Joint Distribution Committee (JDC) maintained that each one 'is preoccupied almost to the point of morbidity with the past. He is always ready to recount in minutest detail the events of his past or the past of his relatives'.[26] This verdict minimized the vigorous and often divisive political debates that took place following Hitler's defeat. In particular (as one spokesman put it), DPs 'decided to renounce our former nationalities, and to declare our Jewish Nationality. We were willing to be stateless until a Jewish homeland was created in Palestine'. The DP camps contributed 13,000 troops to the Zionist cause.[27] Their vision was finally realized in May 1948, but not without further bloodshed and suffering.

WAR AND POPULATION DISPLACEMENT IN PALESTINE

By 1947 Jewish paramilitaries such as the implacable Irgun were at war against the embattled British administration, leaving the British to try to protect their own forces rather than to intervene on behalf of Palestinians. In November 1947 the United Nations voted to create a Jewish state with a population of 538,000 Jews and a substantial minority of 397,000 Palestinian Arabs, while the corresponding Palestinian state would accommodate 804,000 Arabs and just 10,000 Jews. The

---

[24] UNRRA Archives, S-0402-0002-05, Subject Files of Repatriation Section Central HQ 1945–47, Infiltrees, 28 December 1945–6 August 1946; Cohen, *In War's Wake*, 126–7; Arieh Kochavi, *Post-Holocaust Politics: Britain, the United States and Jewish Refugees, 1945–1948* (Chapel Hill: University of North Carolina Press, 2001), 163, 178.

[25] Holian, *Between National Socialism and Soviet Communism*, 162–9.

[26] Irving Heymont maintained that 'you can't live in the shadow of the past forever'. Hitchcock, *Liberation*, 324, 327.

[27] Holian, *Between National Socialism and Soviet Communism*, 157; Feinstein, *Holocaust Survivors*, 292.

UN proposal accelerated the decision of the *Yishuv* (Jewish settlers) to confront the Palestinian population in such a way as to minimize their presence in a Jewish state. Violent clashes lasted from December 1947 until 14 May 1948, when British troops finally left and Israel became independent. However, peace did not materialize. Instead war broke out between Israel and neighbouring Arab states. The conflict lasted a further 12 months, but divided views and military weakness deprived them of influence over the final settlement that determined the frontiers of Israel. Egypt appropriated the Gaza strip, while King Abdullah claimed the West Bank on behalf of Jordan, expelling several thousand Jews in the process. Most Palestinians were left high and dry.

Early in 1948 well-off Palestinians moved to places of safety in Lebanon or Jordan where they had property and relatives and where they expected to shelter until it was safe to return. The situation took a dramatic turn for the worse during the spring. Protracted battles in 1948 displaced at least 750,000 Palestinians, equivalent to half the estimated Arab population of Palestine (another 156,000 Palestinians stayed put) (see Map 5). More than 400 villages and several urban neighbourhoods were destroyed. Zionists claim that Israel was not responsible for the Palestinian refugee problem because the war was forced on Israel; refugees were also described as 'victims of their own aggression'.[28] A more temperate Israeli argument is that Arab states encouraged the indigenous population of Palestine to leave in order to ease the passage of their troops in fighting Jewish soldiers. This too is hotly contested. The historian Benny Morris famously laid bare the archival evidence of violence against Palestinian Arabs on the part of the Israeli Defence Force with the active connivance of Zionist leaders. Morris now dismisses claims of a clearly formulated plan prior to the outbreak of war, but his original research provided abundant evidence of concerted expulsions rather than 'spontaneous' flight. Plan D (Dalet) in March 1948 gave the green light to expel Palestinians from their villages lest they become a base for Arab attacks on Jewish militias. How many privileged Palestinians expected to be gone for just a few weeks is not certain, but their flight convinced those of more humble background to follow suit.[29]

For their part, Palestinians maintained that they were the victims of Zionist aggression, to which Arab states, hopelessly at odds with one another, made a feeble response. They also pointed to the direct pressure exerted on local people by Israeli troops. Rumours of massacres certainly played a part. There was clear evidence of atrocities committed by Jewish forces, notably in the village of Deir Yassin on 9 April 1948, where the Irgun and Stern Gang massacred at least a hundred unarmed men and perpetrated rape in what the Israeli government continues to describe as an 'incident'. Another massacre took place at Ayn al-Zaytun in May. War between the forces of a fledgling Israeli state and the indigenous Arab population became a licence for the Haganah (Jewish militia) and Israeli Defence Force (IDF) to target Palestinian villages and expel their inhabitants.

---

[28] Robert Fisk, *Pity the Nation: Lebanon at War* (André Deutsch, 1990), 46.
[29] Benny Morris, *The Birth of the Palestinian Refugee Problem Revisited* (Cambridge: Cambridge University Press, 2004).

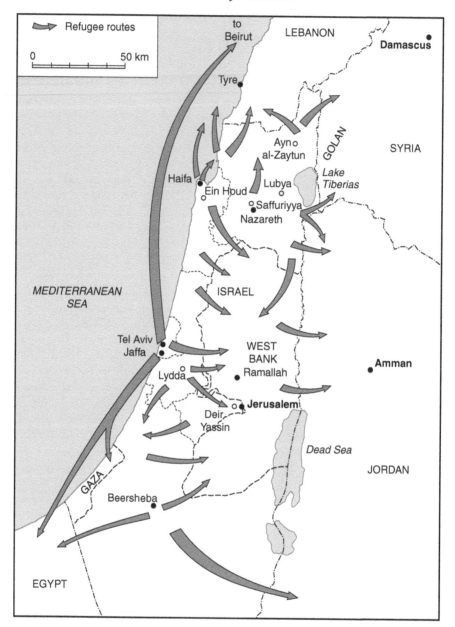

Map 5: Map of Palestinian Refugee Movements, 1948

Zionist forces consistently prevented refugees from returning to their homes, and Jewish immigrants took their place in towns such as Haifa and Acre.[30] This turned displacement into a fait accompli.

Palestinians went from one village to the next in search of sanctuary and in the hope that circumstances would soon improve and enable them to return. One refugee described his odyssey as follows:

> I was the last to leave our village, Saffouriyeh [Saffuriyya]. I stayed in Nasra until the Jews took it, then I took refuge in Hmeimeh. I didn't want to go to Lebanon, because I knew Lebanon and Syria from 1936 when I used to go to buy guns there. From Hmeimeh I went back to Acre, from Acre to Saffouriyeh, I and my wife, then from Saffouriyeh to Aloot. My brother advised me to go to Bint Jbeil but I said 'I don't want to see Lebanon'. The Jews began to search all the houses looking for men who had fought in '36 and '48. I began to fear for my life. It was only then that I decided to leave'.[31]

Others told similar stories of multiple journeys and of Jewish soldiers who prevented them from returning to their villages: 'your village is deserted from now on', a Palestinian recalled being told when he was forced to leave Galilee at the age of fifteen. He returned clandestinely to recover flour, blankets and livestock that had been left behind in the rush.[32]

Refugees were embroiled in further violence. Some ended up in villages that fell within the jurisdiction of the new state of Israel which declared their original homes to be military zones, making it impossible to access familiar places that they could see from their window.[33] Their children and grandchildren try to understand the specific circumstances that led to this disaster. Randa, who was born in Israel in 1958 to a refugee family that lived in Haifa, learned how her grandfather had been tricked by a Jewish partner into signing away his land in 1948. She felt that his lack of education played an important part in his undoing:

> I can say that I am angry with my family, with my grandfather, yet I look at it historically, at what the Turks and British have done, and people's ignorance. They did not study. The Jews came from Europe, with their education and class. They had seen the large world while people here were sitting under trees.

Others too believed that 'being simple' had blighted their parents' capacity to respond.[34]

The Palestinian refugee crisis thus followed 18 months of uninterrupted violence. Diplomatic action came to naught. The British government formulated a

---

[30] Cohen, *In War's Wake*, 144.

[31] Rosemary Sayigh, *Palestinians: from Peasants to Revolutionaries* (Zed Books, 1977), 87.

[32] 'Refugee Interviews' *JPS*, 18, no.1 (1988), 158–71, at 160–1.

[33] Rosemary Sayigh, 'Palestinian Camp Women as Tellers of History' *JPS*, 27, no.2 (1998), 45–6; Ilan Pappe, *The Ethnic Cleansing of Palestine* (Oxford: Oneworld, 2006), 195–8.

[34] Efrat Ben-Ze'ev, 'Transmission and Transformation: the Palestinian Second Generation and the Commemoration of the Homeland', in André Levy and Alex Weingrod (eds), *Homelands and Diasporas: Holy Lands and Other Places* (Stanford: Stanford University Press, 2005), 123–39, at 125–6.

plan in July 1949 whereby 100,000 Palestinian refugees would be settled in Iraq (partly, as was said, to 'transform its economy'), in exchange for the transfer and settlement of Iraqi Jews in Israel whom Iraq regarded as 'communists'. But Israel regarded this as extortion, and wished to avoid any obligation to repatriate 'surplus' Palestinian refugees in order to equalize the transfer arrangements. The proposal never got off the ground.

The prospect of a Jewish state led to other kinds of aggression. Long-standing Christian communities in the region suffered at the hands of Jewish extremists who suspected them of being in league with Arab countries. Jews who had lived for generations in the Middle East were now exposed to violent action when Arab states expelled Sephardi and Mizrahi Jews following the 1948 war. Taking into account other displacements, including those during the Suez debacle in 1956–57, at least 400,000 Jews fled Iraq, Yemen, Egypt and elsewhere. Iraqi Jews were harassed by officials who pictured them as fifth-columnists, de-naturalized them and froze their assets (Jewish community leaders in Baghdad blamed Zionist extremists for putting them in an impossible position). Thus radical changes to the map of the Middle East exposed Jews and Christians as well as the Arab population of Palestine to the uncertainties of forced migration.[35]

Subsequent episodes magnified the scale of displacement. Following the Six-Day War in June 1967, between 300,000 and 400,000 Palestinians fled from Gaza and the West Bank when these lands were occupied by Israel; more than a third of these were '1948 refugees' who had lived for two decades under Egyptian or Jordanian administration respectively. Israeli officials contemplated moving Palestinians from Gaza to the West Bank in order to forestall the creation of what they termed a 'refugeestan', but the preferred solution was to encourage them to go to Jordan. Many did so, and others fled to Lebanon, but a million people stayed where they were and found their lives transformed for the worse; they joined the so-called 'Arab Israelis' (or 'non-Jewish minority') who lived within the state of Israel. Over time, partly because of the strain on local resources, relations between the two groups of Palestinians deteriorated. Arab villagers described the newcomers as 'refugees', a term that carried connotations of helplessness and burden. Arab Israelis in turn felt doubly rejected, both by the state and by Palestinian organizations that claimed to speak on their behalf.[36]

---

[35] WCC Archives, File 425.1.032, Palestine folder, Svenska Israelsmissionen to Elfan Rees, 22 March 1948; Moshe Gat, *The Jewish Exodus from Iraq, 1948–1951* (Frank Cass, 1997); Yehouda Shenhav, 'The Jews of Iraq, Zionist Ideology and the Property of the Palestinian Refugees of 1948: an Anomaly of National Accounting' *International Journal of Middle East Studies*, 31, no.4 (1999), 605–30.

[36] Janet Abu-Lughod, 'Palestinians: Exiles at Home and Abroad' *Current Sociology*, 36, no.2 (1988), 61–9, at 63; Nur Masalha (ed.), *Catastrophe Remembered: Palestine, Israel and the Internal Refugees* (Zed Books, 2005); Fatma Kassem, *Palestinian Women: Narrative Histories and Gendered Memory* (Zed Books, 2011).

THE POLITICS OF RELIEF AND 'DEVELOPMENT'

The process of resettling Holocaust survivors attracted plaudits for its relative speed and effectiveness. A psychiatrist praised 'the transformation of [Jewish] orphans from the savage, half-animal, conditions in which they were found after the war to the balanced, sociable, hard-working conditions in which one finds them in the *kibbutzim*'.[37] By contrast, the plight of Palestinian refugees was portrayed from the outset in terms of humanitarian disaster. One journalist described 'scores of trucks jammed with women, children and old men, and piled skyward with household belongings' on the road from Jaffa, a major commercial centre, to the township of Lydda, whose population increased from 16,000 to 70,000 virtually overnight. The winter of 1948 was cold and damp, and refugees without sufficient means suffered great hardship, the memory of which remained with them forever.[38]

With the conflict in full swing, the International Committee of the Red Cross, the League of Red Cross Societies (LRCS) and Quakers (the British Society of Friends and the American Friends Service Committee (AFSC)) flocked to the scene, joining long-established organizations such as the Church Missionary Society. Near East Relief, the US organization with 30 years' experience of assisting Armenian refugees in the Middle East, chipped in. The LRCS paid tribute to 'those men and women who came from far away to a part of the world unknown to most of them to do a job in the field', and made much of the need to 'explain its task to the refugees'. Both are interesting statements of how officials understood their relationship with displaced persons.[39] Photographs recorded the names of dedicated Red Cross doctors and nurses who worked alongside unnamed refugees, patronizingly described as 'admiring [the] gifts' and 'eager to learn'. A very different account by the Swedish photographer Per-Olow Anderson (see earlier in this chapter) portrayed Palestinian refugees as individual human beings, albeit trapped in a terrible situation.

At the request of the UN, the AFSC assumed a prominent role in Gaza where its Quaker Palestine Unit (QPU)—the 'kewpies'—compromised on core Quaker principles by working alongside the Egyptian military in Gaza, as they did with the Allied forces in Europe and in India. Their mission to promote peace and justice took second place to the provision of emergency assistance.[40] The AFSC distributed food packages and set up temporary shelters, latrines and schools. Quaker relief efforts were supplemented by more substantial Egyptian aid in Gaza following the 1952 revolution that brought Gamel Abdul Nasser to power. Nasser's government organized 'mercy trains' carrying goods donated by

---

[37] Shephard, *The Long Road Home*, 395–6.
[38] Schechtman, *Population Transfers*, 121.
[39] LRCS, *Report of the Relief Operation in Behalf of the Palestine Refugees, 1949–1950* (Geneva: Red Cross, 1950), 5, 11; Winifred Coate correspondence, Jerusalem and East Mission Collection, St Antony's College, Oxford, Box 73, file 2.
[40] Ilana Feldman, 'The Quaker Way: Ethical Labor and Humanitarian Relief' *American Ethnologist*, 34, no. 4 (2007), 689–70.

Egyptians. Later on Egypt developed a range of welfare services for the entire population of Gaza.[41] The World Council of Churches sought to keep Palestinian refugees in the limelight on the grounds 'that the problem of displaced persons in the Holy Land [should] be given the same international aid which has been given to displaced persons in Europe'.[42]

Geopolitics, including the politics of international aid, further complicated the picture. From the outset Israel relied heavily on foreign aid particularly from the USA and the Federal Republic of Germany. Arab countries did not enjoy anything remotely comparable, although they were not completely overlooked. UNICEF contributed food, blankets and medical equipment. In November 1948 the UN created a specialist agency (UN Relief for Palestine Refugees) with a temporary mandate to provide emergency relief for Palestinian refugees. Lawyers acting for the IRO argued that Arab refugees were the result of war operations and did not fall within the wording 'persecution or fear based on reasonable ground of persecution' (the formulation used to determine the status of DPs in Europe). However, given that they were 'willing but unable' to return to their homes, and that this was tantamount to having a 'fear of persecution', Palestinian refugees had, according to IRO legal opinion, a valid claim to be regarded as political refugees. These debates did not see the light of day, and the IRO and the UN resolved instead to concentrate on material assistance.[43]

In 1949 the UN Security Council established the United Nations Relief and Works Agency for Palestine Refugees in the Middle East (UNRWA). The choice of title reflected a view that temporary relief provided by the AFSC and other bodies should be replaced by longer-term economic and social assistance in order 'to prevent conditions of starvation and distress and to further conditions of peace and stability'. One priority was to register those 'whose normal residence was Palestine for a minimum period of two years immediately preceding the outbreak of the conflict in 1948 and who, as a result, has lost both home and means of livelihood'. The agency concentrated on male heads of household; women were not entitled to their own ration cards unless they were widows. Counting heads proved extremely contentious. Better-off refugees regarded registration and inclusion on the ration rolls as humiliating; other refugees believed that it was a prelude to curtailing UN aid. There were numerous stories of 'abuse' of the system for administering rations, and Quakers in particular had grave misgivings about being made to trim the numbers entitled to relief. When the census was completed, UNRWA found that it had 910,000 refugees on its books. (There are now around four million.)[44]

Much of UNRWA's funding came from the US State Department, whose solicitude (as one official put it) 'partly based on humanitarian considerations, has

---

[41] Julie Peteet, *Landscape of Hope and Despair: Palestinian Refugee Camps* (Philadelphia: University of Pennsylvania Press, 2005), 57–61.

[42] WCC Archives, File 425.1.032, Palestine folder, A.C. MacInnes to Norman Goodall, 7 August 1948.

[43] Cohen, *In War's Wake*, 146.

[44] WCC Archives File 425.1.047 Refugees Near East 1949/50. In 1982 UNRWA decided to restrict entitlement to rations to 'hardship cases'.

additional justification [because] the refugees serve as a natural focal point for exploitation by Communist and disruptive elements'. Certainly the United States, by a considerable margin the biggest contributor to UNRWA, found it a useful instrument of leverage in the Middle East. A proposal in 1961 to cut America's payment led the State Department to point out that UNRWA supported refugees at a cost of just nine cents per day, not a bad investment (he said) for an agency that 'has been remarkably successful in keeping the potentially explosive refugee problem under control'. UNRWA also contributed to economic and political stability in Jordan, an important American ally in the struggle against the Soviet Union. International aid was crucial in other respects as well: throughout the 1950s and 1960s US experts believed it unlikely that Gaza, for instance, could sustain the current level of refugee settlement without massive external assistance.[45]

NGOs were supposed to adopt a politically neutral stance on the question of Palestinian refugees, but the dreadful conditions they encountered led some of them to criticize the countries most closely involved. The Church Missionary Society alienated Israel, Jordan and Syria by suggesting that Palestinian refugees should be consulted about their wishes. Writing in 1952, Samuel Morrison from the WCC suggested that Jordan's policy confirmed 'the convictions of the refugees that the Arab states in general are looking at the refugee problem not so much from the angle of the interests of the refugees themselves but from that of their own selfish interests'. He recommended an urgent programme to train refugee 'teachers and social workers [who] are in key positions to direct the thinking of the refugees into constructive channels, to expose the fallacies of communism'. Of emigration he wrote that 'it would be a curious irony of history if the ingathering of the Jews from their dispersion among the nations were only to be achieved at the price of the dispersion of the Arabs of Palestine over the face of the globe'. The best hope was for an Arab Palestine, linked economically to Israel for mutual prosperity. Both sides must 'bury the hatchet. [It is] for the Arabs to realise that Israel has come to stay and for the Jews to understand that without the cooperation of the Arab states their country cannot be economically viable'. No such solution materialized.[46]

Palestinian refugees reacted ambivalently to UNRWA. They tore up registration cards—as the head of one well-to-do household exclaimed, 'I remained in Haifa until the last day for the sake of Arab Palestine; is the result to learn how to beg or how to get a card for flour and food? Even if my children starve to death, I won't register any of them'.[47] Good intentions notwithstanding, the UN had no means of addressing property issues. Class, generational and gender differences complicated matters. One elderly Palestinian lamented that he could not take his land with him whereas his daughter's husband was able to take his degree certificate

---

[45] Phillips Talbot to Stuart Symington, 13 September 1961, NARA, RG 59, General Records of the State Department, Bureau of Near Eastern and South Asian Affairs, Office of the Country Director for Israel and Arab Affairs, Box 1, Folder UNRWA 1961; UNRWA, *From Camps to Homes: Progress and Aims of UNRWA in the Middle East* (Beirut: UNRWA, 1951).
[46] WCC Archives, File 425.1.047 Refugees Near East 1949/50, Samuel Morrison (Near East Christian Council). [47] 'Refugee interviews', 171.

when he left. The older man continued to wait in the hope that his land would be restored to him one day. Meanwhile his son-in-law managed to get ahead by making use of his portable qualifications.[48] The complexity of these negotiations left UNRWA bemused and ultimately impotent.

UNRWA ration cards became a vital element in securing food, decent medical care and rent-free housing, and even a form of collateral against which money could be borrowed. It served as 'a badge of identity [whereas] the identity card (*hawiyyeh*) was derided by Palestinians. It was the host state telling you, "you don't belong here, you are an alien"'. The ration card meant international recognition. But rations also meant having to accept the arrangements made by external agencies, which operated with tables of calorific requirements rather than culturally acceptable foodstuffs. As Julie Peteet points out, 'a multitude of new items appeared in the Palestinian lexicon' including latrines, delousing, powdered milk and distribution centres. More was at stake than the administration of relief. Palestinian men sent women or children to collect the rations in order to avoid the shame of being made to queue for food.[49]

Not being able to grow one's own food had cultural and psychological consequences. Mourid Barghouti described his shame at having to buy olive oil rather than being able to press it from his own olive groves. Refugees in Lebanon added that, 'unless you grow it yourself you can't be sure where it came from'. Others spoke of struggling to find fresh herbs and vegetables to add to burghul wheat: '[O]nce our father went to Damascus and brought back a fish. The people of the village said, "Come and see these Palestinians eating snakes!" They'd never seen a fish before'.[50] Later on they traded the rations for items they preferred to eat, and in time new sources of income enabled refugees to exercise greater choice. None of this altered Palestinians' sense of basic injustice. Relations between the agency and refugees left much to be desired. UNRWA employed Palestinian refugees, but the top posts in UNRWA went to non-Palestinians, so there was always asymmetry. Complaints fell on deaf ears.[51]

RESETTLEMENT IN PRACTICE

Repatriation foundered on the rock of Israeli intransigence. A UN Conciliation Commission for Palestine worked fitfully in 1948–49, and Israel reportedly offered to repatriate 100,000 refugees in 1951, but nothing came of these initiatives.

---

[48] Lena Jayyusi, 'Iterability, Cumulativity, and Presence: the Relational Figures of Palestinian Memory', in Ahmad H. Sa'di and Lila Abu-Lughod (eds), *Nakba: Palestine, 1948, and the Claims of Memory* (New York: Columbia University Press, 2007), 107–33.

[49] UNHCR Records and Archives, Fonds 11, Series 1, Folder 13/31/1 GEN, Algerian Refugees; Peteet, *Landscape of Hope and Despair*, 74, 76.

[50] Peteet, *Landscape of Hope and Despair*, 76–80; Sayigh, Palestinians, 125; Barghouti, *I Saw Ramallah*, 61–2.

[51] Benjamin Schiff, *Refugees unto the Third Generation: UN Aid to Palestinians* (Syracuse: Syracuse University Press, 1995), 141–2. UNRWA currently employs 29,000 Palestinian refugees on its programmes.

Palestinian refugees had no choice but to make the best of things in the West Bank, Gaza, Jordan, Lebanon, Syria and Egypt. Bitter disputes arose between the Arab governments and the United Nations. Host governments insisted that the refugee problem was the responsibility of the UN which had (they argued) approved the creation of the state of Israel and should therefore assume the cost of maintaining the refugees. Since host countries argued that the refugees had a right to return, they could claim that the modest provision they made was consistent with that stance. This is not to say that the reception accorded to Palestinian refugees was either uniform or unchanging. Generally speaking Syria (whose government placed arable land at the disposal of 100,000 refugees) and Jordan offered a more hospitable environment than Lebanon whose government feared that their presence would undermine the fragile foundations of the Lebanese state.

First-generation refugees responded to relief and rehabilitation efforts by insisting that refugee camps provided temporary accommodation rather than permanent homes. Mahmoud Issa remembers that as a young boy he pestered his father to buy a refrigerator, a washing machine and a television, only to be told that 'it will be easier, when the time comes, to return home without these cumbersome belongings'. Other sources confirm the unwillingness of refugees to install ovens and other accoutrements that implied 'resettlement'; the unmistakable refusal to entertain a permanent relocation was coupled to the affirmation of a right of return.[52] Refugees in the Dayr 'Ammar camp in the West Bank regarded the UNRWA-built nursery as a manifestation of potential 'rootedness'; in 1955 they promptly destroyed it. Five years later the Muslim NGO Jami'at al Islam (JAI) complained that UNRWA was cooperating with voluntary agencies such as the YMCA to persuade young refugees to settle in host countries. JAI accused it of 'using the tools of vocational, recreational, and athletic activity to persuade impressionable young people that the road to normality lies in a direction away from the ideals of their fathers. Arab youth are being told that they must foreswear all hope of regaining what was unjustly taken from them and seek instead new homes in other lands.'[53]

From the early 1950s, as it got down to the business of 'works' rather than 'relief', UNRWA provided an impressive programme of social, medical and educational services in the West Bank. Free schooling helped sustain Palestinian identity and provided young men with qualifications (including instruction in the English language) that enabled them to find employment further afield. Girls too received primary and in some cases secondary and even tertiary education, albeit with an overriding emphasis on clerical and secretarial qualifications, as well as qualifications in childcare, hairdressing and dressmaking. A residential training centre was opened in Ramallah in 1962, providing more than 600 girls at a time with 'the opportunity of building a productive life away from the misery

---

[52] Mahmoud Issa, 'Resisting Oblivion: Historiography of the Destroyed Palestinian Village of Lubya' *Refuge*, 21, no.2 (2003), 14–22, at 15; Bisharat, 'Exile to Compatriot', 212.
[53] UNHCR Records and Archives, Fonds 11, Series 1, Folder 13/31/1 GEN, Algerian Refugees. The complaint went unanswered.

and despair of the refugee camps which have been their homes ever since they can remember'. With knowledge of infant care and cleanliness, girls were expected to return to their homes and have a 'constructive' effect on other members of the refugee community. UNRWA sponsored a huge educational effort, complete with films and prizes for the cleanest baby and the best kept road.[54] This formed part of a broader project by UNRWA to 'civilize' the Palestinian peasantry. Demoralization would be overcome by modernization.

A study in the mid-1960s of refugees originally from the Bayt Naballah-Lydda region and who were now living in a refugee camp at Jalazun close to Ramallah found that they derived a modest but perceptible improvement in their living conditions by entering the labour market. However, they were not allowed to own land in the West Bank and depended on local people for credit and other forms of assistance. They suffered a catastrophic loss of status. Jalazun's refugees also described a difficult relationship with the local population, many of whom called them 'trespassers', 'gypsies', and 'fruit thieves'. Locals accused them of having 'sold land to the Jews, and now you come to squat on our land', an unfair charge given that they had little choice. They had, it was said, lost the right to call themselves 'Palestinian', because their action in fleeing the violence in 1948 had demeaned the very name. Their children did not escape being told they lived in 'borrowed homes'. Countering that sense of dislocation and dishonour, one refugee asserted that 'there is no such thing as the West Bank; it is part of Palestine', affirming a link between displacement and collective national identity.[55]

Something similar took place in Gaza where the outbreak of war saw 250,000 refugees flee to this small strip of territory that had been home to around 80,000 native inhabitants. Refugees were obliged to make do with temporary accommodation in schools, mosques and makeshift shelters in caves or deserted military barracks. Some slept on the beach. They complained of being reduced to begging. Dysentery and cholera took their toll. Relations between Palestinian refugees and locals were tense, because farmers lost access to lands that came under Israeli jurisdiction in 1948 and the influx of refugees drove down wage rates. Locals claimed that refugees had abandoned their homes and thereby 'betrayed' the Palestinian cause. As one refugee recalled, 'they made us sleep under the olive trees. In the morning we told them that we want water to wash and drink, but they told us that we had to leave—that we were the Palestinians who had left our villages and come here'. They recollected this as a time of profound humiliation.[56]

The emerging distinction between 'recognized' refugees and the impoverished local population, who were not entitled to ration cards, magnified mutual hostility. As Ilana Feldman puts it, 'Gaza's population categories have been derived from

---

[54] Kjersti Berg, 'Gendering Refugees: UNRWA and the Politics of Relief', in Nefissa Naguib and Inger Marie Okkenhaug (eds), *Interpreting Welfare and Relief in the Middle East* (Leiden: Brill, 2008), 149–73.

[55] Shimon Shamir, 'West Bank Refugees: Between Camp and Society', in Joel S. Migdal (ed.), *Palestinian Society and Politics* (Princeton: Princeton University Press, 1980), 146–65, at 156.

[56] Ilana Feldman, 'Home as a Refrain: Remembering and Living Displacement in Gaza' *History and Memory*, 18, no.2 (2006), 10–48, at 27.

legal definitions that do not quite apply in this territory (international refugee conventions), shaped by institutions that do not have jurisdiction over it (UNHCR) and influenced by long absent political forms (the sovereign state).' Over time, humanitarian relief efforts orchestrated first by the Quakers and then by UNRWA, with their emphasis upon systematic registration and monitoring became a kind of substitute government. This posed particular difficulties for Quakers, who were accustomed to think not in impersonal bureaucratic terms but as caring individuals who sought to forge a close relationship with each refugee.[57]

Jordan's population doubled in size in the space of just 12 months. Municipal authorities were quickly overwhelmed, and the urban infrastructure all but collapsed. Around 140,000 refugees, most of them from rural origins ended up in camps, while the rest found shelter in villages. The Jordanian military insisted that refugees be kept well away from border areas, creating resentment among Palestinians who interpreted this as a sign that the regime had no interest in enabling them to regain their property. The police and army closely monitored political activity in the camps (George Habash, the founder in 1967 of the Popular Front for the Liberation of Palestine (PFLP), worked as a doctor in one of UNRWA's camps in Jordan during the 1950s.) Economically, Jordan afforded little scope for agricultural development, although it capitalized on UNRWA development project aid for various irrigation and highway projects and funding for a Jordan Development Bank. One important concession came in December 1949 when most refugees were granted full citizenship and the right to a Jordanian passport, until such time as they could return to Palestine. Some refugees enrolled in the Jordanian army. But job opportunities were hard to come by. UNRWA's ration cards mattered (as was said) 'as much as God'. Even with sustained development assistance there would remain significant unemployment.[58]

Israeli diplomats hoped that Jordan would cooperate with Germany in sending 'surplus' refugees to work in the Federal Republic. Many seized this opportunity, and others went in search of work in Kuwait. Their remittances helped ensure the survival of family members who stayed in the refugee camps.[59] During the Six-Day War around 200,000 refugees from the occupied West Bank (some of them 'vintage' refugees from the war 20 years earlier) fled to neighbouring Jordan where, in makeshift camps, they became the target of Israel's attacks on the Jordanian army. Two-thirds moved to squalid settlements in Amman, Irbid and elsewhere.[60] Men who left the West Bank for Jordan nearly 20 years earlier in order to seek work in the Gulf States quickly returned to their villages on Jordanian passports to collect their families and take them to Amman. Most refugees expressed a wish to return

---

[57] Ilana Feldman, 'Difficult Distinctions: Refugee Law, Humanitarian Practice and Political Identification in Gaza' *Cultural Anthropology*, 22, no.1 (2007), 129–69, at 135.

[58] F. Witkamp, 'The Refugee Problem in the Middle East' *REMP Bulletin*, 5, no. 1 (1957), 3–51; Avi Plascov, *The Palestinian Refugees in Jordan 1948–1957* (Frank Cass, 1981), 16, 44–8, 92–103.

[59] Falestin Naïla, 'Memories of Home and Stories of Displacement: the Women of Artas and the 'Peasant Past' *JPS*, 38, no.4 (2009), 63–74.

[60] Peter Dodd and Halim Barakat, *River without Bridges: a Study of the Exodus of the 1967 Palestinian Arab Refugees* (Beirut: Institute for Palestine Studies, 1968).

to their original homes, resume their normal routine and re-establish community ties. However, the disclosure in 2012 of the negotiating position of the Palestinian Liberation Organization (PLO) shows that the Palestinian leadership has abandoned any hope of return, while the Bush administration in 2008 contemplated the movement of refugees to distant locations such as Chile.[61]

By contrast, 100,000 refugees in Lebanon were stateless 'foreigners' (*al-ajanib*), although Palestinian Christians received Lebanese citizenship on arrival. Palestinians were subject to tight restrictions on employment and on owning land and other property. Nor were they entitled to social security. Instead their welfare was mostly entrusted to UNRWA which managed 17 official refugee camps, some of which had been occupied by Armenian refugees before the war, a reminder of Lebanon's previous history as a refugee-receiving state. Administrative convenience was the main justification for UNRWA's arrangements, namely to ensure that refugees could be counted and given identity papers by the authorities in Beirut. Other refugees settled on the outskirts of towns such as Tyre and Sidon until they were detected and moved on by local police. Countless unofficial settlements were also scattered across the country. From the outset refugees spoke of unsympathetic villagers who exploited their vulnerability and held them in contempt, and of obstacles to getting anything other than unskilled and casual jobs.[62]

Overcrowding and deprivation in Lebanese camps did not curtail refugees' creativity. Rows of tents gradually gave way to cement structures. Camps came to resemble a labyrinthine maze. UNRWA officials reported in 1967 that 'progress was being made towards the economic rehabilitation of the camp inhabitants' and that some of the refugee camps had developed into thriving communities.[63] New arrivals were crammed into any available space and, because the Lebanese authorities refused to extend the surface area to accommodate the growth in numbers, refugees had no option but to add new storeys to the makeshift structures. They retained the original names of the villages they left in 1948, reinforcing an affiliation to ancestral lands and symbolizing a kind of resistance both to integration (*towteen*) and to emigration. Shops bore the names of villages or broader designations such as 'Return' and 'Palestine'. Refugee camps also produced or reinforced local stereotypes, for example that refugees from Nablus were cunning and even ruthless in business affairs. As in Jordan, camp organizers also set great store by sporting prowess, particularly boxing and gymnastics, as a means of asserting physical strength in the midst of evident 'national weakness', as happened among Jews in German DP camps in 1945.[64]

Boxing gloves soon ceased to be the weapon of choice. Camps such as Shatila made a perfect environment for the growth of armed resistance by Fatah militants

---

[61] <http://www.guardian.co.uk/world/2011/jan/25/palestine-papers-refugees-south-america>.

[62] D.B.H. Vickers, 'The Refugee Problem in the Lebanon' (1951), typescript in Bodleian Library Special Collections, MS. Eng. c. 4706; Jihane Sfeir, *L'exil palestinien au Liban: le temps des origines, 1947–1952* (Paris: Karthala, 2008).

[63] Edward Buehrig, *The UN and the Palestinian Refugees: a Study in Non-Territorial Administration* (Bloomington: Indiana University Press, 1971), 124.

[64] Sayigh, *Palestinians*, 109; Peteet, *Landscape of Hope and Despair*, 110–24.

who mounted dozens of operations inside Israel from bases in Lebanon, leading to massive retaliation from the Israeli air force. The disparity between UNRWA educational provision and the underdeveloped Lebanese school system gave rise to acute tension. Even more disconcerting was the presence of predominantly Sunni Muslim refugees who posed a challenge to Lebanon's multi-confessional state. Lebanese workers and the middle-class resented the competition from Palestinian labourers and entrepreneurs. An ominous sign of trouble to come was the rise of Christian Phalange militias in Beirut who targeted refugees in the run-down district of Karantina in January 1976. Equally alarming was the accusation levelled at UNRWA by Israeli government officials that it was 'inadvertently preparing a generation of educated youth for secular, militant nationalist activities'.[65]

By the late 1970s Palestinian refugees had become embroiled in Lebanon's murderous civil war, partly sustained by Israel whose leaders wished to undermine the PLO, which was responsible for attacks on Israel.[66] This conflict led to the Israeli invasion of Lebanon in 1978 and again in 1982, culminating in destruction of camps in Southern Lebanon in June and bloody massacres in the Sabra and Shatila refugee camps in September at the hands of the Phalange and with the backing of the IDF. Shatila was transformed from a dynamic site of 'embryonic state-building' to a site that embodied a complex mixture of 'hope and despair'.[67] In other interviews, a young fighter spoke hopefully of living not in a refugee camp but a 'training camp'. But despair was etched on the face of a Palestinian woman who could not bury her husband and sons who were killed by the Phalange: '[W]hen I go to the graveyard I just throw the flowers and hope they land on the right places'.[68] Her lament corresponded to the bitter experience of those who survived the Holocaust in East-Central Europe but whose loved ones disappeared without trace.

LEGACIES: PAST AND PLACE

It is an incontrovertible fact that the *Nakba*, magnified by the events of 1967, the consequences of the civil war in Lebanon and the Israeli response to the first and second Intifada remains the most intractable of all episodes of twentieth-century population displacement. The Palestinian refugee crisis affects international relations more than any other situation referred to in this book. It was not always so. An American Quaker wrote in 1959 that:

We must always remember a regrettable fact about relief and rehabilitation of war sufferers. It represents a healing of wounds which should never have been inflicted. In Israel the AFSC is playing a reconciling role between two peoples both of whom claim

---

[65] Peteet, *Landscape of Hope and Despair*, 88, 109–10; Sayigh, *Palestinians*, 127; Rebecca Roberts, *Palestinians in Lebanon: Refugees Living with Long-term Displacement* (I.B.Tauris, 2010), 69–91.

[66] The PLO was founded in 1964 and incorporated Fatah, the Palestinian National Liberation Movement, formed earlier by Yasser Arafat.

[67] Peteet, *Landscape of Hope and Despair*, 17.

[68] Fisk, *Pity the Nation*, 400.

the same land as their own. Israeli and Arab social workers, visiting Greek and Italian community developments under AFSC auspices, have grown together in much more than professional competence.[69]

Other observers offered a much less hopeful assessment: there was already talk in the 1960s of a 'hard core' of Palestinian refugees, equivalent to the 'DP problem' in Europe.[70]

Displacement produced a rich cultural legacy. Writers in the Jewish diaspora have authored poignant accounts of cultural life in Eastern Europe between the two world wars, although these are inevitably framed by the Holocaust.[71] (Russian Jews who migrated to Israel during the 1970s and 1980s by contrast showed no evident warmth towards their place of birth.) Among Palestinians such as Samir Khaled, music and cookery books demonstrated a strong sense of attachment reflected in recollections of 'a sweet life [where] our village was a park and our grapes like gold'. Other authors associated the apparently mundane taste of figs, melons and pomegranates with childhood memories of the Palestinian village or with parental evocation of a pastoral landscape. Ellen Kettaneh Khouri, who was born in May 1948, insists that this is not nostalgia but 'a mixture of *huzn* (sadness) and yearning. It is missing something you don't have, and maybe never had'.[72]

Poetry endorsed these sensual images of (in the words of Jabra Ibrahim Jabra) a 'land of ours where our childhood passed/like dreams in the shade of the orange grove/among the almond trees in the valleys'. The peasant became the symbol of Palestinian nationalism, as in Tawfiq Zayyad's poem, 'On the trunk of an olive tree', which provides the narrator with the only means of expressing his anger at having been displaced: 'I shall carve my story and all the seasons of my tragedy/my sighs/my grove and the tombs of my dead/I shall carve the number of every usurped plot.../I shall carve Dayr Yasin, it has taken root in my memory'.[73] Other refugees constructed 'a more self-conscious relationship to place [and] to reconcretise a connection to the land that had been violently sundered'. Memories of the 1936 revolt against British rule were important in making that connection.[74]

Refugeedom had a marked effect on commemorative activities, although the dominant myth of the *Nakba* took some time to establish itself in Palestinian consciousness. Some refugees refused to embrace the term because they associated it with a permanent uprooting.[75] In spite of or perhaps because of the absence of state

---

[69] Editorial by Colin Bell, *AFSC Bulletin* (Fall 1959), 1.

[70] *World Refugee Report: Annual Survey Issue, 1966–1967* (New York: USCR, 1967), 17.

[71] Ewa Hoffman, *Shtetl: The History of a Small Town and an Extinguished World* (Secker and Warburg, 1998).

[72] Feldman, 'Home as a Refrain', 19; Nadia Latif, 'Making Refugees' *The New Centennial Review*, 8, no.2 (2008), 253–72; Dina Matar, *What it Means to be Palestinian: Stories of Palestinian Peoplehood* (I.B.Tauris, 2011), 62.

[73] Parmenter, *Giving Voice to Stones*, 43, 75–6.

[74] Bisharat, 'Exile to Compatriot', 217.

[75] Diana Allan, 'Mythologising Al-Nakba: Narratives, Collective Identity and Cultural Practices among Palestinian Refugees in Lebanon' *Oral History*, 33, no.1 (2005), 47–56; Ahmad H. Sa'di, 'Catastrophe, Memory and Identity: Al-Nakbah as a Component of Palestinian Identity' *Israel Studies*, 7, no.2 (2002), 175–98.

sponsorship a steady outpouring of literature, film, music and artwork helped establish the framework of a national culture that has 'rootedness' at its core and displacement as its tragic antithesis. Unfortunately the Palestinian Film Archive, established in 1976 to provide a 'people's cinema' of the Palestinian struggle, was wrecked six years later during the terrible siege of Beirut. One documentary that survived is Mustafa Abu Ali's *They Do Not Exist* (1974), about conditions in Lebanon's refugee camps and the lives of Palestinian guerrillas. Other films include the same director's *Scenes from the Occupation in Gaza* (n.d.); *The Key* (director, Ghalib Sha'ath, 1976) set in Lebanon's camps; *Haifa* (director, Rashid al-Mash'harawi, 1995); and *My Very Private Map* (director, Subhi Zabidi, 1998). Significant figures from an earlier generation include Sulafa Jadallah, Hani Jawhariya, Khadija Abu Ali, Rafiq Hijjar, Nabiha Lutfi, Fuad Zentut, Jean Chamoun and Samir Nimr. A series of books by prominent exiles such as Edward Said, including a text accompanying the remarkable photographs of Jean Mohr, as well as Ghassan Kanafani, Mourid Barghouti and Ghada Karmi exemplify a rich body of work seeking to express myriad aspects of the experience of displacement. Since 2002 the anthropologist and film maker Diana Allan has recorded personal testimony in the refugee camps in Lebanon, uncovering well-rehearsed performances on the part of self-appointed spokesmen on the one hand, as well as more informal and less 'polished' accounts on the other.[76]

A sharply defined sense of estrangement suffuses much of this work. Estrangement was accompanied by a sense of a forsaken homeland. Ghada Karmi (b.1939) has spoken eloquently and tenderly of the vibrant social and cultural life in cosmopolitan Jerusalem where she spent her first nine years surrounded by Muslim, Jewish and Christian neighbours, before being swept up by her parents and taken to Damascus and later on to London in a 'hasty and untidy exit'. Writing of her friends and acquaintances, she suggests that their 'stories all had the same ending'.[77] Edward Said's memoir tells of his Aunt Nabiha, who assisted refugees in Egypt and considered their enforced alienation:

> Much of her time in the awful decrepit slums she visited would be spent convincing the women left behind with screaming, underfed children that they did *not* need more medicine. Prescriptions and, preferably, money for patent medicines had the status of a miracle cure for these poor women, and it was not until a few years ago that an acquaintance who survived those early days explained to me that what every one of the destitute and powerless looked for was a drug that might induce forgetfulness, sleep or indifference.

This initial desire to forget yielded to an intense wish to remember, a project to which Said himself made an immense contribution.[78] Other memoirs are written in a different register. The rupture of social relations had sometimes unexpected and momentous consequences for women. In her moving autobiography the

---

[76] Diana Allan, 'The Politics of Witness: Remembering and Forgetting 1948 in Shatila Camp', in Sa'di and Abu-Lughod (eds), *Nakba*, 253–82.
[77] Ghada Karmi, *In Search of Fatima: a Palestinian Story* (Verso, 2002), 123, 145.
[78] Edward Said with Jean Mohr, *After the Last Sky: Palestinian Lives* (Faber, 1986), 116–19.

Palestinian poet Fadwa Tuqan (1917–2003) described how refugees crowded in to her home town of Nablus where the disruption of household structures enabled women—'faceless victims with no independent life'—to play a public role in Palestinian society, such that 'when the roof fell in on Palestine, the veil fell off the face of the Nablus woman'.[79]

Kanafani's short stories such as 'Letter from Gaza' (1956) engaged with the bitter meanings imparted to displacement, particularly by older Palestinians who had to confront their children with the realities of refugeedom. Kanafani (1936–72) was 12 when his family was forced to leave Palestine. (He was killed along with his niece in his booby-trapped car in Beirut, where he was working as a journalist on behalf of the PFLP.) The protagonist in 'The Land of Sad Oranges' (1958) describes how, 'as I left the house behind, I left my childhood behind too'. Elsewhere Kanafani dwelt on journeys in search of work, as in his novella, *Men in the Sun* (1962) which recounts a desperate attempt by three Palestinian men to get to Kuwait to look for work. The driver of a water tanker agrees to smuggle them across the desert from Basra to Kuwait, but before they reach their destination the men are suffocated when the driver is held up by Israeli guards who taunt him about his lack of sexual prowess, the result of injuries he sustained during the war of 1948. When he finally reaches his destination he leaves the bodies of the three men in a rubbish dump. 'Returning to Haifa' (1969) tells of a Palestinian couple who find that the baby boy they thought had been killed in 1948 was adopted by Holocaust survivors from Poland and has grown up to be a proud Israeli soldier. Their tense encounter in 1967 is resolved when the young man's birth parents are left with no other option but to pin their hopes on the Palestinian liberation movement.[80]

Many artists spoke of the centrality of the *Nakba* in their creative work, as well as the importance of a continuing sense of attachment to the homeland. The artist Suleiman Mansour (b.1947) is best known for his painting entitled 'Carry On', depicting an old man who carries Jerusalem on his back, an expression of the refugee's ordeal and the importance attached to the Dome of the Rock. The dramatic setting and the colours used in another of his paintings, 'To the Unknown', bear a striking resemblance to the well-known work of Marc Chagall. Other paintings include 'Homage to the Martyrs'. Ismail Shammout (1930–2006) who was expelled as an 18-year old from Lydda by Israeli troops, and who made his way to Cairo after living briefly in a camp in Gaza, painted one of the most famous pictures of the Palestinian exodus in *Where to...?* Cast in socialist-realist mode, it shows a bedraggled father with three small children who have left their town behind and are heading to an unknown destination. The famous cartoonist Naji

[79] Fadwa Tuqan, *A Mountainous Journey: the Life of Palestine's Outstanding Woman Poet* (The Women's Press, 1990), 106, 113. Compare Isabelle Humphries and Laleh Khalidi, 'Gender of Nakba Memory', in Sa'di and Abu-Lughod (eds), *Nakba*, 207–27.

[80] Ghassan Kanafani, *Men in the Sun and Other Palestinian Stories* (Heinemann, 1978); Ghassan Kanafani, *Palestine's Children: Returning to Haifa and Other Stories* (Boulder: Lynne Rienner Publishers, 2000), 149–96.

al-Ali (1937–87) was born in a village close to Tiberias that was demolished in 1948. He moved to a refugee camp in South Lebanon, before settling in Tripoli where he trained as an electrician. Naji began by painting 'disjointed fragments of broken mirrors glued into old frames...screwing metal bars across the mirror so that viewers would see themselves locked in prison'.[81]

Place figured in this process no less than time. Artists such as Jumana al-Husseini (b.1932) composed figurative paintings of Jerusalem and Jericho: 'I found Palestine again on canvas. I live my youth, my early days there—all the memories, the birds, the flowers, the butterflies, the greenery, the Dead Sea, the windows, the doors, the skies of Palestine. This is where I found myself'. In later life she developed a strikingly beautiful abstract style. In 2001 the Bethlehem-born artist Emily Jacir created a 'refugee tent' as an embroidered 'Memorial to 418 Palestinian villages which were destroyed, depopulated and occupied by Israel in 1948'. Finding it impossible to contemplate embroidering all the names by herself, she enlisted volunteers from Lebanon, Syria, Morocco, Tunisia and elsewhere to complete the task. In choosing to make a tent rather than a more permanent fixture, Jacir explicitly sought to encapsulate a sense of the possibility of 'return'.[82]

Mourid Barghouti poses important questions in his account of returning to Ramallah: 'A visitor? A refugee? A citizen? A guest? I do not know'. Return is invested with profound emotional turmoil: 'we had had to bear the clarity of displacement and now we had to bear the uncertainty of return as well'. He speaks of 'absentee love' as the condition of being an exile: '[T]he long Occupation has succeeded in changing us from children of Palestine to children of the idea of Palestine', an idea that is upsetting as much as it is alluring.[83] These reflections are about time, place and belongings: memories of dispossession entail recalling the moment of displacement as well as the loss of tangible assets. Palestinian memories have been closely connected to place and place names in Palestinian refugee consciousness and thus also of the keys to their property which were retained because, refugees explained, 'we locked our door and kept the key, expecting to return'.[84] Keys and maps acquired a complex symbolic significance: they connected refugees with their property, but they also had the potential to trap refugees in a congealed past. As Edward Said put it, 'sometimes these objects, heavy with memory—albums, rosary beads, shawls, little boxes—seem to me like encumbrances. We carry them about, hang them up on every new set of walls we shelter in, reflect lovingly on them'. He added that 'then we do not notice the bitterness, but it continues and grows nonetheless. Nor do we acknowledge the frozen immobility of our attitudes. In the end the past owns us'.[85]

[81] <http://www.shammout.com/>. Shammout inspired other refugees to try their hand. See Kamal Boullata, 'Artists Re-member Palestine in Beirut' *JPS*, 32, no.4 (2003), 22–38, at 28–9.

[82] <http://homepages.gac.edu/~lwren/AmericanIdentititesArt%20folder/AmericanIdentititesArt/JacirEmily.html>, last accessed on 11 June 2012.

[83] Barghouti, *I Saw Ramallah*, 11, 61–2, 73.

[84] Susan Slyomovics, *Object of Memory: Arab and Jew Narrate the Palestinian Village* (Philadelphia: University of Pennsylvania Press, 1998), 54.

[85] Barghouti, *I Saw Ramallah*, 23; Said, *After the Last Sky*, 14–17.

Mapping the consequences of displacement was closely linked to this intense historical awareness. More than 400 Palestinian villages were destroyed or badly damaged during the war of 1948. Deir Yassin was renamed Givat Shaul, 'a mere suburb of Jerusalem, its main street a line of petrol stations, garages and high-rise apartment blocks, more like the Edgware Road or Brooklyn than the scene of a mass murder'.[86] It was repopulated with Jewish refugees from Romania, Poland and Slovakia. All traces of the Arab inhabitants of the village of Saffuriyya in Galilee were erased by the Jewish National Fund; the travel brochure makes much of the Roman archaeological remains but does not mention the original Arab settlement.[87]

Another obliterated site was the twelfth-century Arab village of Ein Houd ('Ayn Hawd) in the mountains south of Haifa whose inhabitants traced their ancestry back to one of Saladin's generals who had been granted land during the Crusades. The village which according to an official travel guide 'had partly fallen into ruins' was appropriated by the new state. It too underwent an official reincarnation. In 1953 the government decided to 'preserve' it as an artists' colony and training centre. Renamed Ein Hod, it became home to a group led by the Dadaist artist and architect Marcel Janco (1895–1983), a refugee who narrowly escaped the Holocaust in his native Romania. The new owners, who included other refugees from Central Europe, incorporated scattered stones from the original village in order to retain elements of the old architectural forms, even preserving these features (as they put it) 'like a reservation of the [Native American] Indians'. The village mosque was turned into a restaurant and bar, unashamedly named 'Bonanza', which became a popular destination with visiting celebrities such as Eleanor Roosevelt, the Marx Brothers and Danny Kaye. What makes this example especially interesting is that Ein Hod was not the only new element in the Palestinian landscape. The original villagers of Ein Houd moved to a nearby hill where they built a settlement that they named Ein Houd Al-Jadīdah. Its status remains uncertain; for years it had no running water, electricity or access roads. The memorial book to the village of Ein Houd made it possible to recount vivid stories from its medieval and recent past, and indirectly demonstrated how the arrival of one refugee population was associated with the partial expurgation of the other.[88]

Like Armenian, Jewish, German, Cypriot and other refugees, Palestinians devoted considerable effort to the creation of village books that commemorate abandoned settlements. This project has gone hand in hand with making a photographic record of sites in order to 'breathe life into a name'.[89] At Birzeit University Sharif Kanaana directed a team of Palestinian scholars who compiled several hundred such volumes. These books are a lament for a world that has been lost—'all that remains'—not unlike the *yizkor bukhn* that recall Jewish life

---

[86] Fisk, *Pity the Nation*, 23.

[87] Matar, *What It Means to be Palestinian*, 42, 53.

[88] Slyomovics, *Object of Memory*, 25.

[89] Walid Khalidi, *All That Remains: Palestinian Villages Occupied and Depopulated by Israel in 1948* (Washington DC: Institute of Palestinian Studies, 1992), xvii.

in the shtetls of Eastern Europe before the Second World War. In the Palestinian case they have also recreated the physical appearance, the kinship networks and the trades of the old village as part of a deliberate attempt at what Ghada Karmi terms 'surrogate re-population'.[90] Intimate knowledge of the village in these gazetteers establishes an 'authority to know' and a claim to have the land restored to Palestinian ownership.[91] In a similar enterprise, Raja Shehadeh describes the unhindered journeys that lasted for days during his youth when he could easily traverse the hills and valleys around Ramallah, and that are now more or less impossible. The author contrasts the pastoral landscape of the countryside he knew as a boy, which was filled with flowers, olive bushes and vines, with today's polluted and fenced-in landscape, the consequence of Israel's pursuit of territorial aggrandizement and control.[92]

Tactile association with the lost villages went hand in hand with a sense of having forfeited strong social and cultural ties. Refugees from villages in the West Bank described a lush landscape that contrasted with the drab neighbourhoods in the Jordanian capital Amman. Not only was the land fertile, it also conferred a sense of being 'blessed' by one's surroundings and one's neighbours, in contrast to their current situation. It was very different for Jewish refugees who survived the Holocaust: those who were born in Poland, for example, reflected on their escape from hostile neighbours. Time has not healed the rifts of displacement. If, to begin with, Palestinian memories of good neighbourliness extended to Jews—'many still speak with appreciation of many of their Jewish friends and how well Jews and Arabs could have lived together, had it not been for the aspirations of the Jewish and Arab leadership', wrote an American Quaker in 1949—six decades of humiliation have obliterated such sentiments.[93]

Something of the intensity of Palestinian memory work emerges in Mahmoud Issa's project to explore the history of Lubya, a small village in Galilee that was home to around 2,700 people in 1945, including his parents who subsequently moved to Wavel refugee camp in Baalbeck, Lebanon. Israeli officials demolished the village in 1948 and rebuilt it as a kibbutz to house Jewish immigrants from Britain. It is now a tourist stop on the road from Haifa to Nazareth. Issa reconstructed what he could of the intricate social relations in Lubya. His interviews with former residents suggested that some historical events, such as Salah al Din's (Saladin's) battle of Hittin in 1187 and Napoleon's march through the village on his way to besiege Akka (Acre) were 'enthusiastically recounted' as if part of their personal heritage. Refugees retained a keen sense of time and place.[94] Likewise,

[90] Karmi, *In Search of Fatima*, 186; Jack Kugelmass and Jonathan Boyarin (eds), *From a Ruined Garden: the Memorial Books of Polish Jewry* (Indianapolis: Indiana University Press, 1998).

[91] Rochelle Davis, 'Mapping the Past, Re-creating the Homeland: Memories of Village Places in Pre-1948 Palestine', in Sa'di and Abu-Lughod (eds), *Nakba*, 53–75, at 60.

[92] Raja Shehadeh, *Palestinian Walks: Notes on a Vanishing Landscape* (Profile Books, 2007).

[93] Salim Tamari and Elia Zureik, *Reinterpreting the Historical Record: the Uses of Palestinian Refugee Archives for Social Science Research and Policy Analysis* (Jerusalem: Institute of Jerusalem Studies, 2001), 126; Rochelle Davis, *Palestinian Village Histories: Geographies of the Displaced* (Stanford: Stanford University Press, 2011), 190–1.

[94] Issa, 'Resisting Oblivion', 17.

villagers from the West Bank village of Artas located the upheavals in 1948 and 1967 in the context of previous events such as the invasion in the 1830s by Egyptian forces led by Ibrahim Pasha who expelled them from their homes.[95] In these ways, history is continuously being reinterpreted; a command of factual knowledge from the distant past helps to underscore and validate claims to the 'homeland'. Even the momentous significance attached to 1948 has not loosened other rich and extensive webs of meaning. This memory work was no less pronounced among Jews who commemorate their Central and Eastern European forebears and the terrible destruction of European Jewry. Unhappily the commemoration of their arrival in Palestine went hand in hand with erasing traces of the Palestinian past. Mahmoud Darwish spoke of his encounter with a young Jewish boy who was amazed to learn that the stones on which they stood were the remnants of a Palestinian Arab village and not, as he had been led to believe, the ruins of a Roman settlement.[96]

In time the catastrophe of 1948 took its place among other crucial episodes, such as the violent invasion of refugee camps and the first and second Intifadas. Palestinian freedom fighters were often unwilling to commemorate the *Nakba* because they construed it as a moment of weakness and shame that needed to be exorcised. Lament turned into a more politically conscious programme of organization and militancy, designed to support *al-awda* or return. But these projects did not always make headway. A study of refugees in the West Bank found that after 40 years some of them had grown 'committed to a "return" to Palestine conceived abstractly', as if a virtual homeland had become the chief point of reference.[97] Yet more troubling to the nationalist project was that some younger refugees manifested indifference, as did boys in Shatila who were more interested in games of pinball and the teenager who countered, 'Shit to the right of return, we want to live!', expressing a different kind of estrangement that needs to be taken seriously. More complex still were the attitudes of Palestinians who were able to return to Palestine—or more commonly to visit it for the first time—following the Oslo Accords in 1993. Some of the so-called 'Aideen', senior returnees who joined the Palestinian Authority after having lived in Tunisia, were despised by local Palestinian residents. The children of the Aideen found it confusing to adjust to life in a land that had often been portrayed in a romanticized fashion, even if they too affirmed a deep attachment to the 'homeland'.[98]

Edward Said wrote that 'there are many different kinds of Palestinian experience, which cannot all be assembled into one. One would therefore have to write parallel histories of the communities in Lebanon, the occupied territories and so on. It is almost impossible to imagine a single narrative'. He continued, 'since the main features of our present existence are dispossession, dispersion, and yet also a kind of power incommensurate with our stateless exile, I believe that essentially

[95] Naïla, 'Memories of Home', 66.   [96] Parmenter, *Giving Voice to Stones*, 2.
[97] Bisharat, 'Exile to Compatriot', 234.
[98] Juliane Hammer, *Palestinians Born in Exile: Diaspora and the Search for a Homeland* (Austin: Texas University Press, 2005), 93–8; Allan, 'Politics of Witness', 261.

unconventional, hybrid and fragmentary forms of expression should be used to represent us'. Among Palestinian refugees in Lebanon, according to Diana Allan, 'cultural transmission is occurring less through an oral, performative tradition that memorialises 1948 than fragmentary moments that make up the idiomatic fabric of everyday life'. This is a salutary reminder of differences of gender, status and age, as well as of differences between refugees who fled to the West Bank, Gaza, Jordan or Lebanon, and the Palestinians who already lived there, and between refugees and those who were internally displaced. Older women in Shatila adopted the structures of traditional story-telling to make their accounts memorable, whereas younger informants preferred the heroic narratives of Palestinian radicalism. Others manifested a less secure attachment to the national narrative. Women who belonged to the half-obscured Palestinian minority inside Israel had to come to terms with the fact that the state recognized only one narrative, and it was certainly not the *Nakba*.[99]

CONCLUSIONS

Displacement has marked the history of both Jews and Palestinians alike. The worldwide population of Jews stands at approximately 14 million, of whom six million live in Israel and a substantial number in North America. There are more than 9.5 million Palestinians worldwide. Nearly four million live in desperate straits in Gaza and in the West Bank, and close on five million in neighbouring Arab states as well as in other parts of the globe. Around one million Palestinians live in Israel itself, not all of them as refugees but as socially marginalized and politically powerless. Nowhere in the Middle East can it be said that Jews and Palestinians lead a secure existence, Jews because they feel threatened by adjacent states and Palestinians because they lack a state of their own.

Generally speaking Jews and Palestinians experienced displacement as a painful and disfiguring process. The contours of displacement were marked before 1948 when Palestinian farmers migrated to towns and cities in search of a better life. The same applies to Jews who settled in Palestine long before the Holocaust. Jewish experience was closely linked to transcontinental migration and to devastating Nazi resettlement programmes. The Holocaust and the events of 1948 turned the worlds of Jews and Palestinians upside down in a way they could not have anticipated. Large numbers of Holocaust survivors found a home in the new state of Israel where memories of pre-war life have been institutionalized in museums, libraries and archives containing precious items saved from Nazi Germany. Most Palestinians had to flee. Their objects of memory are

---

[99] Said, *After the Last Sky*, 6; Allan, 'Mythologising Al-Nakba', 49; Kassem, *Palestinian Women*, 64–81.

equally precious, but they are hidden from view because the lack of a state means there is nowhere to display them publicly.

Palestinians are acutely aware of the conditions that created their prolonged displacement, even though most of those alive today had no direct experience of the *Nakba*. The same applies to Israelis, who live in a state that rejects any responsibility for the plight of Palestinians. Of far greater significance is the legacy of the Second World War that ultimately sustains Israel's legitimacy. David Grossman has written of how, 'in so many Israeli homes, a thread of deep anxiety was stretched out, and with almost every move you made, you touched it. Even if you were very careful, you still felt that constant quiver of a profound lack of confidence in the possibility of existence'. Grossman became aware of life's fragility. The knowledge of what happened—or what was vouchsafed—was of fundamental importance as survivors and their children confronted life choices.[100] Israel's guardianship of Jewish identity is nevertheless problematic, as we shall see in chapter 8 when discussing the 'rescue' of a group of Jews from an unlikely quarter.

By the middle of the twentieth century it was clear that the fortunes of Jews and Palestinians were closely entwined in terms of conflict. The battle lines were described by Barghouti in his comments on Yitzhak Rabin's appropriation of the discourse of suffering: '[H]e knew how to demand that the world should respect Israeli tears, and he was able to present Israel as the victim of a crime perpetrated by us. He changed facts, he altered the order of things, and he presented us as the initiators of violence in the Middle East. The Israelis occupy our homes as victims and present us to the world as killers'.[101] The war of words and weapons continues unabated. One telling example was the furore caused by John Adams' compelling opera, *The Death of Klinghoffer* (1991), based on the hijacking by the Palestine Liberation Front of the cruise ship Achille Lauro in 1985. Adams included a moving lament entitled 'Chorus of the exiled Palestinians', which led amongst other things to a fatuous charge of anti-Semitism, his critics disregarding the fact that this passage was immediately followed by a 'Chorus of Exiled Jews'.

The historian can at least point out common experiences of persecution and commemoration. Consider Naji al-ʿAli's description of his famous cartoon creation:

Handala was born ten years old, and he will always be ten years old. At that age, I left my homeland, and when he returns, Handala will still be ten, and then he will start growing up. The laws of nature do not apply to him. He is unique. Things will become normal again when the homeland returns. I presented him to the poor and named him Handala as a symbol of bitterness. At first, he was a Palestinian child, but his consciousness developed to have a national and then a global and human horizon. He is a simple yet tough child, and this is why people adopted him and felt that he represents their consciousness.[102]

---

[100] 'Confronting the Beast', *The Guardian*, 15 September 2007.
[101] Barghouti, *I Saw Ramallah*, 177–8.
[102] <http://www.handala.org/handala.html>.

'Simplicity and toughness' will surely be recognizable to Israelis who stop to reflect on the broader meaning of these attributes. The image of a refugee who 'never grew up' encapsulates the lives that were forfeited prematurely by Jews and Palestinians alike. It has a universal quality, describing the sense of being suspended in mid-air or—in Barghouti's phrase—trapped between commas.

5

Midnight's Refugees?
Partition and its Aftermath in India and Pakistan

[In answer to the question, 'What were you doing on 15 August 1947?']
What do you think we were doing? Wondering where we'd be the next day,
whether we'd be able to stay on, even in this place. That's what we were doing

(Atam Singh, Sikh shopkeeper)

INTRODUCTION

In South Asia, as in the Middle East, the retreat from empire reshaped the relationship between population and territory. Widespread violence accompanied the division of India in 1947, unleashing mass displacement as people from different
ethno-religious backgrounds fled either towards Pakistan or India. Broadly speaking the 'refugee problem' was contained within South Asia. Whilst this placed
enormous strain on the resources of both countries, the emergence of a regional
refugee regime helped define India and Pakistan as sovereign nation-states. In other
words relief efforts required and enabled India and Pakistan to establish their legitimacy by making material provision for refugees and finding them a place in the
new society. The formation of new states went hand in hand with the management
of refugees on behalf of the nation.

Partition constituted the first but not the last territorial reconfiguration of
the Indian sub-continent. Less than a quarter century later Pakistan itself broke
asunder. Bangladesh's war of independence created a crisis second only in magnitude to that of 1947. The number of refugees shot up from 120,000 to three
and a half million within a matter of weeks in the spring of 1971. Key questions
once again came to the fore: who belonged to the nation and who did not?
What responsibilities did the state have towards refugees, and vice versa? What
role might international organizations and NGOs play in the crisis? What views
did refugees hold of their predicament and what hopes for the future did they
entertain?

The territorial division of India in August 1947 had devastating and largely
unforeseen consequences. The suddenness with which British officials reached a
decision—at the start of the year they spoke vaguely of leaving India 'no later than
June 1948'—reflected but also provoked an outpouring of hostility between

Hindus, Sikhs and Muslims. As violence intensified so, too, did support for an accelerated partition as the best prospect for restoring a semblance of normality. Sir Cyril Radcliffe chaired a commission that drew up the proposed boundary between the two new states. Radcliffe left India after a few weeks without a hair out of place; millions of others did not have such a lucky escape.[1] The terrible violence that accompanied Partition formed the backdrop to a much greater movement of refugees. Around 850,000 refugees moved from Pakistan to India in just 42 days between mid-September and late October 1947. Much of this upheaval occurred in Punjab. In Bengal, by contrast cross-border movement was less rigorously enforced and migration in both directions assumed a different pace compared to the west.[2]

Notwithstanding the accumulating evidence of inter-communal tension, the signatories to the agreement that divided the Raj did not expect the transfer of power and the partition of India to be accompanied by a mass movement of population. Partition was conceived as a means of preventing migration on a large scale, because the borders would be adjusted instead. Minorities need not be troubled by the new configuration. As Pakistan's first Prime Minister, Liaquat Ali Khan, affirmed, 'the division of India into Pakistan and India Dominions was based on the principle that minorities will stay where they were and that the two states will afford all protection to them as citizens of the respective states'. This view was widely shared on both sides. But the arrangement whereby more than two-thirds of India's Muslim population were assigned to Pakistan, leaving a sizeable Muslim minority in India, was not regarded as immutable. Indian Prime Minister Jawaharlal Nehru said that 'we expected that the partition would be temporary, that Pakistan was bound to come back to us'.[3] Contrary to his expectations, the separation of Pakistan and India proved to be not provisional but permanent.

The process of nation-building in India and Pakistan assumed that refugees would conform to government expectations to be grateful for relief and to become accustomed to rehabilitation. Such assumptions did not include the expectation that refugees would speak on their own behalf. What did this imply for refugees' testimony? In recent years oral historians have begun to pay attention to popular memories of Partition, including the stories told by female survivors and by those who came to their assistance. This historiography forms part of a broader argument about the nature of suffering and 'victimhood' that continues to resonate in the turbulent party politics of India, Pakistan and Bangladesh. The history of displacement from above and from below has inevitably been politicized.[4]

---

[1] W.H. Auden's poem, 'Partition' (1966), made this point in blistering fashion.

[2] Joya Chatterji, 'The Fashioning of a Frontier: the Radcliffe Line and Bengal's Border Landscape, 1947–1952' *MAS*, 33, no.1 (1999), 185–242; Yasmin Khan, *The Great Partition: the Making of India and Pakistan* (Yale University Press, 2007), 129, 156.

[3] Tahir Hasnein Naqvi, 'The Politics of Commensuration: Violence of Partition and the Making of the Pakistani State' *Journal of Historical Sociology*, 20, nos.1–2 (2007), 44–71, at 59; Alok Bhalla, *Partition Dialogues: Memories of a Lost Home* (Oxford: Oxford University Press, 2006), 46.

[4] Ian Talbot and Gurharpal Singh, *The Partition of India* (Cambridge: Cambridge University Press, 2009); Zolberg, Suhrke and Aguayo, *Escape from Violence*, 136–45.

The drama of Partition was brought to life by novelists, photographers, film makers and others. British civil servant Penderel Moon compared the violence to the atrocities committed during the Napoleonic Wars as drawn by Goya.[5] Renowned contemporary photo-journalists including Margaret Bourke-White and Sambhu Saha created images of refugees in different settings. Henri Cartier-Bresson took photos in one of the enormous refugee camps in Delhi as well as of Muslim refugees on crowded trains destined for Lahore. They appeared alongside his photos of market scenes and princely ceremonies, as if he wanted to set the violence of Partition against a broader background of more tranquil 'tradition'. Later on the UN and NGOs and the government of India reproduced powerful photographs of suffering in Bangladesh and India to legitimize their intervention. These representations affected the form and extent of relief efforts and assessments of the future prospects for refugees.

PARTITIONING PUNJAB

The decision to enforce a partition of India was announced on 3 June 1947. This was not a foregone conclusion. In 1940 leaders of the prominent Muslim League advocated a 'Pak Commonwealth of Nations' with Muslim-majority populations in delineated territories including 'Pakistan', 'Bangistan' and 'Osmanistan'. Two and a half months after giving notice of partition, and immediately following formal independence, officials made public the demarcation of the new borders. Gone was the idea of a patchwork of Muslim polities. Pakistan now emerged as a bifurcated state divided between West Pakistan, created from the North-West Frontier Provinces, Baluchistan, Sindh and West Punjab, and East Pakistan on the other, comprising East Bengal and the Sylhet district of Assam. Some Hindu politicians and officials affected a relaxed attitude towards partition, loftily arguing that 'Hindustan is the elephant and Pakistan the two ears. The elephant can live without the ears'.[6] This peremptory suggestion failed to take account of the violence and mass migration that preceded and followed the division of the Raj.

Politicians were overtaken by events. No sooner had the new border commissions began their work but migration occurred on a massive scale. Contemporary descriptions evoked a sense of panic as news reached remote settlements of the decisions taken in the corridors of power and of growing mass violence. Outbreaks of violence between Hindus, Sikhs and Muslims were already commonplace in the final months of the Raj. The level of violence was far greater in Punjab than elsewhere. Muslims fled from Bihar to Western Punjab at the end of 1946 and during

---

[5] Khan, *The Great Partition*, 129.

[6] K.M. Panikkar, quoted in Khan, *The Great Partition*, 87. 'Pakistan' is a compound term coined by Rehmat Ali in 1933, referring to Punjab, Afghanistan, Kashmir, Sindh and Baluchistan. Partition created sovereign Indian enclaves within Pakistan and vice versa.

the first half of 1947, whilst Sikhs and Hindus moved in the opposite direction. In March 1947 Rawalpindi was aflame. Around half a million Muslims and an equal number of Hindus fled their homes before the handover of power in August 1947, expecting to feel safer in areas where their community was in the majority.[7] The announcement of the British withdrawal precipitated jockeying for position between rival politico-religious groups and militias in the midst of disintegrating political authority and uncertainty about the dividing line between the two proposed states. Decisions about state frontiers, particularly in the Punjab, infuriated those Indians who wanted a very substantial 'elephant' and Muslim League leaders such as Mohammed Ali Jinnah and his followers who anticipated large 'ears'.

In all, around 7.5 million Hindus and Sikhs and six million Muslims crossed the newly created borders of India and Pakistan between 1947 and 1951 (see Map 6). More than four-fifths of this total crossed the frontier between India and West Pakistan in Punjab, where Radcliffe's line placed 27 per cent of Punjab's Muslim population under Indian administration and one-third of its Hindu and Sikh population under the authority of Pakistan. In Amritsar, where Muslims made up nearly half the total population of the city before Partition, only a tiny handful remained. This is not to say that people moved directly from one country to the other; Muslim households spent months in temporary camps in India, in the expectation that they would not need to relocate permanently. Jinnah himself expressed the hope that 'officials of the opposite community [in Punjab] would at a later stage come back'.[8]

Both governments arranged hundreds of convoys by train and lorry, or by foot. Railway staff worked overtime to keep the 'refugee specials' going. A Military Evacuation Organization was established by mutual agreement on 3 September 1947 to arrange for the organized transfer of refugees in Punjab. Eye-witnesses described never-ending lines of refugees moving in both directions along the Great Trunk Road. In September a huge fleet of 400,000 people moved from Lyallpur in West Punjab to India, taking eight days to pass through a given point; officials had an immense job arranging for rest stops, food and medical aid, as well as keeping the different convoys apart. People took to the airwaves of All-India Radio to seek information about family members. Nor did the uncertainty cease once refugees reached a place of relative safety. Local newspapers reported desperation both on the faces of the refugee 'influx' and of officials and charity workers. In Delhi the correspondent of *The Times* (London) wrote of refugees as 'carriers of infectious disease and mental derangement'. Graphic accounts helped validate bureaucratic intervention in order to assist the displaced survivors, who were deemed incapable of managing their own affairs. A visiting American psychologist described 'a group of straggling sufferers trying to pull together the fragments of a life lost, and unable

---

[7] Ravinder Kaur, 'The Last Journey: Exploring Social Class in the 1947 Partition Migration' *Economic and Political Weekly* (3 June 2006), 2221–8.

[8] Gyanendra Pandey, *Remembering Partition: Violence, Nationalism and History in India* (Cambridge: Cambridge University Press, 2001), 41.

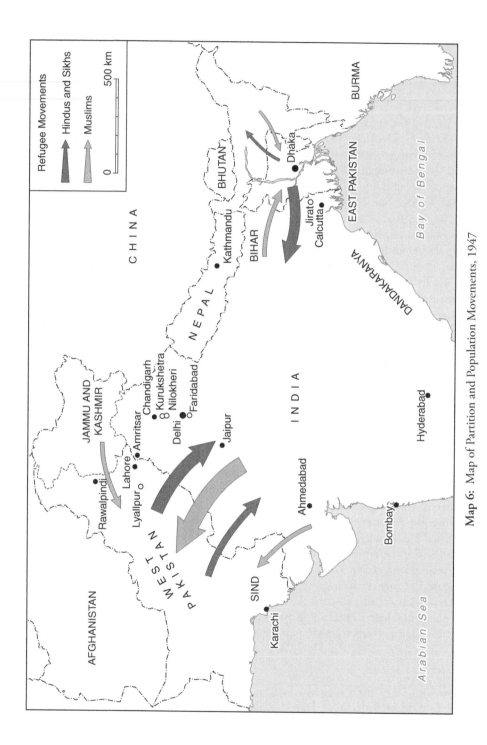

Map 6: Map of Partition and Population Movements, 1947

to do so', clearly implying that refugees faced an uphill and perhaps impossible struggle to recover their composure.[9] This underestimated their resourcefulness.

The idea of an abrupt migration or *raula* in Punjab captured official and popular imagination alike. Most officials in the dying Raj were unprepared for the violence and the intensity of population displacement. Officials described it as a 'vivisection' and even as a 'holocaust'.[10] The Director-General of the Office of Rehabilitation expressed a widely-held view about the flight of Hindu and Sikh refugees from West to East Punjab:

> The hand that was sowing the seed in the fields in the morning was hurriedly packing in the afternoon. When at the time of evacuation the farmers yoked their bullocks to the carts which formed their mile-long caravans they looked wistfully at their houses, granaries full of wheat, and orchards of oranges which they had planted with so much care. The only choice before them was to say goodbye to the land of their birth. When their world turned upside down, the refugees, especially in the villages, were completely unprepared for the enormous calamity of displacement which had befallen them.[11]

Abrupt it may have been, but Partition formed part of a long history of migration in Punjab. Sikh farmers from around Amritsar settled in the famous canal colonies on the North-West frontier in the late nineteenth century, until Partition forced their descendants to return to a 'home' they had never known. Hindu farmers who cultivated the rich cotton and wheat fields in West Punjab likewise ended up returning to their ancestral villages as refugees. Thus the drama of Partition in Punjab took place on a stage that had already witnessed significant demographic disturbance.[12]

PARTITIONING BENGAL

In contrast to Punjab the situation in Bengal was a great deal more fluid—an Indian social worker who became a government minister described it as 'a case of slow poisoning'.[13] But we should not underestimate the impact of violence immediately before and after the British withdrawal. In Calcutta, the Muslim League called for a day of 'direct action' on 16 August 1946 in support of a Muslim state.

---

[9] Gardner Murphy, *In the Minds of Men: the Study of Human Behavior and Social Tensions in India* (New York: Basic Books, 1953), 167.

[10] Ravinder Kaur, *Since 1947: Partition Narratives among Punjabi Migrants of Delhi* (New Delhi: Oxford University Press, 2007), 188; U. Bhaskar Rao, *The Story of Rehabilitation* (Delhi: Department of Rehabilitation, 1967), 1; Mohinda S. Randhawa, *Out of the Ashes: an Account of the Rehabilitation of Refugees from West Pakistan in Rural Areas of East Punjab* (Chandigarh: Public Relations Department, 1954), 12–25.

[11] Randhawa, *Out of the Ashes*, 33.

[12] Uditi Sen, 'Dissident Memories: Exploring Bengali Refugee Narratives in the Andaman Islands', in Panayi and Virdee (eds), *Refugees and the End of Empire*, 291–44; Amrith, 'Reconstructing the "Plural Society"'.

[13] Ritu Menon (ed.), *No Woman's Land: Women from Pakistan, India and Bangladesh Write on the Partition of India* (New Delhi: Women Unlimited, 2004), 201.

Impoverished Muslim labourers attacked Hindu shopkeepers, leaving at least 5,000 people dead. Three months later, pogroms in Noakhali, East Bengal, resulted in similar casualties when a small number of Muslim demagogues incited the crowd to terrorize the population and demanded that Hindu women convert. Often construed as 'irrational', from the point of view of the perpetrators these attacks on private property were carefully considered tactics to compel owners to abandon their homes and businesses, which they duly did.

A two-way flow took place as Muslim officials who had been employed by the Raj now moved to East Pakistan in the hope of maintaining their status, an important reminder that some people looked upon Partition as an opportunity and a blessing rather than as a dead-end or curse. Although on average 12,000 refugees moved each day from East Pakistan to India in 1948, many more stayed where they were. Nevertheless, tensions between the Hindus who remained in East Pakistan on the one hand, and Muslims who remained in India on the other, ran high: anti-Hindu riots in East Pakistan in 1950 were for these people the final straw. As realization dawned that they faced social humiliation and economic marginalization, the exodus became unstoppable.[14]

Although some Hindu families anticipated a difficult time if they stayed in East Bengal, most expected the plans to be overturned and resolved to stay in their own homes and await the reunification of the country. Until the early 1950s, individual Muslims and Hindus, their status uncertain and contested, shuttled back and forth across the border between India and East Pakistan. Migrants did not require passports until 1952, although both governments introduced permits in 1948 in an attempt to regulate cross-border travel. Thereafter those who overstayed, including Indian Muslims who visited relatives in Pakistan before returning to India, were liable to be deported. This was a shocking introduction to the realities of post-imperial state formation. Not for nothing did people lament the immutable and impermeable line that now demarcated India and Pakistan.[15]

The government of West Bengal distinguished between 'victims of communal violence' and economic migrants who hoped to improve their prospects by crossing the border. Ministers argued that newly arriving migrants from East Pakistan were not exposed to communal violence and therefore had no claim on government funds; there was a grain of truth in this charge, insofar as many workers crossed the frontier to take advantage of new employment opportunities. Underlying these tough new responses was the view that West Bengal could not cope with a large influx of Hindu refugees. Nehru shared this opinion, although his main motive was not to antagonize Pakistan by implying that East Pakistan was making life intolerable for the Hindu minority. The government of West Bengal hoped to deter refugees from leaving East Bengal by making it clear that they could expect

---

[14] Penderel Moon, *Divide and Quit: an Eye-Witness Account of the Partition of India* (Delhi: Oxford University Press, 1962).

[15] Vazira Fazila-Yacoobali Zamindar, *The Long Partition and the Making of Modern South Asia: Refugees, Boundaries, and Histories* (New York: Columbia University Press, 2007), 205–8.

unfavourable conditions should they opt for India. Tens of thousands of Hindus who reached the outskirts of Calcutta by steamer or on jungle pathways were held at a reception centre at Sealdah railway station for months whilst officials decided their fate. The authorities distinguished between 'genuine' and 'undeserving' claimants, rejecting the claims to relief payments of those who failed to register with the authorities before the end of 1948, on the grounds that they had missed their chance.

These deterrents had little effect. By the middle of 1948 the number of refugees who entered West Bengal topped the one million mark, and two years later this figure had trebled. In April 1950 Nehru signed an agreement with Liaquat Ali Khan, his opposite number in Pakistan, giving migrants on both sides the right to return to their homes and have their property restored to them. However, the loss of status and income faced by middle-class Hindu families in East Pakistan meant that they had little choice but to leave and to make use if possible of the connections they had built up in the past. In all, some 4.2 million Bengalis left East Pakistan between 1947 and 1962.[16]

Elsewhere a foretaste of things to come emerged in Kashmir about the unresolved status of refugees who fled to West Pakistan during the war that India and Pakistan fought in November 1947 over the princely states of Kashmir and Jammu. Border towns quickly expanded in size. By 1949 the total including in Pakistan-administered Azad Kashmir numbered 582,000 refugees, more than half of whom were living in camps organized by the government in Lahore on the understanding that 'temporary rehabilitation' would cease when the war ended and they could go back to their homes. Others were displaced within what became the Indian-administered territory of Jammu-and-Kashmir, where they squatted on land that had been vacated by refugees who fled to Pakistan. Sixty years on, their number has grown through natural increase, and their 'temporary' status has in effect become permanent.[17]

RELIEF MEASURES AFTER 1947

In Pakistan much of the responsibility for emergency provision fell upon the new provincial government in West Punjab, but the refugee crisis provided Jinnah with an opportunity in November 1947 to express his faith in the 'morale, fortitude and courage displayed by the refugees', adding that they should help one another and insisting that 'nothing is going to shake Pakistan'. Muslim refugees had made a 'sacrifice' that should be recognized by those who had not been uprooted.[18] Officials

[16] Joya Chatterji, '"Dispersal" and the Failure of Rehabilitation: Refugee Camp-dwellers and Squatters in West Bengal' *MAS*, 41, no.5 (2007), 995–1032; Prafulla K. Chakrabarti, *The Marginal Men: the Refugees and the Left Political Syndrome in West Bengal* (Calcutta: Naya Udyog, 1999), 11–22.

[17] Vernant, *The Refugee in the Post-War World*, 766–7; Cabeiri deBergh Robinson, 'Too Much Nationality: Kashmiri Refugees, the South Asian Refugee Regime, and a Refugee State, 1947–1974', *JRS*, 25, no.2 (2012), 344–65.

[18] Saleem Ullah Khan, *The Journey to Pakistan: a Documentation on Refugees of 1947* (Islamabad: National Documentation Centre, 1993), 294–5.

described the newcomers as *muhajirs* who had incurred enormous losses on behalf of their fledgling state. One outcome was that the local authorities in Karachi who complained that the city was 'overflowing' and unable to accommodate any more refugees faced the wrath of newly legitimized *muhajir* spokesmen who played on the idea of their 'sacrifice' for the nation, a stance that was later institutionalized in the Muhajir Qaumi Movement, which now complains that the Pakistani state treated the 1947-vintage refugees as second-class citizens.[19]

In India, too, rhetoric was accompanied by material assistance. A new Ministry for Relief and Rehabilitation on 6 September 1947 managed 45 refugee camps in East Punjab alone, providing temporary accommodation for between 10,000 and 50,000 refugees apiece. At one stage the government administered 160 camps housing 1.2 million refugees. A huge camp near the holy city of Kurukshetra north-west of Delhi took on the appearance of a tented city with schools, hospitals, clinics and shops that at one stage served a quarter of a million refugees. The government made emergency services available including facilities for Hindu and Sikh women to terminate the pregnancies that resulted from rape at the hands of Muslim men.[20]

The crisis provided an opportunity for domestic NGOs to present themselves as part of the new order. In Pakistan Begum Liaquat Ali Khan (wife of the Prime Minister) headed the Pakistan Voluntary Service which distributed food, clothing and medicine. Jami'at al Islam (JAI) administered camps for Muslim refugees, amongst whom it sought donations for its cause. In India the Rashtriya Swayam-sevak Sangh (National Volunteers' Union, established in 1925) administered refugee camps, and lost no time in using its position to assert the superiority of Hindu religion and culture.[21] Social workers from the Tata School of Social Sciences in Bombay and the Indian Boy Scouts helped administer Kurukshetra camp. External organizations such as the YMCA, Catholic Relief Services and the Quakers provided food and medicine. Richard Symonds, who assisted with famine relief in Calcutta in 1942–44, returned in 1947 to work with the Friends Service Unit in Delhi, Punjab and Kashmir, where he praised the work done by Indian and Pakistani troops to provide a safe passage to trainloads of refugees.[22]

By and large international assistance was disappointing. Europe was preoccupied with its own 'DP problem'. Events in the sub-continent did not directly connect with Cold War concerns, nor did the USA associate the crisis with its 'strategic interests', as it did in Korea and the Middle East. India's Minister of Relief and Rehabilitation regretted that 'the powerful tide of international help flowed past the vast area of our own tragedy without as much lapping at its fringes'. The 1951

[19] Zamindar, *The Long Partition*, 238; Ian Talbot, 'A Tale of Two Cities: the Aftermath of Partition for Lahore and Amritsar, 1947–1957' *MAS*, 41, no.1 (2007), 151–85.

[20] Rao, *The Story of Rehabilitation*, 46–7; testimony of Jogendra Singh, in Menon, *No Woman's Land*, 187–94; testimony of Mrs Kuljeet Kaur, in Ian Talbot and Darshan Singh Tatla (eds), *Epicentre of Violence: Partition Voices and Memories from Amritsar* (Delhi: Permanent Black, 2006), 135–41.

[21] Jean A. Curran, 'The RSS: Militant Hinduism' *Far Eastern Survey*, 19, no.10 (1950), 93–8.

[22] Richard Symonds, *In the Margins of Independence: a Relief Worker in India and Pakistan, 1942–1949* (Oxford: Oxford University Press, 2001), 43, 70.

Convention made no provision for refugees in the Indian sub-continent. India and Pakistan refused to sign, complaining about its European focus but also encroachment on state sovereignty. UNHCR therefore had no role to play.[23] The two governments trod a difficult path, on the one hand resisting external interference but hoping on the other for a contribution from wealthy Western countries.

In this unfavourable situation, UNICEF, the ICRC and the World Health Organization (WHO) spoke of being overwhelmed by the scale of the task. The British Red Cross launched hospitals and dispensaries. Individual relief workers (including the wife of the last Viceroy of India, Edwina, Countess Mountbatten who chaired the emergency United Council for Relief and Welfare at Nehru's request) acted on their own account. Indian women worked tirelessly in Punjab helping to arrange health care and education. Subsequent accounts of 'rehabilitation' construed this in terms of the refined sensibilities of individuals: 'What one needed here were virtues alien to bureaucratic routine—sympathy, understanding, great compassion, the urge to succour and sustain, attributes almost of divinity'. Women's groups mobilized to supply food, shelter and medical care to the refugee camps, frequently drawing on the organizational experience they acquired during the Bengal famine of 1943.[24]

India and Pakistan duly made legislative provision for Partition refugees. As explained earlier, the government of West Bengal limited its obligations by restricting assistance to those who had been displaced before the end of June 1948. In Pakistan all citizens, including Hindus, were expected to contribute to the Jinnah Fund to assist refugees from India. Little information is available about the overall impact of Partition on the budget of either state, but it must have been considerable; according to one source the Indian Treasury spent the equivalent of $67 million in 1950 prices (322 million rupees) on refugee camps alone in 1947–50.[25]

The two governments eventually agreed a complex compensation package for those who lost property as a result of Partition. India passed the Displaced Persons (Legal Proceedings) Act in 1949. Pakistan issued a property ordinance in 1950 followed by the Displaced Persons (Compensation and Rehabilitation) Act in 1958. Under the terms of these acts refugees were deemed to be people who fled 'civil disturbances or the fear of disturbances'. In practice this meant that India recognized Hindus and Sikhs as 'displaced persons', whereas departing Muslims were defined as 'evacuees', whose flight enabled non-Muslims to be settled on the vacated property. Attempts to manage the financial consequences were contentious: the Indian government complained of a serious imbalance, because the value of the property that Hindu and Sikh refugees left behind in Pakistan far exceeded that of Muslims who fled India. Another key component in the bilateral agreement was the insistence that 'non-agreed' refugees should stay where they were; but those

---

[23] Rao, *The Story of Rehabilitation*, 3; Loescher, *UNHCR*, 57.

[24] Joya Chatterji, 'Right or Charity? The Debate over Relief and Rehabilitation in West Bengal, 1947–1950', in Suvir Kaul (ed.), *The Partitions of Memory* (Delhi: Permanent Black, 2001), 74–110, at 88.

[25] Vernant, *The Refugee in the Post-War World*, 746.

who did so found themselves at a disadvantage when it came to redistributing the assets that the Hindu population left behind following their departure for India.[26]

In the midst of this violent turmoil, displaced people tried to affirm a sense of self-worth. Hindus who fled East Pakistan rejected the term 'refugee', claiming instead that they were forced to leave in order to help build the new state of India: '[W]e did not (as one organisation put it) fight for independence in order to lead the lives of beggars'. They demanded compensation, not charity. Appealing to the history of nineteenth-century migration to the canal colonies a Punjabi farmer wrote many years later of how he countered the taunts of onlookers by saying 'we are not refugees, we are your brothers, and now we have come back to our native lands', but that ' "refugee" was a tag we carried [and] whenever the term was mentioned, we felt ashamed'.[27] Only when making an ironic comment on the lack of official recognition did they speak of themselves as 'refugees' in need of protection (*sharanarthi*), a term that carried demeaning connotations. Normally they claimed to be *bastuhara*, meaning people who had lost their home, hearth or 'foundations' (*bastu*), or *pursharthi*, believers in self-help.[28] Erstwhile government officials who moved from India to East Pakistan similarly refused to be labelled as refugees—refugees were those 'who had to run away for some reason'—and instead described themselves as 'optees' who staked a legitimate claim to citizenship.[29]

Refugees displayed contrasting modes of petitioning government officials. One anonymous activist wrote in the following terms in 1948:

> I am coming from Frontier Province [Pakistan] where I worked in the Congress for about 26 years. My work was appreciated by the Provincial Congress as well as by our great leader, Pandit Jawaharlal [Nehru]. I remained in jail several times in connection with the civil disobedience movement. I came here with bare head and three clothes on my body. I am seeking the way to serve my motherland under Congress discipline but regret to say that still I could not find way to start. Nobody knows me here and my work done in the Congress fold in my dear Province. Here in UP [Uttar Pradesh] I want to pass my further life [but] the Congress organisations are ignoring me. Now I am 56 and forcibly exiled from my home [and] I am wandering disappointed. Will you kindly advise me what to do and where to do in this critical moment of my life? I have also extreme heart still to serve my national country.

Another spoke on behalf of a broader community (Panchayat), in a letter submitted in 1948 to the Prime Minister of Bombay: 'Though all of us have lost everything, we have not lost faith in Providence and endeavour. Though poor we would hesitate to be a burden on your most benevolent Govt. We have been by nature most docile and immobile in our trade and traditions. We therefore request that a

---

[26] Tahir Naqvi, 'Migration, Sacrifice and the Crisis of Muslim Nationalism' *JRS*, 25, no.2 (2012), 474–90.

[27] Pippa Virdee, ' "No Home but in Memory": the Legacies of Colonial Rule in the Punjab', in Panayi and Virdee (eds), *Refugees and the End of Empire*, 175–95, at 188.

[28] Kaur, *Since 1947*, 183–4; Ram N. Saksena, *Refugees: a Study in Changing Attitudes* (Bombay: Asia Publishing House, 1961), 47.

[29] N. Mahbubar Rahman and Willem van Schendel, ' "I Am Not a Refugee": Rethinking Partition History' *MAS*, 37, no.3 (2003), 551–84, at 564.

portion of one [of the above named camps] be given to our Panchayat people all in a Group in one camp, on rental system. This will facilitate us to retain our old customs, trade and traditions and brotherhood and shall be able to help each other through thick and thin'.[30]

These were not isolated instances of collective self-assertiveness. Refugees from East Bengal organized themselves into camp committees (see later in this chapter). In West Pakistan, Muslim refugees who reached Karachi complained about the difficulty of getting compensation for the property they lost, and the corruption involved in reaching a settlement. Similar stories emerged in India. Sometimes refugees' anger culminated in direct action, as in protests against the living conditions that they were expected to tolerate. But this was a dangerous course to pursue. In Jaipur, for instance, organized protests in 1949 led to the deaths of 15 refugees at the hands of armed police who were called in by the Ministry of Relief and Rehabilitation, another indication that the dangers faced by displaced persons could come from any quarter.[31]

FROM 'REHABILITATION' TO 'DEVELOPMENT'

The political, economic, social and demographic impact of displacement plays an important part in the story of Partition. How could it be otherwise, when every tenth person in Pakistan was a refugee (in Karachi and Lahore the proportion rose to at least half) and when something close to one-third of Delhi's inhabitants were refugees? Delhi lost 330,000 Muslim inhabitants, but by 1955 its population had increased to 1.7 million, nearly twice as great as its pre-Partition size. The population of Bombay rocketed from 1.4 million on the eve of Partition to 2.3 million in 1950, a net increase all the more remarkable for the forced departure of most of its Muslim inhabitants. The situation in Calcutta was particularly unstable, but it created opportunities for refugees to make their mark in more ways than one. It became a magnet for middle-class refugees and for artisans from East Bengal with contacts in the city. Other refugees followed in their wake, keen to maintain a distinction between themselves and plebeian newcomers. Displacement entailed rapid downward social mobility for some of the *bhadralok* class (genteel folk or 'middle-class' professionals). But others set up 'welfare associations' and 'protection societies', trading on their status as displaced people—overtly so, as in the case of the 'Refugees Old Motor Parts Dealers' Association'.[32]

Squatters who fled from East Bengal established impromptu colonies. In the late 1950s Delhi became the site of the East Pakistan Displaced Persons' Colony (now Chittaranjan Park), home to Bengali government officials. Earlier still, refugees in

---

[30] Urvashi Butalia, 'An Archive with a Difference', in Kaul (ed.), *Partitions of Memory*, 74–110, at 219, 224–5; Kaur, *Since 1947*, 186.

[31] Khan, *The Great Partition*, 173–5.

[32] Ravinder Kaur, 'Distinctive Citizenship: Refugees, Subjects and Post-colonial State in India's Partition' *CSH*, 6, no.4 (2009), 429–46, at 431.

Calcutta appropriated land around the local airport and on an abandoned US army base as well as *waqf* land that formerly belonged to Muslim charitable foundations, declaring it 'empty space'. A resident of Viveknagar Colony in South Calcutta described chopping down trees and clearing a space, 'levelling the land and dividing it into small plots, laying down lanes and roads. I moved there with my mother, sister and brother. My mother was able to get one plot and we became part of this colony'. They pointedly named the colony after the Bengali word for 'conscience' (*vivek*), to remind the host population of their obligation to refugees. A determined group took over vacant land in a Calcutta suburb and allocated plots to fellow refugees on a first-come first-served basis, naming the new settlement Azadgarh, literally 'bastion of freedom'. Careful preparatory work included making surveys and taking photographs of the terrain: there was nothing haphazard about their action. Other colonies were named after heroes of the resistance to British rule.[33]

By the late 1950s there were around 400 of these private 'sponsored' colonies, together with a similar number of government colonies. An official inquiry spelt out the important differences between these self-settled refugees and those who were housed by the government in designated camps. Refugees in Azadgarh took pains to defend their homes from government attempts to move them elsewhere. They elected committees and levied self-imposed taxes to help dig wells, build roads, schools, clinics, clubhouses and theatre companies. Refugees spoke of the 'green and peaceful' surroundings that made a pleasant contrast with overcrowded Calcutta. They had no wish to renounce these conditions. They mobilized in self-defence, supported by the United Central Refugee Council and the Refugee Central Rehabilitation Council, which agitated for compensation and in due course for government recognition of rights to jobs, land and housing. Women fought off attacks, often at great personal risk, from agents employed by absentee landlords (*zamindars*) to drive them away.[34]

Before long these colonies became a fertile recruiting ground for the Communist Party whose members offered tangible support and helped to maintain the morale of refugees, including displaced Muslims. They agitated for improvements to infrastructure and helped to organize cooperatives and schools, filling the gap left by other political parties, including the Congress Party, in a process not unlike the politics of inter-war Greece. Joya Chatterji has argued that 'the construct of rights which evolved out [of] the successive refugee campaigns came to be part of an increasingly broad-based and inclusive political programme in a welfarist and even socialist mode'. This was linked to an analysis of the failure of political leadership. As one Punjabi refugee wrote in 1947, 'the entire EVIL lies in the separation theories (i.e. communal award, vivisection of country on religion basis, exchange of population, and accepting religion as the basis for Nation etc.). Would those

---

[33] Romola Sanyal, 'Contesting Refugeehood: Squatting as Survival in Post-Partition Calcutta' *Social Identities*, 15, no.1 (2009), 67–84.
[34] Gargi Chakravartty, *Coming Out of Partition: Refugee Women of Bengal* (New Delhi: Bluejay Books, 2005), 52–63.

talking so high try to fit the Refugees shoe on their own feet for a while and then express how comfortable they are?'[35]

At the same time, ideas of spontaneity and chaos provided a pretext for the construction of organized encampments where officials could temporarily impose a degree of order before dispersing unruly refugees to more remote regions where they would exercise a less disruptive influence and begin the process of 'rehabilitation'. The Indian government expected refugees to build new camps according to blueprints that were designed by officials who took no account of refugee wishes; one camp at Jirat in West Bengal, built to accommodate rural refugees who arrived from the East in 1950, was established on malarial marshland, at a distance from Calcutta that made it impossible for refugees to travel in search of work. Other camps were set up to enable refugee labour to be employed on road-building and canal construction. A contemporary report drew attention to poor physical and mental health but attributed this to 'infantilisation' rather than to government ineptitude. A government minister regarded the camps as 'the show window of the Ministry's herculean labours' and a 'laboratory for the experiments in abiding rehabilitation that were soon to be undertaken on a large scale'. This social experiment was all the more necessary in the light of 'psychological disturbance' and 'reason overthrown' that refugees were deemed to have experienced. Rehabilitation was connected to the prospect of 'independent living'.[36]

After the first flurry of emergency relief measures, in March 1948 the government in Delhi turned its attention to vocational training, education and employment. Japanese technicians helped train skilled mechanics and metal workers to replace the Muslim workers who had since gone to Pakistan. As indicated earlier, this was also conceived as a necessary basis for 'rehabilitation', meaning not just the provision of education and skills but the inculcation of habits of citizenship. The process would take time: Horace Alexander, author of an informative early study of Indian policy, wrote that 'the vast majority of the so-called "hard core" of urban refugees can only be self-supporting when new towns have been built'. The government looked askance at refugees who continued to depend on state support; the minister responsible for their welfare urged that 'gratuitous relief' be discontinued, in order to give 'the drone' (sic) a chance to 'rehabilitate himself' outside the camps. By 1955 these efforts were coupled to a so-called National Discipline Scheme designed to promote physical fitness, self-discipline and self-reliance. Mohanlal Saksena invited India's social workers to identify themselves with refugees 'who have lost their all and who are still probing in the dark, without any hope of redemption'.[37]

---

[35] Kaur, *Since 1947*, 188–9, capitals in the original; Chatterji, 'Right or Charity?', 97.

[36] Rao, *The Story of Rehabilitation*, 46–7; Biraja Guha, *Studies in Social Tensions among the Refugees from Eastern Pakistan* (Delhi: Government of India Press, 1959), 2–14; Chatterji, 'Dispersal' 1011–17; Ian Talbot, 'Punjabi Refugees' Rehabilitation and the Indian State: Discourses, Denials and Dissonances' *MAS*, 45, no.1 (2011), 109–30.

[37] 'The Last of the Noble Lights of Freedom' (a tribute to M.L. Saksena by his son), Saksena Papers, Nehru Memorial Library, Delhi; Government of India, *Rehabilitation Retrospect* (New Delhi: Ananda Press, 1957), 31; Horace G. Alexander, *New Citizens of India* (Bombay: Oxford University Press, 1951), 35; Kaur, 'Distinctive Citizenship', 435.

The governments of both countries as well as semi-official agencies such as the Indian Cooperative Union began to link relief to a broader conception of state intervention and a commitment to 'development'. One indication was the appointment of the first Director-General of Rehabilitation to the Indian Planning Commission.In practice, the resources that the state poured into these programmes favoured better-off refugees who could take advantage of their contacts and educational qualifications. Development projects were infused with a patronizing stance towards lower-class refugees and villagers who lived a life of 'narrow monotony'. Government ministers and NGOs complained about a lack of entrepreneurial ambition among these refugees and hoped that support for cottage industry would provide the necessary stimulus, although the production of quilts, soap and shuttlecocks was small beer compared to the grandiose vision of state-led development. As Yasmin Khan argues, 'Partition could be regarded as an opportunity if refugees who were part of the old, unmodernised, agricultural order could become industrial workers, working on large public works projects'.[38]

In Indian-ruled East Punjab the land abandoned by Muslim farmers was assigned to refugees, following a laborious statistical procedure, with the result that landless labourers and artisans were able to establish themselves on smallholdings. Cooperatives were encouraged, and refugees received loans to buy seed, livestock and equipment. Similar provision was made in Pakistan where contemporaries spoke of the 'splendid response [by refugees] who courageously engaged in occupations completely strange to them'.[39] Wells were dug, and new dams brought electricity to villages for the first time. Farms were consolidated into larger units. Accounts of the new Indian township at Nilokheri, where refugees built homes, shops and factories with government aid, connected its future to a transformation in the personality of the refugees. Horace Alexander spoke in terms reminiscent of early Soviet planners when he described the need for young men to become 'machine-minded'; 'the Nilokheri trainee is not considered fully trained until he understands the whole mechanism, until he can "feel with" the machine he is helping to make. He must try to impart "soul" into machines'. Nehru agreed, adding that Nilokheri was a community development project that blazed the trail for refugee 'rehabilitation'.[40]

A particular source of pride to the Indian government was the Dandakaranya Development Authority in Orissa, which was conceived in 1958 as a means to resettle 25,000 refugee families from East Pakistan in 'a sort of backwater that the tides of modern civilisation passed by'. With the help of overseas agencies such as Church World Service, trees were felled and new villages were established—as it was said—'planned to the last detail'. Lutheran World Relief described how its

<hr />

[38] Khan, *The Great Partition*, 172–3, 229; Gyanesh Kudaisya, 'The Demographic Upheaval of Partition: Refugees and Agricultural Resettlement in India, 1947–1967' *South Asia*, 18, Special Issue (1995), 73–94, at 80; Samir Kumar Das, 'State Response to the Refugee Crisis: Relief and Rehabilitation in the East', in Ranabir Samaddar (ed.), *Refugees and the State: Practices of Asylum and Care in India, 1947–2000* (New Delhi: Sage, 2003), 106–51.
[39] Alexander, *New Citizens of India*, 22, 29–45; Vernant, *The Refugee in the Post-War World*, 764.
[40] Alexander, *New Citizens of India*, 40; Murphy, *In the Minds of Men*, 193, 200.

'Project Daya' ('mercy' in Bengali) would contribute to the 'rehabilitation of these uprooted, plundered, profaned and disinherited people—re-establishing them in responsible social positions'. Dandakaranya, it added, will provide unreclaimed land 'inhabited largely by small groups of aborigines'.[41] Here as elsewhere, 'rehabilitation' was defined in relation to refugees' incapacity, contrasted with the heroic endeavour of relief workers and government planners: one visitor did not hesitate to draw attention to the 'misery' of refugees that was 'seen only by the missionary or the itinerant welfare worker who sacrifices his own personal comfort to visit these forsaken areas in his deep love for humanity'. Dandakaranya was, however, only a qualified success. Refugees—prompted by the Communist Party's tactics of undermining the ruling Congress Party—rejected it in favour of the Sundarbans, the reclaimed mangrove swamps of the Bay of Bengal whose environment was more familiar to them, or opted for the Andaman Islands.[42]

In Pakistan, too, the arrival of refugees had an unsettling effect on the political establishment. The authorities in Sindh claimed that the region was already overcrowded and the local elite locked horns with the newly-arrived refugees (*muhajirs*) who accused provincial leaders of failing to perform their 'patriotic' duty by making adequate provision for them. Local elites regarded the vocal newcomers as a Trojan horse that threatened to shift the gravity of power away from Sindh towards the newly designated capital of Karachi, which is indeed what happened. Ordinary residents resented the intrusion of newcomers who betrayed any signs of privilege; there were complaints that 'idlers and misfits' hoped to make an easier life in Pakistan by cashing in on the new country's sense of obligation to fellow-Muslims. To be sure, the refugee population included wealthy merchants who hoped to prosper in Pakistan where they no longer faced direct competition from Hindu rivals. Out of these complex struggles emerged an oligarchy that cultivated close ties with the Pakistani military and benefited from government subsidies.[43]

This turbulent politics went hand in hand with economic transformation. Hitherto thriving towns in Punjab faced economic ruin. The widespread violence in 1947 devastated the physical infrastructure and created an appalling housing crisis in cities such as Lahore, which was now assigned to Pakistan and lost much of its earlier elegance. Prior to independence Amritsar had been a key transit point for goods that were despatched to Europe and the Middle East; now it belonged to India. Partition ruptured established commercial links—Amritsar's textile mills depended on supplies of dyes from Karachi and cotton from the canal colonies in West Punjab—and led to a net outflow of population that emptied the town of its Muslim artisans (tanners, weavers, dyers, blacksmiths and potters) and traders, leading to a shortage of labour and turning Amritsar into a less important border town. Pakistan, like India, adopted a Five-Year Plan (1955–60) which financed

[41] LWF Archives, Geneva, Box 36, Newspaper Clippings, India.
[42] Alok Kumar Ghosh, 'Bengali Refugees at Dandakarayna: a Tragedy of Rehabilitation', in Pradip Kumar Bose (ed.), *Refugees in West Bengal: Institutional Processes and Contested Identities* (Calcutta: Calcutta Research Group, 2000), 106–29.
[43] Sarah Ansari, *Life after Partition: Migration, Community and Strife in Sindh, 1947–1962* (New York: Oxford University Press, 2005); Naqvi, 'Migration'.

large-scale urban housing projects that were designed to inculcate a 'feeling for the dignity of manual labour'.[44]

Following the military coup in 1958 that brought General Ayub Khan to power, the government espoused a 'back to the land movement'. Planners welcomed the opportunity to reshape the layout of villages on more 'rational' lines. Refugees established new factories in the much enlarged city of Lahore, where textiles and carpet making took off in a big way. Their firms frequently bore the name of the village that their refugee owners left behind in East Punjab, just as refugees did in other settings. Elsewhere too, the new arrivals had a positive effect over time. In Uttar Pradesh, for example, they made and sold optical goods, bicycles, sports equipment and pens in fast-growing towns such as Agra and Meerut, thereby helping to diversify the urban economy. Meanwhile Muslim refugees who arrived in East Pakistan from India set up in business as bakers, tailors, barbers and bangle-makers. They established savings cooperatives. New styles of dress and food—the kebab is a notable example—were introduced. The rickshaw became a common sight on the streets of Pakistan's towns. In short, they made a dynamic contribution to economic and social life.[45]

For all its devastating consequences in terms of loss of life and livelihood, Partition also had the capacity to transform lives in unexpected directions. Some social and economic levelling took place in rural society as a consequence of Partition, and changes in land tenure helped launch the 'Green Revolution'. Research in the 1970s concluded that Punjabi and Sikh refugees were risk-takers. This entrepreneurial streak manifested itself in claims to a kind of invulnerability, paradoxical as it might seem: '[W]e have [said one refugee] gone through so much—what more can happen to us? No-one can do anything to us that can be more terrible than has already occurred. Once everything was taken from us, and we have come back from pennilessness to prosperity. If we lose it all again we could do it once more'. It helped that they also cultivated contacts with local politicians who could assist them to channel this 'aggression' into productive activity.[46]

Fresh job opportunities became available to Punjabi women. The Ministry of Relief and Rehabilitation created a women's section to train prospective teachers, nurses and clerical workers. Female police officers were recruited from the ranks of refugees to help trace girls who had been abducted. Women went out to work in order to replace the income lost when male family members were killed. Female refugees from East Bengal entered white-collar occupations, and their example encouraged West Bengali girls to follow suit. Many mothers insisted that their daughters receive a proper education. In Bihar, widowed Hindu refugees from the new state of (East) Pakistan were regarded as 'unrehabilitable' (sic) by virtue of having lost the chief breadwinner; they were confined to 'Permanent Liability Camps'. Reliant upon state welfare, they nevertheless regarded official assistance as

---

[44] Vernant, *The Refugee in the Post-War World*, 764.
[45] Rahman and van Schendel, 'I Am Not a Refugee', 568–9.
[46] Stephen L. Keller, *Uprooting and Social Change: the Role of Refugees in Development* (Delhi: Manodar Books, 1975), 116, 178; Stein, 'The Refugee Experience', 323.

a debt that society owed them and not the other way round. When the state threatened to close the camps, the women mobilized to defend their rights. Something similar happened in Delhi, where the government instituted a 'widows' colony' for the exclusive use of women whose husbands had been killed. Its inhabitants described a paternalistic regime that reproduced the traditional seclusion of widows whilst providing them with job opportunities. Elsewhere too, women derived a greater sense of self-worth. Namita Chowdhury described how the squatter colonies in Calcutta sustained a 'richness of mind. We were like wild flowers scattered in the forest, growing on our own, without any constraints'. Partition and refugeedom delivered emancipation of a sort.[47]

Another transformation affected the sub-continent's landscape. Officials in the Indian Ministry of Relief and Rehabilitation entertained hopes of creating model villages in Punjab on the ruins left behind during the chaotic 'evacuation'. Plans included improved irrigation, sanitation and transport access. Surviving drawings showed a preference for a radial design with the village hall, school, dispensary and cooperative store at the hub. The Indian government planned the construction of at least 14 new towns to house at least 400,000 refugees who lost their homes when they fled from Pakistan. The settlement at Ulhasnagar ('City of joy') in Maharashtra, a former army transit camp built by the British during the Second World War was expected to accommodate 130,000 refugees, mostly from Sindh. Other new towns included Faridabad in East Punjab, and Nilokheri and Habra Baigachi near Calcutta, to accommodate 10,000 and 40,000 refugees respectively. Horace Alexander described these ventures as 'the fulfilment of a dream'—the dream of people such as S.K. Dey who started a training centre in Kurukshetra and, with Nehru's backing, settled refugees on reclaimed land in 1948 where they 'blazed a trail'. Alexander was especially impressed by the fact that 'young Brahmins [were] at work as shoemakers—outcastes' work'. He waxed lyrical about the 'great experiment' at Faridabad with its potential for 'mental rehabilitation', particularly of women and children who were given the opportunity to participate in art and drama projects. Model towns in his view paved the way for model citizens.[48]

The most famous new settlement was in Chandigarh in East Punjab, which was expected to house 60,000 refugees and to provide Punjab with the capital that it lost when Lahore was assigned to Pakistan. Chandigarh's fame derived from the involvement of the eminent foreign architect Le Corbusier who envisaged a modern city that would symbolize India's 'freedom, unfettered by the traditions of the past [and] an expression of the nation's faith in the future'. More prosaically, Nehru hoped that it would provide refugees with jobs in the construction industry in the short term. Construction began in April 1952. It was a landmark project, carefully choreographed and given some publicity by the leading member of the Magnum photographic agency, Ernst Scheidegger, whose images evoked the hectic construction involving tens of thousands of Indian labourers, male and female. Le

---

[47] Chakravartty, *Coming Out of Partition*, 101; Talbot and Singh, *The Partition of India*, 108–9.
[48] Alexander, *New Citizens of India*, 38–9, 48–9, 114.

Corbusier enthused about Chandigarh, writing to his wife that 'we're in the midst of an eternal landscape. Everything is calm, slow, harmonious, lovable'. He spoke of Chandigarh as 'an architectural symphony'. The city was officially inaugurated in March 1955, on which occasion Nehru suggested that 'You may squirm at the impact, but it makes you think and imbibe new ideas, and one thing that India requires in so many fields is to be hit on the head so that you may think'. Nevertheless, amongst the talk of an architectural showpiece it was easy to forget the irony that the creation of Chandigarh depended upon removing the local peasantry who had farmed the land for generations. Some 6,000 families were forced to leave their homes under the terms of the colonial Land Acquisition Act (1894); they were allowed to remain as 'government tenants' only until such time as building work began. Nor does the story end there. In 2011 Chandigarh's buildings were being looted in order to sell valuable Le Corbusier furniture and other items at international auction: designer manhole covers commanded particularly high prices.[49]

Pakistan built new settlements such as Nazimabad, a suburb of Karachi, the population of which tripled between 1947 and 1952. The settlement consisted of low-rise blocks laid out on the characteristic grid pattern; refugees were given little choice but to move to this purpose-built accommodation. Other 'colonies' sprang up in the early 1950s, with names that reflected the places from which the refugees originated.[50] The government enlisted the services of a Greek engineering and town planning firm that had experience of working on refugee projects in Athens. Elsewhere too, new settlements took the names of the ancestral village, or commemorated freedom fighters and social reformers. Municipal authorities in Calcutta and Delhi have lately drawn up plans to 'redevelop' the old refugee dwellings to make room for new housing projects and shopping malls to cater for the wealthy Indian diaspora.[51] Such are the ironies of population displacement.

REPRESENTATIONS OF DISPLACEMENT

In characterizing Partition as an abrupt rupture, contemporary observers referred to a collective 'madness' that seized all communities: 'passions once aroused are hard to quench'. Other cultural meanings were ascribed to population displacements. Indian officials, journalists and others commonly asserted a basic difference between refugees in the west and the east. Punjabi refugees emerged as stoic figures, incapable of 'stoop[ing] to charity':

[49] Nihal Perera, 'Contesting Visions: Hybridity, Liminality and Authorship of the Chandigarh Plan' *Planning Perspectives*, 19 (2004), 175–99, at 194; Ernst Scheidegger, *Chandigarh 1956: Le Corbusier and the Promotion of Architectural Modernity* (Chicago: Chicago University Press, 2009), 27, 37.

[50] Ansari, *Life after Partition*, 140–2.

[51] Pablo Bose, 'Dilemmas of Diaspora: Partition, Refugees and the Politics of "Home"' *Refuge*, 23, no.1 (2006), 58–68, at 65–6.

Never would their proud hands be stretched out to receive alms. No work, however seemingly low, would they despise. They represented the fine core of the Punjabi peasantry, to whom honest labour is the flower of human dignity. Rehabilitation in their case was easy, for they met Government's efforts more than half-way. They resumed their old, simple, graceful ways of living as if nothing had ever disturbed the even tenor of their existence. They were of the breed of heroes, though their stories have not been told in epic and song.[52]

These men and women had contributed to the development of the canal colonies in the nineteenth century and could therefore draw upon a tradition of hard graft, 'sturdy independence, uprightness, directness of speech and courage'. An official account of rehabilitation was filled with photographs of refugee 'types', distinguished-looking men who gaze into the distance as if to demonstrate their determination. Significantly the only photograph that runs counter to that image, entitled 'derelicts', showed a bedraggled woman and child.[53]

Bengali refugees on the other hand were represented in a different light, having become 'devitalized'. U. Bhaskar Rao, author of an informative study of rehabilitation that allowed refugees no speaking part, expressed this clearly:

Refugees in the East came from a different milieu; the influences that moulded their lives were different. East Bengal was comparatively poor, with an economy less diversified than West Punjab's. The person displaced from East Pakistan had been exposed to devitalising, demoralising forces much longer than his western counterpart had been. When he finally escaped to asylum in India he was completely shattered in body and spirit, all initiatives, all capacity for self-adjustment drained out of him. Here was a mood most frustrating to the rehabilitation effort.[54]

Critics saw them as the embodiment of longstanding regional and ethnic stereotypes. Refugees from East Bengal were taunted as rice eaters, 'bheto Bangal', who gradually learned to eat roti. Calcutta residents made fun of their 'rustic' accents, dismissing them as country cousins. Popular newspapers and periodicals published cartoons showing West Bengal as a hospital patient suffering from 'refugee-itis' and asking the 'doctor' in charge (that is, the Chief Minister) whether the 'case' was hopeless. These modes of representation formed part of a broader notion of the beleaguered, passive and 'effeminate' Bengali. Such distinctions were part of the common currency of Western discourse. The Lutheran educator Herbert Stroup painted a tendentious portrait of the Bengali refugee who had once been proud but was now 'humbled and embittered. His long presence in refugee camps has paralysed his will to succeed. Now he teaches his children the techniques of successful begging'.[55]

---

[52] Rao, *The Story of Rehabilitation*, 8, 37–8.
[53] Randhawa, *Out of the Ashes*, 30, 42.
[54] Rao, *The Story of Rehabilitation*, 148, 155.
[55] LWF, Box WS V.3.b, Service to Refugees, Material Relief, India, 1954–62, 'Project Daya (Mercy)', January 1960. I draw also on an unpublished paper by Nilanjana Chatterjee, 'Interrogating Victimhood' (n.d.), available at <http://www.swadhinata.org.uk/document/chatterjeeEastBengal%20 Refugee.pdf>.

Careful probing by Urvashi Butalia and others affords a glimpse into the relatively unexplored world of Sikh experience. In a dramatic intervention, Sardar Ganesha Singh, Joint Secretary of the Central Hindu/Sikh Minorities Board, wrote in 1947 to the Deputy Prime Minister in the following terms:

> As you are aware, the minorities of this province have made such heroic sacrifices which have got no parallels in the history of India. But now, at the time of India's rejoicing, we are left in the sinking boat. You have handed us over to the butchers, who are thirsting for our blood …You people are standing aside and asking us to stay there, but so far we do not see if you have taken any step to think of us. Our conditions will be like jews [sic] in the Hitlerite regime.[56]

Singh pleaded not to be abandoned. His apocalyptic reference to the extermination of European Jewry suggests that Sikh leaders understood that the security of an entire population was at stake, although in the light of their actions against female members of their own community the reference to 'butchery' sends shivers down the spine.

Much of the violence of Partition took the form of sexual exploitation and humiliation. Young refugee women were thought to be vulnerable to organized sex trafficking. As one welfare worker recalled, 'the main aim was to rescue the women and make sure that they didn't go astray. All these brothel people would wait at the platform trying to grab them; we had to make sure that they were not taken away'. But the issue was not just about the risks from predatory men. The plight of female refugees was ascribed to the dissolution of paternal control. Now 'complete strangers huddle together…women who used to live behind closed doors are today moving about freely and mixing with all sorts of people'.[57] As in Armenia, officials were quick to take up the cause of 'rescuing' abducted women. The two governments came to a preliminary agreement in December 1947. India passed an 'Abducted Persons Recovery Act' in 1949, which set up a substantial investigative apparatus, building upon the work undertaken by organizations such as the Indian United Council for Relief and Welfare. Officials compiled lists of abducted women, usually widows who had been 'appropriated' by men from their own village in order to acquire their property. Between 1947 and 1956 some 22,000 Muslim women were 'recovered' from India, while 8,000 Hindu and Sikh women returned from Pakistan. But many Hindus converted to Islam and married Muslim men, by all accounts making a reasonable life. Ritu Menon's aunt settled quite happily in Karachi even if, as she describes it, her new family disdained her musical aspirations: 'I brought my sitar but my husband said you'd better hide it, people will say I've married a courtesan'.[58]

---

[56] Butalia, 'An Archive with a Difference', 230–1.

[57] Syed Sikander Mehdi, 'Refugee Memory in India and Pakistan', in Glasson Deschaumes and Rada Ivekovic (eds), *Divided Countries, Separated Cities: The Modern Legacy of Partition* (New Delhi: Oxford University Press, 2003), 85–95, at 88; Gautam Ghosh, ' "God is a Refugee": Nationality, Morality and History in the 1947 Partition of India' *Social Analysis*, 42, no.1 (1998), 33–62, at 50.

[58] Ritu Menon, 'The Dynamics of Division', in Deschaumes and Ivekovic, *Divided Countries, Separated Cities*, 115–29; Vernant, *The Refugee in the Post-War World*, 740.

The entire issue was politicized. It symbolized a catastrophic loss of trust between the two countries, where the restoration of women's 'honour' entailed reclaiming these 'unfortunate victims of communal frenzy' for their respective nation. In Pakistan a visiting religious scholar from Iran was presented with a group of refugee women who had just arrived in a lorry from East Punjab, although the Indian representative in Lahore complained that the entire scene had been stage-managed by Pakistani officials in order to give a one-sided picture of 'Pakistani Muslims having suffered untold horrors at the hands of Hindus and Sikhs'. In more strident terms the Hindu fundamentalist Rashtriya Swayamsevak Sangh (RSS) denounced 'Napakistan' ('impure Pakistan') for having behaved in a barbaric fashion but the RSS also poured scorn on the government of India for having failed to protect India's women. The state needed to be 'virile' rather than feeble in its response. Tellingly, the prevailing rhetoric highlighted the image of 'Mother India' in such a way as to downplay the circumstances of individual women, including 'resisting cases', in favour of a generalized depiction of female victimhood.[59]

Partition imposed an immense cost on refugee women and turned them into symbols of national dishonour and patriotic duty. At stake was the idea of the 'martyrdom' of women who killed themselves rather than run the risk of being assaulted, abducted or killed, or who were killed by family members who took it upon themselves to prevent the honour of their womenfolk from being sullied. One Sikh man who put to death dozens of female family members described himself as their 'saviour'.[60] But as Butalia points out, the extant accounts were provided by men who partook of a nationalist discourse. In talking of suicide we are left with more questions than answers: 'If the women were aware of the discussions, perhaps even involved in them, can we then surmise that in taking their own lives they were acting upon a perceived (or rather, misperceived) notion of the good of their community? Did their deaths corroborate the ideology—and were they a part of this ideology?—that the honour of the community lay in "protecting" its women from the patriarchal violence of an alien community?'[61]

PARTITIONING PAKISTAN

The settlement in 1947 did not create a stable situation in Pakistan. Relations between West and East Pakistan had never been smooth. At the outset, Jinnah imposed Urdu as the state language (Bengali gained recognition as a second official language in 1956), and the government in Karachi did little to disguise its contempt

[59] Pippa Virdee, 'Negotiating the Past: Journey through Muslim Women's Experience of Partition and Resettlement in Pakistan' *CSH*, 6, no.4 (2009), 467–84, at 471–2; Khan, *The Great Partition*, 179.

[60] Ritu Menon and Kamla Bhasin (eds), *Borders and Boundaries: Women in India's Partition* (New Brunswick: Rutgers University Press, 1998), 50.

[61] Urvashi Butalia, *The Other Side of Silence: Voices from the Partition of India* (Hurst and Co., 2000), 168–9.

for East Pakistan. Bengali nationalists claimed that they were the victims of 'colonial' exploitation that left the East impoverished and marginalized. It did not help that Muslim refugees from India were immediately offered jobs and land in East Pakistan, causing resentment among the impoverished Bengali population. In January 1964 riots in Calcutta compelled Muslims to sell up and flee to East Pakistan. Copycat killings took place in Dhaka, provoking an exodus of Bengalis in the opposite direction. Another destabilizing factor derived from the presence of the Urdu-speaking Muslim Bihari community, around one million of whom migrated in 1947 from India to East Pakistan, where they worked for a pittance in the jute mills of Dhaka. Tension between Bengalis and Biharis increased during the 1960s when Bengali nationalist politicians demonized Biharis as an enemy within, liable to lend support to West Pakistan in its determination to bring the East to heel.[62]

In late 1970 the situation reached a crescendo. Politicians in East Pakistan berated their Western counterparts for failures of leadership during a terrible cyclone that killed half a million people and left seven times that number homeless. Elections in that year revealed widespread public support for the breakaway Awami League, which was swiftly banned by the Pakistan government, whose declaration of martial law prompted the League to declare an independent People's Republic of Bangladesh ('native land'). In the ensuing civil war, soldiers on both sides committed atrocities. The intellectual elite of East Pakistan faced severe retribution from the Pakistani army for supporting independence. Bengali women suffered brutal and humiliating treatment from the same quarter: many left for West Pakistan with their abusers rather than suffer rejection by their families. Bangladeshi troops likewise systematically mistreated Bihari women whom they regarded as the embodiment of the enemy within.[63]

The presence of several million refugees on Indian soil allowed politicians in Delhi to claim that Pakistan was using refugees as a means of overwhelming India's resources, while Pakistan for its part maintained that India permitted the new liberation army of Bangladesh (*Mukti Bahini*) to use refugee camps as a base from which to launch attacks on the defenders of the status quo. But Prime Minister Indira Gandhi whilst recognizing their propaganda value—at one stage she called them 'our partners'—had no wish to see a long-term refugee population on Indian soil. Claiming that as 'victims of war' they were Pakistan's responsibility, she announced in June 1971: 'I'm going to send them back', echoing sentiments expressed by her father a generation earlier. Her stance was also consistent with Indian policy in the 1960s which deterred refugees from crossing the border and resettled those who did in distant locations. Nevertheless, Gandhi's hopes of stemming the movement of these 'intruders' proved in vain, in as much as the government in Rawalpindi was happy to see the back of those it called 'Hindu traitors'. Faced with overwhelming numbers the government of India reluctantly decided to

[62] Sumit Sen, 'Stateless Refugees and the Right to Return: the Bihari Refugees of South Asia' *IJRL*, 11, no.4 (1999), 625–45; 12, no.1 (2000), 41–70.

[63] Yasmin Saikia, 'Beyond the Archive of Silence: Narratives of Violence of the 1971 Liberation War of Bangladesh' *History Workshop Journal*, 58 (2004), 275–87.

keep the border open. By July the total number of refugees stood at close to seven million, excluding internally displaced people.[64]

India held these refugees in 900 transit camps along the border in Assam, Tripura and West Bengal where they received ration cards but had no right to look for jobs. Three million people lodged with host families. Those settling in Calcutta faced a frosty reception from residents including first-generation refugees from East Bengal who regarded the newcomers as their social inferiors and as carriers of infectious diseases. Others were ordered to move to Dandakaranya (see earlier in this chapter) or shipped as far afield as Sri Lanka, where Muslim villagers in Puttalam extended a welcome to 60,000 refugees before turning their backs on them, blaming them for all manner of misfortunes such as the depletion of fish stocks. Clashes erupted elsewhere. U Thant, the UN Secretary-General, established the East Pakistan Relief Operation under Robert Jackson who had a background in refugee relief in post-war Europe. UNHCR mounted a 'Focal Point operation' to coordinate assistance, marking a departure in its remit. Indian trade unions and businesses and the Red Cross urged the public to give generously, reminding them of the trauma of Partition. Photos of children living inside sewers added to the sense of catastrophe. Oxfam, Lutheran World Services and CARE also provided emergency relief. The combined relief effort masked the determination of Indian officials to return refugees to their homes at the earliest opportunity.[65]

Full-scale war between Pakistan and India broke out in December 1971. By the middle of that month the total refugee population stood at an estimated ten million. Following a ceasefire in January 1972 they began to return to the new state of Bangladesh, with ICRC and UNHCR assistance and Indian government funds. In January the daily average of repatriates was running at 200,000. By March seven million refugees had been repatriated. Much to the relief of the Indian government, which expressed alarm about the impact of the crisis on its development objectives, the process was largely completed by 1974. The Bangladesh government established holding camps and drew upon UN relief funds to help rebuild the infrastructure.[66]

The formation of the new state of Bangladesh left the Bihari population stateless. Half a million Biharis were transferred to detention camps in and around Dhaka. Pakistan agreed to admit 175,000 of them in the course of the next two decades. Those who managed to make their way from Bangladesh to India incurred

---

[64] Louise Holborn, *Refugees, a Problem of Our Time: the Work of the United Nations High Commissioner for Refugees, 1951–1972* (Metuchen: Scarecrow Press, 1975), vol. 2, 754; K.C. Saha, 'The Genocide of 1971 and the Refugee Influx in the East', in Samaddar (ed.), *Refugees and the State*, 211–48, at 213; Antara Datta, *Refugees and Borders in South Asia: the Great Exodus of 1971* (Routledge, 2012), 21–6, 59.

[65] Gideon Gottlieb, 'The UN and Emergency Humanitarian Assistance in India-Pakistan' *American Journal of International Law*, 66, no.2 (1972), 362–5; Datta, *Refugees and Borders*, 131–7, 141–5.

[66] Pia Oberoi, *Exile and Belonging: Refugees and State Policy in South Asia* (New Delhi: Oxford University Press, 2006); Thomas W. Oliver, *The United Nations in Bangladesh* (Princeton: Princeton University Press, 1978).

the wrath of extremists in the Bharatiya Janata Party (BJP). This became the most egregious protracted refugee situation in Asia. At the end of the century some 250,000 Bihari refugees were still living in 60 large camps (including the ironically-named 'Camp Geneva') awaiting, so to speak, repatriation to Pakistan, a country that had no wish to admit them despite their protestations that they were 'stranded Pakistanis'. The situation only took a turn for the better in 2007 when Bangladesh began to remove restrictions on the political and economic rights of Biharis. This does not exhaust the consequences of the Bangladesh war of liberation. Those Hindus who had remained in West Pakistan but moved to Rajasthan in 1971 became known as 'Pak oustees' whom India refused to recognize as refugees because they held Pakistani passports. One further disquieting element was that India's Muslim population stood accused by some Hindu politicians of supporting Pakistan in its attempt to forestall the creation of Bangladesh. By these various means, population displacement was once again linked to questions of citizenship and loyalty.[67]

PARTITION REFUGEES: LEGACIES AND COMMEMORATION

Officially-sanctioned commemorative activity of this violent displacement took a muted form. A handful of authorized accounts described government initiatives, but these belonged to a civil service tradition that celebrated the bureaucratic concern and the power of expertise to overcome obstacles. More tangible expressions of displacement were less common. A 'martyrs' monument' was erected in Chandigarh to draw attention to the suffering of refugees in Punjab, but otherwise India built no memorial to the victims of Partition until a nondescript edifice went up in Attari, Punjab, in 1997. In 2005 the president of Pakistan laid the foundation stone of an expensive monument in Lahore, Bab-e-Pakistan ('Gateway to Pakistan'), built on the site of the Walton refugee camp and including an exhibition devoted to the suffering of Muslim refugees.[68] Some commemorative ceremonies take place in private: Sikh refugees in Delhi organize an annual event at the Gurdwara in Bhogal Market, Jungpura, where they recite the painful experiences of women in Rawalpindi during 1947.[69]

Artists, film makers, novelists and others were less reticent about acknowledging the experiences of Partition refugees. Jogen Chowdhury painted portraits of refugee women in 1947, while Satish Gujral painted swirling images with titles such as 'Dance of destruction' and 'The snare of memory'. No less compelling were the

---

[67] Urvashi Butalia, personal communication; Michael Gillan, 'Refugees or Infiltrators? The Bharatiya Janata Party and "Illegal" Migration from Bangladesh' *Asian Studies Review*, 26, no.1 (2002), 73–95; Datta, *Refugees and Borders*, 80–1, 156–9, 174–5.

[68] Ravinder Kaur, *Since 1947: Partition Narratives among Punjabi Migrants of Delhi* (New Delhi: Oxford University Press, 2007), 10; Khan, *The Great Partition*, 200–1.

[69] Information courtesy of Urvashi Butalia.

works of novelists such as Khushwant Singh (b.1915) whose *Train to Pakistan* (1956) is set in the small village of Mano Majra on the Punjab border with a mixed Sikh, Muslim and Hindu population. Against a backdrop of mounting 'communal' violence and attempts to derail trains carrying refugees, Singh weaves in stories of individual male predators: one official hopes to seduce a young Muslim girl whose words, 'I want to go home', take on a fresh meaning as trainloads of refugees move across the frontier. The book ends with the brutal eviction of Muslim farmers, notwithstanding their lament, 'What have we to do with Pakistan? We were born here... We have lived amongst you as brothers'.[70]

A graphic account by Shahid Ahmad Dehlavi, *Dilli ki bipta* ('Delhi's calamity', 1948), described the forced removal of Muslims from the city and contrasted it with the Indian 'Mutiny': '[T]he devastation of 1857 paled before the ravages of September [1947]'.[71] Some authors lamented the life they were forced to abandon, the abundant harvests in 'Golden Bengal', tolerant neighbours and pleasurable social intercourse. Asked to reflect on his life prior to Partition, the novelist Intizar Husain mentioned his devout Shia Muslim father who maintained excellent relations with his Hindu neighbours; like most Muslims he shopped in Hindu-owned establishments where the shopkeeper commanded their respect. Husain himself recalled his Hindu teacher with great affection. The family's decision to leave Uttar Pradesh for the 'Pakistan' city of Lahore was not taken lightly, but—like so many others—they expected to return shortly.[72] A famous short story, 'Toba Tek Singh' by Saadat Hasan Manto (1912–55) imagined an 'exchange of lunatics' who asked 'How could they be in India a short while ago and now suddenly in Pakistan?'.[73]

Other representations have been equally complex. Partition was construed as a traumatic rupture, displacement as an event whose enormity was difficult if not impossible to grasp. In 1950 the Bengali newspaper *Jugantar* ('New Era') serialized essays submitted by Hindus who arrived in Calcutta. They were replete with nostalgia for East Bengal but also infused by a sense of the trauma of displacement, seeing 'the event causing the pain as a monstrously irrational aberration'.[74] Balwant Anand, a young Indian man fresh out of Cambridge University and installed in a college in Lyallpur (Faisalabad), wrote a memoir describing his relationships with Muslim friends and his attempt to come to terms with refugees in a makeshift camp where Punjabi 'individualism' required the imposition of discipline in the chaotic 'refugee city'. He left a gripping account of what would now be called people trafficking, as unscrupulous travel agents auctioned scarce space on the planes leaving for Delhi. Anand's characterization of the emergency as an 'avalanche' echoes descriptions of the Russian refugee crisis in 1915. His book ends on a happier note as he accompanies a convoy of refugees from Lyallpur via Lahore to Amritsar and 'home', a deliberate narrative device to suggest the ultimate validation

---

[70] Khushwant Singh, *Train to Pakistan* (Delhi: Roli, 2006), 100, 126.
[71] Pandey, *Remembering Partition*, 136.
[72] Bhalla, *Partition Dialogues*, 18, 77–91.
[73] <http://www.sacw.net/partition/tobateksingh.html>.
[74] Dipesh Chakrabarty, 'Remembered Villages: Representations of Hindu-Bengali Memories in the Aftermath of Partition' *South Asia*, 18, Special Issue (1995), 109–29, at 113.

of Partition.[75] A generation later Manas Ray described 'growing up refugee' in Calcutta where his *bhadralok* family settled in 1947. He recalled a home in which the Singer sewing machine and the Encyclopedia Britannica took pride of place, reminders of the fact that his parents managed to retrieve something during their hasty exodus from East Bengal. He describes encounters with plebeian refugees who lived cheek by jowl in the squatter colonies. This thriving community subsequently gave way to a regulated suburb where local government bureaucrats held sway and where scant traces of the old refugee colony now survive.[76]

Anand and Ray were relatively privileged individuals. How less well-off refugees understood Partition is revealed in oral testimony. An Indian carpenter, Faryad, recalled that 'we had thought that once Independence came, the streets of Delhi would be paved with gold, awash with milk. Instead all we saw was rivers of blood'.[77] Accounts such as this rely for their narrative power on the depiction, on the one hand, of hazardous journeys to a place of relative safety and, on the other, of thriving communities rent apart without warning. Hindu refugees recounted tales of a lush and fertile countryside in East Bengal that contrasted with the pitiful conditions they experienced in West Bengal, whose 'stagnant' canals reminded them of magnificent rivers in the land of their birth. Their memories of ancestral villages reserved little or no place for Muslim neighbours. Not all testimony was registered in a single key, however. Refugees from East Bengal who settled in the Andaman Islands, the site of British colonial convict settlement during the nineteenth century, reminisced not about the homes they left behind or about the refugee camp, but about the challenge and excitement of being pioneers, which disconcertingly included bemoaning the mass arrival of Tamils and others during the 1970s.[78]

Some authors introduced a comparative element, for example portraying Hindu refugees as 'the new Jews' (the title of a 1950 play by Salil Sen), supposedly neglected by government relief schemes that disproportionately benefited refugees from Punjab. Punjabi refugees in Delhi described the chaotic drama of displacement amidst worsening Hindu-Muslim relations which they located in what was now construed as a long 'history of oppression' and inter-ethnic strife. This 'master narrative' operates alongside evidence from different informants who spoke of friendship between Sikhs, Hindus and Muslims, for example in Amritsar where, as a teacher put it, 'we used to study together with Muslims, became friends, even eat sometimes'.[79] Nevertheless an overwhelming narrative of antagonism exerts a powerful influence. The staunchly nationalist BJP insists upon a particular reading of

[75] Balwant Singh Anand (1961), *Cruel Interlude* (Bombay: Asia Publishing House, 1961).

[76] Manas Ray, 'Growing up Refugee' *History Workshop Journal*, 52 (2002), 49–78.

[77] Butalia, *The Other Side of Silence*, 149.

[78] Dipesh Chakrabarty, *Habitations of Modernity* (Chicago: Chicago University Press, 2002), 115–37; Uditi Sen, 'Dissident Memories: Exploring Bengali Refugee Narratives in the Andaman Islands', in Panayi and Virdee (eds), *Refugees and the End of Empire*, 291–44.

[79] Sardar Jagdish Singh, 'The Partition Memories of an Eminent Educationist', in Talbot and Tatla, *Epicentre of Violence*, 106–16.

Partition in which Muslim 'perfidy' called for a robust response in defence of Hindu faith and culture. This has become a one-dimensional history. Much the same applies to the Bengali nationalist narrative that dominates public discourse in Bangladesh.

The silver screen afforded the greatest dramatic possibilities. The great film director Ritwik Ghatak (1925–65) was born in Dhaka and moved to Calcutta with his family when he was a young boy in order to escape the worst of the Bengal famine. Ghatak was not the first film maker to bring the experiences of Partition refugees to life: Nimai Ghosh who worked with the Indian People's Theatre Association, directed a film called *Chinnamul* ('Uprooted', 1950), which dealt with the displacement of refugees from East Bengal. Ghosh's film used documentary footage as well as scenes with non-professional actors, including Ghatak himself in a minor role.

Much better known was Ghatak's own remarkable trilogy of films made in the early 1960s. Like *Chinnamul*, Ghatak's *The Cloud-Capped Star* (*Meghe Dhaka Tara*, 1960) tells of a *bhadralok* family from East Bengal whose members made their way to suburban Calcutta where they settled in a claustrophobic refugee colony. The household relies upon the pay-packet of the daughter Neeta (played by the Bengali actress Supriya Choudhury whose family were refugees from Japanese-occupied Burma), even more so when her father injures himself. Partly at her mother's insistence she renounces any chance of furthering her studies or finding happiness in order to support her parents, her sister and her self-absorbed musician brother. Neeta's suffering intensifies when she contracts tuberculosis. In the bleak final scene cry she shouts defiantly, 'I want to live! I want to go home'. *Subarnarekha* (1962), another poignant and subtle portrait of displacement, was set on the banks of the Subarnarekha River and the 'New Life Colony' in Calcutta. Iswar and his younger sister Sita take a young boy Abhiram under their wing. As they grow up, Sita and Abhiram fall in love, but their relationship is jeopardized by revelations about Abhiram's origins. They settle in Calcutta and have a child, Binu. When Abhiram is murdered, Sita finds work as a prostitute; she kills herself after realizing that her first customer is Iswar, who has taken a break from his job working as a cashier at an iron foundry. The film ends with Iswar's decision to adopt Binu, having lost not only his job, but his sister and brother-in-law too. Ghatak's films raised questions about the impact of displacement on social status and personal conduct, particularly of women. Ultimately he seems to suggest that Partition was one dramatic moment in the history of modern rootlessness, and that Bengal is being torn apart both by Partition and by decadence afflicting the country and its people.[80]

---

[80] Bhaskar Sarkar, *Mourning the Nation: Indian Cinema in the Wake of Partition* (Durham, NC: Duke University Press, 2009), 177–85, 200–29.

CONCLUSIONS

It is an over-simplification to say that the formation of India and Pakistan created 'midnight's refugees'. Partition was the very antithesis of a clean territorial split. Instead it was a bloody and prolonged process particularly in Bengal where its wounds took a long time to heal. Mass movements of people were accompanied by brutality and loss of life, and by representations of displacement as an almost insuperable 'problem'. The difficulties it posed resurfaced during the 'second partition' in 1971 that gave birth to the state of Bangladesh.

The legacy of violent state formation rubs shoulders with an alternative reading of Partition, construed not so much as a necessary step to forestall even greater bloodshed (which it clearly failed to prevent) but as a phenomenon that helped to bring about a political, social and economic revolution. Refugeedom allowed government officials to harness the Indian public to 'the saga of reconstruction' and ideas of economic development. But these plans affected refugees unevenly. Camps such as Kurukshetra housed the least privileged people until such time as they could be dispersed throughout India. It took determination to resist these state-driven schemes or bend them to one's own wishes. Partition also did little to improve the status of displaced Dalits ('Untouchables') in East Punjab, whereas reserves of social capital enabled wealthy Muslim refugees to settle relatively easily in cities such as Lahore. These examples can be multiplied many times over. Class mattered.[81]

Politics added other dimensions too. The purpose of relief and rehabilitation was to create new citizens with 'a high sense of moral values and a consciousness of the tradition and heritage of the country'.[82] Refugees were enlisted in the project of nation state-building, as pliant subjects but also as people who had the potential to shake host populations out of their 'slumber'. Partition affords another instance of the ways in which the category of refugee was made by and in turn helped constitute the state. To be sure, the course of patriotism did not always run smoothly. Radical politics in the squatter colonies in Calcutta sustained a vibrant cultural life too. This dynamism resembled the Balkans where refugees from Asia Minor infused Greek politics in the interwar years with a militant edge.

Claims for 'recognition' arising from Partition continue to be an important element in the politics of modern India and Pakistan. In West Bengal the descendants of those who fled from East Pakistan in 1947 framed their experience as a 'sacrifice' and a 'debt' that needed to be repaid. In Pakistan the Muhajir Qaumi Movement spoke on behalf of *muhajir* refugees from India who felt themselves disenfranchised; it continues to claim that they made an incommensurable sacrifice in the name of Pakistan, which the government in Islamabad has failed to acknowledge. In India's southern states, Muslim migrants who divided their time between India and the Gulf states have been urged by the BJP to 'go home' to Pakistan (a country

---

[81] Gyanendra Pandey, ' "Nobody's People": the Dalits of Punjab in the Forced Removal of 1947', in Bessel and Haake (eds), *Removing Peoples*, 297–319.
[82] *Rehabilitation Retrospect*, 34.

of which they have no direct knowledge), in a clear indication of how understandings of Partition can continue to be deployed in a wholly uninformed yet politically explosive manner.

Partition and population displacement thus came to occupy centre stage in the making of both India and Pakistan, with the result that other episodes and other memories have been effaced, including memories of the kindness shown by Muslims to Hindus and vice versa. Refugees' accounts drew upon a broad repertoire of calamity, as when Hindu refugees from East Bengal made sense of their expulsion by locating it within a narrative of the suffering of Bengali Hindus as a whole. Historians and officials too played a part in rendering Partition as a calamity and in ascribing qualities to its architects and victims. Sometimes they alluded to events in Europe. An Indian official likened Muslims in East Pakistan to the Nazi 'Herrenvolk' on the grounds that they dominated their Hindu neighbours and made their lives intolerable. Another asked readers to 'imagine what would have happened if instead of a few hundred thousand people who fled from Europe to Britain during the dark days between 1934 and 1939, the number of refugees had included the whole population of Norway or Denmark. [Then] we can get some idea of the problem which faced this country in 1947', which in India meant 'a transfusion of new blood; the whole body of the country has benefited from it'.[83]

Likewise the eminent Bengali historian Sir Jadunath Sarkar told an audience of East Bengal refugees in 1948 that they were welcome in India, because they could help to revive the local economy. But he did not leave matters there. In a striking comparison he referred to Jewish farmers in Palestine who would, in his words, provide 'a spark of light in the midst of the mess of Muslim misgovernment and stagnation'. He warned that 'Eastern Bengal is going the way of Palestine without the Jews. We must make our West Bengal what Palestine under Jewish rule will be, a light in the darkness of medieval ignorance and theocratic bigotry'. Deploying more ancient allusions he praised the impact of Huguenots in Britain and of Puritan settlers in North America. On this basis he urged West Bengalis to 'graft this rich racial branch upon its old decaying trunk and rise to a new era of prosperity and power'.[84] Unfortunately he could only extend his appreciation of the newcomers' potential contribution by dismissing the attributes of an entire population. Displacement announced the possibility of self-realization, but in a highly selective manner.

---

[83] Guha, *Studies in Social Tensions*: viii; *Rehabilitation Retrospect*, 98.
[84] Chakrabarti, *Marginal Men*, 23–4.

6

War and Population Displacement in East Asia, 1937–1950

After weapons of war have been scattered in the countryside,
Flesh and blood were fleeing on the roads

(Du Fu)[1]

INTRODUCTION

War and invasion, revolution and the formation of new states set the scene for population movements in the Far East in the middle of the twentieth century. China felt the full force of Japanese imperialism, as Korea had done at the beginning of the century. Japanese troops invaded China in 1937, causing 300,000 civilians to seek sanctuary in the foreign concessions in Shanghai and millions more to flee into the interior. The total number of refugees in wartime China may have reached 95 million. Even allowing for approximation and an unknown element of double-counting this extraordinary figure equates to one-quarter of the country's population. In some provinces the proportion was closer to one-half. Nor did other locations escape the consequences of war. The rapid conquest of British-ruled Burma by the Japanese army in 1942 caused civilians to seek refuge in India. Overseas Chinese who fled to China when Japan seized Hong Kong, Macau, Thailand, Burma and other territory found their return blocked when nationalist regimes asserted their authority after the war.[2]

Japan's defeat in 1945 put paid to its empire in South-East Asia. In Korea the USA and USSR agreed to divide the war-torn country in two as a temporary stopgap. Hundreds of thousands of Koreans who had been forcibly removed to the Japanese mainland and made to work as forced labourers were now able to return to their homes, whilst Japanese settlers were evicted in turn.[3] Korea was described

---

[1] Du Fu (712–70) was a Tang dynasty poet. Keith Schoppa, *In a Sea of Bitterness: Refugees during the Sino-Japanese War* (Cambridge, Mass: Harvard University Press, 2011), 171.

[2] Diana Lary, *The Chinese People at War: Human Suffering and Social Transformation, 1937–1945* (Cambridge: Cambridge University Press, 2010), 27, 175–6; Amrith, *Migration and Diaspora in Modern Asia*, 96–102; Adam McKeown, 'Conceptualising Chinese Diasporas, 1842–1949' *Journal of Asian Studies*, 58, no.2 (1999), 306–37.

[3] Lori Watt, *When Empire Comes Home: Repatriation and Reintegration in Postwar Japan* (Cambridge: Harvard University Press, 2009).

as 'one of the blackest spots in the world'.[4] The Korean War (1950–53) turned lives upside down once more, pitting ideological antagonists and their proxies against each other. Refugees from the fighting in North Korea swelled the population of South Korea by at least one-fifth in the early 1950s.

An even greater upheaval took place following the establishment of the People's Republic of China (PRC) in 1949. Anticipating defeat in the struggle for control of the country, 10,000 members of the opposing Nationalist (Guomindang) forces retreated from Yunnan to Burma, because they believed that Burma offered the best prospect of eventually returning to China. Armed refugees mounted guerrilla actions from Burma against the PRC, before moving to Northern Thailand a decade after the revolution. The military and civilian elite made their way to Taiwan. Ordinary civilians sought refuge in Hong Kong. Their numbers grew as a consequence of the Great Leap Forward in the late 1950s and the Cultural Revolution in the mid-1960s. What would become of them?

Revolution in China had other repercussions, some well-known and others less familiar. The PRC launched a military offensive in the remote Tibet Autonomous Region (TAR). When China intensified its grip in the late 1950s, around 70,000 refugees fled to India and Nepal. Half a century on, around 120,000 Tibetans are living outside the TAR, although it remains home to 4.6 million Tibetans. The refugee crisis has been kept in the public eye by a carefully orchestrated campaign. Other upheavals hardly registered on the international agenda. White Russians who fled to China 30 years earlier in similar circumstances were admitted to the Philippines, where they created a theatre, a Russian Orthodox Church and even a local police force. Others who were stranded in China were eventually permitted to leave under the auspices of the UN during World Refugee Year in 1959–60.[5] Even less talked about was the readiness of the PRC to assist ethnic Chinese who faced persecution at the hands of right-wing authoritarian regimes. Some 100,000 ethnic Chinese were forced out of their homes and businesses in Indonesia in 1960 by the ultra-nationalist Sukarno regime. Only decisive action by the PRC rescued them from this predicament by 'repatriating' them to China. This shed a very different light on the policies of Communist China.[6]

Conspicuously missing from humanitarian relief efforts was the International Refugee Organisation (IRO) and its successor, UNHCR. The IRO confined itself to refugees in Europe. UNHCR was well aware of the scale of population displacement in Asia, but its hands were tied by the 1951 Convention. Apart from a brief foray into Hong Kong, UNHCR kept out of these refugee crises, making it necessary to devise a series of regional responses. This did not mean that geopolitical considerations were absent: on the contrary, Cold War rivalries loomed large in framing refugee policy.

---

[4] Colin Bell, 'Thoughts on the Future of the Far East Programs', May 1947, AFSC Archives, Foreign Service 1947-India-Policy.

[5] Amir A.Khisamutdinov, 'Russkie emigranty na Filippinakh' *Voprosy istorii*, 8 (2003), 141–6.

[6] Glen Peterson, 'The Uneven Development of the International Refugee Regime in Postwar Asia: Evidence from China, Hong Kong and Indonesia' *JRS*, 25, no.3 (2012), 326–43.

Much of the responsibility for alleviating the suffering of refugees was devolved upon the military (especially in Korea) and NGOs. Refugees too developed a range of self-help strategies, relying upon family networks or their own wits. But there was a broader agenda. In China and Korea the devastation of the country-side and the mass movement of refugees afforded an opportunity to reconstruct economy and refashion society—at least, so it appeared to Western politicians and non-governmental agencies. Millions of dollars poured into the reconstruction of China until 1949. The Allied army of occupation controlled much of South Korea's economic and social life until such time as the UN could rebuild the country. Although China and North Korea were ultimately 'lost', South Korea became a close ally of the United States. Refugees played a role in this overarching project as pitiful but also as deserving and potentially responsive candidates for 'modernisation'.[7]

NGOs expressed misgivings. In part this was simply about the scale of the problems in Asia. According to Colin Bell, 'the chronic nature of much of the distress in Asia has contrasted with urgent and abnormal need in Europe, which appeared capable of solution within a reasonable time, and towards the solution of which we could make a significant contribution'. He stressed that Asia's refugees 'are our brothers' whose needs could not be ignored.[8] Fellow Quakers offered a more pointed critique: '[W]e have backed governments that do not have the sympathy and support of their peoples. While the peoples themselves are probably anti-communist, we have offered them no acceptable alternatives to communism'. People, he added, needed 'food and education' but also 'liberal government' of the kind that was noticeably absent in Korea and Hong Kong.[9] Other faith-based organizations were less squeamish about throwing in their lot with the struggle against communism in East Asia and enlisted refugees in this task.

WAR, REVOLUTION AND POPULATION DISPLACEMENT IN CHINA

To bring China into the story as a refugee-creating state solely after the Second World War is to overlook the fact that China had itself been a site of internal population displacement on a large scale. Prolonged Japanese occupation and civil war brought about enormous internal movements of people, with upwards of 30 million people displaced by 1939. The mass flight began in the summer of 1937, when officials and other members of the elite escaped towards the centre of China. Japanese bombs, as well as well-founded fears of the behaviour of enemy troops, induced ordinary citizens to flee to the countryside, in the hope of being able to return shortly. A few wealthy individuals managed to reach Hong Kong. Continued

---

[7] Ekbladh, *The Great American Mission*, 114–52.
[8] Bell, 'Thoughts on the Future of the Far East Programs'.
[9] Consultative Committee on Foreign Affairs, Confidential memo on the Korean situation, 13 July 1950, AFSC Archives, Foreign Service 1950 Country—Korea, Inter-office memos.

hostilities meant that most refugees were unable to return to their homes. A year after the Japanese invasion hundreds of thousands were still living in abandoned buildings and alleyways.[10]

Inevitably many Chinese were unable to flee. Japanese officials attempted to alleviate food shortages in Shanghai and other cities by forcing migrants to return to their homes, although many of them preferred the relative security of life in Shanghai to the uncertainty of further displacement. The Shanghai International Red Cross and native place associations (*tongxianghui*) came to the rescue of those who were trapped inside the Japanese noose. An important role was played by the Red Swastika Society, a group of elite and moderately well-off Chinese who collaborated with the occupation regime, but who provided basic relief services to refugees as well as assisting them to return to their homes. Religious societies also supported around one million refugees in Zhejiang province, although twice as many received no assistance whatsoever, and the relief effort dwindled after 1942.[11]

In unoccupied China, the mass movement of internally displaced people continued unabated over the next three years. No sooner had they reached one place of safety but refugees were moved on again, either because the front came closer (or there were rumours that it was about to do so), or because local communities made them unwelcome. As the diarist Jin Xihui put it, 'ordinarily, in both day and night travel, people feared ghosts. Now, given the frightening aspects of war, ghosts were no longer the threat'. The result was an unending odyssey that involved millions of people. Families were separated, sometimes for good.[12]

At least five million peasants also lost their homes and livelihoods (and nearly a million were drowned) because of the decision to breach the dikes of the Yellow River in the summer of 1938 by China, in a desperate attempt to hold up the enemy's advance by 'replacing troops with water'. Around 70,000 square kilometres were affected. Survivors of the flood-induced displacement were forced to settle in West Henan and Shaanxi provinces or in more remote areas, where they were expected to cultivate waste land and thereby contribute to their survival and to the war effort. The government settled 50,000 people on the Huanglongshan Project in Shaanxi province, whose population increased by more than one-third to 14 million. The environmental consequences of such hasty land clearance programmes were deeply damaging. In 1945 some six million people from the flood-affected region were counted as homeless refugees; many suffered from endemic infectious disease.[13] Three hundred miles to the west of Shanghai, the city of Wuhan, to

---

[10] Lary, *The Chinese People at War*, 22–9; Schoppa, *In a Sea of Bitterness*, 60–84.

[11] Patricia Stranahan, 'Radicalisation of Refugees: Communist Party Activity in Wartime Shanghai's Displaced Persons Camps' *Modern China*, 26, no.2 (2000), 166–93; Schoppa, *In a Sea of Bitterness*, 53–7; Toby Lincoln, 'Fleeing from Firestorms: Government, Cities, Native Place Associations and Refugees in the Anti-Japanese War of Resistance' *Urban History*, 38, no.3 (2011), 437–56.

[12] Schoppa, *In a Sea of Bitterness*, 12–15, 35–7, 102.

[13] Diana Lary, 'Drowned Earth: the Strategic Breaching of the Yellow River Dyke, 1938' *War in History*, 8, no.2 (2001), 191–207; *China's Relief Needs* (Washington D.C., National Planning Association, 1945), 42–5; Micah S. Muscolino, 'Violence against People and the Land: the Environment and Refugee Migration from China's Henan Province, 1938–1945' *Environment and History*, 17, no.2 (2011), 291–311.

which hundreds of thousands of other refugees fled, became a dynamic and cosmopolitan site of new projects in health and welfare. The Red Cross and Chinese municipal authorities provided some assistance, but refugees were often forced to rely on their own initiative. Overseas Chinese were cut off and unable to send money or relief packages. Local people played a prominent role in assisting refugees, not unlike the work performed by their counterparts in Russia's voluntary organizations during the First World War.[14]

In broader terms, refugee relief became deeply politicized. In Shanghai's refugee camps the Chinese Communist Party forged a united front with the anti-communist Guomindang but used the opportunity to gain the support of refugees by an astute mixture of patriotic propaganda and practical assistance, such as the resettlement project at Nanniwan in Shaanxi province. Communist officials sought to return refugees to their homes rather than resettle them in remote parts of the country. The Party gained new recruits in Shanghai, where refugees and other civilians came to believe in the Party's competence and 'humanitarianism', as well as its commitment to driving out the Japanese army. Scorched earth policies and mass evacuation—such as the lovely city of Guilin in autumn 1944—were reluctantly accepted. This left a difficult legacy when the war came to an end. Only when UNRRA launched a massive rehabilitation programme could a start be made on rebuilding infrastructure, beginning with the Yellow River dikes.[15]

The return of refugees was equally painful. Those who had fled treated with contempt those who remained behind; the former felt that they had borne the brunt of suffering during the war. When they returned, they wished to reclaim what they viewed as rightfully theirs.[16] By these means the mass internal wartime displacement of population inflicted permanent damage on countless lives, turned households and the entire society upside down, and contributed to the revolution in 1949.

KOREAN REFUGEES: FROM 'RELIEF' TO 'DEVELOPMENT'

The 35-year Japanese occupation of Korea ended in 1945. As in Germany, the territory of Korea was divided pending the outcome of discussions on the formation of a unified state. The UN General Assembly recognized the Republic of Korea in December 1948. In June 1950 North Korean troops crossed the 38th Parallel with the support of Chinese armed forces who now confronted US troops on Korean soil. Prior to the invasion around 650,000 people fled from the North to the southern half of the country, although this figure was disputed by the US army, which believed that local authorities inflated the total in order to secure additional relief supplies. According to the UN, South Korea was home to 5.3 million refugees by

---

[14] Stephen R. MacKinnon, *Wuhan, 1938: War, Refugees, and the Making of Modern China* (Berkeley and Los Angeles: University of California Press, 2008).
[15] Stranahan, 'Radicalisation of Refugees', 177–80; Lary, *The Chinese People at War*, 92, 153.
[16] Lary, *The Chinese People at War*, 181.

July 1951, of whom 1.8 million were living outside the provinces where they ordinarily lived, 1.9 million were within such provinces, 1.2 million were originally from Seoul, and 0.3 million were from North Korea. No-one knew how many refugees there were in the North. It may be that between six and eight million people left their homes before the opposing sides agreed to an armistice in July 1953. For the remaining decade, South Korea was a country of refugees.[17]

The Korean crisis demonstrated the continued importance of geopolitical considerations in determining the extent to which the resources of rich countries would be harnessed to refugee relief. Following the start of hostilities, the US-led United Nations Command (UNC) provided aid to civilians caught in the combat zone. In September 1950, responsibility for civilian relief was transferred to the United Nations Civil Assistance Command in Korea (UNCACK), a unit of the United States Eighth Army in Korea. The presence of American soldiers encouraged prostitution and black market transactions from which refugees did not exempt themselves. Refugee children from poor families could not afford to attend schools and worked as street cleaners or shoe-shine boys to earn money. Obviously little of this surfaced in the official record. UNCACK instead publicized its campaign to inoculate people against smallpox and typhoid. It operated like a mini-state. Some of its personnel were drawn from the Red Cross and from the IRO, but most came from the military, and they did not take kindly to civilians who refused to obey orders to move to specified locations in the south of the country instead of seeking to return to their homes close to the demilitarized zone.[18]

Those refugees from the North who were regarded as a 'security risk' were immediately placed in camps. UN welfare workers encouraged refugees to stay with family or friends, on the grounds that experience with DP camps in Europe had done little to promote individual responsibility. Around half made their way to urban centres, putting the infrastructure under great strain and creating an underclass in overcrowded cities such as the port city of Pusan, where the pre-war population of 500,000 may have trebled by 1951. The city authorities were overwhelmed and left refugees to their own devices, allowing them to take over municipal buildings and factories. Inflation was rampant. Water was rationed. Refugees in Pusan complained that they were at a disadvantage compared to those in camps who could be assured of shelter and a hot meal. Seoul, in the centre of the country, had been 'well steamrollered three times' and had become a 'ghost city [in which] a population of refugees from within the city and from the north ekes out a bare existence, trying to find lost children, waiting for help from wherever it may come'. According to Korea's Ambassador to Washington, 'we are confronted with the problem of caring for the victims of war who cannot help themselves in the face of

---

[17] Bruce Cumings, *The Origins of the Korean War, volume 1: Liberation and the Emergence of Separate Regimes 1945–1947* (Princeton: Princeton University Press, 1981), 54–60. UN estimates from Joseph Lehmann, Executive Director of ARK, 'Report on Field Trip to Korea', 2 November 1951, AFSC Archives, Foreign Service—Korea 1947–2002.

[18] UNCACK was renamed Korean Civil Assistance Command (KCAC) in 1953. Vernant, *The Refugee in the Post-War World*, 779.

the disaster which has overtaken them and for which they are in no wise responsible. They have left their homes, taking with them only what they could carry in their arms. The children, the aged and the sick are in need of medical attention'. Interviews with refugees painted a picture of arduous journeys by rail, road or boat during the winter of 1950. Women struggled to hold on to their young children as they travelled in crowded boats and trains—like a 'dark fog with no light', as one refugee described it—towards the relative safety of Seoul. Messages about missing persons were scribbled on the walls of public buildings. One refugee recalls that 'we lived like insects'.[19]

In December 1950 following the North Korean attack on the Republic of Korea in June, the new United Nations Korean Reconstruction Agency (UNKRA) was launched, with a mandate 'to plan and supervise rehabilitation and relief'; it became fully operational when the armistice was signed. Most of its funding came from the USA and its personnel were subordinated to the US army. As in Germany in 1945, restrictions, for example on access to civilians, caused concern among relief workers. But UNKRA developed a far-reaching agenda. According to UNKRA's director of Public Information and Liaison, 'Korea presents a unique opportunity in the Far East. It is ripe for an economic and cultural renaissance of the first order, which could have effects all over the Far East'. The displacement of civilians during the war provided an opportunity to rebuild society whilst simultaneously being 'a most effective way of halting communism in Asia'.[20] It helped that (in the words of UNKRA's director) Korean refugees demonstrated 'fortitude and [an] indomitable spirit. They have suffered indescribably, but they are amazingly strong and hopeful for the future'.[21]

Alongside UNKRA, NGOs demonstrated an increased readiness to venture beyond the European continent, brought together under the umbrella of the Korea Association of Voluntary Agencies. American Catholic organizations invested heavily in refugee relief, although Catholic Relief Services painted a picture of immense need that had yet to attract widespread publicity, partly because (as they put it) the Korean refugee preferred to suffer in silence. The Lutheran World Federation was another important presence. The idea of the distressed but inherently proud refugee underlay the decision by the American missionary Bob Pierce to

---

[19] Jonathan Rhoads and Lewis Waddilove, 'Report on a Mission to Korea', December 1952, AFSC Foreign Service—Korea 1947–2002; Memo to UN Security Council, 31 July 1950, Records of UNKRA S-0526-0027-0008 (Civilian relief to Korea—General policy, 1 August 1950–31 January 1953); Janice Kim, 'Living in Flight: Civilian Displacement, Suffering, and Relief during the Korean War, 1945–1953' *Sahak Yonku (Review of Korean History)*, 100 (2010), 285–327; Ji-Yeon Yuh, 'Moved by War: Migration, Diaspora and the Korean War' *Journal of Asian American Studies*, 8, no.3 (2005), 277–91.

[20] Memo on briefing by Don Pryor, UNKRA, New York, 22 June 1953, NCWC Office for UN Affairs, CUA Archives Washington, Collection 10, Box 170, Folder 5, Korean Relief 1950–53. Steven H. Lee, 'The UNKRA in War and Peace: an Economic and Social History of Korea in the 1950s', in Chae-Jin Lee and Young Ick Lew (eds), *Korea and the Korean War* (Seoul: Yonsei University Press, 2002), 357–96.

[21] J. Donald Kingsley, 1951, LWF Archives, Box 36, Newspaper clippings, Folder, 'Refugees, General, 1948–1957'.

establish World Vision. Journalists too focused on the figure of the abandoned child. Save the Children opened health clinics and attached particular importance to improving health education, by organizing lectures and slide shows and paying for Korean doctors to train in Hong Kong. American Relief for Korea (ARK) brought together the US government and private charitable organizations (the Hollywood film star Douglas Fairbanks became its public face) and arranged for the delivery of clothing and other items to Korean civilians. The USA alone supported Korea to the tune of around $330 million in just three years.[22]

Following relief work in Germany, Palestine (Gaza), China and India, the Quakers also became involved. The Friends Service Unit established orphanages, neighbourhood centres, clinics and hospitals, and trained local nurses, midwives and anaesthetists in Kunsan, home to around 33,000 refugees. Much was made of the fact that refugee groups were provided with building materials, trained by local Korean builders, and encouraged to construct their own homes. Documentary films advertised success stories to audiences in North America. But Quakers agonized about the role they were expected to play: 'Do we fall into a routine of "supplementing" large-scale governmental efforts, sometimes eating and sleeping in barbed wire compounds? After a generation of this with a great many people making a career out of foreign aid and refugee services, one can't escape that new insights are demanded. It is a haunting feeling'.[23] From this point of view it was vital that refugees should play a part in their own rehabilitation through dignified and cooperative labour, so much at odds with prevailing government corruption associated with the clique around President Syngman Rhee. The AFSC privately denounced his bloated army that consumed resources that might have gone into education and training: 'the military, political, economic climate is not receptive to the longer range community development type of programme that Friends might otherwise consider carrying on'. Still, they remained directly involved until the end of the decade, in the hope of creating something of 'permanent value'.[24]

The alleviation of suffering in Korea, as in Germany, relied in the short term on an awkward collaboration between the military leadership and non-governmental relief workers. A more durable solution hinged on sustained economic growth that generated additional jobs. In the early 1950s this prospect seemed far off. The Korean economy depended heavily upon foreign aid. Refugees from North Korea indirectly benefited from this largesse, as well as from non-governmental philanthropy, and over time they prided themselves on becoming successful entrepreneurs. By contrast, internally displaced Koreans paid a heavier price in terms of material deprivation, which they mitigated by assisting one another. They suffered in silence because Rhee curbed civic organizations and political parties.

---

[22] Benthall, *Disasters, Relief and the Media*, 156; Rachel M. McCleary, *Global Compassion: Private Voluntary Organizations and U.S. Foreign Policy since 1939* (Oxford: Oxford University Press, 2009), 74.

[23] Louis Schneider to Frank and Julia Hunt in confidence, 11 November 1954, AFSC Archives, Foreign Service 1954—Country reports—Korea—Visitors.

[24] Louis Schneider to Frank Hunt, 30 October 1953, AFSC Archives, Foreign Service 1953—Country reports. The AFSC established a presence in North Korea in the 1970s.

HONG KONG: A 'PROBLEM OF PEOPLE'?

If we discount repatriation, the defeat of those opposed to the revolution in China left them with three options for resettlement, only two of which were viable. The least realistic was the possibility of settling outside the region. The US Immigration and Naturalization Service vetted any prospective immigrant who claimed family ties with Chinese Americans, believing this to be part of an attempt at Communist infiltration. Other non-communist states likewise regarded refugees from China with suspicion, although countries such as Australia and Canada were keener to resist the mass immigration of people of Asian descent on purely racist grounds. There was no equivalent here to the policy of admitting European 'escapees' from communism. The American administration adjusted its immigration quota only slightly to provide for refugees from Chinese communism, causing one US congressman to observe in 1953 that doing nothing would 'serve notice [to] those with yellow skin that you cannot join the white man's club. Where will these people look in such an event? The answer is obvious: to the club organised by Uncle Joe Stalin'.[25] But this view cut little ice. Why not (he was told) let the Chinese refugees throw themselves on the mercy of the Nationalist government in Taiwan or seek sanctuary in Hong Kong?

In fact around 100,000 Nationalist Army officers as well as civil servants did move to Taiwan, where they established a government-in-exile, the 'Republic of China', which became a thorn in the flesh of Beijing as well as the colonial administration in Hong Kong. Although making up only 10 per cent of Taiwan's postwar population, the exiles exerted a political and cultural influence out of all proportion to their size, reinforcing authoritarian rule in the ROC, which regarded itself as the guardian of Chinese nationalism, as expounded by Sun Yat-sen, and Confucianism, at the expense of indigenous Taiwanese tradition. Yet their relationship with the native population was an uneasy one. They were described as *waishengren*, 'people from outside the province of Taiwan', and this isolation persisted. A decade after their arrival the leading intellectual Wang Hongjun offered the caustic assessment that, 'If you ask them where they came from, why they came, where they're going, they have nothing to say'.[26]

Meanwhile in Hong Kong the numbers confronted the colonial authorities with a 'problem' that they could not ignore. Around 700,000 Chinese refugees fled the mainland for the adjacent British colony of Hong Kong, most of them between 1949 and 1951. The colony's population had been much depleted when, following the Japanese invasion and occupation, one million Chinese fled to the mainland. This outflow was now reversed. By 1951 its population had doubled to 2.3 million. Natural increase accounted for some of this growth, but most of it was due to

---

[25] Gil Loescher and John A. Scanlan, *Calculated Kindness: Refugees and America's Half-Open Door, 1945–Present* (New York: Praeger, 1986), 238.

[26] A-chin Hsiau, 'A "Generation in-Itself": Authoritarian Rule, Exilic Mentality, and the Post-war Generation of Intellectuals in 1960s Taiwan' *The Sixties: a Journal of History, Politics and Culture*, 3, no.1 (2010), 1–31, at 14.

immigration—in 1956 one in three residents in Hong Kong counted as a refugee. They were expected to return to the mainland rather than attempt to settle in the colony. Once it became clear that they had no intention of doing so, the British chose to avoid using the term refugee, a key consideration being that no offence should be caused to the People's Republic by implying that it persecuted anyone. Taiwan had no such qualms, seeking to make political capital out of the flight of refugees. The British complained that the Nationalists were seeking to 'foment intrigue'—there was an element of truth in this accusation—thereby jeopardizing Anglo-Chinese relations. The upshot of this difficult balancing act was that the colonial administration increasingly described the newcomers as 'illegal' immigrants and 'squatters' whose economic motives deprived them of entitlement to protection under the 1951 Convention.[27]

Included in the total number were members of Shanghai's erstwhile mercantile elite, many of whom were active in cotton-spinning and already familiar with the economic scene in Hong Kong where they had made valuable contacts. Some fled before 1949, in anticipation of the Communist victory, although they hedged their bets and until 1952 entertained hopes of returning to the mainland. After a while they enjoyed an environment favourable to capitalist enterprise, including 'liberal' labour legislation, advantageous terms for leasing land and an abundant workforce.[28] Other family members joined them after the PRC came to power, a move that convinced the colonial authorities that the influx of refugees was more a function of family reunification and economic aspiration than political persecution.[29]

Whereas wealthy business people soon found their feet, those of more modest means encountered a chilly reception from the colonial government. The governor, Alexander Grantham, set the tone by commenting that he did not want the colony to become 'a glorified soup kitchen for refugees from all over China', since they were 'not our own people'. Grantham maintained that poor economic conditions in China and not persecution led these 'traders and travellers' to cross into the colony; he comforted himself with the belief (or hope) that most would return once they found life difficult in Hong Kong. His administration introduced entry permits and identity papers.[30] Grantham's successor, Sir Robert Black, argued that the colony faced an economic challenge and that it was unwise to dwell 'on the circumstances of the mass exodus from Communist China', lest it complicate diplomacy. Thus, he continued, 'the Hong Kong refugee problem is in fact identical

[27] Glen Peterson, 'To be or not to be a Refugee: the International Politics of the Hong Kong Refugee Crisis, 1949–1955' *Journal of Commonwealth and Imperial History*, 36, no.2 (2008), 171–95.

[28] Siu-Lun Wong, *Emigrant Entrepreneurs: Shanghai Industrialists in Hong Kong* (Hong Kong: Oxford University Press, 1988).

[29] Agnes S. Ku, 'Immigration Policies, Discourses, and the Politics of Local Belonging in Hong Kong, 1950–80' *Modern China*, 30, no.3 (2004), 326–60.

[30] Hu Yueh, 'The Problem of the Hong Kong Refugees' *Asian Survey*, 2, no.1 (1962), 28–37; Chi-Kwan Mark, 'The "Problem of People": British Colonials, Cold War Powers and the Chinese Refugees in Hong Kong, 1949–1962' *MAS*, 41, no.6 (2007), 1145–81; Christopher A. Airriess, 'Governmentality and Power in Politically Contested Space: Refugee Farming in Hong Kong's New Territories, 1945–1970' *Journal of Historical Geography*, 31, no.4 (2005), 763–8.

with the complexity of problems created by a rapidly swollen and rapidly increasing population'. According to Black:

> We are not a staging post on a great migration; we are a terminus and a goal. We cannot let ourselves be transformed into a camp with all its nomadic and temporary implications, the object of fleeting charity, a soup-kitchen queue for those less fortunate than we are, as they pause here, waiting to know whither they can go. We are a community who have had some measure of success, the fruits of resource and enduring efforts.

Black concluded that 'we are not (repeat not) callous, calculating capitalists who deny the rights of those still living in our slums to better housing. Our calculations we direct, we hope in a realistic and unsentimental way, to discovering how to fulfil our humanitarian role within the boundaries of this small geographical location'.[31] Tougher rules on immigration in 1962 were portrayed as protecting the 'special' character of the colony, although these measures did not deter successive contingents from trying to get into Hong Kong.[32]

The very real plight of refugees in Hong Kong did not escape the notice of UNHCR. A report prepared on its behalf left its readers in no doubt that these refugees required urgent attention, but it took until November 1957 for the UN General Assembly to decide that 'the problem of Chinese refugees in Hong Kong is such as to be of concern to the international community' and to urge the High Commissioner to 'use his good offices' to secure financial resources to contribute to their relief in situ. They were, it appeared, now de facto refugees, although the colonial authorities continued to insist otherwise. Nor did the UN take a view on the legal status of those who fled. In this situation a great deal of the day-to-day responsibility for assisting the refugees fell upon voluntary organizations which entered the field with a self-proclaimed 'humanitarian' mission.[33]

Doubtless it helped that most newcomers proved more resourceful than Grantham and Black anticipated or were led to believe. An article in a Catholic newsletter praised their resilience, adding that the 'noble' Chinese refugees envisaged Hong Kong as 'the city of freedom and hope'. 'A Chinese family arriving in Hong Kong did not go to a welfare organisation for aid; instead, the family members, one and all, went into the alleys and dumps of Hong Kong in search of boards, crates, wire, tin and tarpaper. This they laboriously carried to a hillside where they ingeniously constructed a hut'. According to one refugee, 'Here I can do what I want', even if it meant living in a makeshift hut. The author concluded optimistically by suggesting that Catholic relief work 'has so aroused the interest of the refugees that great numbers of them are turning to Catholicism. In this free world of Hong Kong, they see love expressed through the priests and sisters whose

---

[31] Speech to the Hong Kong Legislative Council, 1 March 1961, TNA CO 1030/1311.
[32] Laura Madokoro, 'Borders Transformed: Sovereign Concerns, Population Movements and the Making of Territorial Frontiers in Hong Kong, 1949–1967' *JRS*, 25, no.3 (2012), 407–27.
[33] Edvard Hambro, *The Problem of Chinese Refugees in Hong Kong* (Leiden: A.W. Sijthoff, 1955); UNHCR, Fonds 11 Series 1, 15/2/1. Hambro's report was translated into Chinese by the Free China Relief Association.

lives are devoted to helping them in their trouble'. The Maryknoll Sisters organized youth clubs and set up a family counselling service to inculcate good citizenship, and stressed that refugees had made the right choice in escaping from Communism. There were rich pickings for the Catholic Church and its anti-communist crusade.[34]

The support given to Chinese refugees by churches and secular organizations dismayed colonial officials because they raised the prospect that refugees would put down 'roots', although NGOs were more concerned that 'the youth is entirely confused, disappointed and virgin soil for any radical philosophy of life promising them a better future'. Only after a terrible fire in the squatters' camp of Shek Kip Mei on Christmas Day 1953 and riots in 1956 did the colonial administration adjust its policy, by agreeing to fund the construction of seven-storey 'H blocks' in Kowloon to offer greater protection against fire and the spread of infectious disease, and thus to benefit the resident population at large. In 1964 the government evicted squatters from Wong Tai Sin and relocated 180,000 in the high-rise 'resettlement estates' of Chi Wan Shan ('Mercy Cloud Village'). Private sector investment in housing also made a big difference, as it did in South Korea. The colonial government agreed to provide land to refugees from neighbouring Guangdong. Gradually the authorities in Hong Kong came to regard integration as a 'durable solution'—not that this prevented them from rounding up unwanted migrants and sending them back to China, particularly when large numbers of people entered the colony following the Great Leap Forward and the ensuing famine in 1962. In the medium term the situation eased thanks to the rapid growth of the Hong Kong economy to which refugees contributed by making clothes, electrical products and plastic goods for export, with a similar outcome to that of West Germany.[35]

How was population displacement understood by those most directly affected? Chinese nationalist opponents of the PRC who sheltered in Burma and Thailand described an arduous escape from Yunnan and the attempt to sustain as normal a life as possible. In Burma they were assisted by longstanding Chinese migrant communities, who saw them as guardians of Han identity—'informants often mention that their villages are like small Chinese societies'.[36] They framed exile as an expression of the fight against communism (profits from the trade in narcotics helped) and sustaining a sense of 'tradition', including Buddhist belief. Their hatred of communism and affection for pre-revolutionary rural Yunnan remained undimmed, in ways that recall the worldview of Russian émigrés after 1917. Today it

---

[34] Mgnr. John Romaniello, 'A Missionary's Experience with Chinese Refugees in Hong Kong' *Migration News*, 7, no.1 (1958), 12–13; Cindy Yik-Yi Chu, *The Maryknoll Sisters in Hong Kong, 1921–1969: In Love with the Chinese* (New York: Palgrave Macmillan, 2004), 106.

[35] Pastor Ludwig Stumpf to Henry Whiting, 12 October 1954, LWF Archives, Box WS/V.2.a, Resettlement Offices, Hong Kong, 1954–1967; Wong, *Emigrant Entrepreneurs*, 16–18, 37–8, 176–7.

[36] Wen-Chin Chang, 'From War Refugees to Immigrants: the Case of the KMT Yunnanese Chinese in Northern Thailand' *IMR*, 35, no.4 (2001), 1086–105, at 1097. During the 1980s ethnic Chinese fled from Burma to join these refugees in Thailand.

is cemented by memorial books—clan genealogies—that affirm 'the achievements of our ancestors [and] educate the offspring to retain Han history and civilization'. These books, carefully copied from scarce texts that survived destruction, support a history not so much of flight in 1949 as of heroic Han migration to Yunnan under the Ming Dynasty.[37]

We know little of the attitudes of other refugees. It would be an over-simplification to assume a 'refugee mentality' that contributed to the absence of political activism, particularly when the British discouraged political organization and expression in Hong Kong, as did Syngman Rhee in South Korea. The Nationalist Free China Relief Association maintained a presence in some of the refugee settlements, and this was one outlet. Although refugees do not appear to have written about the homes they left or their journey to Hong Kong, they nevertheless registered a presence in cultural as well as economic terms. Film and popular music brought a more dynamic edge to the colony's hitherto conservative cultural scene. Like the *rebetika* music brought from Asia Minor, audiences in the 1950s and early 1960s lapped up popular songs such as 'Shanghai by Night' composed by refugees. The same enthusiasm manifested itself in respect of Mandarin films, until they too were eclipsed by Western products. In the absence for whatever reason of personal testimony, and of significant commemorative activity, this dynamism indicates that refugees left their mark on the history of Hong Kong.[38]

DISPLACEMENT, DIASPORA AND VALORIZATION: TIBETAN REFUGEES

At the end of the 1950s, as the claims of Korea and Hong Kong on international public opinion weakened, the flight of Tibetan refugees began to grab the headlines. In 1959, following a concerted attempt by the Chinese Communist Party and the People's Liberation Army to transform social and economic relations in Tibet, tens of thousands of Tibetans followed the Dalai Lama into exile in neighbouring India, Nepal, Bhutan and Sikkim, in the belief that they would soon be able to return. (Others, of course, opted to stay in Tibet, and about their experiences we know next to nothing.) Although their motives were mixed, refugees often mentioned religious persecution, as well as 'increasing hardship and mental torture' according to one unidentified farmer who fled in 1971. Some had fought against the Chinese army of occupation, while others wished to evade the collectivization of their livestock. By 1960 around 45,000 refugees were registered in India, 25,000 in Nepal and 4,000 in Bhutan; an additional 14,000 fled to the

---

[37] Wen-Chin Chang, 'Home Away from Home: Migrant Yunnanese Chinese in Northern Thailand' *International Journal of Asian Studies*, 3, no.1 (2006), 49–76, at 66.

[38] Benjamin K.P. Leung, *Perspectives on Hong Kong Society* (Hong Kong: Oxford University Press, 1996), 64–5; Janet Salaff, Siu-Iun Wong and Arent Grove (eds), *Hong Kong Movers and Stayers: Narratives of Family Migration* (Urbana: University of Illinois Press, 2010), 102. Second-generation refugees did however protest against Beijing after the Tiananmen Square massacre in 1989.

Portuguese colony of Macao. Smaller numbers added to the exile population later on. India's Buddhist heritage was thought to provide a point of cultural and religious contact.[39]

In Nepal the refugees were regarded as temporary visitors to be looked after by the local Red Cross or the Tibetan Refugee Aid Society of Canada, whose founder provided an excellent summary of their social world. Those who reached India were assisted by various private bodies and by the Ministry of Rehabilitation (chapter 5) which placed refugees in transit camps. Anticipating Chinese spies in their midst, the government in Delhi dispersed refugees rather than leaving them close to the border. Another factor was the government's wish to discourage political agitation among Tibetan refugees by insisting that the admission of refugees was a purely 'humanitarian' gesture. India and Nepal—like the British in Hong Kong—regarded the internationalization of the crisis as an unwelcome development that threatened to damage relations with China. Other governments betrayed no such anxiety. From the outset the USA looked upon refugees as pawns in the struggle against communism, and thus deserving of substantial financial support. In 1959 the CIA created a front organization, the American Emergency Committee for Tibetan Refugees, which offered clandestine support for the resistance army on Tibetan soil, the Chushi Gangdrug, some of whose members escorted the Dalai Lama to safety in 1959. This strategy continued until the early 1970s when the USA sought a rapprochement with China.[40]

Informal settlements sprang up in India and Nepal, but living conditions left much to be desired. The Indian government wanted to tread carefully lest it encourage the belief among Bengali refugees that Tibetans received preferential treatment. For his part, the Dalai Lama feared that the refugees would 'be dispersed and then sink to the level of the poorest Indians'.[41] These anxieties were not unfounded. A confidential UNHCR memorandum argued that visitors to India got a distorted picture of the situation, because they visited picturesque Tibetan hill stations at which children enjoyed good health, whereas remote and disadvantaged places escaped their attention. Here refugees were put to work on arduous road construction projects in the Himalayan region, living on site in flimsy tents and without access to medical care. The author spoke apocalyptically of 'the social downfall of the Tibetan refugees', far exceeding all other post-war refugee problems, adding that 'when I saw the situation of the Tibetan refugees, six years after their arrival in India, I was struck by the similarity with the problems in Europe in 1951, six years after World War 2'. Although the Indian government had done a reasonable job, since 1963 'no new initiatives of any size have been undertaken', something that

---

[39] Margaret Nowak, *Tibetan Refugees: Youth and the New Generation of Meaning* (New Brunswick, N.J.: Rutgers University Press, 1984), 11.

[40] George Woodcock, 'Tibetan Refugees in a Decade of Exile' *Pacific Affairs*, 43, no.3 (1970), 410–20; Carole McGranahan, *Arrested Histories: Tibet, the CIA and Memories of a Forgotten War* (Durham, NC: Duke University Press, 2010).

[41] High Commissioner, New Delhi, to Commonwealth Relations Office, London, 2 June 1959, TNA FO 371/145388; Edward Sniders, UK Permanent Delegation, Geneva, to Selwyn Lloyd, 22 September 1959, TNA FO 371/145404.

Indian officials attributed to the shortage of land and the influx of 900,000 refugees from East Pakistan. He concluded that international support would contribute to their integration, provided UNHCR embarked on 'planned development', an indication of the connection that was being envisaged between individual refugee 'rehabilitation' and nationwide economic modernization.[42]

Public opinion in the West soon began to pay close attention to the plight of Tibetan refugees. Ethnic stereotyping affected contemporary attitudes. Those who made their way to Nepal were described as an inherently 'nomadic' population who were deemed to be less susceptible to psychological damage than Europeans. One condescending report suggested that they 'withstood wonderfully well their miraculous journey through the Himalayas'.[43] This did not lessen the responsibilities of foreign philanthropy which took its cue from the notion of a Buddhist utopia, popularized by the novelist James Hilton before the Second World War and turned into a celebrated film, *Lost Horizon*. Sentimental attachment to this 'Shangri La' combined with Cold War considerations helped engineer international support. In 1960 World Refugee Year enabled sympathizers to provide Tibetan refugees in Nepal with literacy classes, so that following their 'eventual return [they might] be the torch bearers to lead their country to peace and prosperity'. But this was not a uniform view. One British official advocated resettlement in a newly-built 'Tibetan town' housing 25,000 people in Punjab or Himachal Pradesh, which could 'absorb the unrehabilitated [sic] refugees working at present on the roads as well as such of the colonists who have found agricultural work uncongenial or unattractive'.[44] The World Council of Churches also supported resettlement projects, including better facilities for health care and vocational training, lest Tibetan refugees form a 'hard core' and fall victim to what was called the 'refugee psychosis'. Some of these initiatives had lasting consequences. Within a few years the government-in-exile established schools whose teachers inculcated the 'cultural uniqueness' of Tibet and imposed sanctions on recalcitrant students. In Nepal, Swiss relief workers helped Tibetans to develop a thriving carpet weaving industry, with the backing of foreign capital and expertise. Repatriation vanished from the diplomatic lexicon.[45]

In the longer term Nehru's decision to admit the Dalai Lama and his followers made it possible to develop Tibetan culture in exile. The chosen site was the Northern Indian settlement of Dharamsala (in Hindi this conveys the idea of a guesthouse or 'temporary abode') whose monasteries had been built by Tibetan migrants

---

[42] K. Brouwer, UNHCR representative in The Hague, 15 March 1965, Fonds UNHCR 11, Series 1, 1951–70, 15/GEN/TIB, Tibetan refugees, 1959–67.

[43] UNOG Archives, ARR 55/0088, File Box no. 046; Dwight D. Eisenhower Presidential Library, White House Central Files, 1953–61, Official File, Box 579 (Refugees-DPs 1958–60), Folder 116-G 1959–60.

[44] Report by Maurice Frydman, April 1964, Fonds UNHCR 11, Series 1, 1951–70, 15/0/IND/ TIB, Tibetan refugees in India, 1959–65, Folder 3; Dibyesh Anand, *Geopolitical Exotica: Tibet in Western Imagination* (Minneapolis: University of Minnesota Press, 2007).

[45] Memo by W.S. Kilpatrick, Director, Service to Refugees, WCC, Geneva, 29 January 1962, Box WS V.3.b, Service to Refugees, Material Relief, India, 1954–62.

in the nineteenth century. Its facilities were initially lamentable. The Indian government initially issued refugees with ID cards and prevented them from acquiring farm land or owning a business. In due course, refugees came to regard the cards not as demeaning but as a token of pride, affirming their decision not to renounce their refugee status. Over time, this 'temporary abode' took on a more permanent appearance and settlement became the new mantra; in 1969 Tibetan refugees were permitted to work without hindrance and to own land. From time to time new groups of refugees made their way into India. Dharamsala acquired the name 'little Lhasa in India'. It housed the renowned Library of Tibetan Works and Archives. 10 March became the annual day of commemoration of the moment when Tibetans followed the Dalai Lama into exile—organizers of the first demonstration were keen to ensure that publicity material was made available in English in order to maximize international publicity for this event. Since then the date has been fixed as 'National Uprising Day'.[46]

Among Tibetan refugees a distinctive politics was associated with ideas of home as 'sacred space'. Elderly refugees described a 'life [that was] smooth and well regulated by the forces of nature. Floods, earthquakes and foreign invasions were considered as indicative of a disruption in the relationship between the divine forces and us mortals'. Tibetan exiles denounced the desecration of their homeland as a consequence of Chinese administration. But refugeedom exposed divergent opinions between pro-Western Tibetans who have embraced a democratic outlook and ordinary Tibetans who continue to endorse a tradition in which kinship and patronage are paramount. Older Tibetans bemoan the fact that the young generation 'do not understand what we have gone through in life; they are far more attracted to material things. The love that we have for our land is missing in them'.[47] Veterans of the Chushi Gangdrug resistance feel that their actions have been forgotten by the creation of a dominant narrative of non-violence. The Dalai Lama lamented what he regarded as a tendency for Tibetans who remained behind to 'think and behave like Chinese', while Tibetan exiles who arrived in Dharamsala in the 1980s and 1990s were mocked for their 'Chinese ways'. One refugee described how he became 'properly Tibetan' by learning patriotic songs—'I got better at it as I did it again and again'.[48]

Even if the prospect of a return to 'free Tibet' appears remote, nevertheless investment in cultural programmes contributed to a sense that Tibet is 'alive' among its exiled communities. This has sometimes taken surprising forms. Dharamsala is now the site of the annual 'Miss Tibet' competition. According to its website the winner in 2008 was Sonam Choedon who was born in 1990 in Kham, Eastern Tibet. 'She is a student, has studied up to class 8 in Tibet. She is fluent in Chinese as well as Tibetan. She came into exile in India in June 2008 in search of better

---

[46] Nowak, *Tibetan Refugees*, 33–4; Honey Oberoi Vahali, *Lives in Exile: Exploring the Inner World of Tibetan Refugees* (Routledge, 1999), 95–6.

[47] Vahali, *Lives in Exile*, 9, 15.

[48] Emily Ting Yeh, 'Exile Meets Homeland: Politics, Performance and Authenticity in the Tibetan Diaspora' *Environment and Planning: Society and Space*, 25, no.4 (2007), 648–67, at 653, 662.

opportunities for education. Her hobbies include dancing, reading and studying languages. In the future she would like to become a dance teacher and also work on languages. She would also like to use her life and strength to help others in need as people have done for her when she first arrived in India'. Choedon praised the relevance of Gandhi to the Tibetan people: 'Gandhi is the most important freedom fighter of India. He fought with non-violence. His Holiness the Dalai Lama is following his path and pursuing the Middle-way approach to resolve the Tibetan issue.' However, she said that she had not been able to study Gandhi in Tibet and was 'speaking from the brief knowledge I have gained and heard after coming into exile'.[49]

For Tashi, a young Tibetan in Dharamsala, educational provision exposed a paradox:

> Our school principal was Tibetan but she could only speak Chinese. That is one reason why our parents sent us to India; in this school we are learning about our history and also Tibetan language. And now I am in India I am also learning Chinese. I think going back to Tibet will be very difficult but if I can go back in the future I think I should know Chinese.[50]

Some refugees thus developed a more cosmopolitan outlook. Older people found this troubling. One elderly refugee described how, having settled in Bhopal he developed a greater understanding of his Indian neighbours, such that 'without really knowing it, we had begun to eat like Indians, speak like them, dress and even laugh like them . . . it was only when people remarked that we had adapted rather well that I sometimes felt uncomfortable'. He turned down the offer of a plot of land in a neighbour's village and returned to Dharamsala: 'Why had I come to India? To forget? Who was I? What was my past?'[51] The point is that it would be a mistake to regard settlements such as those in Dharamsala or Nepal as the embodiment of a stable, unproblematic and uncontested Tibetan identity, even if foreign friends of Tibet might wish it otherwise. Displacement exposed divergent views about 'authenticity'.

CONCLUSIONS

War, occupation, civil war and revolution constituted the matrix of mass population displacement in South-East Asia in the middle years of the twentieth century. The lengthy struggle to dislodge Japan from its grip on mainland China produced the greatest mass movement of refugees in modern history. Civil war exposed irreconcilable political and ideological differences; as in Russia in 1917–21, one result was an exodus of people opposed to the revolutionary project. Western public opinion portrayed the government of Communist China in negative terms,

---

[49]   <http://www.misstibet.com/>.
[50]   <http://news.bbc.co.uk/1/hi/world/asia-pacific/7926559.stm>.
[51]   Vahali, *Lives in Exile*, 21–3.

but this was a somewhat simplistic appraisal, neglecting the role of communist forces in defeating the Japanese. Nor should the flight of Nationalist forces and civilians obscure the fact that most Chinese got on with their lives as best they could.

The Cold War determined the way in which the refugee crisis was framed and addressed, not only by governments but by NGOs. Conservative voluntary agencies such as World Vision and Catholic Relief Services made no secret of their anti-communist stance, which coloured their attitude towards Chinese, Korean and Tibetan refugees. Western relief workers did not all sing from the same hymn sheet: Quakers in particular denounced the authoritarian and corrupt regime of Syngman Rhee. However, these failings were not the sole preserve of the political leadership: the unconventional behaviour of some refugees also contributed to what was widely perceived as 'moral degradation'.

Although Western sympathy for Tibetan refugees owed a good deal to the 'Communist menace', their high place in the international pecking order, out of all proportion to their numbers, was reminiscent of public support in the West for Armenian refugees earlier. They benefited from the readiness of foreign sympathizers to associate themselves with the preservation of Tibetan culture in exile. To a lesser extent this was also true of Korean refugees, whose Catholic faith ensured backing from the influential Catholic lobby in the USA. Religious ties and cultural sentiment thus helped shape the contours of humanitarianism. Some groups were better placed than others to trade on positive representations of their predicament.

Refugees in South Korea and Hong Kong made use of entrepreneurial skills and seized new economic opportunities. In both societies, the economic 'miracle' in the later 1950s and 1960s helped to alleviate the material misfortunes of refugees and contributed to their local integration. Foreign aid and government investment contributed to economic reconstruction, helping to keep conservative forces in power. Elsewhere in South-East Asia the outcome was less favourable to refugees. For all the virtues that were ascribed to Tibetan refugees, the story was of hardship and uncertainty. Very few Asian refugees were admitted to the USA or Commonwealth countries, which modified their exclusionary policy only in the late 1970s in response to the exodus of refugees from Vietnam (chapter 7).

Bringing this chapter to a close only serves to expose the lack of anything like a full social and cultural history of displacement in South-East Asia. There are nevertheless some pointers. We are beginning to understand how difficult it was for Korean refugees to negotiate the upheaval of war and forced migration. It is less clear how plebeian Chinese refugees came to terms with their bleak experience of life in Hong Kong. Diaries written by Chinese merchants and teachers have survived from the Second World War, throwing light on their experiences of displacement including changes in gender relations brought about by mixing peasants and middle-class students: a displaced sociologist wrote of the impact this made on household relations: 'My landlady is able to learn from my wife the way of bringing up children. And, owing to my constant interference, the beating of his wife by my landlord has become less frequent'.[52] We know that Tibetan refugee communities incorporated a history of life before the Chinese occupation into their interpretation of exile. The politics of social and cultural life is transparent: while China proclaims its role as liberator from feudal rule and 'obscurantism' in old Tibet, the exiled followers of the Dalai Lama bemoan the 'slavery' now imposed by Chinese rule. This is a contested history of displacement, and it does not always lend itself to informed debate. But it shows that the past is of paramount importance.

[52] Lary, *The Chinese People at War*, 83.

PART III

REFUGEES IN THE GLOBAL COLD WAR AND ITS AFTERMATH

One cannot run from one's own past

(Johannes Østrup)

Previous chapters demonstrated that wars, the clash of ideologies and the formation of new states contributed to widespread population displacement in the first
half of the twentieth century. Although self-preservation provided one motive for
flight, governments targeted entire groups of people in pursuit of political, social
and economic transformation. The dissolution of empires and the creation of
nation-states produced enormous demographic upheaval. During the 1950s the
struggle against colonialism extended to large parts of the globe. A refugee crisis in
North Africa where Algerian nationalists fought to overthrow France's grip on their
country was one outcome. Independence struggles in other parts of the Third
World had similarly turbulent results. Communism too captured popular imagination throughout the Far East, in China and North Korea, in Vietnam and
Cambodia, and in Ethiopia. Social relations were turned upside down by concerted campaigns against property owners, not just the wealthy elite but peasant
farmers and petty traders as well. The situation was complicated by the global Cold
War, because the superpowers invested in conflict by arming proxies in the Third
World and sustaining clients who had fled abroad. In the case of Afghanistan, the
Soviet attempt to shore up a communist regime had long lasting consequences in
terms of population displacement.

The end of the Cold War in the 1990s witnessed a shift from a bipolar world in
ways that are still being worked out at the level of states and in diplomatic engagement. One strand of thought maintains that ideological divisions have been replaced
by a new struggle construed as 'culture' versus 'barbarism', manifested in a discourse
that asserts the values of 'civilization' as opposed to 'ancient hatreds' and religious
'fundamentalism', although this would come as a surprise to those who denounced
Ottoman atrocities in the late nineteenth century in similar terms.[1] Another line of
argument holds that the post-Cold War era spawned a new style of warfare fuelled by
a combination of localized grievances and struggles on the one hand, and access to
globalized resources on the other. In fragile states, such as Somalia and Bosnia, new
warriors secured funding from the proceeds of organized crime, from supporters
in the diaspora and by siphoning off substantial amounts of humanitarian aid for

[1] Mark Duffield, *Global Governance and the New Wars: the Merging of Development and Security*
(Zed Books, 2001).

military purposes. In these violent settings, dominated by paramilitaries, mercenaries and warlords, civilians served as a resource to be conscripted or taxed. UNHCR officials speak of intervening in conflicts that recognize no distinction between military personnel and others, making it difficult to assist 'genuine' refugees.[2]

It is easy to be seduced into thinking that the tectonic plates shifted fundamentally towards the end of the twentieth century, but the extent of the upheaval can be exaggerated. As we have seen, both world wars blurred the distinction between uniformed combatants and civilians. Orchestrated attacks on civilian targets took place during the First World War and its aftermath. The brutal Russian Civil War was fuelled by rival ideologies, conducted by paramilitaries as well as organized armies, and sustained by foreign intervention. Ethnic cleansing in Bosnia-Herzegovina had antecedents in the early twentieth century, and its purpose was as transparent then as it was in the 1990s. The main difference is that warlords now find it possible to gain access to external resources on a much larger scale than hitherto, including resources destined for displaced civilians.

The capacity of international and inter-governmental organizations to manage the consequences of refugee crises increased rather than diminished in the second half of the twentieth century. One hallmark was the extension of UNHCR's remit beyond Europe. This new dispensation first emerged in North Africa in the late 1950s, when UNHCR assisted refugees in Morocco and Tunisia fleeing the Algerian war of independence, citing a willingness to use 'good offices' to support those who did not fall within its mandate.[3] This was only the first step in charting an increasingly global course that by the end of the millennium encompassed great swathes of sub-Saharan Africa, South-east Asia and Latin America. Questions arose about the appropriate 'durable solution' to pursue in each case—whether repatriation, resettlement or local integration—and how this might square with the interests of host states and countries of prospective immigration. Inevitably decisions reflected not the wishes of UNHCR, but the interests of member states, each of which affirmed its sovereignty in respect of decisions over asylum.

UNHCR thus had to tread carefully. It engaged awkwardly with governments in South-East Asia that expressed considerable doubts in the 1970s about their ability to cope with large number of refugees from Vietnam and Cambodia. The delicate balance between advocacy and respect for state sovereignty continues to preoccupy UNHCR. In the new millennium its spokespersons point to the persistence of protracted refugee situations and advocate 'international solidarity, co-operation and responsibility-sharing', all of which have been in short supply in the post-Cold War era. They lament the lack of 'clear parameters [to] describe how states should help one another with hosting refugees' and the crisis in the global economic order that fosters even more restrictive policies on the part of countries of prospective asylum.[4]

---

[2] *The State of the World's Refugees 2012*, chapter 1; Chandler, 'The Road to Military Humanitarianism', 693; Mary Kaldor, *New and Old Wars: Organized Violence in a Global Era* (Cambridge: Polity, 2001).

[3] Cecilia Ruthström-Ruin, *Beyond Europe: the Globalization of Refugee Aid* (Lund: Lund University Press, 1993).

[4] *The State of the World's Refugees 2012*, chapter 8.

Already in the 1960s and 1970s voices within UNHCR and in NGOs began to suggest that the nature of the 'refugee problem' had changed. Louise Holborn maintained that decolonization meant coming to terms with very different challenges than those confronted by the aftermath of war in Europe. African refugees were predominantly subsistence farmers or herdsmen who lacked contact with 'modern society', unlike their counterparts in Europe. Refugee movements in Africa, she went on, 'occurred in an entirely different political, economic, social and cultural context [and] the characteristics of the African refugees themselves and the absence of institutional infrastructure presented a refugee problem of a new nature and of new dimensions'. Other scholars shared the view that the phenomenon of 'new refugees' bore little resemblance to previous patterns of displacement, in so far as the numbers were far greater and because refugees from less developed countries ('preliterate mountain tribesmen') lacked cultural or ethnic ties with host societies in Europe and North America that encountered them in greater numbers.[5] This interpretation exaggerates the differences of scale and obscures similarities in policy over time. The number of refugees in sub-Saharan Africa was considerable, but so too was the magnitude of displacement in Europe and in China at the end of the Second World War. Nor should one minimize the difficulties that confronted refugees and DPs earlier on, including the need to improvise 'institutional infrastructure'. Finally, 'new refugees' who sought to settle in distant locations did not necessarily lack kinship ties, precisely because they favoured destinations where they could count on diasporic connections and networks.

Humanitarian organizations increasingly described their work with refugees as a part of a commitment to long-run economic development as well as short-term relief. They justified programmes of economic and technical assistance as a means of enabling refugees either to resettle or—preferably—to repatriate, since aid packages would induce the country of origin to take refugees back and to generate the kind of stability that would forestall further displacement.[6] All the same, this focus on development per se as a means of addressing protracted refugee crises was not a complete departure from past practice. During the 1920s, for instance, the League of Nations advocated investment in Greece to assist the integration of refugees from Turkey. These programmes incorporated a technocratic agenda of 'rehabilitation', implying that refugees could become fully-fledged members of society once they had been helped to get over the trauma of displacement. In this sense UNHCR followed in Nansen's footsteps.

NGOs acquired a global reach. In the inter-war period, they were dominated by special-interest organizations that assisted Armenian, Russian, Spanish and Jewish refugees, in some cases drawing on the knowledge and expertise of refugees themselves. From the 1950s onwards, the largest NGOs did not confine their attention to one group but instead adopted a more universal focus, garnering huge resources from donors and in many cases lucrative contract work on behalf of international

---

[5] Holborn, *Refugees*, 825–7; Stein, 'The Refugee Experience', 330.
[6] Coles, 'Approaching the Refugee Problem Today', 391.

organizations. All too often, however, their evolution along the lines of 'modern-ization, standardization and professionalization' went hand in hand with an increasing distance between NGO field workers and ordinary refugees.[7]

The institutionalization of assistance thus provided refugees with limited opportunities to influence policy-makers. Attempts have been made to address this issue, for example by committing resources to the dissemination of eyewitness testimony; the websites of UNHCR and leading NGOs such as Oxfam indicate the importance that they attach to refugee stories. The Evelyn Oldfield Unit com-missioned a community project to collect the 'untold stories of refugees who have settled in London since 1951', including Chinese, Eritrean, Ethiopian, Kurdish, Tamil and Ugandan refugees. The UNHCR now presents a 'Gallery of Prominent Refugees' who have 'achieved special status within a community because of their achievements, or because they have overcome hardship to build a new life'. But these attenuated vignettes are carefully framed by external agencies to garner a positive response to their work from host governments and donors rather than to provide an opportunity for unfettered self-expression, still less to involve refugees in the decision-making process.[8]

Beyond this specific purpose, two other points can be established with some certainty to demonstrate the significance of attempts to engage with the past. First, refugee leaders looked to history as part of a campaign to turn the tables on their rivals. In parts of sub-Saharan Africa, for example, refugee historians located dis-placement and incarceration along a broad chronological spectrum of victimiza-tion. Prolonged exposure to refugee camps intensified these sentiments and provided an opportunity to mobilize mass opinion for political purposes. The genocide in Rwanda made clear the painful consequences of articulating extreme views of ethnic differentiation among refugees who had been radicalized over many years of exile.

Second, the descendants of displaced and resettled refugees who took a close interest in the experiences of their parents and grandparents could now capitalize upon new information technologies to share their findings and reflect upon their experiences. This was facilitated by the opportunity to return to the places that were left behind, whether in Cyprus, Vietnam and elsewhere. Not for the first time, commemorative activity highlighted collective trial and tribulation. In a par-ticularly dramatic instance, the collapse of the Soviet Union enabled the descend-ants of deported nationalities to draw attention to the suffering of individuals and communities during the Stalin era, and where possible to secure recognition and restitution. Whether as part of external humanitarian or diasporic endeavours, the accounts provided by refugees continued to be subsumed in a broader enterprise.

[7] Barnett, *Empire of Humanity*, 219.
[8] Prem Kumar Rajaram, 'Humanitarianism and Representations of the Refugee' *JRS*, 15, no.3 (2002), 248–64. See <http://www.refugeestories.org/> for the exhibition at the Museum of London (2006–07) with oral testimony collected by the Refugee Communities History Project. For UNHCR see <http://www.unhcr.org/pages/49c3646c74.html>.

7

'Villages of Discipline'

Revolutionary Change and Refugees in South-East Asia

Those vicissitudes we have experienced
Cause our hearts to break

(Nguyen Du)

INTRODUCTION

Forty years ago, war and foreign intervention in South-East Asia filled the pages of the global mass media. It is not hard to understand why. Violent rivalry between established regimes and their revolutionary opponents, backed by the world's superpowers, led to social and demographic disaster. Communist victories in South Vietnam, Cambodia (Kampuchea) and Laos in 1975 displaced two million people to neighbouring states and resulted in internal flight on an even greater scale. Vietnamese refugees made hazardous attempts to flee by boat; many did not survive the journey. In Cambodia the victorious Khmer Rouge inflicted enormous damage on the population, including the country's Vietnamese, Chinese and Muslim minorities: 'to keep you is no benefit, to destroy you is no less', went the slogan. Vietnam's invasion of Cambodia at the end of 1978 culminated in mass exodus to camps along the Thai border of a mixed population of survivors of the genocide and remnants of the Khmer Rouge who sought to regroup. These dramatic episodes were once common knowledge, but the experiences of refugees from Vietnam and Cambodia presently command scant attention in the Western world.

Other crises were much less talked about at the time because they did not easily map on to the East-West confrontation. Political leaders in post-independence Burma set about reshaping state and society, with disquieting results for ethnic minorities that had been relatively privileged under British rule. Persecution reached its peak in 1978, when the government of Burma targeted the 800,000-strong Rohingya Bengali-speaking Muslim minority, declaring them to be 'non-nationals'. Their flight to neighbouring Bangladesh brought them into direct contact with an already impoverished host population (chapter 5). Controversially, UNHCR argued that few Rohingya refugees had a legitimate claim to recognition and pressed them to accept repatriation without giving adequate assurances about their security. Thousands who refused to return faced an uncertain future in refugee camps in Bangladesh or Malaysia, victims of yet another aggressive state-building project.[1]

Whereas the situation in Burma garnered little international attention, Vietnamese and Cambodian refugees became the focus of emergency relief efforts and 'durable solutions'. Efforts to solve these crises were mired in controversy. In the case of Cambodia, the US administration refused to countenance Vietnamese and by extension Soviet control of Cambodia: refugees became pawns in the Cold War whom it was politically convenient to support in the camps whether they were Khmer Rouge warriors or civilians. By contrast UNHCR committed itself to their repatriation on the grounds that it was safe to return to Cambodia irrespective of the influence wielded by Vietnam.[2] Cold War considerations also loomed large in respect of Vietnamese refugees. In the late 1970s American leaders proclaimed their readiness to admit refugees from Vietnam on the grounds of protecting human rights, not just showing favour to prominent anti-communists. The result was the admission of former military officers and Vietnamese fishermen alike, despite public misgivings.[3]

The reduction in Cold War animosity and an increase in asylum applications led the US administration to place stricter limits on immigration although not before 1.4 million refugees had been admitted. In 1988, those fleeing Vietnam, many of them by boat, were held in detention centres, where officials decided who qualified as refugees. UNHCR participated in this deterrent regime, securing the agreement of Malaysia and Indonesia to a 'Comprehensive Plan of Action' which denied refugee status to 'boat people' unless they could prove persecution. An elaborate screening programme underpinned this plan. Those deemed to be 'economic migrants' were promptly sent back to an uncertain future in Vietnam. It was an eerie reminder of UNRRA policy after the Second World War, except that the process now included generous sweeteners to a grateful Vietnamese government.

In the light of these momentous upheavals the time is ripe to offer a fresh assessment of the outcome of refugeedom in South-East Asia. One way of doing so is to adopt a broader historical perspective by relating the drama of war and revolution in the 1970s to earlier and overlooked forgotten episodes of displacement. Postcolonial Vietnam is a case in point. Another is to reflect on refugees' experiences of incarceration. How did this affect refugees' sense of the past and how have their children and grandchildren attempted to address remote experiences? Vietnamese and other refugees such as Hmong were valorized as elements in the global struggle

---

[1] Christopher Bayly and Tim Harper, *Forgotten Armies: Britain's Asian Empire and the War with Japan* (Penguin, 2005), 84–5, 171–2; Maudood Elahi, 'The Rohingya Refugees in Bangladesh: Historical Perspectives and Consequences', in John R. Rogge (ed.), *Refugees: a Third World Dilemma* (Totowa, NJ: Rowman and Littlefield, 1987), 227–32; Sandra Dudley, *Materialising Exile: Material Culture and Embodied Experience among the Karenni Refugees in Thailand* (New York: Berghahn Books, 2010).

[2] Zolberg, Suhrke and Aguayo, *Escape from Violence*, 170–3.

[3] Bon Tempo, *Americans at the Gate*, 146–54.

against communism. Those who were able to flee cultivated a sense of being doubly victimized, not just by communist regimes but by being forced to spend years in camps prior to resettlement. Displacement was associated with a lengthy test of resolve. By contrast the reflections of Cambodian refugees are mostly hidden from history, except insofar as they emerge in the record of relief organizations. In particular there was no Khmer equivalent to the large Vietnamese diaspora whose extensive transnational connections have begun to illuminate refugee experiences.

Ubiquitous refugee camps provided voluntary agencies with access to displaced persons and facilitated a range of educational initiatives and self-help schemes. Refugees took to this activity with gusto, as a means of putting distance between themselves and the regime they fled. Yet refugee camps also exposed them to torment at the hands of local officials who seemed more interested in making their life as unpleasant as possible. Subsequent resettlement is beginning to generate memoir material about the difficult journey into exile and the painful experience of incarceration. The internet has become an important means of collecting information from disparate sources and disseminating it more widely. Subject to several qualifications discussed later on, the meanings that refugees attached to their displacement have begun to emerge.

VIETNAMESE REFUGEES

Vietnam became a French colony in the second half of the nineteenth century. Colonial rule went hand in hand with the organized recruitment of labour; in particular the rubber plantations thrived on indentured labour supplied by the indigenous peasantry. Peasants provided the main support for communist-led resistance to French and then to US occupation. The Second World War weakened France's grip on its colonial possessions. Peasant rebels who backed the Viet Minh fled to neighbouring Thailand to regroup. Vietnam became independent in 1948. The subsequent division of the country into North and South following the Geneva Accords (1954) displaced hundreds of thousands of people. Some 140,000 Viet Minh found berths on Soviet and Polish troop ships and moved to the North. Many more—around 930,000 Vietnamese, the majority of them Catholic peasants—fled in the opposite direction following communist land reform and food shortages in North Vietnam. An additional 55,000 escaped to Thailand. A senior official with the International Rescue Committee put this in context by arguing that 'Vietnamese peasants have gone from the North to the South in search of land and sometimes in search of freedom, for at least one thousand years'. Their 're-markable faces, incredible misery, but no cold and probably no hunger' put him in mind of the European refugees he encountered in 1945.[4]

---

[4] Louis Wiesner, *Victims and Survivors: Displaced Persons and Other War Victims in Vietnam, 1945–1975* (New York: Westport Press, 1988), 9, 109; Odd Arne Westad, *The Global Cold War: Third World Interventions and the Making of our Times* (Cambridge: Cambridge University Press, 2005), 180–5.

Those who settled in the South did not qualify for recognition under the 1951 Convention, because they were internally displaced. Catholic Relief Services, Lutheran World Relief and CARE helped refugees in South Vietnam to enrol on training programmes and find jobs. Keen to keep existing communities intact, the government resettled at least 600,000 refugees on virgin land. Huge development projects were launched at Honai and Go Vap, close to Saigon, and at Cai San near the Gulf of Siam, providing refugees with seven acres apiece to plant rice, bananas, sugar cane and sweet potatoes. This was largely a tactic to keep them out of Saigon, whose population increased by a factor of five since the outbreak of war. In an echo of the rhetoric in Hong Kong and Nepal, the Vietnamese commissioner in charge of land development praised the quality of the refugees, arguing that the success of the programme lay 'in the perseverance and resolute determination of the refugees to give of their best for the reconstruction of their homes and their unwavering struggle against subversive propaganda'. Other sources mentioned 'new refugee settlements [each with] its own schools, markets, infirmaries, churches, pagodas or temples, which are sometimes even better than those in the older indigenous communities'. For these reasons, 'transplantation' was regarded as a success. However, this verdict downplayed continuing tensions between Catholic northerners and the resident Buddhist majority in the South. It also overlooked the fact that the influx of staunchly anti-communist refugees helped to magnify the potential for civil war in Vietnam.[5]

Further upheavals followed as a result of territorial rivalries between Vietnam and Cambodia, which claimed parts of South Vietnam as its own. Vietnamese refugees protested that as 'Cambodians' they had been attacked both by the Vietcong and by forces loyal to the government of South Vietnam. In 1961 Cambodia complained that the government of South Vietnam was following an agenda of 'extermination' in relation to its Khmer minority. With some exasperation, UNHCR responded that the refugees' living conditions were probably no worse than those of the local Vietnamese. Another element in the strategy pursued by President Ngo Dinh Diem was that of resettling refugees and other 'loyal Vietnamese' in the highlands bordering Laos and Cambodia to prevent incursions of communist guerrillas from North Vietnam; this too was designed to relieve the pressure of population in the coastal plains. However, Diem's project alienated the indigenous Montagnard farmers whose land was appropriated for these purposes, and his programme of creating 'agrovilles', designed to enable his regime to keep a close watch on the rural population, also backfired.[6]

Over the next 15 years the population of Vietnam experienced even greater damage. A sustained bombing campaign by the US in 1965 compelled half a million peasants to leave their homes, where they were believed to be targets for 'communist infiltration' by the Vietcong. In 1968 the intensification of the war increased

---

[5] Bui-van-Luong, 12 January 1960, Fonds UNHCR 4, Sub-fonds 1, box 4, File 12/1/14 WRY; Ly-Trung-Dung, 'Integration of Refugees in Vietnam' *Migration News*, 7, no.4 (1958), 11–12.
[6] Wiesner, *Victims and Survivors*, 20–30.

the registered refugee population in South Vietnam from 868,000 to 1,328,000. The bitter divisions created by the war were reflected in rival analyses, which attributed displacement either to military attacks by the Vietcong or to the impact of American military 'pacification' tactics. The government of South Vietnam emphatically defined refugees as 'war victims who leave their homes to escape from communist terrorists or to evade military action', a definition that omitted the fact that around one-tenth of the total displaced population comprised people who had been forcibly relocated by the government of South Vietnam.[7]

In these difficult conditions around 30 separate foreign voluntary agencies invested in refugee relief. The AFSC, Lutheran World Relief and the League of Red Cross Societies supported centres in Saigon, Qui Nhon and Hue whilst criticizing conditions in government-run refugee camps. According to the World Council of Churches, sex work became the norm: 'men work as day labourers in the surrounding villages or wash American soldiers' clothes and cars... many can earn more by buying and selling American goods or getting girls for American soldiers'. Some camps housed up to 25,000 people and became organized communities. Other refugees lived independently with relatives. Much of this has a familiar ring from other episodes of mass displacement.[8] NGOs relied on the US army to transport relief supplies, but they were accused of being too close to the top brass for whom refugees were a valuable source of military intelligence. The presence of refugees attracted shipments of food aid that were quickly diverted to paramilitaries fighting the Vietcong. Certainly the financial ties between the US government and Catholic Relief Services were very close, and the American administration had no difficulty in regarding CRS as an 'integral part of the war effort'.[9]

Following the establishment of the Socialist Republic of Vietnam in 1975 and the government's ensuing relocation programme, more than one million people fled the country (see Map 7). One explanation was that urban residents as well as peasants were expected to move to 'New Economic Zones', established with the aim of increasing food production in remote or war-damaged regions of Vietnam. Entrepreneurs complained of punitive tax rates. Survival depended on transactions in the black market. For many refugees the final straw came when the revolutionary government decided to create 're-education camps' in which up to 100,000 Vietnamese were incarcerated. The refugees were a mixture of Vietnamese and ethnic Chinese, many of whom formed part of the country's commercial elite. Some were admitted to the USA because of a sense of obligation on the part of the American administration towards its former allies. In addition, around a quarter of a million ethnic Chinese moved to China under UNHCR auspices. Hanoi received payments in gold in order to persuade it to allow civilians to leave. More fled

[7] UNHCR London Office memo, 19 September 1968, Fonds UNHCR 11, Series 1, 1951–70, File 15/7, Vietnamese refugees.

[8] Report by Geoffrey Murray, 21 October 1966 and 'An Approach to Post-war Service Priorities in South Vietnam', October 1969, LWF Archives, Box WS V.3.b, Resettlement and Relief, Vietnam, 1966–69.

[9] Nichols, *The Uneasy Alliance*, 102–3.

following the failure of the rice crop in 1977 and the outbreak of hostilities between Vietnam and China in 1979.[10]

Tens of thousands of poorer refugees escaped on unsafe boats captained by inexperienced seamen. Secrecy made it difficult to plan properly. Strangers were thrown together. An unknown number died at sea when overcrowded vessels capsized. These 'boat people' were vulnerable to attacks by pirates. Rape and extortion were commonplace. Refugees met with a largely unsympathetic response wherever they landed. A publicity campaign orchestrated by Parisian activists had little resonance beyond France, where it forced the government to admit more refugees but also split the recently-formed Médecins Sans Frontières (MSF).[11] None of the countries of first destination had signed the 1951 Convention. Malaysia and Singapore turned away refugees until they reached an agreement in 1979 to admit refugees temporarily, subject to steps being taken to resettle them in a third country. Refugees who survived the sea voyage ended up in camps across the region. UNHCR organized so-called transit camps, but an archipelago of closed camps (where refugees had to remain until they agreed to repatriation or were admitted by a third country) was directly administered by the governments concerned. In a disconcerting echo of post-war Germany, protests erupted in the camp at Sungei Besi under the control of the Malaysian government which made living arrangements as basic and tedious as possible, in the hope that word would get back to Vietnam and discourage those others who were thinking of following in their footsteps.[12]

While awaiting decisions about their status, refugees were incarcerated in warehouses, army barracks (as at Kai Tak in Hong Kong) and prisons that housed young offenders and drug addicts. Refugees described heroic attempts to get by in the face of unsympathetic treatment, cramped living conditions and the threat of violence. Unaccompanied children found the experience of isolation extremely distressing. In Sikhiu camp, Thai guards beat refugees for minor infractions and gained a reputation for exploitation and for sexually assaulting women. An ex-army colonel painted a picture of degradation: 'people were so poor, so denigrated, so discouraged by their unknown and uncertain future that they abandoned themselves to vices. Everyone took advantage of any good opportunity that happened to him to exploit to the detriment of others. There was no law in this community. Everyone thought that he was the centre of the universe'.[13] The selection of refugees for resettlement was no less troubling. In Kai Tak, administered by the Red

---

[10] John Knudsen, 'When Trust is on Trial', in Daniel and Knudsen (eds), *Mistrusting Refugees*, 13–35; Kwok Bun Chan and Kenneth Christie, 'Past, Present and Future: the Indochinese Refugee Experience Twenty Years Later' *JRS*, 8, no.1 (1995), 75–94.

[11] Rony Brauman, 'From Philanthropy to Humanitarianism: Remarks and an Interview' *South Atlantic Quarterly*, 103, nos.2–3 (2004), 397–417.

[12] Quynh-Giao N. Vu, 'Journey of the Abandoned: Endless Refugee Camp and Incurable Traumas' *Signs: Journal of Women in Culture and Society*, 32, no.3 (2007), 580–4; Gisèle Bousquet, 'Living in a State of Limbo: a Case Study of Vietnamese Refugees in Hong Kong Camps', in Scott Morgan and Elizabeth Colson (eds), *People in Upheaval* (New York: Center for Migration Studies, 1987), 34–53.

[13] James Freeman, *Hearts of Sorrow: Vietnamese-American Lives* (Stanford: Stanford University Press, 1989), 347.

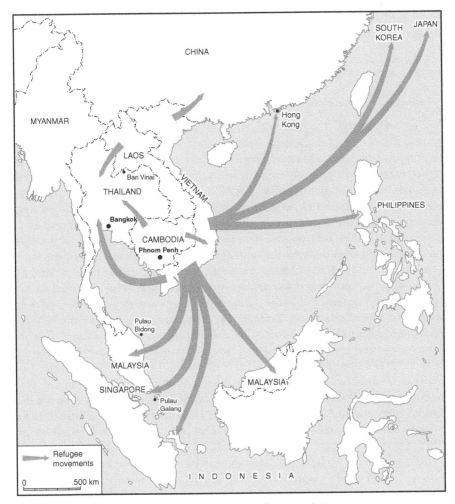

Map 7: Map of Refugee Flows in/from South-East Asia

Cross and the Hong Kong Christian Service, visitors commented on how migration agencies 'skimmed' the qualified refugees, leaving behind a demoralized 'hard core'. In describing the abandonment of some refugees and the widespread collapse of self-discipline, they unwittingly reproduced the terms for DPs trapped in Germany after the Second World War.[14]

One 11-year-old girl who fled with her father (and 150 others, on a boat meant for 40 people) described her arrival on the Malaysian island of Pulau Bidong,

---

[14] Kwok Chan and David Loveridge, 'Refugees "In Transit": Vietnamese in a Refugee Camp in Hong Kong' *IMR*, 21, no.3 (1987), 745–59, at 758.

where she found a lack of adequate housing but an abundance of rats and thieves. Adults spoke of 'social death':

> I just need to get out of hell. I have to get out every day, I need to answer a telephone, type a letter, listen to people who live a normal life, listen to a conversation about normal things, make a cup of coffee. When I return [to the camp] the gate will lock behind me, the freedom still playing on my mind.[15]

Visitors were expected to refer to the inmates as 'asylum seekers' or 'illegal immigrants', since to employ the term 'refugee' was to raise hopes in their mind that their status had been satisfactorily resolved. Refugees fought back and demanded rights, including the right not to be treated as criminals. When one group offered to donate blood to support the Western Allies during the first Gulf War, they were rebuffed by the authorities, fearful that this would be tantamount to recognizing their 'political' status rather than labelling them as trouble-makers or 'illegals'.[16]

Around 100,000 'boat people' were given asylum in Australia, whose government had supported the US campaign against North Vietnam, and others were admitted to the USA and Canada. However, the 'rescue' aroused a great deal of controversy and provoked disagreement as to its rationale, since it seemed to encourage more Vietnamese to make the hazardous journey without any guarantee of success. In a more promising development, the Communist government in Vietnam arranged for the emigration of its citizens who hoped to be reunited with family members, under the so-called 'Orderly Departure Programme', agreed in May 1979. Boat people distinguished themselves from the ODPs: the former 'experienced untold hardships and survived; many took pride in their stamina and resourcefulness. The ODPs were, by implication, soft'. For their part, many ODPs had contacts and knew how to use them in order to speed up the resettlement process; in addition, relatively privileged ODPs had been able to collect more of their personal belongings before leaving Vietnam. An official working for the International Catholic Migration Commission—he might have been speaking of DPs in Europe in 1945—maintained that 'ODPs are a positive force here because they have not learned to behave like refugees. They have not been shredded by institutionalisation'. In his view other refugees needed to learn how to become more 'self-sufficient'. But this dismissive characterization overlooked the resourcefulness with which they had found their way to the Philippines in the first place.[17] The boat became a powerful image, partly because it resonated with American audiences used to stories of the Mayflower as an iconic means of deliverance from

[15] John Knudsen, *Chicken Wings: Refugee Stories from a Concrete Hell* (Bergen: Magnat Forlag, 1992), 36.

[16] Ronald Skeldon, 'Hong Kong's Response to the Indochinese Influx, 1975–1993' *AAAPSS*, 534 (1994), 91–105; Kwok Bun Chan, 'Hong Kong's Response to the Vietnamese Refugees: a Study in Humanitarianism, Ambivalence and Hostility' *Southeast Asian Journal of Social Science*, 18, no.1 (1990), 94–110.

[17] Adelaida Reyes, *Songs of the Caged, Songs of the Free: Music and the Vietnamese Refugee Experience* (Philadelphia: Temple University Press, 1999), 52–3; Benthall, *Disasters, Relief and the Media*, 129–30.

oppression, and partly because it offered a dramatic counterpoint to the famous image of a helicopter rescuing privileged Vietnamese allies from the rooftop of the US embassy in Saigon.

In these holding centres Vietnamese refugees were scrutinized by the grotesquely named 'Processing Community Organisation and Social Services Group', where they were 'prepared' for resettlement. PROCOSS understood its task of contributing to the 'rehabilitation' of refugees by compelling refugees to perform 'labour service', something that they bitterly resented. One camp at Bataan province in the Philippines saw a rapid turnover of refugees. It took on the appearance of a shanty town, with streets called UN Avenue and a central square called Freedom Plaza, 'where boats that had been used to escape were enshrined as memorials'. Here the refugees were 'prepared' for resettlement in the USA. Regular lists were displayed on notice boards to indicate whose request had been granted. The particular purpose of this camp contributed to an atmosphere in which 'refugees showed a pronounced disinterest in getting involved in aspects of [camp] life beyond those requisite for their release'. They reluctantly accepted this administrative routine as part of the package that governed the conditions of being accepted for entry to the USA. Another processing camp, administered by UNHCR between 1975 and 1996, was located at Pulau Galang in Indonesia. Some 28,000 were sent back to Vietnam between 1989 and 1993, having been 'filtered' out. Those who were admitted to the USA or other countries described themselves as 'sojourners' (*Viet Kieu*) who maintained contact with family members in Vietnam, for example by sending them money on a regular basis. Some of these exiles opposed the Communist government, while others made return visits and capitalized on the liberalization of the Vietnamese economy. Most saw themselves as guardians of an 'authentic' national culture.[18]

Vietnamese refugees in Hong Kong nevertheless were adept in devising strategies to survive and avoid being repatriated. A female refugee who reached Hong Kong in the 1990s described how refugees were able to obtain marriage papers to enable them to travel abroad or to trade upon overseas connections. It helped, she said, that 'the camp was like a country, you can find all sort of person, doctors, lawyers. I don't know how they did it'.[19] Refugees and their lawyers learned how to respond to interrogation in such a way as to achieve recognition. Those who failed the test might evade detection by working semi-legally in the Hong Kong economy. Others experienced displacement as a lengthy period of incarceration until such time as they joined the growing refugee diaspora.

---

[18] Reyes, *Songs of the Caged*, 43–6, 49; Rona Fields, 'Life and Death on a Small Island: Vietnamese and Cambodian Refugees in Indochina' *Migration World*, 20, no.5 (1992), 16–20; Lynellyn Long, 'Viet Kieu on a Fast Track Back?', in Ellen Oxfeld and Lynellyn Long (eds), *Coming Home? Refugees, Migrants, and Those Who Stayed Behind* (Philadelphia: University of Pennsylvania Press, 2004), 65–89.

[19] Yuk Wah Chan, 'Revisiting the Vietnamese Refugee Era', in Chan (ed.), *The Chinese/Vietnamese Diaspora: Revisiting the Boat People* (Routledge, 2011), 3–19, at 12.

THE HMONG REFUGEE DIASPORA

The prolonged war in South-East Asia also disrupted the lives of villagers in Laos. Those most affected by the ongoing conflict were Hmong (Meo/Miao), Montagnard and Catholic farmers who engaged in slash and burn cultivation and who therefore habitually moved from place to place. In the early 1960s the American military recruited guerrilla forces from their ranks to help fight the communist Pathet Lao and the Vietcong. Funds granted by Congress to assist Laotian refugees who fled to Cambodia and Thailand were diverted for this secret war. Hmong and Yao villagers suffered the effects of heavy US aerial bombardment designed to demoralize and defeat the Vietcong who travelled in and out of Laos via the Ho Chi Minh trail. The communist triumph in Laos turned Hmong into targets and prompted their mass flight.[20]

One elderly woman, Xiong Vang, described how recurrent conflicts and food shortages in Vietnam and Laos compelled her to move 30 times before she ended up in a large settlement close to the Thai border that went by the name of Ban Vinai, literally 'village of discipline'. Originally the 400-acre site housed 5,000 refugees, but by the mid-1980s a high birth rate meant that its size ballooned to 45,000 inhabitants, making it one of the most densely populated places in the world. Hmong refugees lived reluctantly within this dense social space; three-quarters of all refugees in Ban Vinai lived there for more than 10 years. Daily life did not follow the rhythm of the seasons but revolved instead around a mixture of market transactions, the distribution of UNHCR rations, educating young children, and festivities such as New Year celebrations. Maintaining camp facilities was largely the responsibility of refugees, although they received little recognition and no recompense from the authorities.[21]

Camp refugees formed part of a transnational network. They sold products in distant markets with the help of the Hmong diaspora that kept their cause alive in the United States. Refugees who were admitted to the USA mounted a vocal campaign in support of the admission of family members, which led eventually to the 1980 Refugee Act and a relaxation of entry. Other refugees meanwhile continued to languish in Thai camps. Several hundred Hmong eventually settled as farmers in French Guiana. Ban Vinai remained open until 1992, when the Thai government made arrangements together with UNHCR to repatriate any refugee who had not already been admitted to the United States; thousands of Hmong refugees evaded repatriation by fleeing to the remote hills in Northern Thailand.

---

[20] Alfred McCoy, 'America's Secret War in Laos, 1955–75', in Marilyn Young and Robert Buzzanco (eds), *A Companion to the Vietnam War* (Blackwell, 2006), 283–314; Jeffrey L. MacDonald, ' "We are the Experts": Iu-Mien (Yao) Refugees Assert their Rights as Scholars of their Own Culture', in Ruth Krulfeld and Jeffrey MacDonald (eds), *Power, Ethics, and Human Rights: Anthropological Studies of Refugee Research and Action* (Lanham, MD: Rowman and Littlefield, 1998), 97–122.
[21] Lynellyn Long, *Ban Vinai: the Refugee Camp* (New York: Columbia University Press, 1993), 58, 122, 135.

Thus the collapse of the US intervention and the communist victory in Vietnam and in Laos sealed the fate of the Hmong who became caught up in the great exodus that turned one-tenth of the population of Laos into refugees from communism. However, the Pathet Lao government, backed by its Vietnamese allies, proved durable. Lao refugees who reached the USA had to come to terms with a severe loss of status as they exchanged professional jobs for menial work. Like their Vietnamese counterparts, in recent years they have begun to move back and forth between their homeland and the countries of resettlement, making return visits to keep in touch with relatives who remained behind. The surviving Hmong military leadership denounced Hanoi and demanded that America acknowledge their contribution to the war effort and their subsequent persecution at the hands of the Vietnamese. Non-elite refugees appear to have come to terms with displacement by exploiting diasporic possibilities.[22]

CAMBODIA'S REFUGEES

The refugee crisis in Cambodia originated in the infamous rule of the Khmer Rouge that lasted from 1975 until 1979. The Khmer Rouge leader Pol Pot exploited the widespread suffering caused by the prolonged US bombardment of Cambodia whose purpose was to weaken the supply routes of the Vietcong but whose result was to force hundreds of thousands of people to seek refuge in the capital Phnom Penh. On coming to power the Khmer Rouge ruthlessly targeted 'class enemies' as well as Muslim, Chinese and Vietnamese ethnic minorities whose position was already exposed. A radical programme of de-urbanization removed internally displaced people from the cities and turned the established order upside down. Urban professionals and Buddhist priests bore the brunt of Pol Pot's programme. Priests were executed, temples were pulled down and religious books were destroyed. Anti-Khmer Rouge forces gathered in rapidly expanding refugee camps in neighbouring Vietnam (they housed 160,000 people by 1978), but they could not stop the terror. Eventually Vietnamese troops supplemented by contingents of armed refugees invaded Cambodia at the end of 1978 in order to remove the Khmer Rouge from power. Phnom Penh fell in January 1979.[23]

The defeat of the Khmer Rouge by invading Vietnamese forces helped give birth to an international Cambodian 'refugee problem' as civilians and military forces

[22] Nicols, *Uneasy Alliance*, 132–44; W. Courtland Robinson, *Terms of Refuge: the Indochinese Exodus and the International Response* (Zed Books, 1998), 231–8; Wanni Anderson, 'Between Necessity and Choice: Rhode Island Lao American Women', in Wanni Anderson and Robert Lee (eds), *Displacements and Diasporas: Asians in the Americas* (New Brunswick: Rutgers University Press, 2005), 194–226.

[23] Ben Kiernan, *The Pol Pot Regime: Race, Power and Genocide in Cambodia under the Khmer Rouge, 1975–1979* (New Haven: Yale University Press, 2008).

made their way to the Thai border. This motley group included surviving peasants who objected to conscription, land seizures and requisitioning of food, as well as Khmer forces hoping to turn the tables on the Vietnamese. The border thus became both a buffer zone and a basis for guerrilla resistance to the Vietnamese army, as well as an issue of grave concern for the new government in Phnom Penh. Thailand did not recognize the Cambodians as refugees, characterizing them instead as 'economic migrants' who were to be prevented, by force if necessary, from moving into the Thai interior. Officials in Bangkok also did their utmost to keep outside observers away.[24]

In 1979 thousands of refugees were driven back over the Cambodian border by Thai troops, who were accused of committing atrocities against a defenceless group of people. But the government in Bangkok complained that Western politicians adopted a hypocritical stance in expecting Thailand to accommodate refugees from Cambodia when the West had done little to assist the Vietnamese 'boat people'. At the end of that year, following a renewed Vietnamese onslaught and a desperate food crisis, a second exodus took place. The Thai government relented and agreed that no refugees would be turned back. UNHCR established camps on the Thai border housing 160,000 refugees. (According to some estimates, three quarters of a million refugees lived along the border.) Oxfam, the ICRC and other agencies provided aid to refugees as well as stricken civilians in Cambodia itself, although they had for political reasons to keep the two operations entirely distinct. Refugee relief included a clear political as well as a 'humanitarian' element. For example, the US administration and American voluntary agencies, including Catholic Relief Services and World Vision, capitalizing on years of pro-Thai diplomacy in the Cold War, hoped to cement the basis for anti-Vietnamese resistance among the refugees; collaboration with the Khmer Rouge was a price worth paying to nip Vietnamese ambitions in the bud. This also meant handing over large sums of money to maintain good relations with the Thai government and overlooking the abuse that refugees endured in the camps.[25]

Different political factions controlled different camps. For example the Khmer Rouge dominated the camp in Sa Kaeo; other camps were loyal to former ruler Norodom Sihanouk. The largest camp or 'holding centre' went by the name of Khao-I-Dang. Initially it had a rudimentary infrastructure, but by the mid-1980s, with a population of 60,000, it had developed with UNHCR support a relatively robust economy, with 'flourishing markets, an adequate water supply, excellent feeding facilities, schools, recreational facilities, and even a local Khmer dance academy'. But it also became a byword for rape and extortion.[26] NGOs were omnipresent—40 separate organizations operated in Khao-I-Dang alone by 1980—

[24] William Shawcross, *The Quality of Mercy: Cambodia, Holocaust and Modern Conscience* (New York: Simon and Schuster, 1984), 72–5, 115–23, 169; Cheryl Benard, 'Politics and the Refugee Experience' *Political Science Quarterly*, 101, no.4 (1986), 617–36.

[25] LWF Archives, WS Y.5.1 Emergency projects—Kampuchea, 1979–81.

[26] Ong, *Buddha is Hiding*, 53.

and provided jobs. Other refugees traded with impoverished Thai peasants or engaged in semi-legal or black market activity. Refugees became marginally less vulnerable and, by the same token, cautious about returning prematurely to Cambodia. However, the fact that medical provision was superior to that available to the locals gave Thai politicians a pretext to whip up resentment against the refugees. Consequently refugees who lived in border camps boasting schools, temples, pharmacies, taxi firms, brothels 'could find just about anything they wanted on the border except a safe way out'.[27]

US support for the border camps helped promote anti-Vietnamese activity, and thereby enabled the Khmer Rouge to regroup. In the camps it controlled, the Khmer Rouge managed to appropriate the food aid destined for refugees. This only increased their liability to attack from the Vietnamese and their Cambodian allies. At the same time it was ironic to give these camps greater autonomy, since this merely enhanced the power of the Khmer Rouge. UN officials expressed concern that 'international generosity may have gone too far in terms of the care and maintenance, even spoon-feeding of Cambodians in exile—we wonder if the refugees are now capable of re-acquiring initiative and independence', wrote Sergio Vieira de Mello, although he subsequently decided that they were.[28]

Thai refugee camps served an invaluable administrative purpose for American authorities, because it became possible to identify those suspected of being communists. More subtle processes and procedures were also at work, in that Western NGOs inculcated among refugees the 'appropriate' behaviour that would improve their prospects of qualifying for asylum in the USA by educating them in English and transforming them (as Aihwa Ong puts it) into 'modern human beings'. This practice may have been more straightforward in Khao-I-Dang, which provided a home to refugees from a middle-class background. But the emphasis on individualism challenged Khmer-Buddhist values of compassion and reciprocity that had already been undermined by the ferocious oppression inflicted by the regime of Pol Pot. Another outcome was that women were taught about gender equality, challenging Buddhist Khmer tradition; they had in any case shouldered considerable responsibilities as they entered the camps. Rifts also emerged between people born prior to the Khmer Rouge seizure of power and brought up in the Buddhist tradition, and those who were deprived of the right to practise any religion. Living in refugee camps underlined these transformative experiences.[29]

When Vietnamese troops finally withdrew in 1988, the Khmer Rouge in the guise of the 'Coalition of Democratic Kampuchea' forced refugees to return. Eight years earlier the Khmer Rouge had impressed on refugees in Sa Kaeo camp the alarming ditty that:

---

[27] Robinson, *Terms of Refuge*, 95.
[28] Samantha Power, *Chasing the Flame: Sergio Vieira de Mello and the Fight to Save the World* (Allen Lane, 2008), 85, 122; Terry, *Condemned to Repeat?*, 114–15, 122–5, 132.
[29] Ong, *Buddha is Hiding*, 52–63, 276–7.

Those who go back first will sleep on cots/Those who go back second will sleep on mats/Those who go back third will sleep in the mud/Those who go back last will sleep under the ground.

It is not clear if this was intended as a threat or a realistic assessment of the situation.[30] Several rival groups now jockeyed for position; the Khmer Rouge no longer enjoyed a monopoly of power. In 1991 the United Nations secured the agreement of the various factions to the creation of a new transitional authority that would oversee new elections. A 'peaceful and orderly' repatriation was a vital element in preparing the ground for political change, although the difficulties appeared almost insuperable. A UN survey earmarked land for returnees. Like the Allies in Germany at the end of the Second World War, the UN put on film shows advertising the opportunities presented by repatriation and minimizing the threat in Western Cambodia from land mines and malaria. In March 1992, de Mello approved a plan that gave 362,000 refugees cash to enable them to take their own decision as to where and how to return. UN assumptions that refugees would automatically want to return 'home', that is to their native villages, did not take account of the lack of suitable land. Many repatriants moved to shanty towns where they encountered discrimination and eked out an uncertain existence. The UN made little headway with economic and social reconstruction, pinning its hopes on the political process. Subsequent events showed that political stability was fragile.[31]

CULTURAL REPRESENTATIONS OF REFUGEES AND RELIEF EFFORTS

Much of this recent history was bound up with the refugee camp. The large refugee camp on the island of Palawan in the Philippines had earlier been earmarked for lepers and criminals; the island has since become a popular 'exotic' tourist destination. In the 1980s, Palawan afforded opportunities for Vietnamese refugees to trade and work in the neighbouring towns. Around one third of them became long-term residents, staying for more than a decade. Some children attended local schools. There was a rich cultural and sports programme. Palawan camp also hosted numerous religious and voluntary associations including a Catholic Youth Group, Buddhist Youth Group and a Martial Arts Group. Refugees entertained one another with songs that had been banned by the communist government. Christian evangelical aid agencies also conducted proselytization campaigns. Some refugees chose to be baptised in the belief or expectation that it would assist their passage to

[30] Shawcross, *The Quality of Mercy*, 316.
[31] Arthur Helton, *The Price of Indifference: Refugees and Humanitarian Action in the New Century* (Oxford: Oxford University Press, 2002), 82; Marita Eastmond and Joakim Öjendal, 'Revising a "Repatriation Success": the Case of Cambodia', in Richard Black and Khalid Koser (eds), *The End of the Refugee Cycle? Refugee Repatriation and Reconstruction* (Oxford: Berghahn, 1998), 38–55.

the USA—a particular kind of 'salvation' that carried the implication of setting the past to one side in favour of a 'bright' future. Others 'carefully crafted [a] life history' for the same purpose.[32] This ethnography suggests a correspondence with the DP camps in Europe, insofar as refugees were closely scrutinized for political suitability and signs of physical or mental disability. Resettlement became a distant prospect for those who were deemed insufficiently 'fit', and who continue to live in basic conditions.

Living in camp communities afforded some opportunity to think about the past as well as the future. Refugees from Laos who were held in Ban Vinai looked forward to their eventual resettlement in the USA but reflected too on the lives they lived in Laos before the communist takeover and on an even more distant past in China, which they regarded as their ancestral home. Adult women produced handicrafts for the Thai and American markets; they incorporated references on traditional quilts to their experience of war and displacement, and also included American emblems. The quilt thus embodied a sense of past and anticipated a future resolution of their status. Furthermore, its production and marketing revealed the importance of Hmong kinship networks. But there was another show in town, mounted by relief workers whose 'range of experiences and motivations varied widely from fundamentalist missionaries, Vietnam veterans, world travellers, ex-Peace Corps volunteers, social workers, teachers and others from assorted walks of life and social classes'.[33]

Refugees who arrived in the USA from Vietnam and Laos aspired to be 'accepted' in the host country, and they drew a clear distinction between a hopeful future in North America and a traumatic past. Vietnamese lamented the destruction of village burial grounds, a sense of loss only partly mitigated by a readiness to propitiate their ancestors by making offerings of one kind or another. Others recalled their intense sadness at having been instructed by their parents to pack their bags in a hurry without being able to say goodbye to friends or to complete their education. The anguish was compounded by leaving family members behind as well as a way of life that maintained parental discipline and fostered respect for the elderly. Cambodian refugees likewise found it difficult to regard the past with any degree of contentment. Not only was their experience of life under the Khmer Rouge intensely traumatic, but displacement led them to question cultural assumptions about the period before Pol Pot seized power. According to one scholar, who worked with survivors in North America, Buddhist notions of karma suggested that Cambodians were being punished for transgressions in a previous life.[34]

---

[32] Knudsen, 'When Trust is on Trial', 22; Linda Hitchcox, *Vietnamese Refugees in Southeast Asian Camps* (Basingstoke: Macmillan, 1990), 177–211.

[33] Long, *Ban Vinai*, 85, 108, 184.

[34] Margaret Muecke, 'Trust, Abuse of Trust and Mistrust among Cambodian Refugee Women: a Cultural Interpretation', in Daniel and Knudsen (eds), *Mistrusting Refugees*, 36–55.

Narratives of multiple displacements were common. One Vietnamese refugee described how her family had been displaced more than once:

> My parents were originally from the north. They left the north after the communists killed my grandfather, who was a simple trader. During the war our family moved from place to place in order to escape from the communists, and at the end we lost the war and there was nowhere else to go to, so we went back to our original place in the highlands. So you can see the history of my family—we have been refugees more than once. You can't imagine how hard it was for my family. I was very happy to get out of Vietnam. It was like a thousand kilos was lifted off my shoulders.[35]

Vietnamese who initially welcomed the new regime because it brought the long years of war to an end soon became disillusioned by its policies, which they associated with revenge and corruption rather than justice and reconciliation. From a vantage point in Australia they looked forward to a day when the homeland would become more 'democratic' and less 'corrupt'. They nevertheless retained a connection to friends and family members who remained in Vietnam. These connections often induced feelings of pain at being separated. Interviewing two surviving Vietnamese sisters, the Vietnamese-Australian scholar Nathalie Nguyen writes how family members 'remained silent about central events in each other's lives, either because to speak was too painful or too difficult, or because silence allowed a measure of control over events and was judged to be the best way to protect a loved one'.[36] Accounts written by refugees from Cambodia emphasized mass killing and the drama of escape, but they also testify to a land that was fertile and abundant and a society whose stability reflected Buddhist beliefs and family integrity. Inevitably these ideas were refracted through resettlement in North America, producing contradictory notions about past, present and future.[37]

Like the recollection of life prior to the rupture of displacement, these memories must be evaluated in relation to political projects. This inevitably produces uneven results. We lack testimony from Tibetans and Vietnamese who embraced rather than rejected the communist cause. How displaced Koreans understood their experiences is not any easier to establish. Other unresolved issues included a refusal to speak whether because of 'trauma' (a problematic construct), shame or other considerations including mistrust of the person and therefore also the institution that requires the refugee to provide an account of her or his displacement. Biting one's tongue might be a means of self-preservation. To show one's feelings in a refugee camp ran the risk of being interpreted as someone with psychological 'problems': no-one could afford to be categorized as suffering mental

---

[35] Diane Barnes, 'Resettled Refugees' Attachment to their Original and Subsequent Homelands: Long-term Vietnamese Refugees in Australia' *JRS*, 14, no.4 (2001), 394–411, at 400.

[36] Nathalie Nguyen, 'Memory and Silence in the Vietnamese Diaspora: the Narratives of Two Sisters' *Oral History*, 36, no.2 (2008), 64–74, at 65.

[37] Ong, *Buddha is Hiding*, 29–33; Janet McLellan, *Cambodian Refugees in Ontario: Resettlement, Religion, and Identity* (Toronto: University of Toronto Press, 2009).

affliction that gave immigration officers a pretext to deny that person the chance of being considered for resettlement in the West. In any case the screening process was usually hasty and discouraged refugees from reflecting on the past.[38]

The emergence of a second generation and the rise of the internet helped generate fresh testimony as well as commemorative activity. In the UK the Heritage Lottery Fund supported an initiative of Refugee Action to interview Vietnamese refugees.[39] There is now an online resource of the recollections of Vietnamese boat people who were detained at the uninhabited Malaysian island of Pulau Bidong from 1978 until it closed in 1991, as well as testimony from relief workers from the Malaysian Red Crescent Society. Refugees who ended up there subsequently posted several stories and images on a dedicated website. Pride of place belongs to a photograph of a concrete memorial in the form of a boat. Other photos include underwater shots of a barnacle-encrusted boat.[40] For some refugees, such as Quynh-Giao Vu, Pulau Bidong provided opportunities to study, to learn to look after himself and 'to become an excellent swimmer'.[41]

Pilgrimages now take place to former refugee camps in Malaysia and Indonesia. A report from the former camp at Pulau Galang in Indonesia describes how visitors return to pay their respects to relatives and friends who died in the camp:

> A plaque in front of the graveyard says: 'Dedicated to the People Who Died in the Sea on the Way to Freedom'. Little has changed, according to the visiting former boat people. The Catholic Church and Buddhist temple and the Youth Center in the sprawling camp freshly painted for the reunion. But the scattered wooden barracks once housing the refugees remain in a state of disrepair.[42]

This 'dark tourism' reflects an insistence by the older generation on the correspondence between escaping from communism and drawing on religious faith. It asserts the political significance of these sites of memory, which refugees hope to preserve and which the Hanoi government wishes to see destroyed. It also betrays a degree of anxiety lest the younger generation fail to invest sufficiently in commemorating displacement.

Vietnamese and Tibetan diasporas include refugees who would never entertain returning to a homeland under communist rule, even if it were possible. Others are attracted by the possibility of being able to make a short visit to see for themselves the places that they learned about from first-generation refugees. Cambodian and Vietnamese refugees send remittances to family members. In each case the people

[38] Bon Tempo, *Americans at the Gate*, 158–9.
[39] <http://www.refugee-action.org.uk/ourwork/projects/vietnamese.aspx>.
[40] <http://www.pulaubidong.org/Boat SS 0937 IA - KT 756> (KT = Kuala Terengganu), La Toàn Vinh.
[41] Vu, 'Journey of the Abandoned', 580–4.
[42] <http://www.thingsasian.com/stories-photos/3263>. Ashley Carruthers and Boitran Huynh-Beattie, 'Dark Tourism, Diasporic Memory and Disappeared History: the Contested Meaning of the Former Indochinese Refugee Camp at Pulau Galang', in Chan (ed.), *The Chinese/Vietnamese Diaspora*, 147–60.

who left and returned, as well as those who stayed behind, articulated a complex relationship with the past. Kesang Takla, Minister for Information and International Relations in the Tibetan Government-in-Exile, remembered:

> Annual picnics, festivals and visits to the monasteries, horse-riding; it was very close to nature. Once we arrived in India suddenly everything changed. We travelled by car from Sikkim and I didn't like the smell of the petrol but it was also strangely exciting. I've been trying for a long time to get a picture of the old home but I think it is unrecognisable now. As an exile I suppose in a way I have never felt I have a home anywhere.[43]

CONCLUSIONS

Population displacement in South-East Asia evokes similarities with other episodes and situations. Revolution produced winners and losers. The winners inaugurated programmes for radical social transformation; their opponents kept a low profile or became refugees. Like those who fled Russia after 1917 and China in 1949, refugees from Vietnam and Cambodia included people of relatively modest means; not everyone belonged to the privileged elite. The claim to have fled persecution gave them a degree of leverage in countries of prospective asylum, although this did not allay fears that there might be fifth-columnists in their midst. Other parallels also emerge. Attempts by UNHCR to get refugees to return were reminiscent of the situation facing DPs in Western Europe after 1945. Like their counterparts in the DP camps, Vietnamese and Hmong refugees expressed a desperate wish to avoid repatriation to a communist state, and anti-communist sentiments flourished in the refugee camps maintained by the Hong Kong and Thai authorities. But precisely because the refugees had fled communism, US officials sought to establish the political credentials of those who could be admitted to the USA. Privileged and powerful refugees as well as those with desirable skills were quickly spirited away to safety, sometimes to be debriefed by intelligence officers. Others were detained in camps for much longer. Those who could not construct a convincing case were sent back to Vietnam under the 'Comprehensive Plan of Action' (CPA).[44]

The camps in South-East Asia demonstrated refugees' capacity to fashion a rich cultural life, as they did in Europe after the Second World War. But the restrictions and, above all, uncertainty about the future created conditions in which refugees became extremely anxious. These afflictions lasted not months but years: it was not uncommon for Vietnamese refugees to be confined for a decade, becoming a kind of 'hard core'. Their estrangement from family and friends, which had been fostered by their flight in overcrowded boats, was now compounded by an insecure

---

[43] See her account at <http://news.bbc.co.uk/1/hi/world/asia-pacific/7926559.stm>.
[44] Ferris, *Beyond Borders*, 180–2.

existence in the camps. It took a great deal of individual effort and courage to create a decent life. Those who returned to Vietnam under the CPA were monitored by UNHCR officials, although ironically the biggest problem thereafter was not police harassment but programmes of economic liberalization that disadvantaged single mothers and the sick.

Comparisons between the situation in South-East Asia during the 1970s and 1980s and conditions in Europe after the Second World War make clear the challenges facing these refugees. After 1945 demand for labour in industrialized countries was buoyant, and in some instances (such as in Australia, where Japanese attacks during the war revealed the country's vulnerability), national security considerations helped generate public support for immigration. These concerns all but evaporated during the last quarter of the century. Global recession reduced the demand for immigrant labour, placing refugees in a virtually impossible bargaining position. Détente weakened the drivers of policy in the 1950s. To be sure, Australia continued to provide sanctuary to refugees in significant numbers until the 1990s, under a series of quota agreements. Here, as elsewhere, the tide of public opinion and government policy turned against refugees. The Australian example demonstrates that geopolitics and economic framed programmes of assistance and determined whether refugees would either be resettled, encouraged to repatriate or deterred from fleeing in the first place. The West regarded South Korea, Hong Kong and South Vietnam as strategically significant bulwarks against Communism, and the aid that poured into those countries swelled the resources available for refugee relief. Refugee camps on the Thai border became a means of sustaining anti-Vietnamese activity. But by the late 1980s the Cold War had begun to exhaust its capacity to influence policy. Those who fled from communist rule to adjacent countries and sought admission to third countries had to show that they had suffered direct persecution. If unable to provide this testimony, they faced being repatriated.

Questions remain about how refugees framed their displacement. How did refugees who fled from North to South Vietnam reflect on their lives prior to 1954 and to what extent did they draw upon notions of pre-war culture to negotiate their new environment?[45] How might the history of Cambodian displacement be written into the story of genocide, flight and repatriation or resettlement, in a way that affords them the licence denied them both by Pol Pot and by external relief organizations? We know little of how refugees navigated their return to Cambodia and nothing of the incorporation of their experiences of Khmer Rouge 're-education' camps and in the refugee camps into broader national narratives.

Answers to these questions are thus necessarily provisional. One thing that is clear is that the consequences of the refugee crises in China and South-East Asia were measured not only in the number of refugees and the size of refugee camps but also in new forms of associational activity. No-one could accuse the camps of fostering cultural collapse or economic stagnation. These practices should neither

---

[45] A powerful semi-fictional account is Kim Thúy, *Ru* (Clerkenwell Press, 2012).

be discounted nor romanticized. Refugees from different socio-economic back-grounds spoke of the need to 'stick together': 'we try to help each other because everyone is lonely, everyone has lost their country'. This was not always an elite preoccupation. In Palawan camp, the Vietnamese Refugee Council encouraged a sense of collective national identity by creating a 'little Vietnam', although this project was dominated by former officers in the South Vietnamese army and its description carried connotations of exclusivity. Yet camps also exposed divisions. Refugees from South Vietnam who ended up in Hong Kong drew a distinction between themselves as educated professionals and 'peasants and fishermen' who fled from North Vietnam. Vietnamese refugees from a middle-class background who reached Hong Kong blamed their plebeian neighbours for the unsanitary conditions in the holding centres, even though the main responsibility lay with the government officials who had no wish to make any improvements that might en-courage other refugees to flee.

Other kinds of division manifested themselves in relation to age and gender. Generational distinctions emerged in the rift between the first influx of Karen refugees who fled Burma in the late 1980s and who reached Thailand in 1996–97 reflected the fact that recent arrivals followed traditional religious customs, whereas the more established refugees began to develop something akin to pan-Karenni nationalism. When asked to reflect on his experiences, an elderly Vietnamese refugee who enrolled in college in the USA announced that 'it is hard to study because we do not remember, but we study to forget the past'.[46] The past can evoke painful memories, as if history must be refused rather than embraced. For many Vietnamese women life in refugee camps in Indonesia and Hong Kong held greater danger than the persecution they suffered in Vietnam. Yet profound changes also occurred in gender relations. Cambodian women's lives were turned upside down, because their survival depended upon behaving in a manner that went against traditional norms of female virtue.

Refugees invested heavily in commemorative sites and practices. A Vietnamese American, Trần Trung Đạo, favoured the preservation of monuments to boat people, 'not only in memory of our countrymen but as part of the history of Viet-nam. A hundred years hence, younger Vietnamese will look for Bidong, Galang, Palawan to retrace the steps of those who went before and to overhear the ocean whisper about a woeful and majestic path that was trodden'. Others insisted that the sites should be visited by everyone, not just refugees: 'after all, Vietnamese boat people are a global phenomenon'.[47]

---

[46] Freeman, *Hearts of Sorrow*, 361.
[47] Carruthers and Huynh-Beattie, 'Dark Tourism', 152, 156.

8

'Long Road'

Africa's Refugees, Decolonization, and 'Development'

In spite of the hardship and suffering displacement entailed, exile has opened
our eyes and we have no intention of closing them ever again. We shall only
move forward and never backward

(anonymous Eritrean refugee)

INTRODUCTION

Although news bulletins in the First World might suggest otherwise, the history of
modern Africa amounts to much more than a chronicle of war and displacement.
Media pronouncements regularly reduce Africa's past to a series of reflections on
unalterable deprivation, widespread corruption and unending conflict. A more
informed analysis takes into account the intertwined histories of ethnic groups and
powerful pre-colonial, colonial and independent states, the growth of long-dis-
tance trade and migration including forced migration over several centuries.[1] This
multifaceted history of mobility needs to be acknowledged. One sign of this was
the award in 2009 of the Prix Goncourt to Marie NDiaye for her novel *Trois
femmes puissantes*, whose protagonists include a Senegalese teacher living in France
who decides to embark on a visit to her father's home in Africa. Another was the
success of *Black Mamba Boy*, Nadifa Mohamed's debut novel (2009), which draws
on her father's tales of travelling between Aden and Eritrea in the hope of finding
his own father, weaving into this personal odyssey the violent impact of Mussolini's
attempt to build an Italian empire in North-East Africa. Themes of displacement,
suffering and resolution are threaded through these literary works.

To be sure, the sub-continent has been the site of immense refugee movements;
Africa accounted for more than half of the world's total refugee population at the
turn of the millennium. To understand why this situation came about requires a
historical perspective.

The struggle to throw off colonial shackles generated population displacement
on a large scale. Cold War confrontation spread to Africa, sustaining proxy forces
and helping to fuel internecine conflict. There was no respite during the 1990s and
2000s, when 'new wars' in weak states demonstrated a vicious and uncompromising

---

[1] Hoerder, *Cultures in Contact*, 139–62.

competition for resources between rival paramilitaries.[2] The presence of refugees in adjacent states further destabilized the sub-continent. This happened in two ways. Displacement enabled refugee warriors to regroup in order to overthrow an oppressive regime or restore the status quo ante. This brought unwelcome consequences for the host country. Rhodesian troops regularly crossed Mozambique's border during the 1970s in pursuit of Zimbabwean guerrillas who fought against the white settler regime. In the 1990s, Chad sheltered refugees from the war in neighbouring Darfur, prompting Sudanese troops to attack the camps over the border to frighten or kill their adversaries. Second, the arrival of refugees placed a burden on the fragile infrastructure of host states and the environment. Periodic shortages of food inflamed existing social tensions and political differences. Economically disadvantaged countries struggled to adjust to the influx of large numbers of refugees.

Many African states have simultaneously produced refugees and provided sanctuary to refugees from neighbouring countries. Sudan's protracted civil wars caused refugees to flee in large numbers to Ethiopia, Uganda, Egypt and other states, but Sudan also offered refuge to refugees fleeing the conflict between rebel troops supporting the Eritrean Liberation Front and the combined Ethiopian, Soviet and Cuban forces who aimed to suppress Eritrean independence; furthermore, Sudan accommodated Ethiopian opponents of the Marxist government of Colonel Haile-mariam Mengistu in the late 1970s. Somalia was home to around one and a half million refugees by 1980, most of them dependents of men who had been taken to fight in Eritrea. Meanwhile Somali opponents of the government of Mohamed Siad Barre sought sanctuary in Kenya and Ethiopia, and 300,000 people fled in 1991 in the wake of the coup that unseated Barre and after a severe famine. These displacements need to be located in a broader chronological framework. Throughout the nineteenth century local tribespeople in Mozambique evaded capture by slave raiders by escaping to what is now Zambia. Later on, in order to avoid Portuguese colonial exactions, they migrated to the Zambian copperbelt. Angolan refugees who settled in the western provinces of Zambia to escape fighting between rival liberation armies revisited places they encountered earlier when their country was ruled by Portugal. Susanna Mwana-uta recounted a lifetime on the move from one village to another inside Angola, because of family conflicts, marriages (including with a white Portuguese trader), as well as a succession of wars and peace agreements that took her back and forth between Angola and Zambia. What appear at first sight to be distinctive refugee crises were thus one phase in a succession of cross-border movements reflecting the arbitrariness of colonial borders that separated people with historically close cultural affiliations and economic ties.[3]

---

[2] Zolberg, Suhrke and Aguayo, *Escape from Violence*, 39–40, 120–5; Holborn, *Refugees*, 963–1004; Westad, *Global Cold War*, 207–49; Frederick Cooper, *Africa since 1940: the Past of the Present* (Cambridge: Cambridge University Press, 2002), 104–5.

[3] Julia Powles, 'Home and Homelessness: the Life History of Susanna Mwana-Uta, an Angolan Refugee' *JRS*, 15, no. 1 (2002), 81–101; Oliver Bakewell, 'Repatriation: Angolan Refugees or Migrating Villagers?', in Philomena Essed, Georg Frerks and Joke Schrijvers (eds), *Refugees and the Transformation of Societies: Agency, Policies, Ethics and Politics* (Oxford: Berghahn, 2004), 31–41; Michael Barrett, 'The Social Significance of Crossing State Borders: Home, Mobility and Life Paths in the Angolan-Zambian Borderlands', in Stef Jansen and Staffan Löfving (eds), *Struggles for Home: Violence,*

How did these crises affect the way in which refugees were understood as a 'problem'? A recurring theme concerns the geopolitics of displacement and the causes and consequences of international intervention. One direction points to the history of late colonial rule and to decolonization, to the fact that 'the Western colonial powers who were also among the founding members of the international refugee regime [and] newly independent states sought a means to avoid the embarrassment of treating refugees involving their supporters and close allies as victims of persecution'.[4] The chosen diplomatic route was to empower UNHCR to take 'appropriate' action.

Apart from assisting refugees in the short term, UNHCR also contemplated the 'integration' of refugees in situ. From the 1960s onwards, UNHCR and the NGOs within its orbit argued that durable solutions entailed thinking about the poverty of states in which refugees settled and the impoverished circumstances of states to which they returned. Programmes of long-term social and economic development had great attraction, until they were overtaken by ideas of containment and repatriation that were more attuned to post-Cold War geopolitics and declining international aid budgets. NGOs frequently substituted for weak and impoverished states where ordinary people have been politically marginalized, none more so than refugees.[5]

What of the perspective of refugees themselves? Not all refugees in Africa were confined to camps, but it is nevertheless the case that refugee camps not only served the purpose of managing refugees but also acted as an instrument of political mobilization. The Zimbabwean liberation movement was sustained by histories of resistance to colonial rule; guerrilla leaders in Mozambique, Botswana and Zambia spoke of carrying on the *chimurenga*, the Shona word for the rebellion of 1896. Political leaders knew that guns were not the only resource at their disposal; they also encouraged the creation of an archive. Refugee camps encouraged a social history of displacement. Of course the accumulation of personal testimony did not depend exclusively upon incarceration, but the camp allowed for the dissemination of a shared political and social history. As in other settings, the camp helped validate individual suffering by locating it in a larger struggle for self-expression, including that of the nation. Refugee crises sustained the belief among belligerents that they had 'unfinished business', which made history part of the ideological and political armoury of warring parties.[6]

Hope and the Movement of People (New York: Berghahn, 2009), 85–107; David Newbury, 'Returning Refugees: Four Historical Patterns of Coming Home to Rwanda' *Comparative Studies in Society and History*, 47, no.2 (2005), 252–85.

[4] Loescher, *UNHCR*, 92.

[5] Patricia Daley, 'Population Displacement and the Humanitarian Aid Regime: the Experience of Refugees in East Africa', in Mirjam de Bruijn (ed.), *Mobile Africa: Changing Patterns of Movement in Africa and Beyond* (Leiden: Brill, 2001), 195–211.

[6] Alex de Waal (ed.), *Who Fights? Who Cares? War and Humanitarian Action in Africa* (Trenton NJ: Africa World Press, 2000); Stella Tandai Makanya, 'The Desire to Return: Effects of Experiences in Exile on Refugees Repatriating to Zimbabwe in the Early 1980s', in Tim Allen and Hubert Morsink (eds), *When Refugees Go Home: African Experiences* (UNRISD/James Currey, 1994), 105–25; Jeremy Jackson, 'Repatriation and Reconstruction in Zimbabwe during the 1980s', in Allen and Morsink (eds), *When Refugees Go Home*, 126–66.

COLONIAL LEGACIES: RECURRING THEMES

The consolidation of foreign rule in Africa went hand in hand with population displacement, either as an instrument of colonial control or because it offered a means of escape and a chance to regroup. At the beginning of the twentieth century German troops in South-West Africa (Namibia) suppressed an uprising by Herero farmers who resisted attempts to deprive them of land and cattle; the survivors fled to neighbouring Bechuanaland, where they were promptly enlisted by the British to work in the South African mines.[7] In Mozambique the Portuguese colonial administration maintained its authority by brutal means. Half a million people were forced into fortified village camps where they could be closely guarded. (The same policy prevailed in Kenya during the Kikuyu or 'Mau Mau' rebellion.)

In Portuguese-occupied Angola, a British diplomat who visited the border in July 1961 reported that refugees 'fled in panic [after witnessing] group executions, beatings, theft and destruction, and napalm bombing'. UNHCR kept a low profile for fear of alienating the Portuguese state. Only in secret internal correspondence did the truth begin to emerge about colonial repression: 'It is said that young men with any education or powers of leadership are being selected and shot in order to destroy any leadership among the tribesmen, and that indiscriminate bombing and machine gunning of villages and groups of Africans is being carried out in order to terrorize the population'.[8] The crisis spilled over into the Belgian Congo whence 150,000 Baluba fled in the course of a few weeks (half of them were under 10 years of age), exacerbating a situation in which rival groups fought to control the rich mineral resources in Katanga province. UN officials decided that the needs of Baluba refugees 'cannot be separated from those of the local population [and that assistance to them] must be viewed within the framework of assistance to the Congolese population as a whole'. This doctrine, linking relief programmes and development projects, was enthusiastically embraced by newly independent states and UNHCR. Inter-governmental organizations and NGOs thus turned refugee crises into development opportunities.[9]

Other colonial legacies were equally insidious. New states typically rested on fragile political and economic foundations. Attempts to secure resources for basic infrastructure brought rulers into conflict with powerful local interests that sought to retain their autonomy. Often these rivalries were expressed in ethnic terms, partly because 'tribal' differentiation had been the register in which colonial powers had sought to rule. Chad's difficulties stemmed in part from the impact of French

---

[7] Jan-Bart Gewald, ' "I was afraid of Samuel, therefore I came to Segkoma": Herero Refugees and Patronage Politics in Ngamiland, Bechuanaland Protectorate, 1890–1914' *Journal of African History*, 43, no.2 (2000), 211–34; David Wilkin, 'Refugees and British Administrative Policy in Northern Kenya, 1936–1938' *African Affairs*, 79, no.317 (1980), 510–30; David Turton, 'Migrants and Refugees: a Mursi Case Study', in Tim Allen (ed.), *In Search of Cool Ground: War, Flight and Homecoming in North-East Africa* (UNRISD/James Currey, 1996), 96–110.

[8] J. D. Kelly, 'Report on Refugees from Angola', 26 June 1961, Fonds UNHCR 11, Series 1, 13/7/GEN–15/0/GEN/ANG, Angolan refugees; British Embassy, Leopoldville, to West and Central African Department, 25 July 1961, TNA, FO 371/155062.

[9] Unsigned Report, *United Nations Review*, 9, no.7 (July 1962), 18–20.

colonial policies of divide and rule that favoured the southern savannah which became a centre of cotton and rice cultivation at the expense of the Muslim North, which periodically carried out raids on the South. At independence the southerners alienated their rivals by denying them government posts and introducing discriminatory taxes. This North-South bifurcation contributed to the outbreak of a prolonged civil war in 1965, fuelled by external intervention. Refugees spilled over into Sudan, the Central African Republic, Cameroon and Nigeria.[10] Little news broke beyond the region. By contrast, the crisis in Nigeria, which manifested itself in the decision by leaders of the minority Ibo population to declare an independent state of Biafra in 1967, resonated far and wide. The conflict displaced internally upwards of three million people. It galvanized international public opinion by virtue of astute Biafran publicity efforts—the noted author Chinua Achebe penned a famous poem, 'The Refugee Mother and Child' that drew on Catholic iconography of suffering. Although other African politicians and the UN argued against intervening in a civil war, a group of French doctors denounced the UN and NGOs for standing by whilst civilians suffered. This stance became the launch pad for Médecins Sans Frontières (MSF).[11]

These episodes did not exhaust the legacy of decolonization and state formation. Decolonization had specific consequences for colonists who 'returned' to the metropolis. Its eventual defeat during the Second World War obliged Italy to renounce its colonial possessions in Africa, as well as the Julian Marches and the Dodecanese islands between 1943 and 1954. The Dutch and Belgian governments admitted 'repatriates' from their former colonies in the East Indies and central Africa respectively. They were described as 'national refugees', a device that allowed the UN to disclaim responsibility for crafting durable solutions to their predicament, even as they struggled to gain acceptance in a new and unfamiliar environment.[12]

REFUGEE-GENERATING AND REFUGEE-HOSTING STATES: ALGERIA

Many of the themes just noted are illustrated in Algeria. The Algerian refugee crisis was a conspicuous example of the powerful forces unleashed by the anti-colonial struggle. But it had other implications. The number of refugees who crossed an international frontier was more than matched by the number of internally displaced persons. The crisis marked the start of a connection between UNHCR and NGOs in the Third World that became a hallmark of the refugee regime. It helped drive forward plans for repatriation of Algerian refugees, and thus the need for

[10] Mario Azevedo, *Roots of Violence: a History of War in Chad* (Amsterdam: Gordon and Breach, 2008); Zolberg, Suhrke and Aguayo, *Escape from Violence*, 56–63.

[11] Benthall, *Disasters, Relief and the Media*, 95–108, 124–7; Terry, *Condemned to Repeat?*, 42–3; Chandler, 'The Road to Military Humanitarianism', 683–4.

[12] Ballinger, ' "Entangled" or "Extruded" Histories'?

preparatory measures. Decolonization made it necessary to resettle colonists. Finally, Algeria illustrates the point that African states both generated and hosted refugees: in accommodating Sahrawi refugees later on, Algeria facilitated the construction of Sahrawi refugee identity.

The crisis erupted in 1954 when Algerian nationalists took up arms to end the long French occupation of their country. The bitter war owed much to the fact that the French authorities regarded Algeria as an integral part of France. In response to an insurrection organized by the pro-independence FLN (Front de Libération Nationale), French troops cleared the indigenous population from areas adjacent to the borders with Tunisia and Morocco as part of a 'pacification' strategy; more than three and a half million Algerians were internally 'resettled' in concentration camps between 1954 and 1962. These tactics strengthened popular support for the FLN, which engaged in a brilliant diplomatic offensive. In addition, some 200,000 Algerians fled to Tunisia and Morocco. Several NGOs were involved in the relief of Algerian refugees, including the AFSC, Oxfam, Norway's Redd Barna, and the League of Red Cross and Red Crescent Societies. They pulled no punches, referring to 'the denial of elementary human rights and the legitimacy of the Algerian demand for independence' and to the need 'to alleviate the sufferings of the young men and women who had to leave Algeria as refugees'. In Algeria itself, the Comité Inter-Mouvements Auprès de Evacués (CIMADE), a French Protestant charity, supported Algerians who had been internally displaced and who lived in squalid shanty towns.[13]

At the request of Tunisia and Morocco, UNHCR agreed to extend its 'good offices' formula to North Africa, notwithstanding French objections that Algerian refugees were its citizens. They were finally repatriated from Tunisia and Morocco when Algeria became independent in 1962. UNHCR coupled repatriation to a programme for long-run reconstruction, on the grounds that 'the fate of the repatriated ex-refugees can no longer be disassociated from that of the Algerian population as a whole'. Islamic NGOs advocated a youth programme to provide 'wholesome alternatives to enforced idleness'. Infrastructure projects pointed to an 'overriding concern to provide work so that the unemployed can gain self-respect by supporting themselves'. The Lutheran World Federation funded ambitious reforestation programmes, experimental farms and training centres, as well as clinics, kindergartens and milk stations. This was the start of a commitment to 'development' as a response to refugee crises in Africa, and the secondment of technical experts to get projects under way.[14]

---

[13] 'Algerian Refugees Return—to what?' *Migration News*, 11, no.4 (1962), 22–3; Keith Sutton, 'Population Resettlement: Traumatic Upheavals and the Algerian Experience' *JMAS*, 15, no.2 (1977), 279–300; Ammar Bouhouche, 'The Return of Algerian Refugees following Independence in 1962', in Allen and Morsink, *When Refugees Go Home*, 71–7.

[14] *Algeria, a Cry of Need: a Study Devoted to the Problems of Algerian Refugees Published in Recognition of WRY* (Brussels, World Assembly of Youth, 1960); Felix Schnyder to U Thant, 3 October 1962, Fonds UNHCR 11, Series 1, 13/1/31/ALG; JAI proposal dated 25 February 1960, Fonds UNHCR 11, Series 1, Classified Subject Files 15/64-15/74; Holborn, *Refugees*, 839; Howard Adelman and John Sorenson (eds), *African Refugees: Development Aid and Repatriation* (Boulder: Westview Press, 1994).

Repatriation also took on a different guise. Around one million colonial settlers (*pieds-noirs*) as well as thousands of Algerian 'loyalists' (*harkis*) resettled in metropolitan France at the end of the war—General De Gaulle tried unsuccessfully to persuade the government of Chad to settle them in its desolate northern region. Although they were citizens of France, many *harkis* were unceremoniously directed to camps that had been used to house refugees from the Spanish Civil War.[15]

Little more than a decade after independence, Algeria became host to refugees from another crisis zone. In 1975, on the eve of Spain's withdrawal from its 90-year long occupation of the Western Sahara, Morocco invaded and asserted its territorial claim to lands rich in phosphate deposits. Armed resistance was led by the Polisario Front. Around 130,000 Sahrawi refugees fled to the remote and arid south-west of Algeria. Others remained under Moroccan administration, where their political rights were severely circumscribed. Following a ceasefire in 1991 the refugees expected to return to their homes, but the Moroccan government laid land mines along the border to prevent them from doing so. The result was to perpetuate refugee camps for more than 30 years: each is named after a town in the Western Sahara. Refugees elected a government-in-exile, the Sahrawi Arab Democratic Republic.[16]

The camps cultivated a history of struggle against Moroccan rule that disrupted a harmonious and peripatetic culture: '[W]e had camels and goats, men used to go to towns or cities and return carrying goods that lasted for a month. Women made the tents and took care of everything related to the running of domestic life'. Another added, 'when we moved from one place to another, all the *friq* [tents] moved together, we were like one family'. Older informants who had spent half their life in the camps indicated that the younger generation had gone soft: '[W]e the people of old could stay without food for a whole month or more. Such stamina you will not find in the younger people [who] live in a different and developed age and are exposed to more luxuries'. In part this is a tribute to an educational system that gave children an excellent grounding and allowed students to complete their studies abroad. Returning refugees published newspapers and launched an international film festival in 2003, so there is little evidence of diminution in Sahrawi solidarity or purposefulness.[17]

REVOLUTION AND DISPLACEMENT IN THE HORN OF AFRICA

Displacement in the Horn of Africa pointed to the legacy of not one but two colonial regimes. As an Italian colony, Somaliland provided social and educational

---

[15] Jean-Jacques Jordi, 'The Creation of the Pieds-Noirs: Arrival and Settlement in Marseilles, 1962', in Smith, *Europe's Invisible Migrants*, 61–74.

[16] Dawn Chatty (ed.), *Deterritorialized Youth: Sahrawi and Afghan Refugees at the Margins of the Middle East* (New York: Berghahn Books, 2010), 49–50, 71, 77.

[17] Jacob Mundy, 'Performing the Nation, Pre-figuring the State: the Western Saharan Refugees, Thirty Years Later' *JMAS*, 45, no.2 (2007), 275–97.

advantages to the Mejerteen clan. The subsequent rule of Siad Barre courted the Marehan group instead and made life intolerable for its rivals. Eritrea was also governed by Italy for half a century until the British took over in 1941 and expelled the Italian administration. Initially the Foreign Office envisaged turning Eritrea into a colony for European Jews, but British officials abandoned these plans in 1943. After the war the British planned to re-arrange Eritrea's borders with Ethiopia, Sudan and Kenya, measures that contributed to the creation of a united opposition inside the country as well as to the self-imposed exile of its political leaders. In 1951 the UN imposed a federation on Eritrea and Ethiopia, against Eritrean wishes. Ten years later Ethiopia annexed its neighbour, provoking a lengthy conflict that turned the lives of Eritreans upside down. The ensuing war of liberation only ended in 1993 when Eritrea was finally granted independence. Prolonged violence deprived farmers of cattle and grazing land, and a terrible famine in 1984–85 prompted further flight from Ethiopia. In all some half a million Eritreans fled over the border to the eastern region of Sudan or to Kenya; later on, UN and other assistance programmes made it possible for them to recover some of their assets. Some refugees fled further afield, adding to the large Eritrean diaspora in Western Europe.[18]

Sudan maintained a tough regime for refugees whom it regarded as a security threat and as contributing to unstable relations between itself and Ethiopia. For example, in 1974 the government of Khartoum decreed that they could not own land and had to live on prescribed settlements, the expectation being that this would alleviate economic difficulties in the eastern part of the country and that the refugees would return to Eritrea. Eritrean refugees (*laj'in*) who had settled in Khartoum were made to leave the city, being blamed for all manner of social and economic ills as well as 'moral decay'. There is, however, another reading of Eritrean displacement which places the emphasis on the creation of new social relations among the refugee population. The refugee crisis called into question longstanding kinship and clan ties and undermined the role of traditional village elders. The new contacts and networks in the transit and refugee camps in Sudan sustained a strong sense of national identity.[19]

The revolutionary transformation that took place in the Horn of Africa offers a parallel with events in Russia over half a century earlier. In 1974 Colonel Mengistu seized power in Ethiopia and his Derg regime dominated Ethiopian politics until 1987. The revolutionaries adopted the terminology of the civil wars in Russia and Hungary with their depiction of 'Red' and 'White terror'. Mengistu pressed for the creation of Soviet-style collective farms, and the associated relocation of Ethiopian peasants disrupted the entire rural economy and resulted in mass starvation. Further emergency resettlement took place after the famine of 1984–85. Not everyone left at gunpoint—some younger peasants wanted to make a fresh start elsewhere,

---

[18] Anna Arnone, 'Journeys to Exile: the Constitution of Eritrean Identity through Narratives and Experiences' *JEMS*, 34, no.2 (2008), 325–40.

[19] Gaim Kibreab, 'Resistance, Displacement, and Identity: the Case of Eritrean Refugees in Sudan' *Canadian Journal of African Studies*, 34, no.2 (2000), 249–96.

even if it meant having to encounter hostility from villagers where they were resettled. Members of the old elite fled to Europe and the United States, in another
echo of developments in Russia 60 years earlier. One villager, born in 1969, described how the Derg deprived her family of its land and sent her brothers to fight
in Eritrea; '[B]efore Mengistu everything was cheap, food, clothes, even people
with no education could get a job. With Mengistu everything changed. We had
cattle and started a small farm shop for survival [but] political education was new
to us. I left [for Kakuma refugee camp in Kenya] in 1984'. Some groups prospered
by throwing in their lot with Mengistu, only to become refugees in turn when the
regime collapsed.[20] Those resettled people who were tempted to go back to their
homes had little prospect of benefiting from this new dispensation. Fresh conflict
between Ethiopia and Eritrea in 1998–2000 produced yet more upheaval; thousands of Eritreans fled from the advancing Ethiopian army, while others were sum-
marily deported by the Ethiopian authorities in ways that call to mind Tsarist and
Ottoman practice during the First World War.

The Ethiopian revolution encouraged liberation movements in Eritrea and
Tigray to seek independence. The ensuing struggle produced another refugee crisis,
as Tigrayan leaders urged people to seek sanctuary in Sudan on the grounds that
'conditions favoured extinction: there cannot be a test worse than this. Man dies,
man is born; a village is razed, a village sprouts. But when a people perish that is a
final loss'. Flight became a patriotic duty, albeit one that exposed refugees to further torment. Birhani Paulos, a Tigrayan refugee who reached Sudan in January
1984, described the difficulties he encountered at the hands of Sudanese officials
in Gedaraf: '[T]hey insulted me, and they said: "smell the earth". By this they
meant, "put your face in the dirt and smell that it is not your land" '. Only when it
emerged that he worked for an international organization did they let him go. He
concluded that 'I cannot have a stable plan. Everything depends on the government in Sudan. I am not in my own hands, I am in the government's hands'.[21]
Many refugees died in the camps before they returned to their homes in 1986
under the auspices of the Tigray People's Liberation Front.

THE GREAT LAKES REGION: GENOCIDE AND
POPULATION DISPLACEMENT

Two sites of violence and displacement in sub-Saharan Africa loom larger than all
others in contemporary consciousness. One is Sudan, the other Rwanda and
neighbouring Burundi. The dramatic outbreak of mass murder in the African continent that took place in Rwanda in 1994 was neither 'spontaneous' nor random.

---

[20] Stephanie F. Beswick, ' "If You Leave Your Country You Have No Life!" Rape, Suicide, and Violence: the Voices of Ethiopian, Somali, and Sudanese Female Refugees in Kenyan Refugee Camps'
Northeast African Studies, 8, no.3 (2001), 69–98.

[21] Carole Kismaric, *Forced Out: the Agony of the Refugee in Our Time* (New York: Human Rights
Watch, 1989), 127.

Although its implications only became apparent a generation afterwards, and although it was not internationalized at the time, an ominous refugee crisis flared up in the wake of revolution in Rwanda in 1959. The majority Hutu population sought revenge on the Tutsi minority for having been favoured by Belgian administrators who subscribed to the racist belief that Tutsi were inherently superior to the Hutu by virtue of intelligence and descent (variously supposed to be from ancient Egypt or Ethiopia). The physical features of Tutsis and Hutus could scarcely be distinguished in the way propagandists on both sides maintained (Tutsis were believed to be taller and to have larger noses); they spoke the same language, lived side by side and often intermarried. Nevertheless the colonial authorities introduced identity cards which identified the holder as Tutsi or Hutu, or as a member of the smaller Twa group. During the revolution, Hutu militiamen singled out opponents whom they reviled as 'cockroaches' (*inyenzi*). Sometimes the militias cut off their noses or chopped off their victims' feet in order to 'make them short like the Hutu'.[22]

When Rwanda achieved independence in 1962 around 120,000 mainly Tutsi refugees fled Rwanda for neighbouring Burundi, Uganda, Tanzania and Congo (Zaire). Although many Tutsi stayed put—and it is important to emphasize that only a minority ever enjoyed significant privileges under colonial rule—they risked becoming second-class citizens in Rwanda. Meanwhile exiled Tutsi militants formed a Rwandan Patriotic Front (RPF) with the aim of recapturing power. The regime in Kigali, Rwanda's capital, used the existence of the RPF as a stick with which to beat those Tutsi who remained in Rwanda, enlisting impoverished Hutus in the cause.[23]

Tutsi exiles had something in common with White Russians, who forfeited a privileged position in society when the Bolsheviks came to power in 1917. Unlike the Russians, however, the Tutsis not only anticipated a return 'home' but succeeded in realizing that vision. In exile they conceived of themselves as victims of revolution who sought restitution for the losses inflicted upon them. Ethnicity and social class differences combined to produce a combustible mix. Many Hutus believed that they and not the Tutsi 'invaders from the north' had a privileged claim to Rwanda. Displacement raised the stakes. Although some refugees became relatively prosperous, the majority struggled in the refugee camps. UNHCR officials hoped to help Tutsi refugees in Kivu province to become 'firmly established [since] their misery would perpetuate general chaos, whereas their successful settlement would stimulate general progress'. In Tanzania, the government of Julius Nyerere ordered Rwandan refugees to settle in the north-west of the country and to clear the land. Refugees who resisted this offer faced having food rations withdrawn,

---

[22] The situation was more complex than this summary suggests, because radical elements in the Catholic Church encouraged the 'downtrodden' Hutu to gain an education during the 1950s, thereby creating a 'counter-elite'. See Newbury, 'Returning Refugees', 270–2.

[23] Gérard Prunier, *The Rwanda Crisis: History of a Genocide* (Hurst, 1998), 35–54; Rachel van der Meeren, 'Three Decades in Exile: Rwandan Refugees 1960–1990' *JRS*, 9, no.3 (1996), 252–67; Mahmood Mamdani, *When Victims Become Killers: Colonialism, Nativism and the Genocide in Rwanda* (Princeton: Princeton University Press, 2001), 14, 73–5, 101–2, 160–70.

and their leaders were arrested and deported. Officials found it easier to focus on the project of 'development' than on the freely expressed wishes of refugees.[24]

In Burundi, socio-economic differences between Hutu family farmers and wealthier Tutsi cattle and landowners were similarly entrenched by Belgian administration which maintained Tutsi privilege. Independence in 1962 and the collapse of the monarchy three years later brought Tutsi leaders to power. Political instability was heightened by the presence of 40,000 Rwandan refugees by mid-1962 whom UNHCR hoped to confine to the interior in order to forestall cross-border raids. But the policy backfired when in the following year a group of armed Tutsi attacked from Burundi provoking severe reprisals inside Rwanda and leading to a further influx of refugees. Although the newcomers helped introduce improvements to the local Burundian economy, the Hutu locals resented the connections that Tutsi refugees quickly forged with banks, churches and NGOs, regarding this as a sign that Hutu subordination and Tutsi superiority would be reinforced in Burundi. When the majority Hutu population turned on their rivals in 1972, the Tutsi fought back, killing between 80,000 and 250,000 Hutu whom they demonized as 'pythons'.[25]

Around 200,000 Hutus, including traders, civil servants, priests and teachers, crossed the border into Tanzania. For many of them it was a profound shock: '[A]rriving in the area of settlement we got scared to death. It was in the middle of nowhere. Never in our lives had we seen such thick forest inhabited by wild animals, snakes, and big biting flies'.[26] The Tanzanian authorities directed them to build clinics, schools, roads and other infrastructure funded in large part by UNHCR, and to become self-sufficient in food as well as producers of coffee and tobacco for export. Complaints surfaced that 'we are the granaries of the Tanzanians. We are qualified workers, and they know it. They are savage. They do not want us to leave their country. We cultivate a lot, they eat a lot. We feed all the poor regions of Tanzania. We have become their slaves. We have been given a pet name here, "the tractors"'. Tanzanian officials reportedly looked askance at attempts to sustain secondary education in the camp at Mishamo, Rukwa province: '[T]hey think if we are educated we will not cultivate anymore, that we will go and fight in our own country'. Refugees who moved to Dar-es-Salaam in search of work had to maintain a secretive and fragile existence. There were thus strict limits to Tanzania's open-door policy.[27]

Against this harsh backdrop, examples of resilience and dynamism came to the fore, as in the story told by Innocent, who fled Burundi in 1995 for the relative safety of Tanzania:

---

[24] Fonds UNHCR 11, Series 1, 1951–70, 15/SA 'Refugees from Rwanda—Resettlement in Africa'.

[25] René Lemarchand, *Burundi: Ethnic Conflict and Genocide* (Cambridge: Cambridge University Press, 1995); Peter Uvin, *Life after Violence: a People's History of Burundi* (Zed Books, 2009), 10.

[26] Marc Sommers, *Fear in Bongoland: Burundi Refugees in Urban Tanzania* (New York: Berghahn, 2001), 37–41.

[27] Malkki, *Purity and Exile*, 41–2, 119–20, 136–7; Sommers, *Fear in Bongoland*, 13; James Milner, *Refugees, the State and the Politics of Asylum in Africa* (Houndmills: Palgrave Macmillan, 2009), 109–14; Hanne Christensen, *Refugees and Pioneers: History and Field Study of a Burundian Settlement in Tanzania* (Geneva: UNRISD, 1986), 137.

I was transferred to a camp for 1972 refugees who had a right to plots of land. I, too, eventually managed to get one. I cultivated it and sold my production [sic]. I did some artisan jobs and sold the products and began acquiring a small capital to do a commerce [sic] of dried fish. When returning [to Burundi] two years ago, my money was stolen but I did not abandon the *métier*. I still had my bike and I borrowed money and started a little trade. When the fields started producing well, I sold part of the land to increase my capital, so now I own a boutique and I pay others to help my wife cultivate the lands. I live in my own house.

Since the signing of a peace accord in 2002, which brought the bitter Burundian civil war to an end, the Tanzanian government encouraged half a million refugees to repatriate. Here they were given the chance either to live side by side with farmers who had seized their lands or to be settled in 'peace camps'. Not surprisingly, neither prospect enhanced their sense of security: it does not help that Burundi is one of the poorest countries in the world. But there were personal gains: Innocent added that by returning to Burundi he was reunited with his wife whom he had not seen for seven years.[28]

In 1990 a Tutsi-led incursion by the RPF, with the strong backing of the government of Uganda keen to be rid of armed militants on its territory, facilitated the return to Rwanda of 700,000 largely Tutsi refugees. In the following four years the government of Juvénal Habyarimana (who had held power since 1973) tried to come to an agreement with the RPF. These efforts were undermined by economic decline brought about by a collapse in the price of coffee, the main export commodity, and the decision to devalue the Rwandan franc at the behest of the International Monetary Fund, making imports more expensive. The mass migration of landless peasants from North to South in the early 1990s, often in response to military offensives, magnified local tensions. When Habyarimana was killed in a plane crash in April 1994 along with the president of Burundi, the finger of blame was pointed at Hutu extremists opposed to his attempts to manage the economic and social crisis. The consequences were catastrophic. During the ensuing genocide around 800,000 and perhaps one million people were killed, many of them but by no means all by organized Hutu militias (the *Interahamwe* or 'those who attack jointly'). In Cambodia, it was wise not to be found wearing spectacles; in Rwanda even the size of one's nose made one vulnerable. Few Tutsi and moderate Hutu of any age and gender escaped mutilation or sexual assault. The speed of the killings was matched only by the torpor of the UN. Hutu refugees from Burundi and internally displaced Hutus from the north of the country played a crucial role in the genocide, seeking retribution for years of exile and marginalization.[29]

As the RPF gained the upper hand, inflicting retribution on Hutu citizens, the radicalized *Interahamwe* along with civilians fled west to neighbouring Zaire or east

---

[28] Uvin, *Life after Violence*, 29–30.
[29] Mamdani, *When Victims Become Killers*, 205–6, 214; Newbury, 'Returning Refugees', 275–6; Howard Adelman and Astri Suhrke (eds), *The Path of a Genocide: the Rwanda Crisis from Uganda to Zaire* (New Brunswick, NJ: Transaction Books, 1999).

to Tanzania, an exodus of as many as two million people. In addition, hundreds of thousands were internally displaced. Although probably only one in 20 of those who fled to Congo belonged to the armed forces or militias, most refugees were looked upon as having been complicit in the genocide, a view shared by respected analysts.[30] The establishment of huge new refugee camps on the borders further destabilized the entire region; Hutu refugee militias launched raids on Rwandan territory. Civilians faced deprivation and grave personal risks. In 1996–97 Hutu refugees were attacked by the armies of the new Congolese leader Laurent Kabila and by Rwandan government troops who were intent on revenge. Marie Béatrice Umutesi, a professional social scientist of Hutu background, with good contacts in and beyond Rwanda, wrote a moving account of the struggle to survive amidst hostile rebel militias and suspicious locals, and without adequate support from NGOs. UNHCR rode roughshod over the wishes of refugees and espoused repatriation as the most appropriate 'solution', rewarding villagers who turned refugees over to the authorities. Umutesi reserves some of her most scathing remarks for this 'bounty hunting'. Yet, at the same time as describing the death and disease that ravaged refugees during their retreat, Umutesi also draws attention to the resourcefulness of those like herself who bartered goods, cared for each other and managed to keep one step ahead of their pursuers.[31]

Events in Rwanda thus spilt over into neighbouring states (see Map 8). The continuing violence and instability in the Democratic Republic of Congo has been fuelled by the lucrative trade in gold and diamonds that are mined in the eastern part of the country. Weak state institutions did nothing to bring the violence under control. In Tanzania the UNHCR-administered camps conferred an advantage on refugees from the North who got there earlier at the expense of those from the South of the country. The management of relief thus tended to reproduce Rwanda's regional divisions. In Uganda, a combination of population pressure and political pressure by the government of Milton Obote created difficulties for Rwandan refugees who were treated as scapegoats for the economic crisis in the early 1980s, and who have suffered recently for the same reason. As so often, refugees were also regarded as a 'security risk', meaning that their own security took second place to considerations of state. Many Hutu refugees in camps in Zaire/DCR and Tanzania believed that UNHCR was in league with the Kigali regime to arrange for their repatriation. They wanted to learn at first hand from returnees about conditions in Rwanda, but UNHCR refused to arrange such sessions, on the grounds that this would breach its non-political stance. Umutesi expressed dissatisfaction with UNCHR officials who seemed unable to understand that 'refugees can also be intellectuals not beggars'.[32]

[30] De Waal, *Famine Crimes*, 195–203; Terry, *Condemned to Repeat?*, 2–5, 173–82, 240.

[31] Marie Béatrice Umutesi, *Surviving the Slaughter: the Ordeal of a Rwandan Refugee in Zaire* (Madison: University of Wisconsin Press, 2004), 211; Adelman and Barkan, *No Return, No Refuge*, 140–2.

[32] Johan Pottier, 'Relief and Repatriation: Views by Rwandan Refugees, Lessons for Humanitarian Aid Workers' *African Affairs*, 95, no. 380 (1996), 403–29; Johan Pottier, 'The Self in Self-Repatriation: Closing down Mugunga Camp, Eastern Zaire', in Black and Koser (eds), *The End of the Refugee Cycle?* 142–70.

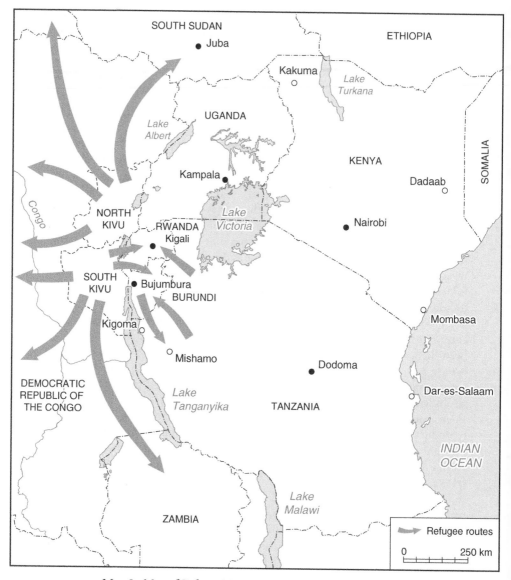

Map 8: Map of Refugee Movements in the Great Lakes Region

Refugees who fled to Kivu following the victory of the RPF and who were then forced to return to Rwanda, faced hostility from people who had occupied their homes with the blessing of the government and who made crude assumptions about their complicity in the genocide. This is precisely what refugees feared, and why UNHCR policy was clumsy and premature. (Wealthier Hutu on the other hand could settle in third countries thereby avoiding these problems.) More than a decade on from these terrible events, North Kivu remains a war zone in which armed Hutu, with access to mineral wealth and other resources, have been able to keep up their fight against the Congolese army and local Tutsi militias, with UN peacekeepers as bystanders, unable to protect the civilian population from violence, abduction and rape. The crisis of mass internal displacement was made all the more volatile by plans to repatriate Congolese Tutsi from Rwanda; this initiative, likewise backed by UNHCR, alarmed ethnic groups such as the Nande and Hutu.[33]

SUDAN: WAR, DISPLACEMENT AND DEVELOPMENT

Independence in Sudan, the second largest country on the African continent, led to a bitter civil war that lasted close on two decades. Religious, economic and cultural distinctions between the predominantly Muslim and relatively developed North, and the 'African' and less developed South, intensified under British colonial rule between 1898 and 1956 that maintained a dual administrative arrangement for the two halves of the country. Until 1946 British officials went so far as to forbid 'northerners' from travelling to the South. The British did little to integrate the immense western region of Darfur into the colonial state, thereby storing up problems for the future. When the British departed, the poverty of the South served to draw attention to its lack of political influence. In this fragile polity, tensions between the northerners and southerners reached boiling point. In 1962 a full blown conflict erupted between a guerrilla army in the South (the self-styled *Anyanya*, or 'snake venom') and the dominant northerners whose forces bombed villagers from the air. Around 20,000 Southern Sudanese fled to Zaire and Uganda in 1964 (when UNHCR first opened an office in Kampala); more followed when peace talks collapsed the following year.[34]

By 1970 UNHCR counted 166,000 refugees in neighbouring states including Uganda, Zaire, Ethiopia and the Central African Republic. A concerted effort was made to arrange for their repatriation in the wake of a peace agreement concluded at Addis Ababa in 1972, the aim of Khartoum being to neutralize any potential incursion from armed refugees in neighbouring states. Education and health care were entrusted to the *Anyanya* under a deal which created a Southern Assembly and a president of the Southern Region. The agreement required 'the whole nation of Sudan' to contribute to the 'resettlement and rehabilitation of refugees'. This was an immense challenge. Internally displaced people far exceeded the recognized refugee population; estimates of the displaced southerners range from 500,000 to one million. To complicate matters further Juba, the chief provincial capital, doubled in size during the war due to an influx of rural migrants brought about by the activities of troops supporting one side or another. Economic and regional divisions persisted, there were too few jobs to go round, and southerners continued to

---

[33] Umutesi, *Surviving the Slaughter*, 92, 209.
[34] Holborn, *Refugees*, 832, 994–7; John R. Rogge, *Too Many, Too Long: Sudan's Twenty Year Refugee Dilemma* (Totowa NJ: Rowman and Allanheld, 1985), 41.

feel marginalized. International NGOs did not coordinate their actions and failed to engage local Sudanese Christian and Muslim organizations. This added to the uncertainty.[35]

In Sudan, economic and political issues were closely linked. UNHCR disposed of substantial resources and could up to a point dictate settlement policy, for example insisting that refugees could not settle closer than 50km to the territorial frontier. This measure was 'intended to reduce political activity by refugees in the country of origin from across border locations and is thereby aimed at preventing tensions between the origin and asylum states'.[36] UNICEF and NGOs including Catholic Relief Services, Church World Service and Lutheran World Relief supported the fragile peace agreement that brought a temporary halt to the civil war.

Refugees in Sudan were vulnerable to exploitation by government officials and landlords who appropriated even the modest belongings of refugees. Animosity increased as pressures on local resources intensified and prices rose. Some of the problems were alleviated by organized settlement schemes funded by overseas aid that regulated employment and supplied basic necessities to refugees, but locals managed to siphon off resources for themselves. Refugees also lost out when they were moved on and deprived of land that they had already cleared and cultivated. The 1974 Asylum Act formally barred them from owning land and other immoveable property. Although the government cultivated an image of generosity, in practice refugees—Eritreans in particular, deemed not just an economic burden but a 'security threat'—faced considerable hardship.[37]

Organized settlement also came at the price of discouraging initiative. The widespread reluctance to involve refugees in the decision-making process allowed officials to claim that refugees had become excessively dependent on state welfare. Many refugees in Sudan settled not in camps but in urban settlements where they eked out an uncertain existence made more precarious by overcrowding. As if to prove the point, the military regime burned down a camp in Khartoum in 1990 inhabited by 30,000 internally displaced southerners. UNHCR attempted to build a working relationship with the government of Sudan by assisting with programmes to support Congolese and Ethiopian refugees on Sudan's territory. UN officials were also involved in economic reconstruction, even though the circumstances did not correspond to the Convention's definition of a refugee situation—High Commissioner Sadruddin argued that there were circumstances (and this was one) where 'displaced persons clearly need some form of international protection'.[38]

In the early 1980s civil war flared up again. The Sudanese People's Liberation Army (SPLA), founded in 1983 by John Garang with backing from the Derg regime in Ethiopia, confronted the government in Khartoum. The conflict was complicated by the prevalence of famine in 1983–84 and by the government's

---

[35] Holborn, *Refugees*, 1358; J.O. Akol, 'A Crisis of Expectations: Returning to Southern Sudan in the 1970s', in Allen and Morsink (eds), *When Refugees Go Home*, 78–95.

[36] Rogge, *Too Many, Too Long*, 60.

[37] Ahmed Karadawi, *Refugee Policy in Sudan, 1967–1984* (Oxford: Berghahn, 1999); Ferris, *Beyond Borders*, 139.

[38] Loescher, *UNHCR*, 153.

decision to arm 'Arab' militias; in practice the two elements were linked. The Arab population of Sudan historically maintained uneasy relations with Dinka and Nuer tribes because of rival claims to land and cattle, and many Dinka pastoralists ended up being enslaved by Arab overlords. The resurgence of civil war brought about a fresh exodus of around 1.5 million people to Zaire, Kenya, Uganda, Egypt and Southern Ethiopia, where refugees were particularly vulnerable. It also generated at least 4.5 million internally displaced people who sought refuge from the government's aggressive counter-insurgency measures and its attempts to conscript civilians, as well as from the requisitioning tactics adopted by the SPLA. Relatively few resources came their way. Those who moved to Khartoum faced fresh problems when the government declared war on the squatter settlements. Refugees who fled to Egypt fared little better. Sudanese refugees in Cairo testified that the stress they suffered from their encounter with UNHCR was second only to the trauma of escape from Sudan, although the 'displacement of anger originally directed at authorities in Sudan towards those in authority in Cairo may in part explain [these] findings'.[39] How the 2011 revolution in Egypt has affected the situation is as yet unclear.

Under international pressure, the government in Khartoum and the SPLA—now deprived of support from Ethiopia—signed a Comprehensive Peace Agreement in 2005, as a result of which refugees began to return to Sudan, albeit under conditions of considerable uncertainty. This fragile situation was more than matched by that in Darfur where the crisis reflected longstanding problems brought about by the pressure placed on local Fur and Masalit farmers by Arab camel-herding tribesmen from drought-affected northern parts of the region who moved south in search of grazing land. Drought appears to have been a major factor in intensifying conflict and encouraging mass internal migration. For example, following the drought in the mid-1980s around 400,000 Arab pastoralists encroached on Fur lands, already struggling to accommodate refugees from the civil war in Chad. More recently the 'pacification' campaign orchestrated by the central government crushed local Fur efforts to secure greater autonomy and unleashed an 'Arab' militia, the Janjaweed, whose name became a byword for mass murder and rape of the 'African' population. There were 600,000 internally displaced people in Darfur by 2004, in addition to 100,000 refugees who crossed into Chad to escape the fighting and to find food. The authorities in Khartoum tried to paint a reassuring picture of Darfur's camps and limited access by foreign aid agencies. This may reflect anxiety in Khartoum that the USA was seeking to use the conflict—not for the first time—to engineer greater influence in Sudanese politics.[40]

Historians cannot yet digest the impact of these upheavals. Nevertheless, oral accounts by Uduk migrants from Southern Sudan described an arduous trek in

---

[39] Susan M. Meffert, 'Feelings of Betrayal by the United Nations High Commissioner for Refugees and Emotionally Distressed Sudanese Refugees in Cairo' *Medicine, Conflict and Survival*, 26, no.2 (2010), 160–72, at 167.

[40] Martin W. Daly, *Darfur's Sorrow: a History of Destruction and Genocide* (Cambridge: Cambridge University Press, 2007), 262–3.

rough mountain terrain and across floodplains, where they were at risk from disease, starvation, banditry and other hazards, including being 'sold to the war' when soldiers went looking for recruits. They recalled this as *bway tur*, 'long road'. The outcome was that 'they found themselves locked into an unpredictable zigzag of journeys' across unfamiliar terrain. Several thousand ended up at a new settlement at Bonga just inside Ethiopia, where UNHCR established schools, churches and sports fields, and where refugees were expected to live independently. Many of them did exactly that, only to find themselves coming under criticism from relief workers for taking steps to secure additional resources by cutting down trees and hunting for food without permission. Females from Southern Sudan who made their way to Cairo found only find poorly paid jobs as domestic servants and were vulnerable to discrimination and exploitation. Their children gained only a basic education because of government restrictions. Egyptian officials refused to recognize the identity cards issued by UNHCR.[41]

The response to challenges faced by these and other Sudanese refugees—such as being required to wait for months to be seen by UN officials—emerged in the testimony collected recently by the US-backed 'Voice of witness' project. Marcy Narem remembered little about the journey from Sudan to Kakuma at the age of five, but described her prowess in the football team, her cautious negotiation of gender relations and the ever-present threat from the indigenous Turkana people. Although she complained that 'since I've been here, nothing has happened to me', nevertheless she aspired to a better life: 'I dream of being a nurse or a pilot. I remember flying to Nairobi, being high up in the sky, and I think it would be so great to be a pilot in a plane like that'. A 20-year-old South Sudanese man who arrived in Kakuma in 1994 commented that after 10 years in the camp, he no longer found 'mutual distrust. Nowadays people have changed. They understand each others' lives...each and every person has an aim to do something'. A South Sudanese woman reported that since reaching Egypt, 'Now I can think of what to do in this world'.[42] Refugees began to fight back. Women's access to income in the informal economy and education enabled them to assert themselves vis-à-vis men whose authority and status were hitherto unquestioned. This empowerment extended also to a more acute historical awareness: one women's self-help group, *Rabita*, discussed the history of Sudan and the complex and often painful relations between northerners and southerners during and after colonial rule, thereby providing them with a clearer understanding of the circumstances that led to the crisis of displacement.

The impact of the virtually uninterrupted wars in Sudan is graphically portrayed in the fictionalized autobiography of a young Dinka boy, Valentino Achak Deng, who fled to Ethiopia and found sanctuary in Kakuma refugee camp in North-Western Kenya before eventually settling in the United States. Kakuma camp was

---

[41] Wendy James, *War and Survival in Sudan's Frontierlands: Voices from the Blue Nile* (Oxford: Oxford University Press, 2007), 113, 120, 150.

[42] Craig Walzer, *Out of Exile: Narratives from the Abducted and Displaced People of Sudan* (San Francisco: McSweeney's, 2009), 245, 249, 435; Jane Kani Edward, 'South Sudanese Refugee Women: Questioning the Past, Imagining the Future', in Patricia Grimshaw (ed.), *Women's Rights and Human Rights: International Historical Perspectives* (Houndmills: Palgrave, 2001), 272–89, at 284.

established in 1992, primarily to house refugees fleeing fighting and scarcity in Sudan and Somalia. It had a population of 90,000 in 2005 when Deng was living there. Valentino Achak poignantly described the moment when he was forced to leave his village in Western Sudan: '[I]t was the beginning of the end of knowing that life would continue'.[43] Officials symbolically conferred a new life on these 'lost boys of Sudan' by giving them all the same birthday, 1 January. Deng's story is one of periodic 'uprooting' and escape, and of the loss of friends and acquaintances to sudden death at the hands of militias. His narrative also embraces chance encounters with people he never expected to see again, and above all it is a story of getting by, falling in love, growing up and seeing the world.

INCARCERATION: A DOUBLE-EDGED SWORD

The experiences of countless refugees in the African continent have been bound up with the refugee camp. Its ubiquity requires an explanation. Bureaucratic opinion maintains that the camp protects refugees from external attack, but this misleading assumption has been painfully exposed on numerous occasions. Camps serve other purposes, however: refugees are easier to manage in an institutional environment than if they are self-settled. We have already seen how camps helped pave the way for repatriation. They also aid the interests of political leaders who can promulgate their message to a captive constituency. For warlords the camp is a means to recruit soldiers. In Zaire, military commanders sustained their position among the massed ranks of Hutu refugees by creaming funds from aid agencies and extorting cash from refugees, as well as drawing on their own foreign bank accounts and the property they had brought with them from Rwanda. It was not just about buying guns and bullets. As one Hutu commander boasted, 'We have the population'. Camp inmates were regularly reminded through press bulletins and radio broadcasts of the need to safeguard the interests of the Hutu 'nation'. Creating this bond became a means of effacing the difference between refugee warriors and civilians, although at least two relief agencies were unconvinced by these cynical tactics: MSF and the International Rescue Committee both withdrew from Zaire, although UNHCR remained on the grounds that it had a duty to protect refugees prior to promoting their repatriation, and other aid agencies invoked the need to provide humanitarian assistance even if it entailed making unpleasant compromises.[44]

Somali experience provides a telling illustration of the reasons for the persistence of refugee camps despite their evident shortcomings. Camps set up in Somalia for ethnic Somali refugees (650,000 people at a conservative estimate) from the disputed territory of Ogaden in 1977–78 allowed President Siad Barre to consolidate his position as leader of a 'greater Somalia' and to tap international aid. The US—keen to support Barre in his rivalry with the pro-Soviet leadership of Ethiopia—channelled

---

[43] Dave Eggers, *What is the What: the Autobiography of Valentino Achak Deng* (Penguin Books, 2006), 75.
[44] Terry, *Condemned to Repeat?*, 166–81; Lischer, *Dangerous Sanctuaries*, 78–97.

this package of assistance via CARE and the World Food Programme. With these resources the camp population set up a health system, schools and workshops. Thousands of Somali citizens who managed to get jobs in the refugee camps were understandably reluctant to renounce them; here as elsewhere, the camps created a role for 'big men' who energetically exploited their position. The government in Mogadishu discouraged alternative modes of existence, because self-sufficiency would undermine the case for emergency financial and material resources from abroad. Another factor supporting international intervention was the widely-held view among NGOs that refugees were too 'traumatized' to take any initiative— these assumptions about 'dependency syndrome' and 'refugee mentality' clearly echoed views about 'DP apathy' in Europe a quarter of a century earlier. Many refugees described camp life as a form of 'slavery' that reminded them of stories of Arab dominance in generations gone by.[45]

The misplaced assumption that high dependency ratios in camps or among self-settled refugees deprived them of a capacity for enterprise is belied by the historical evidence, although this is not to overlook the fact that refugees might emphasize their vulnerability for tactical reasons, such as to improve access to resources. Refugees worked hard to make a living in the hope of accumulating sufficient resources, as for example in the Ogaden where they developed a varied mix of economic activities. Evidence elsewhere supports this finding. Tigrayan refugees survived in overcrowded refugee camps in Sudan, often by circumventing local laws that prohibited them from trading with local townspeople. Refugees also helped one another. Eritrean refugees in Sudan turned to cash crops and adopted new agricultural technologies, proclaiming 'we shall only move forward and never backward'. Many of the 180,000 refugees who returned to Eritrea likewise resolved to make a fresh start.[46]

This is not to say that conditions in refugee camps were anything other than challenging. Somali refugees who arrived in the Dadaab camp complex in Kenya in 1991 stayed for 15 years or more, and managed to survive with difficulty thanks to UNHCR support (including taking jobs as NGO community workers) and remittances from those who had already left. Studies of Dadaab and Kakuma testify to the disciplinary regime of the enclosed refugee camp and the risks to which women were continually exposed.[47] But life in refugee camps was never a catalogue of unmitigated misery. In 2006 the large settlement at Buduburam in Ghana housed 38,000 refugees from Liberia, who turned it into a thriving town with its own temples, mosque, cinema, bank and supermarket. Sudanese refugees who had been settled at Kiryandongo in Masindi district, Uganda, since 1991 did not live a one-dimensional life. In addition to meeting the needs of family members from

[45] David Laitin and Said S. Samatar, *Somalia: Nation in Search of a State* (Boulder: Westview Press, 1987), 125–6; Simon Turner, 'Suspended Spaces: Contested Sovereignties in a Refugee Camp', in Thomas B. Hansen and Finn Stepputat (eds), *Sovereign Bodies: Citizens, Migrants and States in the Postcolonial World* (Princeton: Princeton University Press, 2005), 312–32.

[46] Gaim Kibreab, 'Refugeehood, Loss and Social Change: Eritrean Refugees and Returnees', in Essed, *Refugees and the Transformation of Societies*, 19–30, at 27.

[47] Hyndman, *Managing Displacement*, 93–110, 121–31.

the plots of land assigned to them, they devised a range of entertainments including both poignant songs ('Sudanese live in sorrow') and frivolous pieces.[48] Dances such as the *larakaraka* simultaneously evoked a longing for Sudan and affirmed the possibility of making a decent life in a community of exiles. These cultural expressions are, like political activity, dynamic rather than static. Newer opportunities for social encounter, such as discos, draw attention to inter-generational disharmony that displacement intensified. Refugee life in camps has, so to say, never stood still.[49]

Camps additionally enabled political activists and militants to prepare refugees for future struggle or for eventual 'homecoming'. ZANU-administered camps in Mozambique instructed Zimbabwean exiles in the history of white oppression—not a difficult task in view of the settler regime's fondness for creating tightly controlled 'protected villages' in Rhodesia, as a means of depriving nationalist guerrillas of potential support. (The number of internally displaced people was put at 750,000 in the late 1970s.) The camps across the border became an instrument of political as well as military mobilization, sustaining incandescent rage against white rule and the settlers' monopoly of land that had displaced African farmers earlier in the century. The camp at Wampoa College for example promoted a powerful historical narrative, emphasizing the historic absence of political rights and economic prospects, not to mention the aggression shown by the Rhodesian army to its opponents. Teachers and other professionals trained the next generation and maintained a disciplined regime in exile. As in camps at other times and in other places, vocational training went hand in hand with sports and music. Unhappily the process of return to independent Zimbabwe was hampered by great haste and administrative confusion, which relief organizations such as Lutheran World Federation, the Mennonites, and Zimbabwean church leaders attempted to alleviate.[50] Much of the country was devastated by the war, and extensive rural poverty continued to play havoc with the lives of ordinary peasant farmers. The uncompromising stance of the Mugabe government—typified by its treatment of opponents which reached a crescendo during the war in Matabeleland in 1983–86 and brought about a fresh exodus to Botswana—owed much to the political opinions and educational programmes promoted in the camps and the atmosphere of suspicion brought about by years of enforced exile. The camp hardened political opinions, sustained a history of struggle, and—dare one say—combined bravery with brutalization.

'DURABLE SOLUTIONS'

Recurrent refugee crises in many parts of Africa gave rise to immense relief efforts on the part of UNHCR and NGOs. As we have seen, there was a clamour to

---

[48] This was not the first time that Masindi had been home to refugees: a small community of Polish refugees lived there from 1943 to 1948.

[49] Tania Kaiser, 'Songs, Discos and Dancing in Kiryandongo, Uganda' *JEMS*, 32, no.2 (2006), 183–202.

[50] Janice McLaughlin, *On the Frontline: Catholic Missions in Zimbabwe's Liberation War* (Harare: Baobab Books, 1996).

impose 'durable solutions': repatriation, resettlement or integration. African leaders articulated their own programme. In 1969 the Organisation of African Unity (established in 1963, and renamed the African Union in 2002) agreed a refugee convention that widened the definition of refugees to include internally displaced persons as well as those who crossed an international frontier. The 1969 Convention also took into account the political realities in countries where white settler regimes led pro-independence freedom fighters to continue the struggle in exile. Claims to protection were to be made on the basis of group determination, not unlike the situation in Europe between the wars when Russian and Armenian refugees were regarded as a collective entity. Asylum was seen as a 'peaceful and humanitarian' gesture, not to be construed by any member state as an 'unfriendly act'. Governments agreed to settle refugees in the interior of the receiving country, in order to reduce the possibility that refugees would make cross-border incursions into the country of origin—a significant provision that underlined the security concerns expressed by OAU member states. For 40 years UNHCR has based its actions in the sub-continent on the OAU Convention. When the Convention first came into force, the refugee population in Africa was around 900,000; 20 years later it reached 5.5 million.[51]

However, focusing on external intervention neglected the actions of refugees who provided for themselves. One example emerges from the aftermath of famine in Darfur in 1984–85 which was exacerbated by the presence of large numbers of refugees from the war in Chad. Unfortunately UNHCR adopted a highly restrictive definition of those entitled to receive food aid—focusing primarily on those who conformed to the internationally agreed definition of refugee—and overlooked the needs of others. The outcome was not only widespread casualties that could have been prevented but also a legacy of bitterness between the local population and the newcomers. Addressing the needs of both subsequently involved considerable efforts. Other initiatives included programmes for cross-border assistance in an attempt to prevent farmers whose crops failed from becoming refugees. Since many farmers were nomads, particularly in the Horn of Africa, UNHCR opted to take a leaf out of the book of the OAU, rewriting the rules that hitherto precluded it from assisting internally displaced persons.[52]

Broadly speaking repatriation became the preferred option. The first significant repatriation effort took place in the early 1960s when Algerian refugees returned from Tunisia and Morocco under UNHCR auspices. UNHCR advertised other success stories, such as the organized return of Ethiopian refugees in the 1980s and Mozambican refugees in the early 1990s, and lamented the circumstances that prevent repatriation, as in the case of Eritrean refugees in Sudan, who remained in exile for decades as a result of precarious conditions in their home country. But repatriation was rarely an unalloyed success or a straightforward option. The practical consequences have already been mentioned—and the repatriation of Liberian refugees

---

[51] Fonds UNHCR 11, Series 1, 1/1/71 'Good Offices Policy' (1967–70); Zolberg, Suhrke and Aguayo, *Escape from Violence*, 28–9.
[52] Loescher, *UNHCR*, 303–4.

from Buduburam is another case in point. Poor and war-torn countries have often been overwhelmed by the cost of rebuilding homes and infrastructure. Organized return did not always correspond to the wishes of displaced people: pastoral nomads in the Horn of Africa wanted land for their cattle, rather than to be required to move to a prescribed 'home'. Other considerations also hampered repatriation. UNHCR found it cheaper to maintain Eritrean refugees in situ than to pay for a large-scale repatriation scheme. The government in Sudan came to rely upon UNHCR largesse. In Kenya and Tanzania too, the presence of refugees attracted goods and services that brought tangible benefits to non-refugees as well.[53]

Aid has often gone hand in hand with ideas about 'rational' social organization and economic development. The International Conferences on Assistance to Refugees in Africa (ICARA) convened under UN auspices in Geneva in 1980 and 1984 agreed on the need for investment in infrastructure—education, health and transport—in order to alleviate the burden on host countries. Although little came of these initiatives, the debates drew attention to the link between displacement and development. In Tanzania, which provided refuge to Hutu farmers fleeing the fighting in Burundi in the 1970s, the government in conjunction with UNHCR and the Lutheran World Federation set aside unpopulated forest land at Ulyankulu for refugees to cultivate maize, beans and cassava in accordance with the doctrine of village settlement (*ujamaa*). Programmes for 'rehabilitation' and economic development were designed in part to weaken the pressure for further displacement. By the 1980s this had become accepted doctrine. The development agenda served an important purpose in indicating to officials in the country of settlement that the needs of local people would not be overlooked in the process of assisting refugees. Everyone, that is to say, would be entitled to international aid. In these circumstances UNHCR had to tread carefully because it was not an 'operational' agency; precisely for this reason repatriation commended itself as a preferable alternative to the lengthy commitment to support refugees in the country of first asylum. But by the late 1990s Tanzania had had enough—officially, it reported 800,000 refugees in 2005—and in response to claims from Burundi that it was providing a safe haven for rebel groups, launched a concerted programme to round up Burundian refugees. By forcing large numbers into camps, cutting the size of plots of land reserved for their use and depriving them of wage-earning opportunities in the local economy, the Tanzanian authorities began to look upon incarceration as the prelude to organized repatriation. Something of the same stance applied in respect of refugees from Rwanda. In late 1996 the authorities told UNHCR of their intention to send refugees back. Within a few weeks some 450,000 Hutu refugees had been forced across the border.[54]

Whatever the preferred 'solution', a question mark hangs over the meanings that refugees assigned to places and to their past. The 'place' to which one returned

---

[53] Johnathan Bascom, *Losing Place: Refugee Populations and Rural Transformations in East Africa* (Oxford: Berghahn, 2001); Elizabeth Holzer, 'A Case Study of Political Failure in a Refugee Camp' *Journal of Refugee Studies*, 25, no.2 (2012), 257–81.
[54] Milner, *Refugees, the State and the Politics of Asylum*, 126.

might have become very different from the place it once was, partly because of the damage inflicted by war and partly because newcomers took over the homes and farms belonging to those who fled. It is thus appropriate to think of returnees as 'starting over' rather than 'coming home'. Tigrayan refugees, originally farmers from the highlands who returned from neighbouring Sudan to lowland Ethiopia in 1993, 'were neither creating a new way of life from a clean slate nor going back to a previous state of being'.[55] The past figured in their homecoming as a reminder that migration was a recurrent feature of Tigrayan life. In other circumstances—Rwanda is the obvious case in point—the past acquires a different meaning in relation to repatriation, because 'victims' and 'perpetrators' now confront one another about misdeeds and mass murder. In addition to these political and psychological dimensions, material elements arise from claims for compensation and other kinds of restitution. Sometimes, as in Ethiopia, repatriates were obliged to get used to new farming practices. For all these reasons repatriation has never been a straightforward choice on the part of individuals or a straightforward policy. It has always come at a price, usually paid disproportionately by refugees, and it always entails a complex relationship to the past.

REFUGEE HISTORIANS, REFUGEE JOURNEYS

An intense historical consciousness manifested itself in the situations just described. In Tanzania's refugee camps, to which tens of thousands of Hutu exiles were confined after the bitter conflict in Burundi in 1972, refugees manifested a powerful sense of nostalgia for the coffee fields and the cattle that they had left behind. They hoped to return, provided that Burundi was ruled by a Hutu government and not by Tutsis. But far more was at stake. The camps gave vent to the expression of an exclusive ethnic identity whereby refugees rationalized the discrimination and historic suffering to which they had been exposed. Refugees in Mishamo portrayed themselves as the embodiment of a Hutu nation clearly distinguishable from Tutsi 'interlopers' from the far north. They deployed a strong sense of the past in order to shore up their identity. Specifically they constructed a strongly woven and didactic narrative of political, economic and social marginalization at the hands of Tutsi 'foreigners' to whom negative qualities were ascribed without qualification. Among Hutu refugees this blunt characterization of ethnic difference went hand in hand with an idealization of the distant past when Hutus lived together in peace and a belief that the present torment of displacement cemented Hutu solidarity. History—or rather, a 'mythico-history' now 'seized centre stage' and provided refugees with a morality tale, a way of ordering the world, and a guide to appropriate behaviour.[56]

---

[55] Laura Hammond, *This Place Will Become Home: Refugee Repatriation to Ethiopia* (Ithaca: Cornell University Press, 2004), 15.
[56] Malkki, *Purity and Exile*, 53.

Yet it would be wrong to overlook the cosmopolitan outlook expressed by other refugees. An anonymous Sudanese in Kakuma described his relations with local Kenyans: 'In my life as a refugee, I have come to socialise with people of different cultures, understand them, and appreciate them. And then also I have come to know different political ideas'.[57] Burundi refugees who settled in the Tanzanian township of Kigoma embraced a less rigid identity than their counterparts in refugee camps. Nevertheless, here too 'refugee historians'—self-appointed custodians of the past who occupied a senior position in refugee society—did not hesitate to tell stories of Hutu suffering at the hands of Tutsis. Whether originating from the Lake Region or the highlands, Hutu refugees were enjoined to remember and to avenge their persecution. While making the most of life in 'Bongoland' ('brain-land', the term they gave to Dar-es-Salaam), they looked upon themselves as the real 'owners' of Burundi, whereas the Tutsi were regarded as 'interlopers' who had benefited from Belgian favouritism in the past. In this atmosphere expressions of resolve sounded menacing rather than reconciliatory: the phrase 'never again' acquired a particularly sinister overtone.[58]

In post-genocide Rwanda, the state offers its own version of the past. Deliberate efforts are being made to 're-educate' people in accordance with ideas of reconciliation, 'de-ethnicization' and 'unity' (*ubumwe*). Rwandan citizens are barred from making public reference to their ethnicity, and schools may not teach the history of the genocide. Newly instituted *ingando* or 'transition camps' are designed to inculcate 'harmony'. They promote themselves as part of an 'ancient Rwandan tradition', and their instructors emphasize that colonial rulers pitted Rwandan against Rwandan, an interpretation that oversimplifies a complex history and overlooks pre-colonial divisions, but which clearly serves a political purpose in modern Rwanda, namely to quash difference by government fiat. The project extends not only to the current crop of young citizens but also to older Tutsi who fled Rwanda between 1959 and 1961.[59]

The richest material for the social and cultural historian of refugee displacement emerges in a different context, in relation to Jews in Ethiopia who looked upon themselves to be the descendants of a 'lost tribe' that fled Egypt in 1300 BCE. The men among them worked as blacksmiths or metalworkers, the women as potters; many were also tenant farmers. None of them benefited from the revolutionary changes undertaken by the Mengistu regime, and several thousand took the fateful decision to escape to neighbouring Sudan. En route they were exposed to attack by Ethiopian bandits (*shifta*) and militias to whom bribes had to be paid to allow them to cross the sealed border. One in five lost their lives before reaching Sudan. The authorities in Sudan placed most of them in refugee camps whose conditions were little better than those they left behind in Ethiopia. They suffered infectious disease and dehydration. Some refugees believed they were being deliberately

---

[57] Walzer, *Out of Exile*, 435.
[58] Sommers, *Fear in Bongoland*, 42–64.
[59] Andrea Purdeková, 'Rwanda's *ingando* Camps: Liminality and the Reproduction of Power' Working Paper no.80 (Oxford: RSC, 2011).

poisoned. The Sudanese authorities harassed them and punished any attempt on their part to escape their confinement. They had little opportunity to work either as farmers or as craftsmen. When Israel launched 'Operation Moses' in November 1984, and airlifted refugees from Sudan to Jerusalem via Brussels, the plan was conceived as deliverance from an intolerable situation. The government in Khartoum came under intense US pressure and was in no position to hinder these efforts.[60]

Important work by Israeli psychotherapist Gadi BenEzer, who encouraged young Ethiopian Jews to speak about their ordeal, reveals that they imbued their journey from Ethiopia to Sudan with notions of vulnerability and suffering, but also with a sense of having embarked on an epic adventure that would eventually take them to 'Yerussalem'. They exhibited abundant reserves of personal courage and fortitude, as well as impressive resourcefulness in having secured food, hidden money and disguised themselves from the Ethiopian authorities. Amos recounted in graphic detail his attempts to save his brother from the Ethiopian and then the Sudanese border guards, which ended with them being reunited. It is a tale of near-drowning, thorns in the flesh and bleeding, and incessant running to escape. The narrative is also suffused with Amos's sense of duty towards his brother. Other narratives spoke of 'walking through an unknown land, facing obstacles, enemies, sickness and death [that set them] on their way to becoming Israelis'. For young refugees the flight required them to fulfil adult roles and to learn lessons about responsibility. Boaz organized a group for self-defence against the *shifta*, turning the tables on the soldiers:

> After a short time we started to behave bravely and people started to be afraid of us. We began to act like others around us, lifting up a stick [to fight] and so on. We started to get control over the situation, to be active. People then became afraid of our small group.

These narratives contradict the official view that 'heroic rescue' was the sole prerogative of the Israeli state acting in the interests of incapable refugees. Takaleh described the harsh conditions in the Sudanese camps: 'I learned what it is not to belong', while Tena spoke of learning what the world is like: 'I did not know what bad things were. Now I know everything'. The mental universe of refugees had grown rather than shrunk, and they displayed an impressive maturity and capacity for emotional development.[61]

Episodes of this kind constitute a story of a specific 'homecoming' and resolution that gains credence by virtue of constant retelling of stories of bravery and destiny, particularly at family gatherings and at holiday time. But they also suggest the rehearsal of historical myths, one element of which was the firm belief that their ancestors settled in Ethiopia many centuries earlier. Thus ideas of cohesion and solidarity are reinforced through the construction of a national epic. Tales of

---

[60] Ahmed Karadawi, 'The Smuggling of the Ethiopian Falasha to Israel through Sudan' *African Affairs*, 90, no.358 (1991), 23–49.

[61] Gadi BenEzer, *The Ethiopian Jewish Exodus: Narratives of the Migration Journey to Israel 1977–1985* (Routledge, 2002), quotations at 146, 153, 170.

personal anguish, sacrifice and salvation form part of a collective portrait of suffering, endurance and redemption. The element of myth served as a means of 'opening up a space for the Ethiopian Jews as a group in the Israeli psyche'. That is to say, there was a connection between the Ethiopian Jewish odyssey and deep-seated Israeli notions of Biblical struggle and the modern *aliyot* or immigration episodes. Ultimately, 'being Jewish was experienced not only as a risk factor but also as a major resource for survival'.[62]

Nevertheless this 'homecoming' was not trouble-free. In part this reflected the need to deal with traumatic experiences, but it also had to do with the reception that the refugees encountered in 'Yerussalem'. Israelis found it difficult to come to terms with Jews whose skin colour was black. There was also a widespread perception that they had been 'rescued' by Israelis; although in one sense this was true, it made no room for the intense deliberation and difficulty that went with the decision to flee from Ethiopia to Sudan. Ethiopian Jewish refugees underwent additional humiliation, first by Israeli officials who transferred them to 'absorption centres' for months or even years and then at the hands of religious authorities who required them to 'convert', as if to emphasize their inauthenticity compared to Jews who arrived from the Soviet Union. This added another layer to communication and affirmation of collective endeavour and draws attention to the interplay between different Jewish histories that could not easily be reconciled.

CONCLUSIONS

Political rivalries and state-building, security concerns and competition for resources have combined to ensure that in parts of Africa, as in other parts of the world, displacement has become a way of life. African states struggled to maintain administrative control over their territory in the face of rival and secessionist claims to rich mineral deposits and other resources. When the availability of external development aid and weaponry is taken into account, it is not difficult to see why politics should become so combustible. Population displacement was one outcome. This generalization does not apply to the entire subcontinent. States such as Ghana, Senegal, and Botswana managed the transition from colony to independent state with relative ease, and they have become stable sovereign polities.[63] At present (2013) civil war in Côte d'Ivoire makes things extremely uncertain, but it was not always so. Mozambique was badly affected by the struggle for independence during the 1960s and early 1970s, but it subsequently became a peaceful, albeit economically disadvantaged society, and in 1995 was rewarded with membership of the British Commonwealth (Rwanda was also admitted, in 2009). Tanzania, not

---

[62] BenEzer, *The Ethiopian Jewish Exodus*, 86, 198. The hardship and prejudice that they encountered in Israel are addressed in the film *Va, vis et deviens* (Radu Mihaileanu, 2005), in which the mother of a Sudanese boy disguises her son as a so-called Falasha, entitling him to a seat on the plane to Jerusalem but simultaneously launching him on a troubling journey of self-discovery.

[63] Ghana has accommodated large numbers of refugees from Togo and Liberia.

a wealthy country by any international measure, accommodated hundreds of thousands of refugees without being destabilized, although the government kept a close watch on Hutu refugees from Burundi and life got much harder for refugees in the 1990s, when the collapse of apartheid weakened the claims of refugees to be 'freedom fighters' and their political legitimacy evaporated. But the general point remains: it makes no more sense to describe Africa entirely in terms of its displaced population than it would be to generalize about Europe on the basis of the collapse of Yugoslavia.

Africa also figures in the history of population displacement as a key site of external assistance and the appropriation of the refugee as a de-historicized figure. Africa's large refugee population made it possible for NGOs, UNHCR and other international organizations to expand their operations and to establish greater legitimacy as well as a public profile. They were not disinterested parties. Their growing importance required them to focus on current crises. The expanding machinery of humanitarian intervention discounted the root causes of population displacement and turned the refugee into a kind of blank slate on which could be written plans for integration and development or repatriation. NGOs claimed the right to speak on behalf of the refugee. New states too appropriated the refugee for their own ends. Proto-states took shape in the refugee camp where they were constructed around the history of displacement and a mythico-history that validated their entitlement to a monopoly of territory.

Where does this leave the social history of population displacement in sub-Saharan Africa? This field is largely uncultivated and its contours are not yet clear. Often the sources are difficult to come by. Marie Béatrice Umutesi collected stories from refugees who were held alongside her in the camp at Tingi-Tingi in Zaire, only to find that this precious cargo disappeared during their hurried retreat. This is not the only stumbling block. The performance of external agencies indicates how little scope they afforded refugees to articulate their views. However, some provisional conclusions can be reached. One is the need to set displacement in the broader historical context of pre-colonial and colonial rule. Decolonization provided new states with a chance to redress real or perceived wrongs by turning the tables on ethnic groups that hitherto enjoyed the patronage of colonial rulers. This was the emerging pattern in Chad, Sudan, Somalia and Rwanda.

Beyond this, the complex movements of people in colonial as well as post-colonial times shaped the subsequent course of forced migration. Refugee movements across state frontiers reflected historic economic and personal ties that created nearby affiliations as well as extensive transnational and diasporic connections. Transnational communities channelled resources to displaced people as well as to fund political causes. One telling example is that of Somali refugees in Kenya, North America, and Western Europe, who supported each other in distant places and situated their experiences in a transnational framework. They interacted with one another, with Somali groups in Somalia itself, and with refugees in the huge and overcrowded camps in Ifo, Dagahaley, or Hagadera that form part of the Dadaab complex in Kenya. One woman described how she had worked for 10 years in Somalia on behalf of CARE International, before being forced in 1991 to leave for

Dadaab where her husband had a job with UNHCR. By drawing attention to a nomadic past that was characterized by economic insecurity, she and others 'mobilise[d] images of being adventurous, tough and independent, rather than marginalised, displaced and helpless'.[64] In similar vein, a study of the Uduk people of the Blue Nile suggests that 'the bland language' of humanitarian intervention, with its talk of 'survival' and 'coping', does scant justice to the depth of their cultural imagination and practices, or the intensity of the adventures during their trek across difficult terrain.[65]

Displacement entails thinking critically about the politicization of history. Youthful Zimbabwean exiles grew up in camps in Mozambique or Zambia learning about the brutal occupation of their country and the seizure of land by white settlers. Cameroonian asylum seekers who reached Johannesburg in the mid-1990s aligned themselves with the political struggle in their home country, turning this into the dominant discourse.[66] Hutu refugees in Tanzanian camps emphasized their victim status, but young Hutu men and women in the township lived an adventurous and imaginative life, without necessarily subscribing to ideas of 'ethnic absolutism'. The evidence does not always point in a single direction. Umutesi's riveting personal account (which she combines with an historical analysis) describes 'ordinary' human interaction, with scarcely a mention of Hutu solidarity and manifests a refreshing readiness to engage with and to compare notes with her Tutsi acquaintances. Some refugees hoped to be 'reborn', not as nationalists but as the faithful adherents of evangelical churches. Others gave themselves nicknames—'Rambo', 'Eddy Muffy' [Eddie Murphy] and 'Maiko' [Michael Jackson]—that alluded to Western cultural icons rather than the prescribed Hutu heroes. Unhappily, the social world of these refugees was turned upside down in 1994, and new claims were made on their allegiance, with painful and disturbing consequences.[67]

We need to bring political, social, cultural and economic histories into closer alignment. History affected refugees' relationships with governments and relief agencies, with other refugees, and vice versa. A modern social history of displacement needs to connect the aspirations and actions of refugees, on the one hand, to statist and non-governmental projects and the changing geopolitical agenda on the other. Refugees used existing contacts to gain publicity for their cause or to secure material advantage. Sometimes that resourcefulness is deeply troubling, as in the behaviour of refugee warriors. The difficulties and dangers—the risks that women in particular faced when they collected firewood beyond the bounds of the refugee camp or when they were expected to grant sexual favours in exchange for 'protection'—should not be underestimated. But they do not tell the whole story. Ethiopian women fleeing

[64] Nauja Kleist, 'Nomads, Sailors and Refugees: a Century of Somali Migration' *Sussex Migration Working Paper* no.24 (University of Sussex, 2004), 11.

[65] James, *War and Survival*, xv, 120.

[66] Mario Azevedo, *Tragedy and Triumph: Mozambique Refugees in Southern Africa, 1971–2001* (Portsmouth, NH: Heinemann, 2002); Ernest Pineteh, 'Memories of Home and Exile: Narratives of Cameroonian Asylum Seekers in Johannesburg' *Journal of Intercultural Studies*, 26, no.4 (2005), 379–99.

[67] Sommers, *Fear in Bongoland*, 132–3; Umutesi, *Surviving the Slaughter*, 114–15.

from Mengistu's 'Red terror' described hardship but also spoke nostalgically of the life they left behind. As refugees they demonstrated plenty of resourcefulness. The same was true of Somali women who fled to Kenya in the early 1990s and who reported widespread sexual violence and exposure to HIV/AIDS, but who also participated in income-generating projects and in providing reproductive health care in the refugee camps. Cultural enrichment and personal adventurousness were part of the equation: terms such as deprivation and exploitation capture only a fraction of the refugees' social world.

The results of refugees' efforts to create an historical record of displacement may become better known in years to come. What is already clear is that it behoves us to pay due attention to the multi-faceted histories of migration, including the journeys that refugees made, and their awareness of changes that occurred and how they related to the places, people and lives left behind. It is worth reflecting on the words of Wendy James's Uduk informant who told her about the vibrant cultural life in Bonga, which had become 'home':

> [There is a] kind of new talk which they have invented here in Bonga, the new way of speaking, but this is not just done by children. Grown-ups do this here. They're inventing a lot of new songs, and inventing new ornaments and fashions. It's all just new styles, invented in this place. And the dancing is now different, it is completely new.[68]

This is not to overlook danger or to romanticize displacement, but rather to do justice to the meanings with which it is imbued and the multiple possibilities that it disclosed.

[68] James, *War and Survival*, 224.

9

'Some Kind of Freedom'
Refugees, Homecoming, and Refugee Voices in Contemporary History

We walked a long way on foot, but you've reached some kind of freedom, so you keep on walking

(an unnamed Bosnian Muslim refugee)

INTRODUCTION

Seismic changes took place across the globe towards the end of the long twentieth century. Soviet domination of Eastern Europe came to an end and the USSR itself vanished from the scene, to be replaced by new states. Soviet communism's last hurrah in the Third World sounded as an invasion of Afghanistan, generating a prolonged refugee crisis and a storm of violence in the region that has yet to abate. NATO's decision to respond to the attacks on the USA in September 2011 by launching a 'war on terror' in Afghanistan against mujahideen (refugee warriors) whom they had earlier welcomed as harbingers of anti-communist resistance compounded the crisis of displacement. In Europe the imminent collapse of communism did not lead to pre-emptive invasion and widespread flight as it did in 1956 in Hungary and 1968 in Czechoslovakia; instead the evaporation of Soviet power in Eastern Europe in 1989 was contained by domestic political transformation. However in Yugoslavia all hell broke loose, unleashing the greatest refugee crisis in Europe since the end of the Second World War. Politicians and paramilitaries targeted ethnic minorities and settled old scores. European governments and international organizations did their utmost to keep refugees within the borders of the former Yugoslav state, with some success, although tens of thousands of citizens of the former Yugoslavia sought refuge in Germany and other Western European countries.

These events had the consequence of hiding from view other sites of upheaval, not just in Europe, where the Turkish invasion of Cyprus in 1974 launched a new phase in Greek-Turkish rivalry and a crisis that remains unresolved, but also in Sri Lanka and Bhutan where displaced populations live beyond the international gaze.

The end of communist rule and the formation of new states in post-Soviet space did not culminate in continent-wide migration. Anxieties that territorial refashioning would cause a mass movement of refugees westwards failed to materialize. The numbers were significant only in the case of ethnic Germans who moved from Russia to Germany. Although at one stage EU states provided protection to around 700,000 refugees from the imploding Soviet bloc most of the repercussions of territorial refashioning were confined within new states that emerged out of the Soviet wreckage without provoking serious conflict, with the notable exception of Armenia and Azerbaijan where rival claims to Nagorno-Karabagh led to a refugee crisis. Russia's lengthy attempt to secure control over Chechnya also produced a bitter war that killed and displaced hundreds of thousands of people. Here, too, the crisis was contained at a regional level. Lest this paint too sanguine a picture, it should be remembered that the demise of the USSR created a situation not unlike that in 1918 where new states were populated by substantial non-titular minorities. Around 25 million ethnic Russians were living in ex-Soviet republics other than the Russian Federation, their families having migrated when the Soviet state promoted the industrialization of 'less developed' republics. This serves as a reminder that crises of displacement should be set in a broad chronological context.[1]

In addition to territorial changes, the post-communist political dispensation afforded unprecedented opportunities to publicize and engage with earlier histories of mass population displacement. Survivors of Stalin-era deportations, their children and grandchildren could speak openly of the suffering they endured. Other options opened up too. For example, Crimean Tatars who were deported to Central Asia during the Second World War began to contemplate the possibility of returning to their 'homeland', which now found itself part of independent Ukraine. The leaders of newly independent Baltic States encouraged former DPs who had settled overseas to make a return visit and even to resettle permanently, although relatively few took up the offer in the face of misunderstandings and disputes over title deeds.[2]

The negotiation of memory was not confined to former Soviet states. Yugoslavia's dissolution paved the way for contested interpretations of the post-war history of the Italian-Yugoslav borderlands. Now the talk was of 'history as something to be exhumed, as having been submerged and only now being brought into the light'.[3] Angry debates also ensued in Greece and in the diaspora about the fortunes of Macedonian children who were despatched by the Greek Communist Party to Eastern Europe during the Greek Civil War: right-wing commentators have gone so far as to label this a 'genocide' (see later in this chapter). Another example of post-communist reckoning concerned the fate of 400,000 Karelians who were 'evacuated' to Finland following the Soviet-Finnish agreement of 1944. Early assessments of this transfer suggested that they adjusted quite quickly to life in Finland; in fact the reality was more complex. In the 1990s survivors could retrace the steps taken half

---

[1] Rogers Brubaker, 'Migrations of Ethnic Unmixing in the "New Europe"' *IMR*, 32, no.4 (1998), 1047–65.

[2] Wyman, *DPs*, 9–10.

[3] Pamela Ballinger, *History in Exile: Memory and Identity at the Borders of the Balkans* (Princeton: Princeton University Press, 2003), 12.

a century earlier. A freshly-laid 'trail of the displaced' aimed to 'reawaken' and share memories with the younger generation who were expected to dress for the part.[4] These cultural constructions and practices belong in any discussion of the contemporary refugee regime.

Much of this history is occluded in contemporary public discourse. Certainly from a vantage point in the First World, debates around refugees carry a strong whiff of parochialism. One would hardly know from reading the British popular press that most of the world's refugees struggle to survive far from UK shores. To be sure, newspapers and broadcasters periodically carry stories of human suffering from distant sites of crisis, but public opinion expresses an anxiety about being 'overwhelmed' by refugees and asylum seekers, as if Britain were a vessel at risk of capsizing. The attendant demand for rigorous border controls is matched by claims that Britain had sufficiently discharged its responsibilities towards refugees in the past: the genealogy of 'welcome' is alive and well. (The same discourse operates in Australia too, for example.) In a think-piece on 'the battle at the borders', Jeremy Harding pointed out that many asylum seekers look to the West precisely because of its history of intervention in distant lands: '[T]he West's exertions on far-off battlefields, shaping a world in its likeness, are among the reasons Europe is the place of choice for thousands of people. In ways we fail to acknowledge, we issue the invitation and map their journeys towards us'.[5] Against the backdrop of economic depression, it has become ever more difficult for refugees to obtain asylum. Governments seek to detain and deport promptly those whose claims to recognition are deemed to be unfounded. With little grasp of histories of conflict and dispossession on the part of officialdom, refugees meet with underlying suspicion and outright hostility. But refugees nevertheless achieve a degree of momentum by managing their expectations and confronting the past.

NORTH-WEST FRONTIERS OF DISPLACEMENT

Around five and a half million refugees left Afghanistan, initially after the coup mounted against the old monarchy in 1978 by the People's Democratic Party of Afghanistan, and then in much greater numbers in the wake of the Soviet invasion of Afghanistan in December 1979 and the campaign to suppress resistance to the puppet regime. Taking account of internal displacement and one million estimated war-related deaths, the consequences of the Soviet invasion affected around half the Afghan population. Only during the more enlightened leadership of Mikhail Gorbachev did an agreed withdrawal of troops take place in 1989. Soviet analysts of the crisis dismissed refugees either as members of the old elite who could play

[4] Anna-Kaisa Kuusisto-Arponen, 'The Mobilities of Forced Displacement: Commemorating Karelian Evacuation in Finland' *Social and Cultural Geography*, 10, no.5 (2009), 545–63.

[5] Jeremy Harding, 'Europe at bay' *London Review of Books*, 34, no.3 (2012), 3–11; Guy Goodwin-Gill, 'Asylum 2001: a Convention and a Purpose' *International Journal of Refugee Law*, 13, nos.1–2 (2001), 1–15, at 4.

no role in 'progressive' (that is, Soviet-dominated) Afghanistan or as 'simple folk, deceived or alarmed by reactionary propaganda'.[6] Continued political turmoil throughout the 1990s and renewed conflict among the resistance led to further mass displacement, although many refugees decided to return to Afghanistan following the fall of the Taliban government in 2002. They 'crossed paths with increasing numbers of cross-border migrants, traders and new refugees moving in the opposite direction'. Returnees in turn added to the numbers of internally displaced persons.[7]

Iran and Pakistan as adjacent states became the main destinations for Afghan refugees. The Iranian authorities settled them in poor urban neighbourhoods, where the newcomers took over the jobs of Iranians who were conscripted during the war against Iraq. It helped that for decades Afghan men had migrated in large numbers to Iran for economic, cultural and religious reasons. Faced with this new crisis Iran sought financial assistance from UNHCR, but aid only began to flow in 1983, and whereas $1 billion was earmarked for the needs of Afghan refugees in Pakistan, only $150 million went to Iran. Unwilling to contemplate a large numbers of refugee welfare claimants on its territory, Tehran re-classified them as 'migrants' and in 1996 stopped issuing refugee cards. Educational opportunities were also circumscribed, one consequence being that Afghan refugees made clandestine provision for their children. The offspring of Iranian mothers and Afghan fathers were placed at a particular disadvantage by being denied Iranian citizenship. Iranian public opinion was at best indifferent and at worst hostile to refugees, portraying them as 'dirty' and 'lazy'. One Hazara woman described being trapped between her desperate present circumstances and a hopeless future: 'What can we do? Afghanistan is *kharaab*, destroyed, and it will never get better. Life is so hard here, but it is impossible there. Nowhere is home for us'. A Pashtun refugee compared her former life in Afghanistan with her current situation in a small village in Iran:

> In Afghanistan, we didn't live like this. We had regular homes, not clay and straw shacks. I planted crops and we had plenty to eat. Then the Uzbeks came and took everything and destroyed whatever was left behind. We had to leave. The land is good for nothing now. And my body is sterile. Here, everyone calls me 'the woman who has nothing', because I have no home, no land, no herds.[8]

On the other hand, there is plenty of evidence to suggest that young Shi'a adults made a meaningful life, for instance gathering in coffee shops and libraries where they read their poetry to one another, reaffirming the importance of the poet as a major cultural figure in Afghan and Iranian society. Many young people read and write poems that often explore the pain of exile. Mohamed Kazem Kazemi wrote

---

[6] Vasilii I. Potapov, *Bezhentsy i mezhdunarodnoe pravo* (Moscow: Mezhdunarodnye otnosheniia, 1986), 90–1; Westad, *Global Cold War*, 348–9.

[7] Khalid Koser, 'The Migration-Displacement Nexus and Security in Afghanistan', in Koser and Martin (eds), *The Migration-Displacement Nexus*, 131–44, at 131.

[8] Diane Tober, ' "My Body is Broken Like my Country": Identity, Nation and Repatriation among Afghan Refugees in Iran' *Iranian Studies*, 40, no.2 (2007), 265–85, at 278, 281.

a famous poem in 1991 that alluded to the indifference shown to Afghan refugees by Iranians. There is evidence too of an unfettered and cosmopolitan imagination. In one of his love poems Seyyed 'Asef Hosseini 'compares his suffering for his be-loved to all the suffering in the world, jumping through a dizzying array of im-agery, including recent events in Fallujah and Abu Ghraib, the genocide in Poland, hunger in the Horn of Africa, and the shackled prisoners of Guantanamo'.[9]

Different conditions applied in Pakistan. In the view of some scholars, Muslim solidarity helped ensure that the government committed itself to 'compassion and companionship' with the Afghan refugees.[10] But the material expression of that solidarity did not correspond to the rhetoric. Some 350,000 Afghan refugees in Pakistan—mostly Pashtuns and Baluchis—were housed in 'temporary' refugee camps close to the border or else were expected to build their own homes in the North West Frontier Province and Baluchistan, where pressure of numbers led to shortages of water, wood and grazing land. Refugees were forbidden to buy land or other property in Pakistan. Women (who far outnumbered men) worked on domestic tasks including weaving and embroidery.[11] Higher numbers kept local wages low. Farming skills were forgotten, partly because generous external assist-ance created an alternative economy dominated by racketeering and warfare. More to the point, there were fewer restrictions on political and military organ-ization than in Iran, because the government of Pakistan curried favour with the USA in the late stages of the Cold War, whereas Teheran wanted to maintain cordial relations with its powerful northern neighbour. From their base in Paki-stani refugee camps, resistance factions carried out sustained raids in occupied Afghanistan. This archetypal 'refugee warrior community' lived off enormous quantities of foreign aid, little of which found its way into the hands of ordinary refugees. The flow of aid prepared the ground for the triumphant return of muja-hideen and for the Taliban to assert their claim to be the legitimate rulers of liber-ated Afghanistan.[12]

The political radicalization of Afghan refugees during their enforced exile in Pakistan and Iran had well-known consequences. But important questions about the relationship between returnees and the Afghan population who stayed behind under Soviet occupation are yet to be answered. The situation was com-plicated by the Taliban whose policies forced moderate Afghans to flee to Iran. Children had to endure playground taunts that their country contributed little to human civilization and their parents called for an 'Afghan pride booklet' that would show something of Afghan history and achievements. This is a poignant

---

[9] Zuzanna Olszewska, ' "A Desolate Voice": Poetry and Identity among Young Afghan Refugees in Iran' *Iranian Studies*, 40, no.2 (2007), 203–22, at 220.

[10] M. Nazif Shahrani, 'Afghanistan's Muhajirin (Muslim "Refugee Warriors"): Politics of Mistrust and Mistrust of Politics', in Daniel and Knudsen (eds) *Mistrusting Refugees*, 187–206.

[11] Saba Gul Khattak, 'Living on the Edges: Afghan Women and Refugee Camp Management in Pakistan' *Signs: Journal of Women in Culture and Society*, 32, no.3 (2007), 575–9.

[12] Matthew Fielden, 'The Geopolitics of Aid: the Provision and Termination of Aid to Afghan Refugees in North-West Frontier Province' *Political Geography*, 17, no.4 (1998), 459–87; Rüdiger Schöch, 'UNHCR and the Afghan Refugees in the Early 1980s: between Humanitarian Action and Cold War Politics' *RSQ*, 27, no.1 (2008), 45–57; Lischer, *Dangerous Sanctuaries*, 44–72.

reminder that circumstances can conspire against refugees who seek to maintain a collective self-worth.[13]

Were such a history to be written, previous episodes of displacement in Afghanistan and enduring ties of kinship between refugees and local households would provide an inescapable element. Future historians may detect important differences between the life stories of refugees who spent time in Pakistan's refugee camps and those who were more or less self-settled in Iran. Apart from narrating these recent shocks, room might also be found for the history of Kabul's community, which was swollen by an influx of Jewish refugees from the Soviet Union in the 1920s and 1930s. So far as Afghans themselves are concerned, exile appears to have been understood not only in terms of physical safety but as the necessary precondition for safeguarding Islam. This obligation was deeply embedded in Muslim consciousness, since it belonged to a tradition that went back to the time of the Prophet's *hijrah* (exile). Ironically many Tajik refugees in Pakistan had themselves fled from the Red Army when the Bolsheviks established Soviet rule in Central Asia during the early 1920s, and their descendants helped to buttress the anti-Soviet resistance in the 1980s. Some observers have detected signs of hope in Afghanistan. The Swiss photographer Ahad Zalmaï, who was born in Afghanistan but fled following the Soviet invasion, felt sufficiently confident to make a photographic record, including images of refugees who set up temporary homes in the caves that previously housed the famous Bamian Buddhas before they were destroyed by the Taliban. Afghanistan nevertheless remains a highly volatile reminder of the legacy of the Cold War.[14]

These responses must be set in the context of the turbulent politics of Iran and Iraq. Iran had the misfortune to become embroiled in a long and bitter war with Iraq between 1980 and 1988, when its neighbour took advantage of the political uncertainty brought about by the Iranian revolution. The precise demographic consequences are obscure, but the flight of Iraqi Shiite civilians to Iran compounded the burden caused by the influx of Afghan refugees. Iraq's own internal political crisis generated widespread suffering and population displacement. When the first Gulf War ended in 1991, around 1.3 million Kurds fled from Saddam's Iraq to Iran and 450,000 to the frontier with Turkey. The so-called 'safe haven' for Iraqi Kurds was portrayed as 'humanitarian intervention', although it served Turkey's interests by deterring Kurds from seeking refuge inside the country, which is home to a large Kurdish minority population. The first and second Gulf Wars also had catastrophic consequences for Palestinian refugees who had sought sanctuary in Baghdad after 1948 but who were forced by the fighting over the future of Iraq to shelter in squalid camps inside Syria, such as Al-Tanaf. The US-led invasion of Iraq is widely recognized to have had disastrous results including a refugee population

[13] Chatty, *Deterritorialized Youth*, 152–8.

[14] <http://www.lightstalkers.org/zalmai>; Ahad Zalmaï, *Return, Afghanistan* (Geneva: Aperture Foundation, 2004); Magnus Marsden, 'Muslim Cosmopolitans? Transnational Life in Northern Pakistan' *Journal of Asian Studies*, 67, no.1 (2008), 213–47; Sara Koplik, 'The Demise of Afghanistan's Jewish Community and the Soviet Refugee Crisis, 1932–1936' *Iranian Studies*, 36, no.3 (2003), 353–80.

put at nearly four million (including 1.7 million internally displaced), one in eight of the Iraqi population. The refugee population includes people who worked for US occupation forces as translators or in other capacities, and who fled Iraq to avoid the dangers posed by insurgents who resisted the occupation. But trying to find a safe passage to the USA has been immensely difficult, even more so than for DPs from central Europe and for Vietnamese refugees. Here, too, the elements of a refugee history have yet to emerge.

UNHCR was heavily involved for example in supporting Afghan refugees, at the invitation of a country (Pakistan) that had not signed the 1951 Convention. International NGOs such as MSF and CARE also sought to improve conditions in refugee camps in Pakistan. They included Red Crescent and various organizations with a shared commitment to 'Islamic relief' (*ighatha islamiya*). At one stage Hezb-e Islami maintained 250 schools with 43,000 students in Pakistan. These organizations expressed unease at the scale of Western programmes of humanitarian action and a wish to differentiate themselves from the 'missionaries' and the ICRC. For a while at least, Islamic relief agencies mobilized support across the Middle East and further afield among countries keen to assist refugees and to invigorate the Afghan resistance, thereby hastening the Soviet retreat. This activity was taking place at the same time as the mobilization of transnational Islamic networks in Bosnia (see later in this chapter). Over time, and particularly in the wake of the 'war on terror', it behoved Islamic NGOs such as the British-based Islamic Relief to emphasize their professional expertise and non-political, charitable credentials lest their activities be construed as giving comfort to militants.[15]

What did the management of Afghan refugees imply for self-expression? Only a tentative answer is possible. To be sure, vulnerability remained a serious concern. But long exposure to incarceration whilst it obliged refugees to leave traditional farming life behind nevertheless created thriving communities. But we should not press the point too far, because the camps sustained refugee warriors and new power-brokers whose world-view made it even more difficult for women to express themselves. All this means that although the history and perspectives of Afghan refugees will be difficult to establish, it is likely that the mujahideen among them will doubtless seek to impose their interpretation of the past.

SOVIET DISSOLUTION AND POPULATION DISPLACEMENT

Notwithstanding the intensity of these dramas and their global significance, it is appropriate that this chapter should come full circle by revisiting Europe's experience of mass population displacement. The dissolution of the Soviet Union, long regarded as a stable polity, enabled former Soviet republics to become sovereign states. Tension in the Caucasus between Armenia and Azerbaijan erupted into violence in 1991.

---

[15] Jonathan Benthall and Jérôme Bellion-Jourdan, *The Charitable Crescent: Politics of Aid in the Muslim World* (Tauris, 2003), 52, 69–84; Terry, *Condemned to Repeat?*, 69.

Chechnya has been a running sore. A long-running dispute between the Russian Federation and Georgia turned into open warfare in August 2008, as Russia sought to protect ethnic Russians in the small enclave of South Ossetia. In June 2010 a violent confrontation between Kirgiz and Uzbeks in Kyrgyzstan displaced around 250,000 Uzbeks; tens of thousands fled to neighbouring states. Yet Soviet fission was by and large a non-violent process.

The collapse of the Soviet Union posed particular problems for 25 million ethnic Russians who lived outside the borders of the Russian Federation. Non-Russian majorities in newly independent states regularly made it clear that Russians now occupied a subordinate place in society. As one migrant put it, reflecting on the fact that the borders moved while he had not, 'we suddenly found ourselves immigrants within our own country. But we were still in our own country'.[16] Mounting discrimination caused 10 million people to move to Russia from Central Asia and the Caucasus between 1991 and 2001, either under duress or more commonly because they feared their Russian ethnicity would put them at a future disadvantage. They were initially treated in accordance with the provisions of legislation passed in 1992 which stated that a forced migrant was an individual 'who has citizenship of the Russian Federation and who has left or intends to leave his or her place of residence on the territory of another state or on the territory of the Russian Federation as a result of violence or other form of persecution towards him or herself or members of his or her family'. Persecution included being the target of threats 'in connection with the conducting of hostile campaigns towards individuals or groups of individuals, mass violations of public order or other circumstances significantly restricting human rights'.[17] This neat legal formulation and the recognition of citizenship rights had little meaning for migrants who encountered bureaucratic indifference; worse, the Russian Federation began to prioritize domestic 'security' and the regulation of migration over practical assistance to those who arrived. This calls to mind the situation of Dutch, French, Italian and Portuguese citizens who found themselves repudiated upon their 'return' to the metropolis as 'national refugees'.

The priority of Russian migrants was to establish decent living arrangements, but instead they had to make do with substandard accommodation. To some degree these difficulties were alleviated by various self-help strategies, such as relying on family and other personal connections. Local people resented their presence; it did not help that their arrival coincided with pronounced economic decline in the Russian Federation during the 1990s that put a great strain on all welfare programmes. At the same time, these Russians from the 'near abroad' were also regarded in the first Putin era (2000–08) as a resource helping to offset the decline of the ethnic Russian population. Some of them cultivated a belief that they had a 'higher cultural level' than that of Russians who had lived their lives within the Russian Federation: '[I]t is [as one informant told Moya Flynn] highly qualified,

[16] Moya B. Flynn, *Migrant Resettlement in the Russian Federation: Reconstructing Homes and Homelands* (Anthem Press, 2004), 70.

[17] Hilary Pilkington, *Migration, Displacement and Identity in Post-Soviet Russia* (Routledge, 1998), 37.

cultured, intellectual, well brought up people who have arrived. They want to bring their culture and strong labour potential to the economy and culture of Russia'. Thus migrants claimed the right to support by drawing a distinction between other Russians and themselves, rather than by asserting a straightforward cultural affinity. They were the custodians of the 'real Russia'.[18]

The outbreak of conflicts between newly independent states (such as Armenia and Azerbaijan) as well as within the Russian Federation (in particular, Chechnya) produced displacement and deprivation. When the two enclaves of Abkhazia and South Ossetia broke away from Georgia, 250,000 ethnic Georgians sought safety in other parts of the country; war in 2008 further magnified these numbers. Between 1988 and 1992 around 300,000 ethnic Armenians and 500,000 Azeris fled the disputed territory of Nagorno-Karabagh, the mountainous region administered by Erevan and connected to Armenia by a narrow corridor through Azerbaijan. Both countries found themselves in dire economic straits (Armenia's energy crisis was magnified by the blockade imposed by Turkey and Azerbaijan), making life extremely difficult for everyone. At the start of the millennium Armenia had by far the largest number of recognized refugees per head of population. In Chechnya the brutal conflict between Russian and Chechen forces lasted a decade and a half. It left a terrible legacy. Hostilities commenced in 1995 when Boris Yeltsin ordered Russian troops to suppress the attempt by Chechens to gain freedom from the Russian Federation. The ensuing war displaced some 250,000 Chechens to neighbouring territories of Ingushetia, Dagestan and North Ossetia. Even greater numbers of people sought sanctuary in these adjacent lands when war flared up again in 1999 during the Putin presidency. UNHCR struggled to contain as many people as possible within the borders of Chechnya, but its assistance left a lot to be desired and it was hamstrung by the reluctance of foreign governments to alienate Russia by questioning its claim to sovereignty over Chechnya.[19] As we shall see, Russian-Chechen relations were closely bound up with the history of wartime deportations.

TOGETHER IN DISHARMONY: THE DISSOLUTION OF YUGOSLAVIA

In 1991, following Croatia's declaration of independence, local Serbs established a 'republic of Krajina' and expelled the Croat population from their homes. Further displacement took place when Serbs in turn were expelled from Croatia/Krajina in 1995. Official figures suggest that 200,000 refugees fled the country and 350,000 were internally displaced, while 20,000 lost their lives. The conflict was fuelled by rival claims to land and drew upon religious and cultural differences between Catholic Croats and Orthodox Serbs. Croats expressed a belief that they had suffered from longstanding subordination to local Serbs who dominated the local

---

[18] Flynn, *Migrant Resettlement*, 52, 136.   [19] Loescher, *UNHCR*, 276, 336–7.

Communist Party. In fact, relatively cordial relations had been maintained between Serbs and Croats during the communist era, but the collapse of Yugoslavia
revived memories of rivalries before and conflict during the Second World War,
helping to inflame national differences (Krajina was formally re-incorporated into
Croatia in 1998).

In Bosnia-Herzegovina around 2.5 million people were forced out of their
homes during the war that lasted from 1992 until 1995. Forces loyal to the Bosnian Serb leader Radovan Karadžić were directed by paramilitary leaders such as
the notorious Željko Ražnatović ('Arkan') to rape, torture and murder Bosnian
Muslims in a systematic fashion. UNHCR lacked the wherewithal to prevent attacks on Muslim enclaves in so-called 'safe havens'. Civilians in the besieged cities
of Sarajevo and Tuzla experienced the war not as displacement but as a trap. The
bombardment of the market in Sarajevo in February 1994 caused international
outrage exceeded only by the Serb massacre of Bosnian Muslim refugees in Sre-
brenica in July 1995. Eventually, as a result of international intervention, the
Dayton Accords in December of that year led to the formation of two ethnically-
defined polities, one Bosnian and the other Serb (Republika Srpska). The agreement made provision for people to move to 'their' country, an assumption that
took no account of 'mixed' marriages nor satisfied those who felt an attachment to
Yugoslavia and who now thought of themselves (as one refugee put it) as 'an en-
dangered species'. Some 500,000 people fled Bosnia for adjacent countries including Croatia and Slovenia. An additional 700,000 people took refuge in Germany,
Sweden, Denmark and elsewhere (see Map 9). These population movements were
accompanied by an economic collapse which made it difficult for refugees to receive adequate assistance in places of temporary local asylum in former Yugoslavia.
Providing earlier economic aid might have reduced the tensions that brought the
crisis about.[20]

In Kosovo, the conflict took the form of a bitter struggle between ethnic
Albanians and Serbs, already evident in the communist era and intensified by
discriminatory policies pursued by Serbian authorities after 1989. This led to
the mass exodus of around 400,000 Kosovar Albanians to Western Europe,
North America and Albania during the 1990s. Kosovar authors drew a parallel
with the calamities that befell the local Albanian population during and after
the Balkan Wars at the beginning of the century. Serbian presence was further
strengthened by Slobodan Milošević's decision to settle ethnic Serb refugees
from the wars in Croatia and Bosnia on Kosovar territory. A war in 1998 produced a huge refugee crisis. NATO's bombing campaign early in 1999 was
conceived and implemented as a 'humanitarian war' designed to destabilize the
Milošević regime in Belgrade, but it only magnified civilian suffering on both
sides. A total of 460,000 Kosovar Albanian refugees were displaced when the
air strikes commenced and a further 800,000 subsequently fled to Albania and

---

[20] Ivaylo Grouev, *Bullets on the Water: Refugee Stories* (Montreal: McGill University Press, 2000), 29,
144–51; Stef Jansen, 'The Violence of Memories: Local Narratives of the Past after Ethnic Cleansing'
Rethinking History, 6, no.1 (2002), 77–94; Helton, *The Price of Indifference*, 299.

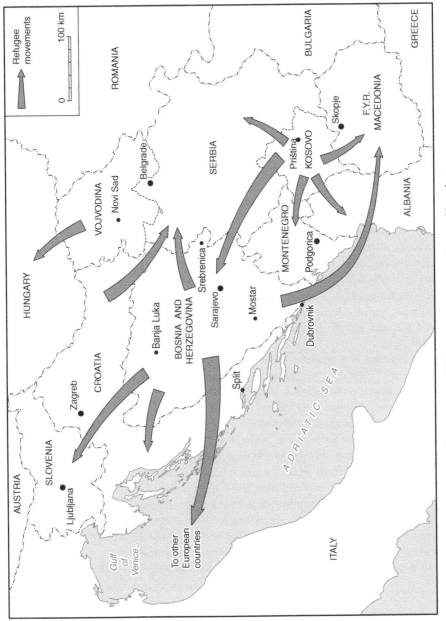

Map 9: Map of Refugee Movements in Former Yugoslavia

Macedonia, neither of which welcomed refugees. When Macedonia closed its border and deported Kosovar refugees to Albania, Greece and Turkey, American officials entertained the possibility of transferring numbers of refugees to the US military base at Guantanamo Bay, where they would not be recognized as refugees under US law. The entire crisis caught UNHCR 'off guard' and exposed a lack of coordination between the military and NGOs, most of whom threw in their lot with NATO in order to get access to refugee camps.[21]

Nor did Serbian civilians escape unscathed. A 35-year old Serb who fled Bosnia and took refuge in Belgrade spoke of the years he had lost to war: 'I was born at the wrong time'. When Serbian troops withdrew from Kosovo, NATO and UNHCR stood by while the Kosovo Liberation Army (KLA) and ethnic Albanians targeted the remaining Serb population and occupied their homes in order to force them to leave Kosovar territory.[22] Surviving Serbs were now confined to enclaves in the interior of Kosovo and the region bordering Serbia itself. Those who fled to Serbia met with hostility from the local population who complained that these 'peasants' enjoyed unearned privileges. Refugees described the toll taken on families living in makeshift accommodation outside Belgrade, pointing out that 'we left houses one thousand times better than here' and bemoaning the likely difficulties in returning to them.[23] Serb sentiments of being victimized were suffused with arguments about historic claims to Kosovo, the territory lost to Ottoman forces in the battle of 1389. They expressed sorrow at having had to abandon Orthodox monasteries and churches as well as their homes in Kosovo. Nationalist politicians reinforced this stance by recalling Serbia's humiliation during the First World War and recycling memoirs of 'Golgotha' for a modern Serb audience (see chapter 1).

The break-up of Yugoslavia led to hastily arranged deals, such as when Croats driven out of Vojvodina—a place familiar with forced migration ever since Germans were forced to abandon their homes and businesses at the end of the Second World War—exchanged their homes with Serbs who left Zagreb. The decision to flee had huge emotional and psychological costs, as in the case of a young Kosovar Albanian who joined his family at the behest of the woman he loved and whom he left behind in Pristina: 'I felt the need to scream like a wild animal when you said goodbye', he wrote. These departures left a bitter taste.[24]

Sometimes the destinations chosen by refugees reflected existing economic ties, as when Bosnian Muslim families joined adult male relatives who worked in Slovenia's third largest town, Celje. Struggling to make ends meet, one mother told a visiting researcher why she encouraged her children to learn Slovenian: 'I would like my children to get the most out of the surroundings they live in. Every culture has its good sides and can offer opportunities for learning. I wish that they would

---

[21] Helton, *The Price of Indifference*, 30–77; Barnett, *Empire of Humanity*, 186–91.

[22] UNHCR, *The State of the World's Refugees 2000*, 234; Helton, *The Price of Indifference*, 68.

[23] Natale Losi, Luisa Passerini and Silvia Salvatici (eds), *Archives of Memory: Supporting Traumatized Communities through Narration and Remembrance* (Geneva: IOM, 2001), 89–90.

[24] Losi, Passerini and Salvatici, *Archives of Memory*, 31.

integrate the new patterns with the old Bosnian ones'.[25] But her willingness to embrace hybridity remained a minority view. Usually displacement reinforced feelings of incomprehension, combined with a sense of national victimhood and staunch proclamations of an eventual return. As a Kosovar woman told her interviewer:

> Well, you cannot describe it. It is awful, very hard to be like that. The name can show you, you know, R.E.F.U.G.E.E. is like the worst thing in the world, so it is something that you cannot describe. You don't have any power and you don't have anything but your soul, your body and nothing else. This is very difficult and very hard for everybody. Even for the people who accepted refugees it was very hard, every time you feel like you are not you. So, every day you feel empty, you feel...I mean it's just very hard; without any power, with nothing.

Her only crumb of comfort came from securing a job with an international aid agency in Kosovo.[26]

The conflict in Bosnia enabled a multitude of Muslim NGOs to advance rival claims to intervene on behalf of Bosnian Muslims who were portrayed as victims twice over: as victims of communism and now as the object of secular and Christian meddling. The Red Cross, MSF and other organizations did not escape the accusation of advancing a Western cultural model. Egyptian and Saudi relief agencies worked incessantly in refugee camps in Croatia and Slovenia, with the blessing of UNHCR, distributing food and medicine and providing counselling services. But these efforts went hand in hand with attempts to enable refugees to return to their homes or to move to Muslim countries rather than remain a beleaguered minority. It is unclear how refugees responded to attempts to foster a 'feeling of community' between Bosnian Muslims and the *umma* or community of believers.[27]

Private initiatives, prompted in part by the constant media attention to the conflict, enabled some refugees to seek asylum in the West. But governments were reluctant to make it easy for refugees to enter, and the oft-repeated claims about the large numbers of 'economic migrants' were reminiscent of rhetoric in the late 1950s. The states of former Yugoslavia shouldered most of the burden, helped by external economic assistance that did not always benefit the people for whom it was intended. Repatriation began in earnest following the Dayton Accords, under which all refugees and internally displaced persons were entitled to return and reclaim their homes. International relief organizations arranged 'go and see visits' to help refugees decide if they wished to return permanently. Many displaced people favoured repatriation in principle—elderly refugees had no wish to die and be buried in a foreign country—but they would only consider returning if there were stable political and social conditions, meaning not just access to jobs and housing

---

[25] Natalja Vrečer, 'The Lost Way of Life: the Experience of Refugee Children in Celje from 1992–1994', in Renata Kirin and Maja Povrzanović (eds), *War, Exile, Everyday Life: Cultural Perspectives* (Zagreb: Institute of Ethnology, 1996), 133–46.
[26] Losi, Passerini and Salvatici, *Archives of Memory*, 70.
[27] Benthall and Bellion-Jourdan, *The Charitable Crescent*, 140–3.

but a more secure framework of government and the prospect of not being victimized. Although thousands opted to remain in Western Europe, more than a million people displaced by the war in Bosnia-Herzegovina decided to go back, half of them to areas where they remained ethnically a minority.

Repatriation was beset by enormous difficulties including having to cope with damage to housing, infrastructure and poor provision of education and healthcare. Simply finding work posed problems. One Bosniak (Bosnian Muslim) family returned to Banja Luka hoping that peace would enable them to recover a way of life that meant they did not have to lock their door at night, but this prospect seemed a long way off. Others reclaimed their houses but sub-let them in order to maintain a kind of 'transnational' existence, as did Bosniaks who fled to Croatia and opted to live there long after the war was over. The important consideration was to keep one's options open, although this was not always possible. Serbs who fled Croatia during the war in 1991–95 faced an uphill struggle to return, not least because the government of Franjo Tudman maintained that Croats should be given priority in the allocation of scarce resources—this being the man who proclaimed: 'We have established a state and now we will decide who are its citizens'. Most Serb refugees settled in Serbia or else remained in a kind of limbo. In Kosovo, where repatriation took place within a matter of months in 1999–2000, the challenges were equally daunting given the lack of a functioning civil administration and the ever-present dangers from landmines.[28]

Some of the difficulties were negotiated imaginatively. The self-styled 'Community of Displaced and Exiled Croats from Vojvodina' required refugees who arrived in Zagreb in 1991 and 1992 to complete a questionnaire before being allowed to join. This had important consequences: 'the brevity and stiffness of the forms have a powerful psychological effect, because it channelled strong emotions and helped the exiles to accept the fact that they were not alone in this experience and that their departure had been inevitable'.[29] The documentation provided for an amalgamation of experience, underpinning a 'community' of displacement. But the process of return posed considerable challenges. The old state no longer existed, and basic infrastructure had been damaged. Refugees were expected to return to a place about which they expressed considerable ambivalence. Returnees were often portrayed as having had an easy time of it in Western Europe, as if having spent several years as a refugee amounted to a luxury compared to the experiences of those who were forced to endure the battle for Sarajevo. Those who remained behind called them *pobjeglice*, people who had fled in order to save their skins and implying a degree of cowardice; they reserved the term *izbeglice* for 'real refugees'. In these

---

[28] Helton, *The Price of Indifference*, 35–50; Anders Stefansson, 'Homes in the Making: Property Restitution, Refugee Return and Senses of Belonging in a Post-war Bosnian Town' *International Migration*, 44, no.3 (2006), 115–37; Marita Eastmond, 'Transnational Returns and Reconstruction in Post-war Bosnia and Herzegovina' *International Migration*, 44, no.3 (2006), 141–66; Ellen Oxfeld and Lynellyn D. Long, 'Introduction: an Ethnography of Return', in Oxfeld and Long (eds), *Coming Home*, 9. For Kosovo, see UNHCR, *State of the World's Refugees 2000*, 241–2.

[29] Nives Ritig-Beljak, 'Croatian Exiles from Vojvodina: between War Memories and War Experience', in Kirin and Povrzanoviĉ (eds), *War, Exile, Everyday Life*, 173–88, at 181.

circumstances, the best (and most charitable thing) one could say, as did Alma who repatriated from Germany, was that 'we have all changed'.[30]

POST-SOVIET MEMORIES AND COMMEMORATION

The dissolution of the Soviet Union made it possible to publicize memories of deportation and resettlement, in ways that would have been inconceivable before 1991. Children could travel to the place of their parents' birth and see for themselves what they had only been told about. Ideas about 'homeland', return and restitution emerged as central issues in post-Soviet life. This is seen most clearly in relation to the Crimean Tatars, who built a thriving Islamic civilization during the Crimean Khanate, only to find it threatened following the annexation of the Crimea to the Russian Empire in 1783. Their presence had tragic consequences in the Soviet 1930s, when the Stalinist state lashed out at national minorities that were thought to be in league with co-ethnics abroad. On 18 May 1944 Stalin ordered the deportation of the Tatars to the Urals and to Central Asia, accusing them of 'treason', although Crimean Tatars were prominent in Soviet partisan detachments. Around 191,000 individuals of all ages—many able-bodied men were at the front, serving the Soviet cause—were given just a few hours' notice to leave their homes on what they came to call this 'black day' (*kara gün*). They were herded on to cattle trucks. Stalin's henchmen violated Islamic traditions, for example by preventing the proper burial of Tatars who died en route, and obliterated Tatar place names, insisting on incongruous new designations such as 'Pretty' and 'Happy'. Mosques were turned into cinemas and storage depots. The Crimean Tatar artist Rustem Eminov, who was born in Tashkent in 1950, depicted this painful episode in a series of paintings: 'I didn't see this, but I *imagined* it within myself from the remembrances of my mother'. In the post-Stalin era, conditions for the Crimean Tatars improved somewhat, and in 1967 the Supreme Soviet of the USSR annulled the charge of treason. But the Soviet government opposed their attempts to return to Crimea, on the grounds that they enjoyed full rights of citizenship in Central Asia, to which the Crimean Tatar leadership retorted that they could trace their ancestry in Crimea to the time of the ancient Scythians, and that Crimea was the 'homeland'.[31]

These painful episodes of communist-era displacement could now be publicly aired and commemorated. The political and cultural consequences were immense. Stories of deportation under Stalin painted a graphic picture of personal and group deprivation. Edward Guzovskii, an elderly Polish man deported in 1935 from the Soviet western borderlands to Kazakhstan, recalled that in Ukraine, 'everything

[30] Anders Stefansson, 'Sarajevo Suffering: Homecoming and the Hierarchy of Homeland Hardship', in Fran Markowitz and Anders H. Stefansson (eds), *Homecomings: Unsettling Paths of Return* (Lanham: Rowman and Littlefield, 2004), 54–75, at 64.

[31] Greta Lynn Uehling, *Beyond Memory: the Crimean Tatars' Deportation and Return* (Palgrave, 2004), 128, 137.

was wonderful, there were peonies, daffodils, chestnuts to pick. I remember sticking my hand deep into my grandfather's beehive and eating the honey by the fistful'. Although he managed to build a Ukrainian-style cottage on the Kazakh steppe and to become the head of a local school, what remains most vivid was the rupture of displacement: '[W]e were given a few hours to pack our things, we travelled a week through Donetsk then Voroshilovgrad and then further until the train stopped, they unloaded us and brought us to a bathhouse. It was something horrible: dirt, steam, nose, people running about overhead. I didn't know whether they were people or demons'.[32]

Many of those like Guzovskii who were deported to Kazakhstan between 1935 and 1941 made their way to Western Europe via the Middle East when the Soviet Union joined the alliance against Hitler. Some of them spent years in isolated settlements in East Africa. Others remained behind. When Kazakhstan became independent its new president expressed the hope that Slavs would depart to their 'motherland'. In post-communist Poland nationalists described exiled families as the 'lost sheep of the Polish nation' (not unlike their counterparts during the First World War—see chapter 1), whose culture had been undermined by Russification. Teachers and social workers were duly despatched to Kazakhstan to promote the Polish language. But this 'return' to Poland was fraught with difficulties, and only 300 out of an estimated 100,000 people of Polish descent in Kazakhstan were accepted by the Polish government during the 1990s: 'They tell us [said one informant] that if you aren't from the Second Republic you are not a Pole'. Having been forced from their homes for spurious political reasons, exiled Poles now faced the prospect of being regarded not as a lost flock but as the black sheep of a post-communist state. There was nothing straightforward about the decision to leave or the decision to stay: ethnic Greek survivors of the Stalinist deportations expressed sadness at the departure of families for Greece, and lamented that 'we are like the Etruscans here, we will soon disappear and no one will know that we have ever lived in Central Asia'.[33]

With the collapse of communism, stories surfaced in the public media not only of the brutality of the deportation and the ordeal of resettlement but of medical experiments and an official campaign of 'extermination'. Crimean Tatar farmers had to take jobs in factories and coal mines in Tashkent and Samarkand. Relations with the local population who shared their Islamic (Sunni) faith appear to have been reasonably good, unlike those with officials in the 'special settlements' where deportees were obliged to live. More importantly, exiled Crimean Tatars managed to sustain a collective national identity. Their knowledge of the Russian language also enabled some of them to get ahead. But the constraints were obvious. Under Soviet rule discussion about the pain of deportation took place largely within a family setting where discretion could be more or less assured; subsequently, the recollections of parents and grandparents helped to shape the cultural framework

---

[32] Brown, *A Biography of No Place*, 142–3.
[33] Eftihia Voutira, 'Post-Soviet Diaspora Politics: the Case of the Soviet Greeks' *JMGS*, 24, no.2 (2006), 379–414, at 386; Brown, *A Biography of No Place*, 232–3.

of the second- and third-generation, as in the case of Eminov. A visiting journalist who reported on the fiftieth anniversary of the deportation was impressed to be told that 'most children say "mama" or "papa" as their first word; our children said "Krym" [the Russian word for Crimea]'. Lilia Bujurova, the acclaimed Crimean Tatar poet, put her feelings into words: 'Don't spare me, don't leave anything out'.[34]

Beyond the discursive realm there were other challenges to confront following the end of the Soviet state. Around 250,000 deportees and their descendants eventually returned to Ukraine. But repatriation posed material difficulties, as it did in former Yugoslavia. Returning Tatars either squatted on vacant land or conducted frustrating and often distressing negotiations with competing (non-Tatar) claimants and the city authorities. Some family members relocated to Ukraine while others decided to remain in Central Asia where housing conditions were more tolerable. Debates within the family about relocation exposed complex emotions. It was perfectly possible for Crimean Tatars to conceive of the Crimean 'homeland' (the *vatan* or *rodina* that evoked sun, water and fruits) and Uzbekistan in broadly positive terms without any contradiction. All the same a tension manifested itself between the nationalist rhetoric of return and a frequently expressed wish to remain in Uzbekistan. As Greta Uehling puts it, 'images of flying back collided with images of houses and homes which cannot be put on airplanes'. A more extreme emotional viewpoint meant feeling 'at home' in neither place. Legal difficulties compounded the difficulty. Thousands of Crimean Tatars were stateless. In 1999 the Ukrainian government insisted that those who resettled in Ukraine had to renounce their Uzbek citizenship. But unlike the indigenous Russian population they failed to establish an autonomous republic or to have their 'national assembly' (*Mejlis*) recognized officially. Caught, so to speak, in the midst of an intense Russian-Ukrainian rivalry, Crimean Tatars insisted on the right to be recognized as indigenous inhabitants of Crimea.[35]

Memories of the forced re-settlement of Chechens and Ingushetians in Siberia and Central Asia during the Second World War likewise sustained feelings of victimization and contributed to the creation of a 'mythico-history'. In Chechnya, resistance to Russian rule during the 1990s and beyond was strengthened by a deliberately cultivated consciousness among Chechens of Russia's occupation of their land during the nineteenth century and of the Stalin-era deportation in February 1944, whose sixtieth anniversary was marked by the European parliament's decision to recognize this as a 'genocide'. Heroic figures such as Imam Shamil (1797–1871) inspired the Chechen resistance.[36] History mattered to the refugees; it was also contested by Russian nationalists who were convinced that Chechens had behaved in traitorous fashion. On the other hand, for reasons that remain obscure, Meskhetian Turks, who also suffered under Stalin, expressed much less anger.

---

[34] From her poem, 'Govori' ('Speak'), translated from the Russian in Brian Glyn Williams, *The Crimean Tatars: the Diaspora Experience and the Forging of a Nation* (Leiden: Brill, 2001), 415, 416.

[35] Uehling, *Beyond Memory*, 115.

[36] Brian Glyn Williams, 'Commemorating "the Deportation" in Post-Soviet Chechnya: the Role of Memorialisation and Collective Memory in the 1994–96 and 1999–2000 Russo-Chechen Wars' *History and Memory*, 12, no.1 (2000), 101–34.

With the demise of the USSR diaspora communities could also travel to the 'homeland' that had hitherto only been accessible in photographs and the stories told by older family members. The descendants of Circassian refugees who settled in Syria, Jordan and Turkey in the late nineteenth century have made 'return' visits.[37] True, a handful of Armenians visited 'Hayastan'—their name for Soviet Armenia—but mass 'diaspora tourism' did not begin until the 1990s, by which time Armenians had begun to head in the opposite direction to settle in North America. Ukrainians, Lithuanians, Latvians and Estonians all participated in organized tours or made private journeys to the land where their parents or grandparents were born, and began to turn the diaries they inherited and the photographs they took into commemorative websites. Other cultural practices echoed those embarked upon by displaced populations elsewhere, such as compiling memorial books, whereby Armenians commemorated the 'lost villages' that are now situated in Turkey. This was just one element of a wide-ranging diaspora activity: for example, the Armenian Relief Society, formed in 1910 by American-Armenians, continues to 'serve the social and educational needs of Armenian communities everywhere'.[38] The diaspora also mobilized at times of crisis, for instance establishing a Fund for Armenian Relief in the aftermath of the devastating earthquake in Armenia in 1988. A key element throughout has been frequent references to the genocide and the fate of survivors.

Elsewhere, too, new political realities encouraged and facilitated a complex confrontation with past experience, previously suppressed or repressed, which often reinforced feelings of individual and collective suffering that contributed in turn to the validation of nationalist claims and the exclusion of other memories. In the Baltic States, well-resourced museums chronicle the deportation experience and describe the Soviet 'occupation' as 'genocide'. These projects went hand in hand with the removal of memorials that do not correspond to the nationalist project. Croats and Serbs manifested radically different understandings of the Second World War, which the former recalled as a time when local Serbs massacred Croat partisans towards the end of the war, while Serbs recollected the murders committed by members of the paramilitary Croatian Ustaša in 1941.[39] (Croat spokesmen also complained about prolonged discrimination under communism.) Wartime upheaval and displacement were connected to strong feelings of loss, 'damage' and victimization. In this respect what Croatian villagers forgot or downplayed—such as the co-existence that manifested itself in inter-marriage or just good neighbourliness—is as significant as what they recollected.

When Latvia achieved independence in 1991 the psychologist Vieda Skultans found that she could carry out research in the country she left as a young baby. Skultans wanted to study the meanings attributed by Soviet-trained doctors and

---

[37] Chatty, *Displacement and Dispossession*, 124, points out that they portray themselves as the progeny of noble-born migrants, in contrast to the supposedly poor and enslaved Circassians who remained in the Caucasus.

[38] <http://www.ars1910.org/>.

[39] The Ustaša movement was founded in 1934 as a Croatian attempt to counter Serb domination of Yugoslavia.

patients to 'neurasthenia' or nervous exhaustion, but she soon found herself engaging with representations of Latvia's past and the history of Latvians who were deported to Siberia or Central Asia during the Second World War and in the final months of Stalin's rule. Drawing upon a series of interviews with around 30 Latvian informants, who either had direct experience of deportation or had otherwise been closely affected by forced migration, Skultans distinguished 'illness narratives' from other kinds of account. An illness narrative conveyed the erosion of meaning, whereas other narratives suggested a capacity 'to retrieve meaning and purpose under the most inauspicious circumstances'. She argued that 'many people with a terrible past do manage to author lives which give a sense of satisfaction and completeness. Those who fail in this enterprise complain not only of the painfulness of past experience but also of the incoherence of their life stories. They have failed twice over, both as agents and as authors'.[40]

Although many of her informants gave vent to a belief that their life lacked coherence, former deportees who embraced the idea of pilgrimage and adventure were better able to adjust to changing circumstances. Personal torment coexisted with a reflective attitude that enabled each of them to evaluate the past and establish a grasp of agency and of a meaningful life. One informant, Solveiga (b.1921), fashioned a dramatic narrative of being deported to Siberia as a 20-year old, her return to Riga and her second period of exile; she recounted a life of stories of misfortune, exploits, 'magical coincidences' and the kindness of strangers.[41] Among other Latvian exiles, particularly those in the diaspora that swelled in size when DPs opted to remain in the West after 1945 in conditions of privation, analogous torments described in the Bible (Israelites in the wilderness) or evoked in Latvian folk tales and songs, afforded a degree of comfort, and have parallels with BenEzer's therapeutic work with Ethiopian Jews who made the difficult journey to Israel (see chapter 8). Skultans's rich ethnography also sheds light on ideas of exile and homecoming. Memories of life in Siberia were bound up with a vast and desolate wintry landscape, which contrasted starkly with the fertile, compact and ordered homeland. Lidija (b.1922) recalled how the water in Lielupe smelled of yellow water lilies: '[W]hen we went barefoot, the meadow flowers clung to our legs, the pollen, flower petals. It was beautiful'.[42] But homecoming proved no less painful than exile. Late Soviet Latvia, with its corrupt officials and declining economy, did not correspond to the pastoral images they kept in mind during the long years of exile. Deportees described their disappointing and painful encounters with Latvians when they returned many years later. Locals accused them of having 'deserved' their punishment ('all the deportees should have been shot'). Yet Latvia remained, for better or worse, 'home'.

Vivid eyewitness accounts testified to the repercussions of violence in former Yugoslavia. Journalist James Dalrymple reported from the border between Kosovo and Macedonia in terms that drew upon images of biblical torment to 'paint a picture' in which the human figure was effaced:

---

[40] Vieda Skultans, *The Testimony of Lives: Memory in Post-Soviet Latvia* (Routledge, 1997), xii.
[41] Skultans, *The Testimony of Lives*, 59–66.   [42] Skultans, *The Testimony of Lives*, 149.

Through the river mist at dawn it looked like an oil painting of Hell, with the added dimensions of smell and sound. The colours came from the clothing of the densely packed human flotsam that filled the wide valley as far as the eye could see. As the rising sun of Good Friday started to reveal this awesome panorama, the image of Golgotha, the hill at Calvary, came easily to mind.[43]

Perhaps he was unaware of the use of Golgotha by eyewitnesses of the Serbian refugee exodus during the First World War. These accounts have been amplified by the testimony contributed by displaced women who survived the onslaught in Bosnia. They paint a graphic picture of how neighbour turned on neighbour, how mothers had to watch the murder of their children, and how Bosnian Muslim survivors (sometimes aided by sympathetic Serbs) hid in the forest for days or weeks at a time. Mixed in with descriptions of these painful scenes are characterizations of the peaceful existence that refugees had to renounce. Thus refugees spoke of having built their own homes and planted fields with crops that gave a good yield. Now, however, they describe a never-ending journey in search of security: one refugee, Ćamka, fled to Slovenia: '[W]e walked a long way on foot, but you've reached some kind of freedom, so you keep on walking'.[44]

Other personal testimony reveals something of the 'memory work' associated with refugeedom. Young Croat children were encouraged to write short accounts of the circumstances surrounding their abrupt departure from their homes. Not surprisingly their stories are informed by images of violence, particularly where close family members were concerned, and by a heroic insistence that they will eventually reclaim their homes. Particularly interesting is the way in which personal accounts corresponded to 'official' discourse and were infused with historic grievances, as in the case of Serbian memories of displacement that connected present suffering to the disasters during the First World War. Material objects also had the capacity to trigger powerful recollections of displacement. Hajrija, a Muslim refugee from Donji Vakuf in Bosnia-Herzegovina who had settled in Islamabad, described her anxiety that her children would forget the town where they were born:

> My husband made a model of our town to keep the memory alive... It takes a long time to build a town because it isn't easy to find the right materials here [in Pakistan]. We had to have red roofs on the houses and lots of green for the trees. The green was particularly hard to find. My husband was very determined. He looked and looked and finally we found some branches that we could cut to look like small trees. We must tend the model all the time because the green turns yellow. My husband made the clock tower separately, so it could sit alone above the town, just like at home.

The inscription on this object read: 'These are our houses, on the land inhabited by our forefathers. We are going back there no matter when and in such a way that we'll be so powerful that no one will be able to force us to leave our land again'.

---

[43] *The Independent*, 3 April 1999.
[44] Janja Beč, *The Shattering of the Soul* (Belgrade: Helsinki Committee for Human Rights in Serbia, 1997), 59.

This resolution echoes similar expressions of intent on the part of Greek Cypriot and Palestinian refugees, while the architectural form corresponds to attempts to recreate in books and films towns in Bosnia that were destroyed in the early 1990s. One such memorial book commemorates the Bosnian Muslim town of Foca-on-Drina whose mosque was dynamited and turned into a car park.[45]

Post-communist political turbulence made it possible to address other episodes of state-induced population displacement. Pursuing these opportunities was neither straightforward nor benign. One neglected post-war situation deserves mention, because it connects with the geopolitics of territorial and social reconstruction, and with contested memories of displacement. It concerns the Julian Marches located between Italy and Slovenia. German troops occupied Italy following its withdrawal from the Axis in 1943, and Italy's capitulation simultaneously provided an opportunity for communist partisans to advance in the entire region. Between 1943 and 1954, when the Allies' regional administration finally came to an end and Tito's Yugoslavia was granted control of part of Istria, a total of 300,000 Italians and 50,000 Slavs fled westwards. Their purpose was to evade the retribution meted out by partisans who threw their fascist opponents—the precise numbers of those judged and punished for being so designated are uncertain—into the numerous karst pits (*foibe*) that are a feature of the Istrian landscape.[46]

The Italians who left Istria after 1945 were officially classified as refugees (*profughi*). They were sent to makeshift accommodation, including former concentration camps, and thence to transit camps before eventually settling in government-built apartments in Trieste or in more distant locations in Italy and even abroad. Luckier ones found lodgings with friends or relatives. Many refugees were still living in camps a decade or more after their displacement. As in other similar situations, life in the camp created a kaleidoscope of experience. Older men and women faced great difficulties as it dawned on them that they would not see their homes again. Among younger refugees in particular, the camp became a place of romance and liberation, where a new world 'opened up', partly by exposing them to Italians from former colonies in Ethiopia, Libya, and the Dodecanese. One woman recalled how 'even the tragedy of the war was for me a curious adventure: bombings, fires, alarms, and flights to the shelter seemed undecipherable episodes that didn't endanger me but rather made my life more interesting'.[47]

A study prepared prior to the collapse of communism found that survivors were reluctant to speak about these events, but a much clearer picture now emerges of how they recollected and represented their experiences. Identifying themselves as exiles (*esuli*), the Istrian refugees told one another stories and poems, and devised commemorative practices that are familiar from other refugee situations, for example, setting up shrines in their new home to honour departed souls or displaying

---

[45] By 1997 Hajrija had moved to Utica, New York, leaving the model town behind. Julie Mertus (ed.), *The Suitcase: Refugee Voices from Bosnia and Croatia* (Berkeley: University of California Press, 1997), 90–1; Slyomovics, *Object of Memory*, 2.

[46] Glenda Sluga, *The Problem of Trieste and the Italo-Yugoslav Border: Difference, Identity, and Sovereignty in Twentieth-century Europe* (Albany: SUNY Press, 2001).

[47] Ballinger, *History in Exile*, 201.

photographs of abandoned villages. Interviews with the children of *esuli* confirm the significance of the lost landscape: one second-generation refugee remembered that his father bought a pair of binoculars to enable him to see the oak tree marking the entrance to the village he had been forced to abandon. Their behaviour reflected a belief that they were victims and martyrs, something that their failure to gain sympathy for their cause in Italy did nothing to diminish. Visual imagery highlighted suffering as 'Calvary' and exodus from 'paradise lost'. Other images portrayed Istria as a mutilated female: a cartoon by *esuli* artist Gigi Vidris represented 'the end of Istria' in the shape of a murdered woman who is overlooked by a skeleton emerging from the *foibe* pointing a bony finger of accusation at the Allies: a highly racialized figure of a Yugoslav partisan is suitably startled and scuttles away. Exiles reinforced the message by asserting that they maintained a 'pure' Italian identity, such that they were made to feel 'strangers in our own home'.[48]

Some *esuli* found meaning in various political activities, including a readiness to entertain irredentist claims on the territory they had abandoned to Yugoslavia. Claims for compensation were still being debated in the 1980s. Whether conservative, liberal or socialist in outlook, the *esuli* were frequently confronted with the charge that all exiles were 'fascists'. These experiences informed their relationship to the past and thus their subsequent representations of displacement. In the light of recent political changes—above all, the collapse of Yugoslavia—the *esuli* in particular portrayed themselves as victims of 'ethnic cleansing'; this proposition, embellished by the terrible stories of the *foibe*, was relentlessly affirmed by exile associations. Among the *esuli* at large, the narrative of 'submersion' occupied a particular significance. It operated on two levels: as an allusion to hidden crimes ('Slav treachery') that needed to be uncovered, and as a way of drawing attention to the mass graves that were the last resting place of Italian victims of (Slovene) partisan violence in the latter stages of the Second World War. Here too, being displaced in Europe implied in the late twentieth century an entitlement to recognition and an opportunity to publicize stories that were either little known or kept to oneself.[49]

Although several hundred thousand Italians fled from the advancing communist forces, others stayed put out of political sympathy with anti-Fascist partisans. Italians who remained in Istria after 1943—and who became known as *rimasti*—articulated feelings of suffering born of persecution during the Fascist era, particularly for those who had espoused progressive politics in the region's villages and towns. Their ethnic origin exposed them to taunts by local Croats and Slovenes that they were 'fascist'. Some were able to participate in cultural events legitimized by the communist state whose officials more or less tolerated the Italian minority in Istria, and others joined communist organizations in order to affirm their political loyalty. But a more complex political and cultural process was also at work. Rejecting the claims of *esuli* that they were 'contaminated' by virtue of their association with the Slovenes and Croats in Yugoslavia—'there are no Italians left in

---

[48] Ballinger, *History in Exile*, 198.   [49] Ballinger, *History in Exile*, 145–67.

Istria', as one exile put it—the *rimasti* expressed pride in the affirmation of a mixed Latin-Slav identity.[50] Although most did not learn to speak Serbo-Croat, they did inter-marry across the ethnic divide. In response to accusations of being indelibly tainted by communism, the Istrian *rimasti* subsequently claimed rather to have been marginalized in Tito's Yugoslavia, thereby enabling them to portray themselves as victims. One element of this self-ascription is an 'interior' displacement in the new Slovenia. This condition includes feelings of loss at the decline of towns such as 'Red Rovigno' (which was a thorn in Mussolini's side, and which was assigned to Yugoslavia in 1947) and a broader lament at being surrounded by the 'ruins' of a once viable community that included an Italian cultural component.

The collapse of Yugoslavia and the end of the Cold War also affected public debate in Greece and Macedonia, and further afield, in relation to the history of the thousands of children who were 'evacuated' from Greece during the civil war and sent to homes in Eastern Europe. This episode was and remains an issue over which opinions are deeply divided. In 1950 the Greek government appealed to the UN to recognize that the evacuation of children by the Greek Communist Party in 1948 amounted to 'hostage taking by Slavo-communists'. Queen Frederica described this as 'genocide'; so, too, did the voluble right-wing diaspora organization of Greek Macedonians, the Pan-Macedonian Association Inc. For its part, the left-wing League for Democracy in Greece, a short-lived body based in London, argued that the evacuation offered Greek and Macedonian children the possibility of a life of 'peace and prosperity'. The Communist Party had undertaken 'a vast humanitarian enterprise'.[51]

Enduring and irreconcilable divisions exposed by the evacuation exposed the complex meanings of 'home' and 'homeland'. Whether these children returned to Greece in the late 1950s (as some did) or remained in the host country, they expressed ambivalent feelings towards the country of their birth. Having spent their formative years in Hungary, East Germany, Yugoslavia and other locations, where they learned a new language and received an education, they discovered a 'second homeland'. The children who returned faced discrimination at the hands of the right-wing government. Returning to Greece exposed complex emotions, as in the case of Stefanos Gikas (a pseudonym) who was born in the early 1940s and evacuated to Budapest before returning to Greece in 1958. He recalls an early childhood not in a society rent by political factions but in an impoverished village. When he returned ('I wanted to go back to Greece, and yet at the same time I didn't'), Gikas was dismayed by the continuing poverty—'all they had was milk'. He was put on a boat to the island of Leros where 'we didn't learn as much. Life in Eastern Europe was better, we were freer then'.[52] Things did not improve when he went back to

---

[50] Ballinger, *History in Exile*, 13.

[51] Danforth and Van Boeschoten, *Children of the Greek Civil War*, 39–40, 268.

[52] The island of Leros was returned to Greece after the Second World War, having previously been under Italian administration. In the 1960s the Greek Colonels used it as a dumping ground for political opponents.

Athens, until he realized that 'a man hires five people, they work, and he earns the most money'. Capitalism became his passport to integration in Greece.[53]

For decades much of this story was kept under wraps, because the governments of Greece and Yugoslavia sought to maintain a reasonable working relationship. In the late twentieth century this began to change. In 1988, shortly before the dissolution of Yugoslavia, the Toronto-based Association of Refugee Children from the Aegean Macedonia organized a reunion for the evacuees in Skopje. The reunion was an occasion for proclamations about the 'exodus' of children who had—as it was said—been rescued from their 'persecution' at the hands of Greek right-wingers. Their suffering during this 'Golgotha' was connected to ideas about the fragile status of Macedonia and the potential for its 'liberation'. Ten years later, when Macedonia had become independent, the country's president spoke of the part played by the evacuation in protecting Macedonia from 'obliteration'. His appropriation of their experience, which he rolled up in the emotionally charged language of 'ethnic cleansing', deliberately overlooked the fact that ethnic Greek children had also been evacuated. Meanwhile, conservative figures continued to trumpet in wholly partial terms the violence inflicted by communist partisans during the Civil War.[54] These politically divisive statements contrast with the dignified stance taken by many of the survivors who did not forget what happened to them but who were willing to be reconciled and who abjured the politicians' divisive rhetoric.

CYPRUS: HOPES ABRIDGED

Amidst these dramatic stories of displacement it is salutary to be reminded that one refugee crisis in Europe has festered for decades without any sign of being settled. Bitterness between the Greek and Turkish communities in Cyprus derived in part from the legacy of conflict on the mainland earlier in the century (see chapter 2). Although this did not stop neighbourly relations from being forged between the two communities on Cyprus, the island was by no means an undisturbed idyll: for example, in 1964 Turkish Cypriots fled after being targeted by their Greek neighbours. Nonetheless, when Turkish troops invaded Cyprus 10 years later the shock was palpable. Around 200,000 Greek Cypriots (two-fifths of the total population) and 50,000 Turkish Cypriots fled their homes in search of sanctuary. Many left within 24 hours of being confronted by the occupation and found temporary shelter with relatives or in makeshift accommodation in zones newly demarcated by the United Nations, expecting to return to their own homes before long. One refugee described how his hasty and surreptitious departure, and the need to grab what belongings he could, made him feel 'as if we were thieving from our own houses', just as Palestinians recalled their experiences in 1948.[55]

---

[53] Danforth and Van Boeschoten, *Children of the Greek Civil War*, 137–46, 194.
[54] Danforth and Van Boeschoten, *Children of the Greek Civil War*, 252–8, 270–6.
[55] Peter Loizos, *The Heart Grown Bitter: a Chronicle of Cypriot War Refugees* (Cambridge: Cambridge University Press, 1981), 105; Peter Loizos, *Iron in the Soul: Displacement, Livelihood and Health in Cyprus* (Oxford: Berghahn, 2008), 140.

The crisis was largely contained within Cyprus itself, although the UN monitored the so-called 'green line' between the two halves of the island. According to international law those who fled were classed as internally displaced persons. Nevertheless, UNHCR took on the task of coordinating emergency assistance. The label of refugee quickly stuck, but Greek Cypriots resented it, because this implied that they were unlikely to be able to return in the near future to what they termed the 'occupied areas' (*ta katexomena*).[56] Refugees also rejected the label on the grounds that it implied a loss of independence, although this did not stop them creating a 'Refugee Committee' to defend their interests. Not all refugees were equally disadvantaged, because some of them owned second homes on the island. Some enterprising refugees traded on their status and established new businesses which they named 'Refugee Kebabs' and 'Refugee Taxis', significantly terms that connoted instant gratification rather than a kind of long-term investment in exile. Villagers—the overwhelming majority—found the move to town hugely disconcerting. It did not help that they met with barely disguised contempt from locals. One refugee recalled that 'You could rarely see discrimination [but] there were people who used to say to their children "eat your food or else the refugee will come and eat it", or pointed their finger at us saying "these are refugees"'. It helped to be able to share sensory pleasures with fellow villagers such as memories of smells from the local bakery and the taste of fruit from the orchards they abandoned.[57]

In response to refugees' demands, the government set aside homes and land abandoned by Turkish Cypriots in order to make affordable public housing available to the newcomers from the North. This programme was underpinned by the provision of $20 million of international aid. Greek Cypriot refugees responded to the catastrophe by encouraging their children to receive an education, drawing either upon government loans or other resources. The authorities in the Greek-administered zone treated the refugees as a resource rather than as a burden: the Orthodox Church invested in factories that recruited refugee workers, and farmers were able to obtain land and thereby prevent their skills from going rusty. Other refugees worked in the booming construction industry or the growing tourist sector. Their children were highly motivated and able to make their way in the world. The outcome had parallels with Germany and South Korea in the 1950s, where an economic 'miracle' contributed to the integration of refugees.[58]

Cypriot history suggests the need to take account of some of the broader implications of population displacement in relation to refugees' adaptability and resilience. While wealthier refugees were able to build homes on land set aside by the government of Cyprus, others were provided with terraced houses on purpose-built estates (*synikismos*). Refugees who lived on these estates lamented the destruction of hitherto

---

[56] Rebecca Bryant, 'Partitions of Memory: Wounds and Witnessing in Cyprus' *CSSH*, 54, no.2 (2012), 332–60.

[57] From an interview with Markos M. aged 72, conducted in July 2011 by Andrea Papaioannou, cited with permission.

[58] Loizos, *Iron in the Soul*, 41–51; Roger Zetter, 'Labelling Refugees: Forming and Transforming a Bureaucratic Identity' *JRS*, 4, no.1 (1991), 39–62.

thriving communities, and they established new relationships only with difficulty. Refugees from the same village managed to stay in touch with one another to the extent of inviting former neighbours to family weddings and funerals. Complaints were heard that these assistance programmes subordinated refugees to a state-led project of development, and that providing refugees with a 'permanent' place to live was a decidedly mixed blessing. Although the state enabled refugees to adjust to the circumstances of displacement, and although economic growth made a difference, refugees' own self-help measures enabled them to come to terms with protracted exile. Religious leaders stressed that they were not alone and enjoyed spiritual protection. But the past retains its capacity to become like a 'splinter of iron which has been trapped inside the now-healed flesh'.[59]

It has proved difficult to translate ideas of return and restitution into action. The partition of Cyprus turned what refugees believed would be turned a temporary sojourn into a lengthy internal exile. When they spoke of 'no going back', refugees employed the phrase in a dual manner, meaning a determination to see through their journey to a place of safety and their despair at the diminishing likelihood of returning for good to their original village. Notices placed by refugees ('temporarily residing in Limassol') only served to draw attention to the fact that—as among Palestinian, Tibetan and other refugees—desire did not easily translate into repatriation. In 2003 the Turkish Cypriot authorities allowed refugees to make short visits to the north of the island. Half of those who made the journey planned to make further visits. Many came away with a renewed and painful feeling that their homes were near yet so far, as well as with disturbing impressions of buildings and cemeteries that had fallen into disrepair and a clear indication of renamed streets and monuments to Turkish 'martyrs'. Others refused the offer of a visit, regarding it as offensive that they were being asked to show their passports in order to gain admittance. One person eloquently described feeling 'tied like another Odysseus who could not accept this degrading process'.[60]

All refugees, whatever their background and whether Greek or Turkish Cypriot, confronted the material consequences of displacement and potential repatriation. The failure of UN mediation in 2004 reflected Greek Cypriot misgivings about the continued presence of 'Turkish settlers' and a lack of clear provision for the unconditional return of Greek refugees. These feelings of bitterness have been accompanied by a realization that there is unlikely to be an easy resolution to displacement. As a result, refugees have adopted an idealized version of home. At the same time, although the death of a loved one, a newspaper headline about the events of 1974 or another screening of the well-known documentary film, *Attila '74* (Mihalis Kakogiannis, 1974) might trigger painful memories, refugees from both communities showed an impressive capacity to get on with their lives, whether in Cyprus or in the diaspora.[61]

---

[59] Loizos, *Iron in the Soul*, 153–62, 186.

[60] Lisa Dikomitis, 'A Moving Field: Greek Cypriot Refugees Returning "Home"' *Durham Anthropology Journal*, 12, no.1 (2004), 7–20.

[61] Roger Zetter, 'Reconceptualizing the Myth of Return: Continuity and Transition amongst the Greek-Cypriot Refugees of 1974' *JRS*, 12, no.1 (1999), 1–22; Nergis Canefe, 'From Ethnicity to Nationalism: Intricacies of Turkish Cypriot Identity in the Diaspora' *Rethinking History*, 6, no.1 (2002), 57–76.

HIDDEN AND EMERGING HISTORIES

Other sites of displacement disclose important aspects of state practice, attempts to forge 'durable solutions', and refugees' engagement with the past.

Some conflicts have been brought to an end by virtue of outright victory for one faction and defeat for the other. The clearest example in recent history is Sri Lanka. Here the prolonged war between the Sri Lankan army and the Tamil liberation movement (the Liberation Tigers of Tamil Eelam, LTTE) displaced 800,000 people internally from a total population of 20 million. Around 100,000 Tamils fled to India during the 1980s and 1990s, where many of them ended up in make-shift refugee camps. In autumn 1990 Tamil warriors turned on the 60,000-strong Muslim population in the North, accusing them of being 'traitors' and giving them only a few hours to leave. Internally displaced Muslims faced hostility from residents in the western district of Puttalam who complained about competition for business and the 'inappropriate' behaviour of refugee women and children—a reminder that displacement has often been associated with moral laxity on the part of the host population. The defeat of the LTTE in 2009 enabled the government of Sri Lanka to confine 300,000 internally displaced people in the innocuous-sounding Menik Farm and in other camps, where officials 'scrutinised' individual refugees.[62]

The implications of the civil war for the Tamil diaspora have been profound. The anthropologist E. Valentine Daniel argued that the first generation of migrants who arrived in Europe in small numbers belonged to the Tamil elite, but manifested an attachment to the state of Ceylon to which they expected to return with the professional qualifications that would cement their role as leaders. During the 1960s and 1970s, the diaspora grew in size with the arrival of student activists who were affiliated to the Tamil nationalist cause; they argued that differences between Sinhalese and Tamils could not be bridged and unlike the elite Tamils found it impossible to conceive of Sri Lanka as a multi-ethnic polity. A third cohort reached the First World in the 1980s, as refugees whom the elite group in the diaspora regarded as 'riff-raff'. Each group invested the past with different meanings: the elite embraced a unified national history of Ceylon, while the student cohort were transfixed by histories of Tamil chieftains and kings. The third group 'opted out of the project of the nation'. The experience of applying for asylum left them feeling cynical about nations and national laws—the realization of a Tamil nation, if it came to pass, would in their eyes simply consolidate the rule of the professional elite. They pursued the relative security that came from getting jobs in the UK economy, and from feeling that they were part of a large and non-territorialized diaspora, rather than entertaining the prospect of a nation-state they could call their own. The only history that meant anything to them was their recent bruising encounters with British officialdom and the Tamil elite.

---

[62] Oberoi, *Exile and Belonging*, 200–31; Joke Schrijvers, 'Fighters, Victims and Survivors: Constructions of Ethnicity, Gender and Refugeeness among Tamils in Sri Lanka' *JRS*, 12, no.3 (1999), 307–33.

It remains to be seen whether this 'national indifference' is a transitory phenomenon within the diaspora.[63]

Like the Tamil conflict, other situations are largely hidden from the international gaze. In the remote kingdom of Bhutan (home to Tibetan refugees since 1959), the king adopted the Orwellian slogan of 'Gross National Happiness' as its guiding principle in the 1990s. Unfortunately the elements of such happiness were not shared equally. From the 1980s onwards the minority Lotshampa population—most of them descendants of migrants from Nepal—found political and social conditions intolerable when the regime insisted on the need for all subjects to sign an oath of loyalty to the monarch and to subscribe to 'national harmony'. The government justified this stringent programme on the grounds that Bhutan is a small state that cannot afford the 'luxury' of cultural pluralism. Anyone opposing these changes was labelled a 'terrorist'. Those who gave notice of their intention to leave Bhutan had to sign a form stating that they left voluntarily. Around 110,000 refugees settled in camps in South-Eastern Nepal during the 1980s, leaving a small number of Lotshampa in Bhutan.

History illuminates this state of affairs in several respects. From their vantage point in the refugee camps, Lotshampa maintain that their presence in Bhutan dates back as far as the seventeenth century, whereas their Bhutanese counterparts detect no trace of a Nepali presence before 1900. Refugees created a 'mythico-history' in which their forefathers were farmers who taught Bhutanese peasants the value of education and progressive agricultural practices. Their feelings of superiority also derived from a belief that they kept themselves apart from mainstream society. For their part, the Bhutanese affirm the superiority of Buddhist religion and culture. However, in the 1950s the monarchy's drive to modernize Bhutan imposed greater central control of the South. Things took a turn for the worse in 1988–90 when the government conducted a census to classify the population into citizens and aliens. Many Lotshampa lost out as a result, and they continued to suffer throughout the 1990s. This proved the final straw.[64]

CONCLUSIONS

In the new millennium humanitarian personnel engaged in a good deal of soul-searching, drawing attention to difficult issues, including factors such as climate change and food scarcities that threaten to bring about more widespread population displacement, inequities in states' asylum procedures, and the 'shrinking of humanitarian space'. It needs to be said that UNHCR and NGOs have at times contributed to such shrinkage by discouraging field staff from maintaining close contact with refugees on a daily basis. In Kampala, for example, the decision to move

---

[63] E.V. Daniel, 'Suffering Nation and Alienation', in Arthur Kleinman, Veena Das and Margaret Lock (eds), *Social Suffering* (Berkeley: University of California Press, 1997), 309–58.
[64] Michael Hutt, *Unbecoming Citizens: Culture, Nationhood, and the Flight of Refugees from Bhutan* (New Delhi: Oxford University Press, 2005).

its local office to a distant part of the city led refugees to claim that 'UNHCR is just running away'. It was often easier to obtain the views of self-appointed spokesmen rather than solicit the opinions of ordinary refugees.[65] UNHCR has been accused of complicity with governments in hindering outside access to refugee camps and hampering independent research. Other shortcomings and abuses have come to light, such as the sexual exploitation of refugees by relief workers. At the same time, warriors have perpetrated attacks on humanitarian personnel. All this paints a depressing picture of the limits to as well as the limitations of humanitarian intervention. Critical voices including those within the agency itself accuse it not of overweening ambition, but of insufficient room for manoeuvre, unprecedented challenges, and a retreat from its mandate to protect refugees in favour of emergency humanitarian relief.[66]

The modern era affords new possibilities for self-expression that derive from more accessible technologies of communication, as well as manifesting what appears at first sight to be a greater attentiveness to refugee testimony. Yet it is worth asking how far we have come since the 1950s, when the UNHCR can still talk in bland terms of refugee life as 'desperately simple and empty'? The Refugee Communities History Project under the aegis of the Evelyn Oldfield Unit seeks to 'counter misapprehensions' and to 'demonstrate the contribution that refugees have made to London', but the focus on 'contribution' inevitably plays down or even discards as unimportant the life they lived hitherto. If history matters, we need to take account of the complexity of these biographies and, in Doreen Massey's words, 'the conjunction of many histories and many spaces'.[67]

What does contemporary displacement imply for refugees? Has the multiplication of resources—crucial in arguments about the efflorescence of 'new wars'—improved things by affording refugees greater access to communication technologies? If so, what uses have they made of these means to advance their claims to recognition and to defend their interests? Elites regularly drew upon ideas of historic catastrophe to justify repatriation and/or restitution, whereas non-elite voices struggled to be heard, sometimes for very practical reasons. Refugees have begun to create websites devoted to the commemoration of displacement. But access to new technologies or even basic means of communication is neither guaranteed nor equally distributed. A female refugee from Ethiopia disclosed that, 'I associate writing with giving good news. I had nothing good to say about the misery of our life. Besides we did not have money to buy stamps', neatly

---

[65] Harrell-Bond and Voutira, 'Barriers to Access'; Kristin Sandvik 'Negotiating the Humanitarian Past: History, Memory, and Unstable Cityscapes in Kampala, Uganda' *RSQ*, 31, no.1 (2012), 108–22, at 116.

[66] Jeff Crisp, 'Why Do We Know so Little About Refugees? How Can We Learn More?' *FMR*, 18 (2003), 55; Alexander Betts, Gil Loescher and James Milner, *UNHCR: the Politics and Practice of Refugee Protection into the Twenty-first Century* (Routledge, 2011); *The State of the World's Refugees 2012* (Geneva: UNHCR, 2012).

[67] <http://www.evelynoldfield.co.uk/rchp/index.shtml>; Doreen Massey, 'Places and their Pasts' *History Workshop Journal*, 39 (1995), 182–92; Nyers, *Rethinking Refugees*, 21.

encapsulating emotional and practical difficulties in creating and disseminating a record of displacement.[68]

The collapse of Soviet communism enabled survivors of Stalin-era deportations and their descendants to visit and sometimes to return to their former homes. Others chose not to exercise this option, and not everyone had the requisite resources. Families were once more broken up when younger members opted to emigrate whilst elderly parents stayed behind. The end of the Cold War opened up the possibility not only of migration but also of commemorating past displacement and engaging with the meaning of 'homeland'. This was not an unmixed blessing. Altered political realities in Eastern Europe brought submerged stories to the surface, albeit in ways that exacerbated rather than lessened political tensions; supposedly ancient antagonisms might be invoked in order to claim privileged treatment or compensation. Political changes laid the foundation for bitter quarrels over the legacy of the Second World War and over the consequences of communist rule, as in the case of the child evacuees from Greece. In Serbia the contested memories of historic battles amplified existing grievances and inflamed relations between Serbs and other ethnic groups in the collapsing Yugoslav state. 'Ethnic cleansing' became a rallying-cry for different campaigns, a rhetorical device in the hands of political leaders who were staking a claim to power. Nor was it just a matter of asserting claims for repatriation or restitution, or at long last being able to draw public attention to immensely damaging historic episodes. The relaxation of constraints on commemoration went hand in hand with a process of forgetting a time when people lived side by side in relative harmony. I return to this repudiation in the conclusion.

---

[68] Helene Moussa, *Storm and Sanctuary: the Journey of Ethiopian and Eritrean Women Refugees* (Dundas: Artemis Enterprises, 1993), 170.

Conclusion: Refugees and their History

It is the misleading familiarity of 'history' which can break open the daily naturalism of what surrounds us

(Denise Riley)

Refugees have been allowed only a walk-on part in most histories of the twentieth century, and even then as subjects of external intervention rather than as actors in their own right. *The Making of the Modern Refugee* argues that they belong to the mainstream rather than the margins. Familiar processes such as war, revolution and state-building take on fresh meanings when examined through the prism of population displacement. Refugees were an integral element in these transformations. They were first targeted, then expelled or 'transferred' because they were deemed not to belong or because they opposed revolutionary projects. Sometimes they were displaced when the borders of their country were redrawn around them to create a new polity. Granted, refugees might flee for their lives when enemy armies trampled over their towns and villages, but it is myopic to think of them as mere flotsam and jetsam, moving 'spontaneously' in search of safe ground. Nor was displacement always a catastrophe; it could be an opportunity to assert claims to political recognition. Where they became part of a new state, refugees shaped government practices by their very presence. They might be portrayed as victims who had finally found a proper berth in the newly-forged nation-state. To be sure, this acknowledgement did not always extend very far or go very deep, and refugees were frequently excised from the history of the state they helped to construct. This makes it all the more remarkable that refugees affirmed a sense of purpose. Notwithstanding the obstacles put in their way, refugees actively participated in interpreting displacement and staking a claim to be taken seriously. In the conclusion I deal with this aspect of refugees and their history.

A refugee-focused history entails considering not only the process of displacement but also the contours of assistance. Here, too, it is difficult to escape the claims made by the modern state. Governments appeal to a history of 'generosity' towards refugees (a history heavily laced with myth), but this frequently serves as a justification for maintaining tough controls on admission.[1] Although humanitarian

---

[1] Loescher and Scanlan, *Calculated Kindness*; Tony Kushner, *Remembering Refugees: Then and Now* (Manchester: Manchester University Press, 2006); Klaus Neumann, *Refuge Australia: Australia's Humanitarian Record* (Sydney: UNSW Press, 2004).

relief efforts were a significant endeavour in their own right, that history too remains under-explored. International organizations and NGOs show scant interest in the past unless making some bland claim about their reputation. It suffices that the world is full of refugees whose needs must be addressed here and now, as though the clock starts again with each new emergency. Humanitarianism concentrates on the present circumstances of refugees and treads cautiously when it comes to thinking about the root causes of displacement. Humanitarian doctrine also succumbs to the temptation to treat refugees 'as if they were *tabula rasa* with no history, past experience, culture, anticipation, skills, coping mechanisms to interpret new situations'.[2] This is a field where history dare not speak its name.

Placing refugees at the centre of historical enquiry exposes certain paradoxes and pitfalls. One risk is taking the refugee label for granted. Labels have consequences. *The Making of the Modern Refugee* problematizes the category by showing how it emerged and shifted over time and place. States, international organizations and NGOs, and refugees too, invested in the term. The refugee crisis in Russia during the First World War introduced a new word into the lexicon, 'refugeedom'. What began as an unsettling episode in a collapsing empire rapidly became a continental and global phenomenon with high political stakes. It was not just a question of numbers, large though these were. Population displacement in the aftermath of both world wars led to the creation of a refugee regime, with a League of Nations office (before 1939) and the UNHCR (after 1951) at its core. As High Commissioner in the 1920s, Nansen attended to specific groups of refugees who had lost the protection of their state. Thirty years later, the United Nations adopted a definition that centred upon the individual victim of persecution. Although diplomats initially took the view that displacement was limited in time and space, events moved faster than they envisaged.

Successive high commissioners repeated the mantra that the UNHCR was non-political. In so doing they discouraged public discussion of the fundamental causes of refugee crises, although in truth political considerations lay close to the surface of this humanitarian diplomacy. The post-1945 regime introduced the principle that to be recognized as a refugee it had to be established that persecution had taken place, and it was no secret that this meant persecution by the totalitarian state. It now sufficed to create a brief personal case note, not to embark on an extended historical analysis. In a similar vein, whether refugees could in practice safely return was a bureaucratic question about the future, not about the past and how it impinged on the present. History was kept out of the picture; it was an unnecessary distraction and an unwelcome complication. Far better to concentrate on vital technical issues—counting heads, delivering food and medicine—and on boosting the profile of the UNHCR by means of campaigns such as World Refugee Year or publicity stunts such as the 'Refugee Run', an annual fixture at the Davos summit in which business leaders and politicians are invited to imagine themselves as refugees.[3]

---

[2] Gaim Kibreab, 'The Myth of Dependency among Camp Refugees in Somalia, 1979–1989' *JRS*, 6, no.4 (1993), 321–48, at 336.

[3] <http://refugeerun.unhcr.org/>.

After the war the numbers and scope of NGOs grew rapidly. They provided the chief conduit for emergency relief and implementing 'durable solutions'. They raised enormous sums of money and employed thousands of staff who moved around with consummate ease. In addition to technical solutions, their actions were informed by religious doctrines (faith-based organizations mushroomed) and cultural assumptions, including an image of refugees as helpless victims who had lost self-control rather than as ordinary people with the capability to surmount the extraordinary difficulties they encountered. Only occasionally—Quakers are a notable example, 'humane and quietly efficient' in Francesca Wilson's words—did humanitarian organizations negotiate with refugees on equal terms, as well as seeking to establish the basis for peace and reconciliation.[4] More often than not, NGOs went looking for expressions of unalloyed gratitude and 'success stories' that would keep supporters happy and staff on their toes. True, refugees were sometimes directly employed on externally-managed relief projects, as in Greece during the 1920s and with UNRWA in the 1950s. Yet generally speaking the relationship between refugees and relief agencies operated asymmetrically, and still does. Assisting refugees implied appropriating their experiences, making assumptions about their bewilderment, and disqualifying them from expressing an opinion of their own.

History directs our attention to the way in which refugees have been valorized by non-refugees and how they valorized themselves in order to negotiate a way out of their predicament. This is partly about the blanket ascription of qualities to displaced populations, making some more deserving of assistance than others. Greek refugees from Asia Minor were portrayed as 'backward' (particularly if they came from the far corners of Anatolia) or, if they originated from Smyrna and Eastern Thrace, as sturdy individualists, 'a progressive factor and a rural element of the first class'.[5] Refugees from the Punjab figured in contemporary descriptions of Partition as capable and independent, whereas their Bengali counterparts did not escape being characterized as 'weak and effeminate'. Armenians drew upon the image of oppressive Turkish rule to depict themselves as the embodiment of Christian civilization and thus deserving of Western humanitarian assistance. Hungarians and Vietnamese Catholic refugees trumpeted their anti-communism as a means of turning themselves into (more or less) desirable refugees. Tibetans made much of their virtues as Buddhist victims of communist oppression, although their positive portrayal also hinged upon embedded cultural references to 'Shangri-La'. Like Armenians, they were hyper-historicized.

Refugees of necessity engaged with the label attached to them. This was only partly about gaining legal status. Recognition in accordance with the 1951 Convention conferred definite advantages, assuming that the host state had signed the Convention. Cultural and political considerations and not just legal status came into play. Officials and employers deemed the Latvian DPs who reached the UK

---

[4] Francesca Wilson, *Aftermath: France, Germany, Austria, Yugoslavia, 1945 and 1946* (Penguin Books, 1947), 130.

[5] Pentzopoulos, *Balkan Exchange of Minorities*, 102.

after the Second World War under the European Volunteer Workers scheme to be economic migrants, whereas they saw themselves as refugees from communism. Sometimes, as with refugees from Bangladesh who arrived in India in 1971, refugees were described as 'war victims', a term that spoke only obliquely of their persecution and implied nothing about any prospective rights. Refugees might be told that they could become citizens, but they faced discrimination and contempt on a daily basis. Those who had to move from Greece to Turkey in 1923 were called *muhacir* or *mübandil*, terms for 'refugee' that differentiated them from locals. Armenian refugees in Cyprus were 'refugees' (*kaghtagan*), not 'natives' (*deghatsi*). Partition refugees loathed being called *haranarthi* ('refugees') and styled themselves *pursharthi*, a term that advertised self-reliance. Nor were pejorative distinctions such as these invariably imposed by non-refugees. Refugees from an earlier vintage did not hesitate to draw a line between themselves and refugee newcomers, usually in detrimental terms. The gap in understanding was even greater where elite migrants confronted later cohorts of refugees.[6]

Specific issues arose for women who were exposed to abduction, degradation and sexual violence. Such risks constitute an important element of the history of refugees and of humanitarianism. Sometimes the consequences of displacement affected their property rather than their bodies, as when Palestinian women lost their dowry wealth in the war of 1948. Ideas of a vulnerable female population did not float freely and were moored to political projects such as attempts to build the nation-state or safeguard the 'nation-in-exile'. The violence done to women and children symbolized the calamity that befell the entire nation, as in the Armenian genocide in 1915 or France's refugee crisis in 1939–40. It strengthened ideas of suffering that could be deployed in fundraising campaigns, usually without any context or explanation, turning refugees into passive creatures. Yet the female encounter with displacement might be deemed shameful enough to hide it from view, as happened to Sikh women and girls who suffered at the hands of their own husbands and fathers during Partition. A gendered history of displacement also discloses that women often took charge of the household and rose to the challenge of dealing with officialdom and relief workers, 'being strong' (*awiyye*) as Palestinian women put it. It allows for women's participation in the armed struggle, as with Tamil Tigers who praised the 'sacrifices' made by female warriors on the nation's behalf. It recognizes the centrality of women's direct involvement in projects of refugee relief, bringing them to the political fore.[7]

To write refugees into history is to take seriously the way in which refugees engaged with displacement. *The Making of the Modern Refugee* has traced the impact of displacement on the lives of refugees but has sought to avoid making trite assumptions about a common experience. Whose experience counts, and why? How,

    [6] Daniel, 'The Refugee', 273–4.

    [7] Fiona Reid and Sharif Gemie, 'Constructing Citizenship? Women, Welfare and Refugees in France, 1939–1940' *Women's History Review*, 20, no.3 (2011), 347–68; James Clifford, *Routes: Travel and Translation in the Late Twentieth Century* (Cambridge, Mass: Harvard University Press, 1997), 258–60.

precisely, is it articulated? Being forced to leave one's home could leave terrible scars. Fear went hand in hand with feelings of profound loss for which a new vocabulary had to be found; Ethiopian refugees used the evocative term *sedetagna* to express how people lost everything that was dear to them.[8] But this has been a starting point of this enquiry, not a foregone conclusion. New experiences and encounters were mediated by various means, including information sources and political propaganda that painted displacement with a palette of mixed emotions including outrage and despair, but also resolution and hope. Emotions might furthermore be rearticulated in the present, for example to instil in children an attachment to a 'homeland' they have never seen. This emotional register forms an inescapable part of the history of displacement. History demonstrates what kind of representation emerged, whose voices gained greater exposure and credence, at what time and under what circumstances.

Displacement did not invariably override other meaningful elements in the social life of those who became refugees. Addressing the circumstances of displacement takes us, so to speak, only so far. There are, it is true, powerful countervailing forces. Refugees regularly turned the spotlight on the moment of their displacement, regarding it as an abrupt calamity that overturned routines and shattered lives forever. Muslim inhabitants of the Ottoman Empire referred to their mass displacement in the Balkans in the wake of the Russo-Turkish War on 1877–78 as the 'great unravelling'. Punjabi spokesmen described Partition as *raula*, a sharp break or 'vivisection'. Palestinians looked upon the events of 1948 as the *nakba*, the disaster that dismantled a traditional way of life and condemned them to a life of torment in exile: Mourid Barghouti speaks of being 'struck by displacement'. Crimean Tatars alluded to *kara gün* or the 'black day', marked by the arrival of NKVD detachments in their village with instructions to deport entire families to Central Asia. Exiled Tibetans observe 10 March as the anniversary of their sudden departure. In these instances, commonly-held expectations of being gone for a matter of weeks dwindled as refugees came to terms with prolonged displacement. The moment of departure acquired particular significance. Patriots advertised the overwhelming abruptness of departure so as to maintain the pulse of commemorative activity with the ultimate aim of recapturing the state.

To probe further the question of how refugees comprehended their displacement is to acknowledge that personal accounts are located in an extensive and intricate web of meaning. Refugees often explained displacement in contingent terms—as a result of being in the wrong place at the wrong time—but also related it to collective misfortune. One can therefore detect an 'engulfment of individual narratives by the collective narrative of history', such as the belief that an entire nation had been targeted and wronged.[9] Hutu refugees who fled Burundi and were cocooned in Tanzania's refugee camps created a 'mythico-history' that purported to validate their claims to the land whilst simultaneously depicting Tutsis as imposters.

[8] Helene Moussa, *Storm and Sanctuary: the Journey of Ethiopian and Eritrean Women Refugees* (Dundas: Artemis Enterprises, 1993), 168.
[9] Skultans, *The Testimony of Lives*, 7.

Other camps—in Baqubah, Argelès, Wildflecken, Kurukshetra, Shatila, Dharamsala, Mishamo and Pulau Bidong—fostered this intense historicity. No-one could accuse these refugees of a dearth of historical consciousness. Tibetan refugees perceived themselves as guardians of a distinctive civilization. Basque refugees constructed a self-image not as victims of Franco but the embodiment of a socialist and republican tradition which they sustained in exile. Armenian refugees interpreted displacement as a state of being rather than as a momentary episode. Diasporic groups were enlisted in this enterprise. Like refugees, they were (in the memorable phrase with which Salman Rushdie introduced *Midnight's Children*), 'handcuffed to history'.

Histories of population displacement need to allow for process as well as rupture. This is not to minimize the impact of being suddenly and violently displaced. Rather, it seeks to contextualize displacement and to challenge overarching narratives of abrupt, traumatic catastrophe. At a basic level this means that displacement could entail a protracted sequence of moves from one place to another. Thinking about process also invites us to consider the connections that refugees capitalized upon. Labouring men who moved to the canal colonies during the era of the British Raj returned to their ancestral villages when Pakistan and India became independent, but cross-border migration here and in Bengal continued, notwithstanding the efforts of government officials to stem this 'long Partition'. Wealthy Palestinian refugees who fled to Beirut in 1948 followed in the footsteps of family members who had forged commercial contacts throughout the Middle East. Refugees from the Spanish Civil War followed the tracks made by earlier generations of labour migrants who moved to France to pick grapes and harvest sugar beet or who sailed to Argentina. Refugees from the bitter civil war in Mozambique fled to Malawi because of a family history of migration. Bosnian Muslim women who were attacked by Serb militias during the war over the carcass of Yugoslavia sought refuge in Slovenia because their menfolk had traditionally found work in Ljubljana. Tunisians fleeing the political turbulence in their country in 2011 made their way to the Italian island of Lampedusa, whence they were despatched to camps on the Italian mainland. Some attempted to get to France via the so-called 'death pass', the mountain path used in the 1930s by Italian exiles who rejected Mussolini's rule.

Thus the trajectories of displaced people rarely had a random character but were instead associated with historic ties, journeys and diasporic formations that can best be understood as 'the culmination of evolving forces operating much earlier than the actual physical migration of people'.[10] As has been aptly said, refugees 'went into exile as persons enmeshed in relationships, and the processes by which they experienced their displacement were indeterminate because of the myriad relationships which they carried with them'.[11] Kurdish refugees numbering about

---

[10] Shami, *Population Displacement and Resettlement*, 4; Peter Loizos, 'Generations' in Forced Migration: Towards Greater Conceptual Clarity' *JRS*, 20, no.2 (2007), 193–209.

[11] Harri Englund, *From War to Peace on the Mozambique-Malawi Borderland* (Edinburgh: Edinburgh University Press, 2002), 4, 33.

30 million people worldwide did not see themselves as belonging to a 'small minority' but as members of a diasporic nation.[12] Similar views were held by Armenians and Jews, Palestinians and Tibetans. These patterns point to the importance of history and ancestry. Ethiopian Jewish adolescents made sense of their hazardous journey from Ethiopia to Israel via Sudan by associating the migration of their forebears with their own resolve. The journey took on the character of an odyssey intertwined with a history of nation and diaspora. Decisions to join communities overseas could nevertheless lead to painful separation, as in the case of children from leftist families who were shipped to Eastern Europe during the Greek Civil War.

To be designated a 'refugee' throughout the twentieth century frequently meant demeaning treatment at the hands of governments and host populations, an obser- vation that is not fundamentally altered by the protection afforded refugees recog- nized under the 1951 Convention or by humanitarian assistance. There never was a golden age for the modern refugee. A sense of mortification figured most strongly among Palestinian refugees who preferred to think of themselves as prospective 'returnees'. Refugees from East Bengal were provided with the acronym 'East Pakistan Displaced Persons' whom West Bengalis mocked as 'East Pakistan Dis- eased Persons'. But the word could also be seized upon by those to whom it was applied: a badge advertising a broader history of national calamity and even a source of collective pride, as with Hutu refugees in Tanzania, or a clever bit of marketing, as with the 'Refugee Taxi' and 'Refugee Kebab' businesses that people from Northern Cyprus established in the southern sector after 1974. Refugees from the East Punjab who settled in Lahore named their businesses and sports clubs after the places they left behind, as in the case of the Amritsar Rovers Hockey Club (this did not stop their children who made good in the 1960s from refusing to be labelled as refugees). The same link between past and present operated among Greek refugees from Turkey who settled in Piraeus. Displacement was framed in complex terms in relation to Jewish DPs, who were invited to look to a future in the new state of Israel forged from the terrible experience of the Holocaust and legitimized by scripture. Dwelling on the past could be a vital element in shaping one's prospects.

The history of displacement is by definition a history of place—of departure and of arrival, sometimes of multiple journeys, and also of staying put. Refugees left their mark on destinations such as Beirut, Kokkinia, Marseille, Bourg-Madame, Chandigarh, Karachi, Hong Kong, Shatila and Masindi. Their descendants too imaginatively reconstructed the places they left behind, investing them with no- tions of beauty, pleasure, fecundity and stability. 'The past [as Salman Rushdie put it], is home'.[13] Home was portrayed as a place where one's ancestors lived, died and were buried, and where one had been raised. It made basic necessities available as a result of working the land alongside neighbours: as one Greek Cypriot put it, 'in Lapithos, fruit and cheese and other food and goods were exchanged or given away

[12] Östen Wahlbeck, 'The Concept of Diaspora as an Analytical Tool in the Study of Refugee Com- munities' *JEMS*, 28, no. 2 (2002), 221–38.
[13] Salman Rushdie, *Imaginary Homelands: Essays and Criticism, 1981–1991* (Granta, 1991), 9.

to friends and relations', whereas 'here everything has to be bought'.[14] Yet the evidence also suggests that some refugees felt a double affiliation: Crimean Tatar deportees spoke of Crimea as a lost land to which they might one day return, but nevertheless evinced a genuine attachment to Uzbekistan. Children evacuated from Greece during the civil war spoke in adulthood of Macedonia as the 'homeland', but in the same breath described feeling 'at home' in Hungary or East Germany. 'Where are you from?' was never an innocent question, nor would it generate a trivial response. Place was both a geographic location and a rich metaphor that expressed varied emotions and experiences.[15]

Some places became a destination for refugees from very different points of origin. This happened in refugee camps as well as cities and countries. In Kenya, Dadaab variously housed refugees from Sudan, Somalia and Ethiopia. During the 1920s Armenians made their way to Lebanon where they transformed the small settlement of Bourj Hammoud into one of Beirut's most bustling suburbs, where they were joined by Palestinian refugees three decades later. Tunisia was successively home to Serbian refugees during the First World War, to Algerian refugees in the 1960s, and to refugees from Libya in 2011. Cyprus was a destination for Armenian refugees in the 1890s and again in the 1920s, and for Jewish survivors of the Holocaust, as well as the site of mass internal displacement following the Turkish invasion in 1974.

The spatial consequences of displacement were poignant and sometimes ironic. Chandigarh was an entirely new city built to accommodate refugees from Pakistan, at the expense of the local peasantry who were displaced to help realize Le Corbusier's grand vision. Sosúa—a symbol of Trujillo's cynical 'offer' to provide a haven for refugees from Nazi Germany—is now a thriving tourist resort offering sand and sex, a 'trans-national town' in which local and global networks intersect. Although the owner of the Tropix Hotel advertises himself as 'a living example of the town's refugee history', fewer than 10 Jewish families now remain as a tangible reminder of the history of forced migration. Other attractions have supplanted these episodes: 'Prepare [says the website of a major travel company] to be enchanted by the friendly islanders, beautiful scenery and hypnotic rhythm of the merengue'.[16]

Refugees established a foothold in new places but also recalled the places they left behind and invested them with meaning, 'playing out the drama of their lives in more than one location'.[17] Memorial books, compatriot unions, visits—virtual or otherwise—and belongings, practices and performances need to be understood in the light of these claims upon the past and the central place that social memory plays in the construction and reproduction of identities. They encapsulate a sense of loss, and may also (re)store a sense of self.[18] Memorial books reconstruct a history

---

[14] Roger Zetter, 'The Greek-Cypriot Refugees: Perceptions of Exile under Conditions of Protracted Exile' *IMR*, 28, no. 2 (1994), 307–22, at 311.

[15] Kassem, *Palestinian Women*, 29.   [16] Gigliotti, 'Acapulco in the Atlantic', 43.

[17] Lincoln, 'Fleeing from Firestorms', 456.

[18] David Parkin, 'Mementoes as Transitional Objects in Human Displacement' *Journal of Material Culture*, 4, no.3 (1999), 303–20.

of the village, enumerate its former inhabitants and their dwelling places, and establish an association between the displaced and their original homes. Han Chinese refugees who fled Yunnan in 1949 recreated elaborate clan genealogies. Websites that draw attention to Armenian sites in the Ottoman Empire as well as Jewish memorial books testifying to life in Eastern Europe before the Holocaust are a didactic means to educate the next generation. Palestinian village books and the books compiled by Greek Cypriot and Bosnian refugees have an overtly political purpose, being informed by the realization that careful investment in the land and the arduous toil of their forefathers had been dissipated. They are not mere gazetteers, but texts that associate place with sensory perceptions—the smell of sea breeze, the taste of lemons, or the sight of a familiar shop. These texts, like the keys to abandoned properties, establish a claim to land that has been forfeited but might yet be restored.

Commemoration invites us to acknowledge amnesia. Official discourses and histories play an important part in blocking out inconvenient truths. The Russian Revolution obliterated memories of population displacement during the 1914–17 war. Patriotic Chinese scholars were silent on the disastrous human consequences of the decision to breach the dykes of the Yellow River in 1938. Fascist and authoritarian regimes adopted the same stance: Mussolini had no wish to be reminded of Italy's defeat and subsequent population displacement during the First World War; Franco drew a veil over the displacement of civilians during the Spanish Civil War—it was left to Spanish exiles in South America to keep the flame alive; and the authoritarian rule of Syngman Rhee kept the school curriculum free from any mention of the distress suffered by Korean refugees. The Gaullist myth in postwar France found no room for official commemoration of the defeat and 'exodus' in 1940, let alone for the events of 1914. The Second World War was recollected as a time of heroic resistance, not demeaning displacement; in any case, the bitter Algerian war shifted the focus to a contemporary crisis.

Authoritarian polities tended to discourage discussion of refugee crises. In addition to Kemalist Turkey, one thinks of Chinese refugees in Hong Kong. Bangladesh appears reluctant to acknowledge that it was founded on population displacement, perhaps because to address this history would be to raise difficult questions around Bihari refugees. It took concerted effort and sometimes political cataclysm to discuss these episodes. The deportation of non-Russian minorities in the Stalin era only attracted publicity following the collapse of the Soviet Union, helping to underscore the legitimacy of post-Soviet states such as Latvia and Lithuania. A new generation in Spain began to rewrite the history of refugees as part of a reassessment of the Franco era, encouraged by the 2007 Law on the Recovery of Historical Memory.

Other kinds of amnesia and censorship are also at work. Refugees often excised from history their former neighbours who had turned upon them at the moment of displacement; their presence in the historical narrative was too disturbing. Following the Greek-Turkish population exchange, the neighbourliness shown by Orthodox and Muslim villagers was rewritten as a history of mutual disdain, or else entirely overlooked in the process of constructing the Hellenic national epic.

Hindu refugees who arrived from Pakistan in September 1947 and moved into Muslim houses in Delhi refused to acknowledge its Muslim past; many Muslims likewise wrote the multicultural elements of Lahore out of history. The state of Israel, with the backing of most of its Jewish citizens, threw its weight behind attempts to transform the landscape of Palestine leaving few traces of its erstwhile Arab inhabitants. Poles who were forcibly resettled from Western Ukraine after 1945 did their utmost to erase the German presence in the 'recovered lands' from which ethnic Germans had been expelled. The displaced might think of themselves as a spectral 'presence', but they turned former neighbours into ghosts as well. This is about rewriting the past for present purposes, a politics of negation and oblivion.[19]

However, there is a cosmopolitan stance that needs to be acknowledged too.[20] Some of the commemorative work undertaken by refugees embodied a different kind of nostalgia, an appeal to a time when neighbours lived in harmony with one another whatever their religion or ethnicity. Elderly Greeks who found sanctuary in the North Aegean island of Lemnos in 1922 spoke subsequently of their friendships with Muslim neighbours in Smyrna. Other refugees introduced more 'worldly' attitudes into parochial host communities: Baltic refugees who reached the Russian interior in 1915–16 were thought likely to introduce more modern farming methods, drawing on a history of agricultural improvement that could be shared with the local peasantry. Some fictional representations of pre-Partition Indian villages described a life of pleasure and abundance that allowed for tolerance between people of various faiths who negotiated their difference on a daily basis. Refugees from Bosnia-Herzegovina described Sarajevo as a cosmopolitan city where Serbs, Croats and Muslims 'were mixed like corn and flour' in the workplace.[21] These generous interpretations of the past challenged ultra-nationalist dogma and projects designed to cement ineradicable difference.

Cosmopolitanism emerged also in the attitudes of relief workers. Quakers protested Allied endorsement of 'competitive nationalism' in Europe's DP camps at the end of the Second World War and urged the need for international reconciliation; Francesca Wilson looked upon the DP camp at Föhrenwald as 'a little UNO'.[22] The Dominican priest Father Georges Pire believed that working with these refugees afforded an opportunity to 'surpass all the barriers that so often cause such deep divisions amongst men. Thus men of very different backgrounds, by uniting sincerely in a common purpose to help other men, discover in themselves a great similarity giving rise to understanding and mutual liking'. Pire described how a 'Europe du coeur' took shape in the refugee villages he sponsored, expressed as a brotherhood of 'all men, working in unison in a spirit of solidarity, serving a cause which is utterly humane and absolutely true'. This spirit had a political component, but it transcended Cold War rivalry on behalf of a universalized humanitarianism.[23]

---

[19] Pandey, *Remembering Partition*, 135, 146; Rebecca Bryant, 'Partitions of Memory', 332–60.
[20] Chatty, *Displacement and Dispossession*, 37, 283.   [21] Grouev, *Bullets on the Water*, 60.
[22] Wilson, *Aftermath*, 124.   [23] Gatrell, *Free World?*, 246.

One must accordingly thread into the narrative of displacement the motivation, orientation and narratives of the numerous individuals who took upon themselves the task of assisting and managing displaced persons in their capacity as psychologists and psychiatrists, doctors, social workers, statisticians, lawyers and engineers, as well as military personnel, policemen and civil servants. The doctrine of intervention was itself connected to the notion of rupture. That is to say, the more that displacement was construed as 'spontaneity', 'panic' and 'trauma', the more it behoved professional experts to introduce a necessary element of control. Intervention was designed to overcome the harmful psychological consequences of displacement and turn refugees into responsible and worthy citizens. Sometimes, as with 'culturally' different refugees, this tested the patience of external aid workers. Writing in 1919, a British army officer prefaced his report on the camp for Armenian refugees at Baqubah by stating that: 'I have had to write from knowledge derived from intercourse with the refugees themselves, much of which on close examination proved to be quite unreliable'.[24] It is not difficult to see how in these circumstances relief workers were able to substitute their own impressions for the insights of refugees.

Refugees regularly encountered humiliation and infantilization; their world having been turned upside down already, they were subject to further kinds of deprivation. Structures and styles of assistance that act upon rather than with the participation of refugees had a corrosive effect: as Barbara Harrell-Bond says, 'it is not that refugees do not need help; they do. The problem is the kind of help they receive, the way help is provided and the role which they are forced to assume to get it'. She maintains that refugees were subjected to a different set of practices in the late twentieth century compared with the 1950s, when they were supposedly granted more autonomy. Refugee camps that are suffused with externally imposed notions of order must bear a particular responsibility for promoting these attitudes, which include judgements about 'traumatized', 'untrustworthy' and even 'subversive' refugees. Yet many relief workers operated with similar suppositions throughout the twentieth century, as did the British psychiatrist who diagnosed a young Jewish DP girl as a disturbed patient on the grounds that she combed her hair with a broken comb and looked at herself in a broken mirror, until a Jewish DP dentist pointed out that he might consider providing her with a decent comb and mirror before assuming she was ill.[25]

The administrative constraints and legal requirements imposed on refugees sometimes enabled engaging with the past for instrumental purposes. Refugees caught up in the upheaval of Partition likened their circumstances to that of Jews in Nazi Germany. Others likewise deployed historical allusion to highlight their predicament or to demand recognition as potential citizens of the country in which

---

[24] Lieutenant H.L. Charge, *Memoranda on the Armenian and Assyrian Refugees* (Baghdad: Government Press, 1919), 10.

[25] Feinstein, *Holocaust Survivors*, 20; Harrell-Bond, 'The Experience of Refugees', 140–3; Harrell-Bond, 'Can Humanitarian Work with Refugees be Humane?' *HRQ*, 24, no.2 (2002), 51–85; Hyndman, *Managing Displacement*, 127.

they settled. Refugees seized upon history as a means of asserting or maintaining claims to restitution, as with 'Partition refugees' who claimed that their pension entitlements were being ignored.[26] Ethnic German expellees who were forced from their homes in Poland and Czechoslovakia in 1945 asked on arrival in Austria to be accorded preferential treatment on the grounds that 'our parents were all citizens of the former k. and k. [*kaiserlich und königlich*] Monarchy. Their achievements in terms of culture and patriotism should be well known to you'.[27] Karen refugees in Myanmar ascribed their persecution partly to their Christian religion, a reminder of their history of association with the British prior to the independence of Burma in 1948. They cultivated a strong sense of ethnic identity in the refugee camps on the Thai-Myanmar border, another indication of how displacement can strengthen collective affiliation.

Refugees were allowed to speak under quite specific circumstances. An emerging oral history provides a point of departure to consider the meanings that refugees attributed to their displacement and to the assumptions that were made about 'homecoming'. How far refugees can claim the mantle of expertise for themselves is also an important issue. Social scientists sometimes urge that refugees should be 'subjects in their own enquiry' rather than objects of study, but in practice scant attention has been paid to verbal exchanges between refugees, or to those between refugees and external agencies. Refugees are frequently required to testify in a prescribed setting that puts pressure on them to establish a story that will carry legal and bureaucratic credibility; at best one might describe this as a sensitive kind of eavesdropping. Legal procedures generated a large (and largely hidden) documentary record into which history intruded selectively.[28] Whereas British government officials betrayed a kind of amnesia about the historically close ties between Britain and colonial Rhodesia, Zimbabwean female asylum seekers refer to Britain's oft-asserted claim to be a country of 'fair play'.[29] Writing refugees back into history means asking questions about the sources at the disposal of the historian. Governments, inter-governmental organizations and NGOs left behind a documentary record. These resources are invaluable but they are limited in scope, and they testify to the power vested in departments of state and humanitarian bureaucracies. Technical experts and relief workers assembled field reports, kept diaries and wrote their memoirs, underlining the privileged stance of these eye-witnesses.

Such first-hand testimony as is available from refugees must be interpreted carefully. There is an expectation on the part of immigration and asylum officers that 'real' refugees should tell a convincing story of the immediate circumstances of their individual persecution. Sudanese refugees complained bitterly that 'UNHCR

---

[26] Kaur, 'Distinctive Citizenship', 437–8.

[27] Tara Zahra, '"Prisoners of the Postwar": Expellees, Refugees, and Jews in Postwar Austria' *Austrian History Yearbook*, 41 (2010), 191–215, at 195.

[28] Didier Fassin and Richard Rechtman, *The Empire of Trauma: an Inquiry into the Condition of Victimhood* (Princeton: Princeton University Press, 2008), 250–74.

[29] Terence Ranger, 'The Narratives and Counter-narratives of Zimbabwean Asylum: Female Voices' *Third World Quarterly*, 26, no.3 (2005), 405–21.

caseworkers always think that any story [we] tell during the interview is a lie'.[30] Refugees and DPs who petitioned the IRO in 1947 had to demonstrate a 'valid objection' to being repatriated to Eastern Europe, and thus needed to construct a credible account for the eligibility officers. This pattern of interrogation persists. Often the resulting accounts are brief and formulaic, because this is what the bureaucratic mind requires in order to reach a decision; other aspects of their life are of no concern. But some refugees might say little or nothing, perhaps because they were traumatized or silenced by officials who had heard enough. Silence can also be a kind of defiance—a deliberate refusal to confess one's private thoughts, or a calculated decision to wait until the time is right: 'silence can nourish a story and establish a communication to be patiently saved in periods of darkness until it is able to come to light in a new and enriched form'.[31] Of Vietnamese refugees who found sanctuary in Norway it is said that 'some cherish the past, while others leave it to itself'. Historians need to understand why, in certain circumstances (as Virginia Woolf once put it), 'language runs dry', but also how it can unleash a torrent of claims and explanations.[32]

The course of population displacement in the modern era is thus complex and contested. So too is the process of writing that history. The answer to the questions posed here about narrating experience is that much hinges on the situation in which refugees find themselves. Writing in 1943, Hannah Arendt described Jewish refugees from Nazi Germany who reached France or the USA (of whom she was one): '[W]e were told to forget. Apparently nobody wants to know that contemporary history has created a new kind of human being, the kind that are put in concentration camps by their foes and in internment camps by their friends. Even among ourselves we don't speak about this past'.[33] For every voice that speaks loudly there are dozens that are suppressed. Many refugees lacked the means to enforce their understanding of what befell them. Their voice might be muffled by earlier vintages of refugees who claimed greater legitimacy and questioned the integrity of those who fled later on—this certainly seems to have happened among refugees from the Spanish Civil War who settled in South America, and among Tibetan refugees in Nepal. Where there exists the capacity for enforcement, refugees may be reluctant to embrace it. Nationalist claims regularly effaced other stories, as in the case of the young Palestinian man who loftily informed his interviewer that 'my mother told us about Palestine, but she didn't know the plots', an important reminder that age and gender play an important part in framing these narratives.[34]

---

[30] Jane Kani Edward, *Sudanese Women Refugees: Transformations and Future Imaginings* (New York: Palgrave Macmillan, 2007), 117.

[31] Luisa Passerini, 'Memories between Silence and Oblivion', in Katharine Hodgkin and Susannah Radstone (eds), *Contested Pasts: the Politics of Memory* (Routledge, 2003), 238–54, at 238.

[32] Knudsen, *Capricious Worlds*, 3; Michel-Rolph Trouillot, *Silencing the Past: Power and the Production of History* (Boston: Beacon Press, 1995), 22–6; Efrat Ben-Ze'ev, Ruth Ginio and Jay Winter (eds), *Shadows of War: a Social History of Silence in the Twentieth Century* (Cambridge: Cambridge University Press, 2010).

[33] Arendt, *Jewish Writings*, 265.   [34] Sayigh, 'Palestinian Camp Women', 42.

To focus exclusively on particular kinds of 'plot', such as concentrating on victimization and deprivation is to miss important features of refugee resourcefulness. Another way of putting this is to say that there needs to be a history of refugee activism, whether it be petitioning, hustling, self-defence or other forms of expression. Vietnamese refugees made every attempt to circumvent restrictions on their departure from Vietnam and to survive in sanctuaries that turned out to be hostile. Umutesi's memoir of her arduous trek to Zaire in the aftermath of the genocide in 1994 testifies to the capabilities of female refugees, without minimizing the deprivation and dangers they faced. Where male adult 'breadwinners' were killed or fled, women assumed positions of responsibility as head of the household or as independent economic actors. Women's groups in refugee camps as well as women's contributions to the work of NGOs have been important hallmarks of change. History invites us to spot these different identities and tactics, and to open up a discussion of contexts and views. It may not be the history we wish to hear. For some refugees, it is as if 'history had seized centre stage', as though 'the events of violence are not past, that they have the potential of becoming alive any moment'.[35] That potential can be troubling when history becomes part of the armoury of mutual incomprehension or provokes a wish for vengeance, whether in Eastern Anatolia in 1915, Rwanda and Burundi after 1972, Kosovo in the 1990s, or among nationalist politicians in India's BJP whose uncompromising stance reflects their background as Partition-era refugees, where 'the victims of today are potentially the aggressors of tomorrow'.[36]

We cannot nor should we strive for a final resolution of all the questions posed by a history of displacement. It is best to contemplate instead what is at stake in maintaining an ongoing conversation, even if this is a dialogue between unequals. Time and again, the terms of the conversation are set not by rank and file refugees but by those who speak and act on their behalf and whose programmes dominate the institutional record. No matter how good their intentions, the appropriation of refugee experience is deeply ironic. Refugees have usually lost enough as it is: must they also forfeit the right to speak for themselves? Does it matter that they offer contrasting perspectives, like the Vietnamese refugee who proclaimed, 'who I am is who I was, and not who I have become', whereas a female refugee in South Sudan took the opposite stance, saying 'now I can think of what to do in this world'? How can they be enabled to speak out, even if this risks reviving disputes and confrontations that gave rise to displacement in the first instance? My hope is that an informed critical history will enrich that conversation and contribute to dissolving the malign manifestations of refugeedom in the modern world.

---

[35] Quotations from Malkki, *Purity and Exile*, 53; Veena Das (ed.), *Remaking a World: Violence, Social Suffering and Recovery* (Berkeley: University of California Press, 2001), xx.
[36] Terry, *Condemned to Repeat?*, 223.

Further Reading

If asked to name a handful of books that have inspired me, I would begin with the work of anthropologists. John C. Knudsen, *Capricious Worlds: Vietnamese Life Journeys* (Transaction Publishers, 2005) is a moving reflection on the experiences of Vietnamese refugees in Hong Kong and Norway. Barbara Harrell-Bond, *Imposing Aid: Emergency Assistance to Refugees* (Oxford University Press, 1986) and Liisa Malkki, *Purity and Exile: Violence, Memory, and National Cosmology among Hutu Refugees in Tanzania* (Chicago University Press, 1995) helped change the way we think about the world of the refugee camp and about refugees in general. Pamela Ballinger, *History in Exile: Memory and Identity at the Borders of the Balkans* (Princeton University Press, 2003) is far more than a 'regional' study. The late Peter Loizos wrote a think-piece, 'Misconceiving refugees?' in Renos Papadopoulos (ed.), *Therapeutic Care for Refugees: No Place Like Home* (Karnac Books, 2002) that encapsulated a lifetime of reflection on displacement, particularly in Cyprus. To these should be added Gadi Ben-Ezer, *The Ethiopian Jewish Exodus: Narratives of the Migration Journey to Israel 1977–1985* (Routledge, 2002).

Historians of refugee crises in Europe and their aftermath are indebted to pioneering works by John Hope Simpson, *The Refugee Problem: Report of a Survey* (Oxford University Press, 1939) and Michael Marrus, *The Unwanted: European Refugees in the Twentieth Century* (Oxford University Press, 2002) both strong on institutional responses, and Eugene Kulischer, *Europe on the Move: War and Population Changes, 1917–1947* (Columbia University Press, 1948), an unsurpassed study of demography and politics. A model study of an intertwined history is Maud S. Mandel, *In the Aftermath of Genocide: Armenians and Jews in Twentieth-Century France* (Duke University Press, 2003). On the Ottoman Empire and Turkey, I recommend Uğur Ümit Üngör, *The Making of Modern Turkey: Nation and State in Eastern Anatolia, 1913–50* (Oxford University Press, 2011); for Russia see Peter Gatrell, *A Whole Empire Walking: Refugees in Russia during World War I* (Indiana University Press, 1999). There is a rich literature on the Greek-Turkish population exchange. The essays in Renée Hirschon (ed.), *Crossing the Aegean: an Appraisal of the 1923 Compulsory Population Exchange between Greece and Turkey* (Berghahn, 2003) are a good starting-point.

Among recent histories of post-war displacement, refugee relief and resettlement, see Anna Holian, *Between National Socialism and Soviet Communism: Displaced Persons in Postwar Germany* (University of Michigan Press, 2011), and Daniel Cohen, *In War's Wake: Europe's Displaced Persons in the Post-War Order* (Oxford University Press, 2012). On Jewish refugees in Germany I recommend Angelika Königseder and Juliane Wetzel, *Waiting for Hope: Jewish Displaced Persons in Post-World War II Germany* (Northwestern University Press, 2001).

There is much to be learned about the geopolitical origins of refugee crises beyond Europe from the path-breaking book by political scientists Aristide Zolberg, Astri Suhrke and Sergio Aguayo, *Escape from Violence: Conflict and the Refugee Crisis in the Developing World* (Oxford University Press, 1989). Essential for understanding the international refugee regime are Claudena Skran, *Refugees in Inter-War Europe: the Emergence of a Regime* (Clarendon Press, 1995) and Dzovinar Kévonian, *Réfugiés et diplomatie humanitaire: les acteurs européens et la scène proche-orientale pendant l'entre-deux-guerres* (Publications de la Sorbonne, 2003) for the inter-war period, and Gil Loescher, *The UNHCR and World Politics: a Perilous Path* (Oxford University Press, 2001) for the UNHCR era. Fiona Terry, *Condemned to Repeat? The Paradox of Humanitarian Action* (Cornell University Press, 2002) is a thoughtful and wide-ranging study of post-Cold War practices. The archives of the League of Nations and UNHCR are an extraordinary treasure trove. The history of refugee relief as seen through the lens of NGOs is still to be written.

Some of the richest literature on population displacement comes from studies of Palestinian refugees. Top of my list are Edward Said and Jean Mohr, *After the Last Sky: Palestinian Lives* (Faber, 1986) and Mourid Barghouti, *I Saw Ramallah* (Bloomsbury, 2004). A good overview is Dawn Chatty, *Displacement and Dispossession in the Modern Middle East* (Cambridge University Press, 2011). Julie Peteet, *Landscape of Hope and Despair: Palestinian Refugee Camps* (University of Pennsylvania Press, 2005) and Susan Slyomovics, *Object of Memory: Arab and Jew Narrate the Palestinian Village* (University of Pennsylvania Press, 1998) are insightful; so, too, are numerous articles by Rosemary Sayigh and Ilana Feldman.

Two very different but equally illuminating books on the Indian sub-continent are Urvashi Butalia, *The Other Side of Silence: Voices from the Partition of India* (Hurst & Co., 2000), a landmark study, and Vazira Fazila-Yacoobali Zamindar, *The Long Partition and the Making of Modern South Asia: Refugees, Boundaries, and Histories* (Columbia University Press, 2007). The historiography is rich and growing all the time. A good summary is Ian Talbot and Gurharpal Singh, *The Partition of India* (Cambridge University Press, 2011).

The Japanese invasion of China has lately been the subject of three books: a masterly overview by Diana Lary, *The Chinese People at War: Human Suffering and Social Transformation, 1937–1945* (Cambridge University Press, 2011) and specialized studies by Stephen MacKinnon, *Wuhan, 1938: War, Refugees, and the Making of Modern China* (University of California Press, 2008), and R. Keith Schoppa, *In a Sea of Bitterness: Refugees during the Sino-Japanese War* (Harvard University Press, 2011). There is as yet nothing comparable on Vietnam, Korea or Cambodia. On Hong Kong in the wake of the Chinese revolution in 1949 we await the publication of an excellent doctoral dissertation by Laura Madokoro. Meanwhile there is Yuk Wah Chan (ed.), *The Chinese/Vietnamese Diaspora: Revisiting the Boat People* (Routledge, 2011).

On sub-Saharan Africa, in addition to Liisa Malkki's work, I learned a lot from the memoir by Marie Béatrice Umutesi, *Surviving the Slaughter: the Ordeal of a Rwandan Refugee in Zaire* (University of Wisconsin Press, 2004) and the essays in Tim Allen and Hubert Morsink (eds), *When Refugees Go Home: African Experiences* (UNRISD/James Currey, 1994), particularly Terence Ranger's reflections on social history.

From the voluminous literature on diaspora and transnationalism, I would single out Aihwa Ong, *Buddha is Hiding: Refugees, Citizenship, the New America* (University of California Press, 2003). The implications of the collapse of communism in Russia and Eastern Europe are spelled out by Pamela Ballinger (see earlier in this section), Greta Uehling, *Beyond Memory: the Crimean Tatars' Deportation and Return* (Palgrave, 2004) and Loring M. Danforth and Riki van Boeschoten, *Children of the Greek Civil War: Refugees and the Politics of Memory* (Chicago University Press, 2011).

Finally, several websites contain valuable material, including documents, maps, photographs and personal testimony. For UNHCR see <http://www.unhcr.org/cgi-bin/texis/vtx/home>. For academic activity, see the website of the Refugee Studies Centre, University of

Oxford, <http://www.rsc.ox.ac.uk/>. For specific situations monitored by Human Rights Watch, go to <http://www.hrw.org/en/category/topic/refugees>. A UK perspective is provided by the Information Centre for Asylum and Refugees, at <http://www.icar.org.uk/index.html>. A new Refugee Archives and History Group has been established by Paul Dudman at the University of East London. For details see <http://refugeearchiveshistory.wordpress.com/>.

Index

Printed and bound by CPI Group (UK) Ltd, Croydon, CR0 4YY